W9-BZU-641

THE BEST BEERS

THE BEST BEERS

1,000 MUST-DRINK BREWS
FROM PORTLAND TO PRAGUE

BEN McFARLAND
TOM SANDHAM

THE THINKING DRINKERS

STERLING EPICURE
New York

STERLING EPICURE
New York

An Imprint of Sterling Publishing Co., Inc.
1166 Avenue of the Americas
New York, NY 10036

STERLING EPICURE and the distinctive Sterling logo are registered trademarks of Sterling Publishing Co., Inc.

Text © 2017 by Ben McFarland and Tom Sandham

All rights reserved. No part of this book may be reproduced, stored in a retrieval system, or transmitted in any form or any means (including electronic, mechanical, photocopying, recording or otherwise) without prior written permission from the publisher.

ISBN: 978-1-4549-2832-4

Distributed in Canada by Sterling Publishing Co., Inc.
c/o Canadian Manda Group, 664 Annette Street,
Toronto, Ontario, M6S 2C8, Canada

For information about custom editions, special sales, and premium and corporate purchases, pleases contact Sterling Special Sales at 800-805-5489 or specialsales@sterlingpublishing.com

Manufactured in China

10 9 8 7 6 5 4 3 2 1

sterlingpublishing.com

A complete list of image credits appears on page 288.

CONTENTS

INTRODUCTION

ADVENTURES WITH BEER

Welcome to the updated version of *World's Best Beers*, a book that was first written almost a decade ago.

In 2009, the craft beer scene was flourishing in areas of epicurean enlightenment all over Europe, America, and elsewhere.

Disillusioned with dull beer, microbrewers were kicking the shins of the mass-producing, multinationals, wrestling beer out of the hands of accountants and returning it to its rightful place as an artisanal product made by actual people who cared about it.

The previous edition proclaimed that, despite a brewing history spanning around 10,000 years, it had never been a better time to be a beer drinker. Well, things have become even better, and the pace at which craft beer has spread around the world since the first edition has been quite extraordinary.

In London, where we're based, the number of breweries could be counted on one hand back in 2009. Now, that amount is set to hit one hundred, and craft beer has become a cornerstone of the capital's rich food and drink scene.

Similar things are happening all over the world, a lot of it inspired by the Americans who fired the starting gun back in the 1980s. Countries that were hitherto bland lands of brewing are now home to thriving beer cultures, and from Portland to Paris and Manchester to Melbourne, the number of microbreweries is on the rise, talk of great beer is getting louder, and the boundaries of what beer can be are being stretched in the fervent pursuit of flavor.

Now very much part of the global consciousness, "craft beer" can no longer be considered a fad, and, while the craft beer "bubble" may occasionally deflate a little, the expectation and desire that beer should be tasty is not going to go away.

After decades of drinking in the dark, a new dawn has risen, and there's no sign of the sun setting on it anytime soon. So, whether you are a seasoned beer aficionado or an occasional imbiber thirsty to discover more, we hope this enlightening tour through the global craft beer scene will provide you with everything you need to know ... and bring on a thirst too.

Cheers,
Ben & Tom
The Thinking Drinkers

THE HISTORY OF BEER

Iran and Iraq are not the easiest places to get a pint these days, but ironically this is roughly where brewing was first born, somewhere between 10,000 and 8000 BC.

Archaeological experts believe beer in this, its earliest incarnation, was a rudimentary gruel made from unmalted grain that would have been magically fermented by yeasts in the air and clay vessels.

But the Sumerians first started brewing seriously, using malted barley that they soaked in water. A Sumerian clay tablet dating back to 1800 BC, provided not just the earliest "official" record of brewing but also the oldest recipe in the world.

It consisted of crushing a bready substance with honey, herbs, water, dates, raisins, and spice, squeezing it through a sheet of straw, and letting it ferment. It probably tasted awful, but it was safer than disease-riddled water and was written down as part of a catchy hymn to Ninkasi, the Sumerian goddess of brewing, that made it easy for people to remember.

As religion, over time, became increasingly interwoven into daily life, beer and those who brewed it took on an emblematic, spiritual dimension. Certain types of beer were reserved exclusively for religious ceremonies, while women, who oversaw much of the brewing back then, were thought to have a deep religious relationship with Ninkasi, who blessed their beer vessels by magically turning grain into giggle-juice.

Beer played a religious role in Europe too, where monasteries were the first commercial brewing operations. Evidence in the Domesday Book of AD1086 records other brewing enterprises, but the monks first made real money (and missionary success) from the mash-fork, especially the Benedictine order.

Monastic brewhouses mushroomed all over medieval Europe, mostly founded near rivers, and many developed their own maltings. Monks oversaw the widespread introduction of hops in AD 1000 and, 400 years later, Bavarian brothers began bottom-fermenting techniques.

The dissolution of the monasteries saw the Church's grip on European brewing loosen, and, by the early 1800s, beer had shifted from ecclesiastical to industrial hands.

TECHNICAL INNOVATION

Prior to the Industrial Revolution, breweries were small concerns whose dark beers, brewed mainly in the colder months, rarely roamed beyond a limited radius of the brewery.

But thanks to a number of groundbreaking industrial advancements, all that changed in the late 1800s when beer became easier to make, store, drink, and transport across long distances.

The advent of the steam engine had given rise to larger-scale production, railroads, and industrial refrigeration (pioneered by Munich's Spaten brewery during the 1870s), while Louis Pasteur lifted the lid on

yeast and enabled brewers to preserve and prolong beer's life.

The introduction of coke as the core fuel gave brewers greater control of the malting process and allowed them to produce paler malt. This, paired with pasteurization and refrigeration, paved the way for helles and pilsners, the golden lagers that took Europe by storm in the second half of the century.

The advent of golden lager was a marketing master stroke, and more than 120 years later, represents the vast majority of the beer drunk worldwide.

The ability to mass-produce lager was behind the post–World War II period of mass consolidation brewing, which saw the emergence of global behemoth brewing businesses.

But since the 1980s, in the reverential hands of a growing grassroots brewing movement, beer has undergone a genteel global revolution.

Historical recipes are being revived and reinterpreted, the art of the old is being merged with the science of the new, and, in their quest for new flavor experiences, brewers are looking both forward and back, as well as to one another, for inspiration, experimentation, and innovation … and it may just be the best time to be a beer drinker since neolithic man first soaked barley in water.

Right: The monks at Maredsous Abbey, a Benedictine monastery in Belgium, have a centuries-long history of beer brewing. Nowadays their beers are brewed for them at the Duvel-Moortgat brewery.

INGREDIENTS Hops

Let's give a big hand for the hop—making beer beautiful since the ninth century. Before the hop reared its conelike head, packed with resins and essential oils, brewers had been adding herbs, flowers, and spices, but while brewers still dip into these ancient recipes, for the most part, the hop has become the seasoning king in beer.

Hops are grown on bines up to 20 feet in height and are a member of the same botanical family as cannabis. They have an interesting medicinal background, having once been prescribed as an aphrodisiac for men, yet an inducer of sleep for women.

History buffs suggest Roman writer Pliny first referenced them in his bestseller *Natural History* back in AD77 to 79, christening them *Lupus salictarius*, meaning "wolf plant," due to their creeping fondness for growing wild among willow trees. But their widespread involvement in brewing didn't materialize for another few hundred years. The earliest evidence of using hops in brewing can be found in ninth-century documents written by Abbot Adalhard of the Benedictine monastery of Corbie in northern France. But German nun Abbess Hildegard of Bingen also deserves a mention; she wrote about them as a preservative for the first time in the tenth century and was also the first person to write about the female orgasm. By the fourteenth century hops had ingratiated themselves with European brewers and were introduced to North America during the 1600s.

Many hail hops as the "grapes of beer," but that is a little misleading. Yes, they're varietal like grapes and provide unique flavors and aromas, but unlike grapes they don't provide fermentable sugars during brewing. Hops are more accurately regarded as the seasoning, bringing balance to a liquid that would otherwise be sweet and syrupy. Picked in the summer, dried and used in pellet or fresh flower form, they give beer its bitter zing and delicate, floral aroma. Hops ward off bacteria and preserve beer too.

Alpha acids and hop oils are the key to the plant's virtues and provide the flavor and aroma compounds that brewers want. While there's been a growing buzz about dual-purpose hops and single-hop beers in recent times, hops can still be divided simply into two categories: bittering/kettle hops and aroma hops. Bittering hops, abundant in alpha acids, are added at the beginning of the boil for bitterness, while aroma hops, oozing with hop oils yet low in alpha acids, tend to be added toward the end of the boil or sometimes in the whirlpool. If dry-hopping, aroma hops can also be added after the wort has cooled, while fresh-hopping involves adding newly picked "wet" hops to the beer. Bitterness is best obtained when brewing begins, but brewers experiment at all stages of the process to achieve other aromas or flavors.

TOP HOPS
A selection of some of the most popular hops in brewing today:

NELSON SAUVIN (NEW ZEALAND)
A talented dual-purpose hop delivering "fresh crushed gooseberries"—a descriptor also used for Sauvignon Blanc grapes.

ZATEC/SAAZ (CZECHIA)
Regarded as the Rolls Royce of hops and a key component of Czech pilsners, renowned for its light, spicy, citrus zest.

CASCADE (USA)
A high-alpha variety with unique floral/spicy aromas mainly due to abnormal levels of some of the essential oils.

FUGGLES (UK)
Once the main copper hop, this aroma idol balances full body with a clean and refreshing quality present in many traditional ales.

OTHER HOP VARIETIES

AMARILLO (USA)
A hop, fully resplendent in tangerine, grapefruit, and lime flavors. One of the most popular American C-hops (floral, citrusy, and aromatic, found in IPAs).

CENTENNIAL (USA)
A dual-purpose hop boasting nearly double the alpha content and floral, citrus qualities of Cascade, one of the other C-hops.

CHALLENGER (UK)
A high-yielding dual-purpose hop with a refreshing, full-bodied rounded bitterness.

CHINOOK (USA)
A high-alpha dual-purpose hop with a very strong, spicy grapefruit character.

COLUMBUS (USA)
A bittering hop generally used as a main copper hop in the form of extracts and pellets because of the high-alpha content.

CRYSTAL (USA)
A craft brewer's favorite due to its versatile profile, this aroma hop imparts herbal and woody notes to beer.

FIRST GOLD (UK)
Suitable both as a general kettle hop (page 16) and also for a late and dry hopping in all types of beer. Includes a citrus note that lends balanced bitterness.

GALENA (USA)
A relative of First Gold, this high-alpha bittering hop is balanced with a strong tomcat/black-currant character.

GOLDINGS (UK)
A delicate aroma variety brimming with youthful fruity lemon/orange zest and smooth almost sweet citrus aromas.

GREEN BULLET (NEW ZEALAND)
A sleek smooth hop whose aroma qualities match its bittering power. Provides pine and lemon.

HALLERTAU (GERMANY)
A delicate, floral, and slightly fruity aroma, traditionally used in lager-type beers.

MOTEUKA (NEW ZEALAND)
An aroma hop that delivers a lovely lime expression.

MOSAIC (USA)
An aroma hop amped up with mango and other tropical and pit fruits.

MT. HOOD (USA)
An aroma hop for a mild and grassy flavor; comes through as delicate, floral, and slightly herbal.

NORTHDOWN (UK)
An excellent all-rounder with good alpha and aroma properties. A richer take on Challenger.

NORTHERN BREWER (GERMANY)
A direct descendant of Northern Brewer (UK), this dual-purpose hop has excellent bittering properties and a cedar aroma.

NUGGET (USA)
A high-alpha hop for great bittering, with a light herbal aroma.

PACIFIC GEM (NEW ZEALAND)
A high-alpha hop, very fruity with celebrated berry fruit aromas.

PERLE (GERMANY)
An excellent enduring-aroma hop, with characteristics as good as those of Hallertau but with a higher alpha-acid content and better yield.

PRIDE OF RINGWOOD (AUSTRALIA)
A bittering hop employed for balance and gentle woody hop aroma. Popular in lagers.

SIMCOE (USA)
A dual-purpose, primarily bittering hop with a clean, pinelike aroma and hint of citrus.

SORACHI ACE (JAPAN)
Loved by brewers looking to add lemon character to farmhouse ales, IPAs, and wheat beers.

SPALT (GERMANY)
Slightly spicy and loved by lagers, this brings both refined bitterness and uplifting aromas to the party.

STYRIAN GOLDINGS (SLOVENIA)
A noble hop and a distinguished variety almost identical to Fuggles, but with a distinctive perfume character.

TARGET (UK)
A high-alpha dual-purpose variety that delivers sage and spice on the nose and a big hit of citrus bitterness.

TETTNANG (GERMANY)
An aroma hop, often used in European lagers and traditional lighter English cask ales.

WILLAMETTE (USA)
A good-quality aroma hop with complex notes working through estery, black currant, and herbal.

OTHER INGREDIENTS

GRAIN

Rice, rye, wheat, oats, sorghum, corn, and spelt are just some of the grains used by brewers, but barley is considered the soul of beer, and, in almost every case, it is the base grain used in brewing.

Barley furnishes beer with the fuel needed for fermentation. It's the source of sweetness, it sculpts the beer's body, adorns it with much of its mouthfeel, and creates a tasty platform on which the other ingredients can perform.

Choosing the specific malts that go into the grist (page 16) is the key component of the brewer's art, and malts can loosely be divided into two groups: base malts and specialty malts. The former tend to be light in color yet high in fermentable sugars and make up most of the grain bill, while the latter, ranging in hue from light-brown to black, shape flavor and color in smaller quantities.

Right: Malted barley, the fuel for fermentation and the soul of beer.
Far right: The mash—where the fermentable sugars are unleashed at different temperatures.

YEAST

Yeast is the most important, interesting, and enigmatic ingredient in beer and perhaps the most fascinating member of the funghi family.

There are thousands of different yeasts that surround us, yet most brewers are interested only in those called *Saccharomyces cerevisiae* which, when presented with sweet wort, munches on sugars like a ravenous Pac-Man, excreting alcohol and belching out carbon dioxide as it goes along.

Yeast also provides beer with a broad range of flavors, some of which are good and some aren't. Yeast is a living organism that undergoes 13 different stages before fermenting. Brewers must ensure that the temperature, oxygen, and sugar levels in the mash (page 16) are all to the yeast's liking, and if they aren't, the yeast will certainly let them know as they fail to ferment.

The brewer's job is to work out when a particular yeast strain flips from friend to fermenting foe. For yeast can be a fickle, feral fellow capable of bringing a brewer sobbing to his knees. If the wrong yeast wheedles its way into the brewing process, funny things will happen during fermentation—and not in an amusing way.

As such, a lot of breweries stick to a single signature yeast for just this reason, but if a brewer wants to explore across different styles then he'll need to work with more than one. This is fine as long as the strains are kept apart. Like a spouse and a secret lover, it's not a great idea to introduce them to each other.

Yeast strains can be loosely divided into two categories: lager

yeast and ale yeast. Generally speaking, ale yeast lends more character to the beer than lager yeast.

- Ale yeast likes things warm (54 to 75 degrees Fahrenheit) and remains buoyant in the fermentation vessel.

- Lager yeast performs better at lower temperatures (34 to 55 degrees Fahrenheit) and prefers to eat in smaller, lighter groups that drop down to the bottom of the fermentation vessel.

Lager yeast is a clipped dinner companion; it will politely polish off everything on its plate, but it won't add a great deal to the conversation. So much so, most won't notice or remember it being there.

Ale yeast, on the other hand, is a far more gregarious guest. Rudely pushing away its unwanted plate of residual sugars (which add sweetness and texture to the beer), it happily mingles with the other ingredients at the table, spicing up conversation with some fruity opinions.

WATER

Water is a critical component of the brewing process, constituting 95 percent of the ingredients and exerting an immense influence on the overall character of beer.

Not all water is the same. The geology of a given geographic area once determined the mineral content, hardness, and softness of the local water, and, before the age of water treatment, it also determined the type of beer that could be brewed.

In the Czech town of Pilsen, for example, water is very soft with barely any mineral salts. As such, the local water complements the delicate hop and measured malt flavors of the pilsner beer style.

By contrast, the mineral-rich high alkali waters of Dublin and London traditionally lent themselves perfectly to the brewing of porters and stouts, while the water in Burton-on-Trent, harder than a gravedigger's heart and high in minerals and sulfates, gave the town's eponymous ale its dryness and sulfuric aroma—known as the "Burton Snatch."

Technology developed over the past 50 years or so means that modern breweries can replicate water from anywhere in the world and alter its inherent hardness, softness, and mineral content according to the style of beer being brewed.

HOW BEER IS MADE

Theoretically, brewing is a fairly simple process, but as any homebrewer can testify, it's far more complicated and nuanced than meets the eye, and titanic tomes exist, far weightier than this one, that delve deep into the art and science of brewing. But, for now, here's a breakdown of the basics of brewing.

MILLING & MASHING

Milling splits the kernel of the grain into grist, which is a granular mixture of husks and fine starchy flour.

The grist is then mixed with hot water in a mash tun to unleash soluble sugars and form the mash; a stodgy, oatmeal-like substance. Different sugars are unlocked at different temperatures, and, depending on the desired style, brewers play around with heat in order to coax out the appropriate sugars.

The mash is then separated from the grain-husk material and sprayed with water in a lauter tun to create the wort—a smooth, sweet molasses-like solution that contains all the sugars and starches required for fermentation. The wort is then sent to the kettle.

BOILING

The wort-filled kettle is brought to an undulating boil that zaps away unwanted yeast prior to fermentation.

Hops are then added. Bittering hops, able to withstand the high temperatures, are added at the beginning of the boil for bitterness and herbal flavors.

Toward the end of the boil, more heat-sensitive hops are added for flavor before aromatic hops are introduced in the last few minutes of the boil, and late hopping occurs as the wort is cooled and prepared for the fermentation process.

FERMENTATION & CONDITIONING

Once the spent hops and any congealed malt are strained away or separated and siphoned off using a whirlpool, the wort plummets in temperature and is pumped into a fermentation vessel, where the yeast, knife and fork in hand and napkin tucked eagerly under its chin, awaits.

For the first hour or so, the wort lies dormant, and there's little sign of any activity. But as anyone who has seen the movie *Jaws* will testify, the dead calm always precedes a thrashing feeding frenzy. Before long, the surface transforms from a millpond to a seething, foaming mass of liquid bubble-wrap that bursts and bloats both wide and high. Things get heated in the eating orgy, but the temperature is controlled using cooling jackets so that the yeast doesn't expire from the excess.

As with humans, alcohol seldom aids stamina, and after a while the yeast really needs to sleep. It tends to lose its appetite and enthusiasm before it has eaten all the sugars, but this is a good thing because brewers require residual sugars to add finesse to the flavor and bulk to the body of the beer.

Right: A small mash tun where grist meets water.
Opposite, top: Overalls? Check. Beard? Check.
Woolly Hat? Check. Fresh craft beer? Check.
Opposite, bottom: Gert Christiaens of Beersel patiently waits for his oak barrels to work their magic on his lambic beer.

FILTRATION, PASTEURIZATION, AND PACKAGING

After conditioning, most brewers seek to create "bright beer" by filtering out all the yeast and undesirable proteins and pasteurizing the beer, essentially exterminating any potential infection by partially boiling it at high heat for 15 minutes.

But in their unwavering pursuit of flavor and freshness, an increasing number of smaller brewers are neither filtering nor pasteurizing their beer and are happy to hand it to drinkers with a hazy appearance. To enable the beer to last longer in the bottle and the keg, "bright beer" is often pasteurized. This destroys any stray bacteria that might infect it once packaged.

In a producer-driven market, uneven flavor undermines the commercial viability of brands, and this method is favored among industrial brewers.

While pasteurization can be frowned upon for removing flavors so carefully produced by the brewer, it doesn't always mean boring beer. Some distinctive beers, well-brewed and crafted with integrity and excellent ingredients, can be pasteurized. That said, a growing number of brewers who are wary of the potential perils of pasteurization are turning to sterile filtration. This removes enough yeast and spoiling elements from the beer to ensure maximum shelf-life without stripping away flavors from the brewing process later on.

BEER
BASICS

STORING, POURING & TEMPERATURE

Packaging, storing, pouring, temperature, and glassware all have a surprisingly significant affect on the entire sensual beer-drinking experience from first sip to the finish—whether on appearance, aroma, or flavor.

STORING

Rather than stockpiling copious cases of beer, buy little and often, keeping it as fresh as possible —as most beer is brewed to be drunk that way.

Fresh beer has two arch enemies: sunlight and oxygen. Oxygen creates undesirable "off" flavors in beer ranging from wet cardboard and leather to lipstick, stale bread, and sherry—and not good sherry.

Overexposure to light, meanwhile, unleashes an unpleasant "skunked" aroma akin to the stench sprayed from anal glands of stressed-out skunks. No one wants that.

The simplest place to store most beer is the refrigerator. Just as cooler temperatures decelerate the deterioration of food, so they do for beer. It's dark in there too—the light does turn off when the door's shut.

Can't fit all your beer in the refrigerator? Then a dry, dark cellar or garage is perfect. Ideally, it should be cool, but unless they're wildly fluctuating don't worry about changes in temperature.

Unlike wine, beer bottles should be kept upright, although a short period of horizontal storage doesn't harm beer unduly.

POURING

The perfect pour should heighten anticipation, create a thirst, and, regardless of style and regional preferences, display a foam head.

Head is good. It keeps the carbon dioxide in and the oxygen out, it's home to some lovely hop bitterness, and, let's be honest, it makes a beer look even more handsome. The general rule of thumb is around two fingers (around 1 inch) of head.

The perfect pour should cater to and control the carbonation of the beer. Some beers are a lot livelier than others. High levels of carbonation can be found in classic Belgian beers, wheat beers, and, of course, some bottle-conditioned ales.

If you're unsure of a beer's behavior, hold the glass at an angle of 45 degrees. Aim the pour at a spot about halfway down the side of the glass. If the beer begins to foam immediately then slow down, slimming the stream.

As the liquid reaches the halfway spot, tilt the glass slowly and carefully toward an upright position. If, in the early stage of the pour, foam isn't forming then slowly tilt the glass upright, heighten the gap between glass and bottle, and accelerate the flow, aerating the beer as it hits the bottom of the glass.

For bottle-conditioned beer, decant all but the bottom inch into the glass—as that's where the sediment resides.

TEMPERATURE

The effect of temperature on the flavor, aroma, look, and feel of a beer is immense.

Cold temperatures enhance carbonation, bitterness, dryness, and astringency, while warmer temperatures accentuate sweetness and acidity, broaden the beer's body, and coax out the complexity.

In general, serve beer between 42 and 55 degrees Fahrenheit. That said, each style has its ideal serving temperature. Delicate light lager styles, such as pilsner and helles and also wheat beers, are best served between 39 and 45 degrees Fahrenheit, while a couple of degrees warmer will mean you get the most from maltier dark-lager styles.

Farmhouse ales perform well at around 46 degrees Fahrenheit, as do lighter abbey ales, Trappists, and sour beers. To really entice the aromatics from the hop-driven pale ales and IPAs, dial it up a further degree or two.

Around 52 degrees Fahrenheit is perfect for darker abbey ales, porters, and stouts (although both suit summer chilling), while the full, flavorsome complexity of barley wines and vintage or aged brews really shines at around 54 degrees Fahrenheit.

Not sure of the optimum temperature? Many brewers will suggest a serving temperature on the label.

BEER EVALUATION

When assessing beer, you should use all your senses. Yes, all of them.

SOUND

The sound of a cork being popped or a beer glugging into a glass is a highly evocative one, while the "Pffft" of a bottle being opened reveals much about the beer's carbonation. If you put a glass of beer to your ear, you can hear the sea. Sometimes. Although it is doubtful that it has much to say about beer to be honest.

SIGHT

Use your eyes. Have a look at the beer. Hold the glass to the natural light, preferably against a white backdrop, and give it a proper look.

It's not just color and clarity you're looking for here, it's the way it moves and keeps its head, the consistency, and the carbonation. All of which communicates a lot about a beer's quality and fidelity to style.

Not all beers should look the same but all of them should make you want to drink them—whether it's a pilsner cascading into a glass and surging up into a tight, white head; the billowing pour of a creamy, velvet stout; or a flickering flame peered through a golden prism of a barley wine.

Looks can, of course, be deceiving, but in general they can tell you a great deal about a beer.

SMELL

Your nose is not just there to keep sunglasses on your face—it's the most important instrument in your analytical arsenal.

Right at the top of your nose is your olfactory epithelium, a ½-inch-squared strip of tissue that analyzes and identifies particular odors. Olfactory experts figure that as much as 95 percent of what one perceives as taste is actually smell, and this is easily demonstrated if you take a swig of a beer while pinching your nostrils.

There are thousands of flavor compounds present in beer that your tongue won't tell you about. Each of beer's four core ingredients creates a wealth of aromas that can contribute to a beer's complex bouquet, not to mention any additional ingredients there may be.

These can evolve according to everything from the height of the liquid in the glass to the temperature of the beer. Drinking a beer straight from the bottle denies these sensations, so pour it into a glass and give it a swirl.

As well as detecting all of beer's aromatic delights, the sense of smell is also crucial in recognizing faults in a beer, flavors that shouldn't be there—like butterscotch, wet cardboard, skunky sulfurous smells, or, perhaps worse, absolutely nothing at all.

TASTE & FEEL

Having appreciated beer's aromas, it's now time to explore its flavor. Taste is a combination of aroma and flavor and can be identified when you drink it.

Unlike wine tasting, you should really swallow rather than spit when tasting beer. Not only is it more enjoyable, but many have claimed that this is because receptors of bitterness, an essential element in beer, can be found at the back of the tongue—with sweetness at the tip; sourness and saltiness filed on either side.

But the general consensus is that the entire tongue can sense all of these tastes more or less equally, so when you taste beer slowly circulate it around the tongue, giving it time to get to know the beer.

Take another sip and it'll tell you more, not just about the flavors but about the texture too. Does it sit on the tongue? Does it feel round? Does it fill the mouth or dissipate quickly?

Don't forget to breathe and open up that retro-nasal passage—essential in assessing flavor when one eats and drinks. Inside the mouth, at the back of the palate, it's an opening to those olfactory receptors first reached during appreciation of the aroma.

Originally a safety net to warn us about poisonous or rotten food, it now sends another important, aromatic message to your brain. So before you swallow, aerate the beer by puckering the lips and breathing in like a backward whistle.

Then, as with life, there's the finish. How does the beer end? Does it fall off a cliff? Or stay longer than the mother-in-law? What are the flavors and the feelings that it leaves you with?

GLASSWARE

Glassware is crucial to the enjoyment of beer, and choosing the right vessel is an important exercise.

Visually, glassware, quite literally, speaks volumes. The iconic imperial pint or swaying stein is a wide-mouthed clamor for carefree consumption, while a tight-lipped snifter talks a little softer of something special to sip and savor.

In addition to the emotional, ritual role of glassware, there's the physical element too. From a sensory perspective, form should follow function. Each glass should be shaped to enhance the olfactory experience of certain beer styles, enhancing aroma and introducing them easily to one's nose.

NONIK PINT GLASS

It couldn't be more British, but this pint glass should only be used for drinking session-friendly beer such as a bitter or a golden ale.

DIMPLED MUG

Purists may not like it, but drinking cask-conditioned beer from this hardwearing ruggedly handsome glass with a handle and a kaleidoscopic charisma just feels right, always.

TULIP/THISTLE

Short of stem and wide of mouth, this swirl-friendly glass suits acutely aromatic beers, its protruding lips opening up the aromas and launching the liquid onto the mid-tongue. Ideal for Belgian ales.

SNIFTER

Warmed up in one's hands, this globular glass ushers aromas toward the nostrils with its inward pointing lips. Ideal for stouts, porters, and barley wines.

FLUTE

A long lithe body lends itself to carbonated beers, foaming a tight head and neatly channeling the aromas. Ideal for fruit beers, lambics, and Flemish reds.

The design and thickness of the glass affect the temperature of the liquid within. A stemmed white-wine glass will keep a weissbier chilled, while a brandy snifter, clutched in one's hands, slowly warms up a Baltic porter and coaxes out its rich complexity.

As you broaden your beer horizons, it's good to grow your glass collection too, and don't be shy to use glassware more readily associated with wine and spirits.

NUCLEATION
Historically, specks of dirt and imperfections in the glass would have enhanced the effervescence of a beer. But with the advent of improved cleanliness, brewers and glass manufactures have been forced to encourage nucleation by scoring the bottom of their glasses to help create a fine-looking fizz.

PILSNER
The classic straight-sided slaker gives drinkers the golden glad-eye and heightens the hop character with its v-shaped top. Best suited to the imbibing of German and German-style helles, pilsners, schwarzbier, and dunkels.

GOBLET/CHALICE
Beloved of the Belgians and often ecclesiastical in appearance, these short-stemmed, broadly brimmed goblets and larger chalices reach out, arms akimbo, offering up all the flavors from within. The wide surface area keeps one's nose close to the aromas, inviting big sips of Trappist beers, abbey ales, and Belgian ales.

WEIZEN
Designed with typical Teutonic efficiency, its shape thrusts a frothy white head upward, unleashing big banana and classic clove characteristics. Use for all types of wheat beer.

STEIN
Designed for drinking and clinking, the thick-walled stein was originally an earthenware Bavarian beer vessel, which, in nineteenth-century beer gardens, sported a thumb-levered tin lid to stop leaves and insects dropping into the beer. Use for Oktoberfest lagers, helles, dunkel, märzen.

GERMAN STANGE (AND OTHER SMALLER VESSELS)
In Cologne, kölsch is always served in straight-sided cylindrical "stanges" while in nearby Düsseldorf, the city's altbier comes in a slightly portlier version. For barley wines and strong beers, try an antique eighteenth century dwarf ale glass or, if you can't find one, a small sherry glass.

BEER STYLES

In the 1970s, prior to the craft brewing revolution, there were no more than 20 or so recognized beer styles, but now, according to America's Brewers Association, there are more than 150, ranging from straightforward pale ales and porters to the frankly esoteric. As craft brewing has become more creative, beers have been reinvented, cross-fertilized, and misinterpreted so often that they're mere signposts of style now.

GRAIN

PORTER & STOUT

Porter was first mentioned in 1721 and became the world's first truly global beer style.

Initially a hoppier, aged version of the popular muggy pub brown beers, the new "porter" beers were highly hopped, brewed with high-roasted malt, and, unlike other beers that were matured in pub cellars, aged at the brewery in 108-gallon casks called butts.

In the late eighteenth century, London brewers such as Truman's and Barclay Perkins began making stronger yet very similar versions of their popular porters that they called, rather cleverly, "stout porters" to differentiate them.

Both beers were often brewed to the same recipe, the only difference being that less water was used to mash the stout, and it wasn't until the mid-nineteenth century that stouts became a distinct and separate style.

Across the Irish Channel in Dublin, meanwhile, a drier stout brewed with roasted malt had become the flagship style of the Guinness brewery and over time, aided by both canny advertising and the missionary zeal of Irish diaspora, became arguably the world's most iconic beer brand.

GERMAN WEISSBIER

German wheat beers get all their banana and clovelike flavor from the use of a unique yeast strain that brings out the true character of the wheat malt used in the brew. The proportion of wheat also tends to be higher in Germany than it is in Belgium, and German brewers would never throw in herbs or spices. Weissbier can either be light or dark in appearance, and most brewers produce two versions: hefe (with yeast) or kristal (without yeast). The latter may look cleaner and clearer, but the former is by far the more flavorsome and popular.

BELGIAN WITBIER

Soft, citrusy, and spiced, with a slightly milky character, few beer styles can slake a thirst more elegantly than a wonderful witbier.

Belgian wits are unfiltered, brewed using more unmalted wheat than their Bavarian brethren, and use spices and fruit—mainly coriander and orange peel—which the Germans simply wouldn't allow.

SAISON

A centuries-old beer style first brewed by farmers to slake the rasping thirst of itinerant agricultural workers, known as *saisonniers,* who toiled over the soil in Wallonia.

Boiled and spiced, it was brewed during the colder months and then stored to be drunk throughout the summer. Rarely reaching a strength above 4% (useful when you're swinging a scythe), saison recipes would depend entirely on which ingredients were close at hand; be they hops, herbs, or spices; barley, rye, wheat, or spelt (a grain that fills out the body of a beer while keeping things "light").

Having almost slipped out of existence in the 1970s, saison has enjoyed a remarkable global renaissance, and fidelity to the loosely defined style remains, ranging from dry thirst slakers to complex characters flowing in flavor, dry spiciness, herbal highs, and yeasty funk.

BIÈRE DE GARDE

Similar to saison, bière de garde is an acutely idiosyncratic style rooted in rustic farmhouse tradition and synonymous with the Pas-de-Calais and Nord regions of northern France. Bière de garde ("keeping" beer) was brewed during the temperate fall and winter when recently harvested hops and barley were readily available. The cool climate created a languid, stable fermentation and purged the process of pesky, bothersome bacteria.

This produced a lean yet luscious liquid sustenance that would last the summer months when brewing was not viable. While typical, "traditional" bière de garde tends to be light copper in color, tangy with a toasted malt character, and has a tight finish and ABV hovering around the 7% mark, it is by no means a style that plays to rigid stylistic rules.

Color can range from dark brown to blonde, either ale or lager yeast can fuel the fermentation, some brewers add spice and sugar, and hop character has traditionally been held back but is more apparent in modern American-accented interpretations.

In France, there are a couple of clear seasonally based bière de garde categories. Winter releases, often called *Bière de Noel,* are rich, strong, malty, and sometimes spiced cockle-warming affairs, while the spring sees lighter, drier yet muscular malty beers whose body is often smoothed out using wheat.

RAUCHBIER

Rauchbier is brewed using a centuries-old process dating back to the days when malt used for brewing was kilned by burning wood, the flame giving each grain a heavily smoky flavor.

The spiritual home of German rauchbier is Bamberg, where an array of smoked beers is brewed using malt kilned over beechwood. For the uninitiated, the smoke character can overwhelm the senses (like drinking a campfire through a barbecued herring that's been swimming in lapsang souchong tea all its life), but perseverance reaps rewards, and soon the smoke fades to reveal sweetness, complexity, and silky texture.

HOP

AMBER/RED ALES

Whatever you do, don't be hoodwinked by the emphasis on hue here. While the reddish tinge to these ales suggests a malt sweetness, most modern amber or red ales are simply tawny-colored Trojan horses for the American hop.

Initially inspired, perhaps, by British bitters, the sweetness in amber ales is more rounded than a red and certainly more session friendly. Red ales, meanwhile, tend to resemble an IPA in everything but color.

Amber ale remains an incredibly popular, indigenous flag-bearer for the American craft brewers, the most famous and commercially successful being Fat Tire, made by New Belgium Brewing, Colorado (see brewery profile, page 202).

INDIA PALE ALE (IPA)

Back in the eighteenth century, when it was the most significant brewing nation in the world, Britain sent huge amounts of India pale ale on a six-month boat journey to Bombay.

Hops and high alcoholic strength gave it the swashbuckling sea-legs to endure the long, treacherous journey. Acting as sturdy ballast, the rocking and rolling in oak rounded off the bitter edges and created a beer of mature oak-aged character.

The heat helped too. Often rising gradually to more than 95 degrees Fahrenheit, it would perform a kind of natural pasteurization, zapping any residual yeast that may have fallen through the filtering process back in London.

It was an enormous success in India, but, by the late 1800s, IPA sales were slumping. It all but disappeared for the best part of a century until the 1990s, when America, its craft brewing scene gathering momentum, enthusiastically adopted it as its own.

The Americanization of IPA, particularly on the West Coast, is the most significant event to have shaped beer in the last 30 years. Not content with reinventing IPA by cranking up the aroma and bitterness with the amounts of American hops, America's craft brewers have doubled it, tripled it, made it imperial, and even taken it into the black.

More than 200 years after English brewers were exporting heavily hopped ales and porters to India, hundreds of British craft brewers are now brewing American-style interpretations of IPA. Yet very little of it, if any, is drunk in India.

PALE ALE

The little black dress of the beer world, pale ale should fill the refrigerator of every beer drinker. Easy-drinking ales of understated and often undervalued excellence, born of the British bitter tradition, pales now encompass a wide range of hues and hop influence. But at their core, pales primarily pivot on sheer drinkability with an elegant equilibrium of malt flavors, delicate, floral–hop bitterness, and an enticing aroma. American and Pacific pale ales tend to hail the aromatic hop with more gusto, and this has given rise to a modern breed of British pales that are low-gravity and sessionable, like a classic bitter but with more contemporary floral and fruity hop character. Pale ale styles are also known as hoppy light ales, golden ales, and session ales.

LAGER

BOCKS

In the fourteenth century, these strong, massively malty beers were exclusive to the north German town of Einbeck, but, following the town's demise in the Thirty Years War, they were revived in Bavaria and are now brewed all over Germany and beyond, mostly as seasonal beers for both winter and spring.

While pale bocks have increased in popularity recently, most bocks are dark in color, brewed with Vienna and Munich malt, a light dusting of hops, and a long lagering period of around 12 to 15 weeks. Drinking between 6.3% and 7% ABV, bocks are rich, warming, and full-bodied with a notably long, lingering finish.

The word bock, a distortion of the "beck" part of Einbeck, translates as billy goat, and the hairy-chinned members of the Bovidae family are often seen on bock beer labels.

CZECH LAGER

Czech lager has its own rather baffling lexicon based loosely on strength and color. While there are many overlaps, idiosyncrasies, and exceptions, these descriptors should simplify any exploration of Czechia's incredible lager brewing tradition.

STRENGTH

Ležák literally means "lager," but, rather unhelpfully, it can be used to describe ale as well. Must be between 11 to 12 degrees Plato (which measures the density of wort) and is usually the flagship beer style for Czech breweries.

Výčepní has a strength from 7 to 10 degrees Plato. Translated as "tap beer" or "draft beer," it can also be bottled and is a hugely popular "style."

Speciáls are big beers weighing in at 13 degrees or above. Often adorned with imagery associated with German bocks—goats, rams, etc.

COLOR

Czech beer (known as pivo) is color-coded too—the boundaries of which can be rather blurry. Světlý refers to "pale-colored" beer and tmavé dictates that the beer should be "dark" while polotmavé has a "half-dark" hue akin to an amber lager. The darkest is cerne, meaning "black," but it often shows up as a lighter beer too.

SUBSTYLES

Kvasnicové: Loved by Czech lager connoisseurs, this "yeast beer" gets its sparkling character from the addition of fermenting wort or yeast prior to kegging—otherwise known as krausening. Confusingly, it's a term sometimes used to mean unfiltered beer.

Nefiltrované: A pivo (beer) that hasn't been filtered after lagering—which generally furnishes it with a fuller, fresher flavor.

Tankova: "Tank beer" that is pumped fresh from the brewery into conditioning tanks within the bar. Benefits from being unpasteurized and therefore has a reduced oxygen exposure.

DUNKEL/SCHWARZBIER

For decades prior to the mid-nineteenth century arrival of pale golden lager, dark lager dominated much of Germany's drinking landscape with dunkel in Bavaria and schwarzbier in Thuringia.

The original Bavarian dunkels, brewed using scratchy and smoky malt, were dark roasty affairs until the latter 1800s when malting techniques, borrowed from British brewers, made mellower amber Munich malt. Combined with cool maturation, this delivered a smooth, deep, less smoky character with a subdued hops.

Schwarzbier, meanwhile, is both historically and stylistically closer to porter than pilsner. Denser and darker than a dunkel, bleeding from light-black into dark-maroon, schwarzbiers are more muscular in mouthfeel too, with a heavier roast going on. The best are balanced out by a muted hop presence. The classic example is Köstritzer (page 108).

GERMAN PILSNER

Compared to Czech pilsners, German versions are often lighter in hue, with daintier aromatics, a similar sure malt backbone, and a very elegant, spritzy bitterness from the Hallertau and Hersbruck hops. There's a lightness to them, with something slightly sulfidic that gives it a more refreshing character —and this comes from very good brewing in cold conditions.

While southern German pilsners make more of the malt, northern German pilsners contain a crisper bitter bite like the breeze that blows off the Baltic coast, the Hallertau and Tettnang hops delivering a distinct grassy hoppiness and a signature snappiness to each sip.

MÄRZEN/OKTOBERFEST BEERS

Back in the Middle Ages and prior to the advent of refrigeration, brewing beer in the summer was problematic due to air-borne

bacteria. So, in March (hence the name), brewers amassed plenty of saleable beer, strong and heavily hopped, to tide them over until fall.

Stored in cold-cellared casks, märzens were full-bodied, malt-accented beers, deep-amber to copper in color with an alcohol content of around 5 or 6%. By October, the summer had finished and the coast was clear to begin brewing again. Brewers cleared out their barrels of märzen beer in order to make room for new beers. Having lots of strong beer to finish off in a hurry was a good excuse for a party ... and thus the Oktoberfest was born.

Today, Oktoberfestbier tends to be a mellower, paler version of a märzen, lagered and matured for between three and four months. Rather confusingly, Oktoberfest beers don't tend to be drunk at the Oktoberfest anymore, with the easier-drinking, lighter helles beers preferred.

Beyond the Bavarian capital's borders, imitations must be called Oktoberfest-style beer, as genuine Oktoberfest beer can be brewed only by the breweries within Munich's city limits.

The meaning of märzen, meanwhile, has morphed and now commonly refers to a lighter, amber-colored beer style originally unveiled by Gabriel Sedlmayer of the Spaten brewery in 1841.

At the same time, Anton Dreher of the Klein-Schwechat brewery in Austria was introducing beer drinkers to his similar maroon, malt-driven Vienna lager that took Europe by storm.

Nutty, slightly sweet, and notable for a refined roast character and lengthy finish, Vienna lager is conspicuous by its absence in its city of birth, yet it's a style that has been embraced with gusto by both American brewers and also Latin America, where the Germanic brewing influence has endured from a few generations ago.

The stylistic lines between märzen, Vienna lagers, and Oktoberfest beers are becoming increasingly blurred and all three can be huddled under the umbrella term "amber lager."

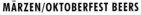

PILSNER

In 1842, a notoriously bad-tempered Bavarian brewer called Josef Groll brewed the world's first pale-colored lager and, in doing so, radically altered the course of brewing history.

Disillusioned with the poor-quality beers that were being produced in the Bohemian town of Pilsen, local merchants (upstanding pillars of the community) commissioned the building of a new brewery and recruited Groll to brew a lager that would rival the märzen beers being brewed in Bavaria and the Vienna styles of Austria.

Groll brought together Bohemia's sensational, spicy Saaz hops, the envy of European brewing; moist Moravian barley and Pilsen water, softer than a bubble bath of kittens—and perfect for lager brewing.

Using brand-new cutting-edge kilning facilities and a malthouse that could produce the same light-colored malt used by English brewers to make their pale ale, Groll created a very clear beer that was laid down for 37 days in extremely chilly, labyrinthine cellars where the bespoke Bavarian yeast could work its magic.

When the first barrels were tapped on November 11, 1842, during the St. Martin's Fair in Pilsen, the world's first clear, golden lager poured forth. It must have been an incredible sight—a translucent, twinkling gold lager served in clear glassware, a novelty at the time.

During the twentieth century, pilsners became a global phenomenon, and pilsner is now a term attributed, rather haphazardly, to hundreds of pale lagers of varying quality brewed all over the world.

Yet it's in Czechia, the beer's birthplace, pilsners can still be enjoyed in their purest form. Referred to locally as světlý ležák (pilsner is considered a brand name), Czech pilsners proudly showcase the signature spicy Saaz hop and get their gorgeous golden hue and muscular malt body from traditional floor malting and decoction techniques, while the deliberate dabbling with diacetyl often bestows the butterscotch flavor upon the beer.

When drawn straight from the chilly tanks in the brewery cellar, unfiltered and unpasteurized, all hazy and daisy fresh, a proper Czech pilsner is one of the greatest elbow-bending experiences you are ever likely to have, thanks to its utterly thirst-quenching properties.

QUENCH

ALTBIER

Altbier is the drink of Düsseldorf, and, like kölsch —its arch nemesis from Cologne—it straddles the two fundamental families of beer: ale and lager.

Brewed like an ale (using top–fermenting yeast) yet conditioned like a lager, alt means "old" and derives from the 1800s, when the proud, traditional brewers of Düsseldorf and its environs stood firm against the tide of new-fangled golden lagers from Munich and Pilsen.

Altbier is served in small, cylindrical 7-ounce glasses called Bechers (tumblers) whose slim shape prevents loss of carbon dioxide, maintains the beer aroma, and maintains the head. It's at its best when drawn fresh and unpasteurized from wooden casks in the city's array of brewpubs (hausbrauereis).

BITTER/BEST BITTER

At a time when acerbic, bitter beers dominate the modern beer scene on both sides of the Atlantic, it's ironic that bitter is seldom mentioned as a beer style anymore.

Yet bitter remains the quintessential cask-conditioned British pint. Classically crisp in hop character and underpinned by a craveworthy malt and a medium body, ranging from gold to copper in hue with medium bitterness, bitter epitomizes the easy-drinking English ale tradition that is under threat from popular highly hopped IPAs.

HELLES

Bavaria's answer to Bohemian pilsner was and still is helles; the original golden German lager first brewed at the Spaten brewery in 1894 and still enjoyed in Bavaria's beerhalls. Drunk predominantly on draft, this light-colored lager glistens in the glass and is softer, slightly sweeter, and less hoppy than a traditional pilsner.

KELLERBIER/UNGESPUNDET

Kellerbier is German lager at its most romantic and rustic and the antithesis of mass-industrialized lager brewing.

Kellerbier is matured in the cellar (it literally means "cellar beer") and is traditionally served unfiltered and unpasteurized in earthenware mugs. Hazy on the eye and full of fruity esters, much of kellerbier's color (similar to a märzen) and body comes from caramelized malt, while a healthy hopping gives the beer its quenching crisp dryness and sprightly aromatics.

At its most authentic, kellerbier is served ungespundet (unbunged). This involves removing the bung from the cask and releasing the carbon dioxide to create a less effervescent beer that is hopped more for purposes of preservation. In terms of mouthfeel and cellarmanship, it's close to British cask-conditioned ale.

KÖLSCH

Brewed like a pale ale yet conditioned cold and long, kölsch stylistically straddles the gap between golden ale and a delicate lager. Bright and brisk, light on the bubbles with a faintly citrusy fruit twist, it can be called kölsch only if it is brewed in Cologne, Germany— thanks to a law passed in 1948.

Brewed with one type of malt and treated to lengthy lager-conditioning, kölsch is always served in a straight-sided, narrow, 7-ounce glass called a stange, which prevents it getting warm. Extremely subtle and delicate with fruity ale-esque flavors, it's light in both body and appearance with subdued maltiness, unobtrusive hoppiness, and plenty of effervescence. While unable to call it kölsch, craft brewers outside of Cologne have been aping the style, sometimes with the use of wheat.

SIPPERS

IMPERIAL STOUT/BALTIC PORTER

Back when London breweries were exporting porters all around the world, in the latter half of the eighteenth century, one of their thirstiest customers was the Baltic region.

These dark beers, dispatched north on Baltic fleets, were brewed much stronger than domestic versions—not because the beers needed to withstand the journey but rather because drinkers in Russia simply liked their beers strong.

These imperial stouts were considered the ports of the beer world; complex, cockle-warming bruiser beers that were smoky and silky with touches of tar and tobacco; velvety vortexes of rich coffee, chocolate, and chicory; perfectly suited to the Baltic and its cold climate.

Unsurprisingly, the popularity of these porters did not go unnoticed by Baltic-based breweries, which began making their own versions. The colder climate and Germanic lager-brewing traditions meant they tended to use bottom rather than top fermentation, and most Baltic porters continue to be lagered in cold conditions, making them a little leaner and less oily and unctuous than the behemoth imperial Russian stouts, yet still remarkably robust.

WHAT'S THE DIFFERENCE BETWEEN PORTER & STOUT?

There's no real difference between porter and stout anymore. Traditionally, stout has always been considered a stronger version of porter, as, in the eighteenth century, the term "stout" was a generic prefix used to describe something bigger and stronger.

But that's not the case anymore. Modern porters can be more potent than stouts and vice versa. In their ingredients, brewing methods, taste, and appearance, the two beer styles are pretty much equally indistinguishable.

BARLEY WINE/OLD ALE

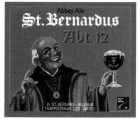

During the eighteenth century, England was often getting into fisticuffs with France, and consequently drinking wine—the enemy's elixir—was regarded as most unpatriotic.

So, in order to challenge "posh" plonk on the tables of the upper class, strong and imposing ales called barley wines were devised and often brewed in aristocratic country houses.

Ranging from amber to deep copper-garnet in color, they're grandiose, mellifluous fellows that dial up muscular malty sweetness and/or heavy hop bitterness.

Barley wines are suited for cellaring, designed to develop maturity over time, and ideally served in a snifter, like a complex port or brandy. Staring into a roaring fire wondering where it all went wrong is optional … but recommended.

BELGIAN ALES

Belgium boasts more indigenous beer styles than any other nation in the world and, unlike its German neighbor, never regulated its brewing with anything as regimented as the Reinheitsgebot.

So why try and classify them here? Well, despite the huge diversity of style, esoteric ingredients, and brewing methods, deep down in the DNA of nearly every Belgian ale there's an off-centered funky fruitiness that can best be described as, well, "Belgian."

Many attribute this common character to famously fruity Belgian yeast strains both during primary fermentation in the brewhouse and then later in the bottle. Other common characteristics include the sparing use of spices; the open addition of sugar and cereal grains to give a beer its sinewy body and high alcoholic content; sweetness before bitterness; bespoke glassware, and also bottle-conditioning.

DOPPELBOCK/DOUBLE-BOCKS

An extra-strong version of bock beer, doppelbock emerged in the late eighteenth century as a potent monastic beer brewed by Franciscan monks. Exceptionally malty with feint bitterness, doppelbocks usually check in at around 7 to 10% ABV with the stronger versions reaching as much as 13%. Darker, maltier, hoppier, more potent, and often recognized by the "–ator" suffix, as in Salvator brewed by Paulaner (the original doppelbock), Celebrator by Ayinger, and Spaten Optimator.

EISBOCK

Intense and intoxicating, icebocks are categorized as some of the world's most potent beers. They achieve their strength from being frozen at the latter stages of maturation. A thick, molasses-like winter warmer with a massive malt profile, a big body, and plenty of alcohol in the mix.

WILD & WOOD

FLEMISH RED ALES

Flemish ales are a funky, age-old fusion of wild yeast, wood-aging, bacteria, and blending. They're traditional, tremendously tart, and seductively sour with a faint farmyard funkiness.

Considered the Burgundies of beer, Flemish red ale is initially brewed using myriad malts, mostly Vienna, and hopped using old hops for preservation purposes rather than for bitterness or aroma.

At Rodenbach, the most famous brewery for the style, mixed fermentation follows using bespoke cultures of mixed yeast—often laced with lactobacilli. A month-long secondary fermentation takes place before the beer is decanted into *foeders*, enormous wooden tuns, where critters come out from the cracks, microflora emerge from the oak, and Brettanomyces brings its funkiness to the party.

Young beers are then blended with old to produce a swirl of sweet dark-cherry, sherry, and balsamic vinegar. An ideal aperitif, great with game, and the Belgian beer style most likely to seduce red wine drinkers.

GOSE

Laced with lactic acid, coriander, and salt, gose is an eighteenth-century regional specialty that nearly died in the 1960s. Sharp, sour, sometimes served with syrup, and synonymous with the East German city of Leipzig, gose has made a refreshing return in its hometown and beyond, with a host of new-world brewers embracing its esoteric character and old-school cache.

LAMBIC STYLES

Lambic is both the generic term for spontaneous beers from this particular part of Belgium and the name given to the base beer. Young lambic is slender and soft, while older lambic is funkier with a bigger Brettanomyces influence.

However, beyond the bars and cafés surrounding the breweries where it's served uncarbonated, most lambics are blended into gueuze.

Gueuze (pronounced "goo-zah") is a bottle-conditioned blend of young lambic (aged for between six and 12 months) and old (oude) lambic (aged in oak for up to three years) to a ratio of one to two.

A greater proportion of older lambic brings more Brett and complexity, while gueuze blended with more young lambic will be softer in character. Blenders strive for a signature style and a certain consistency of flavor from year to year, but every vintage tends to be different—which adds to its allure.

Faro was popular in the nineteenth century, and is lambic beer sweetened with sugar to make it more palatable to the everyday drinker.

Old Ale is an English pre-Industrial Revolution ale stored for long periods in unlined wooden tuns, also traditionally known as "stale" beer. Barrel-dwelling wild yeast gifted it its tart, lactic sourness that tended to be consumed as the spike in a blended porter. While rarely referred to as such, the increasing interest in barrel-aging and wild yeast means old ale is very much at the forefront of craft beer's new guard. For a "classic" English example, however, reach for Westerham's Audit Ale.

THE
WORLD OF
BEER

FEATURED COUNTRIES

1 Britain & Ireland
2 Belgium
3 Germany
4 Czechia
5 Italy
6 Denmark
7 Sweden
8 Norway
9 Finland
10 Iceland
11 France
12 Austria
13 Switzerland
14 Netherlands
15 Spain
16 Portugal
17 Poland
18 Luxembourg
19 Estonia
20 Hungary
21 Malta
22 USA West Coast
23 USA South & Central
24 USA North & Eastern
25 Canada
26 Argentina
27 Peru
28 Brazil
29 The Caribbean
30 Mexico
31 Australia
32 New Zealand
33 Japan
34 Cambodia
35 Sri Lanka
36 Israel
37 South Africa

"You can't be a real country unless you have a beer and an airline—it helps if you have some kind of a soccer team or some nuclear weapons, but at the very least you need a beer."

FRANK ZAPPA

MAKING THE SELECTION

Taste is a subjective sensation, and even if you were to take a hundred beer drinkers and ask them to compile a list of their top ten favorite beers (never mind a thousand) no two lists would be the same. No bad thing, for if we all liked the same beer, life would be dull.

The criterion used for our selection has been, first and foremost, flavor. The worst crime a beer can commit is being forgettable and bland. From the smokiness of a German rauchbier to the dry hop finish of a pilsner, all have taste, and all are memorable in their own ways.

In terms of both styles and geography, the net has been cast far and wide, from the southern tip of Argentina to the northernmost outpost of Scandinavia; with a dazzling array of beer styles, from American IPAs to zoigl, we've done our utmost to capture the amazing diversity of beer.

And what diversity there is. It's madness the sheer amount of lovely beer being brewed out there. Deep-rooted beer-drinking nations continue to thrive, while countries such as Denmark, Italy, and America, once barren beer terrain, are now fertile lands for drinking adventurers.

In terms of ingredients and approach, experimentation is rife; new styles are being created, and traditional styles are being revived, often with an avant-garde twist; brewers are exploring the past but, with modern science, not getting stuck there; and beer is rekindling its kinship with food, placing itself at the forefront of a global gastronomic renaissance.

For ease of reference, then, the thousand-plus beers are listed under country and ranked in alphabetical order. While the style of the beer is mentioned, it doesn't always tell you everything about the beer, so, using a selection of symbols, we offer guidance on when and how to drink it

We've also captured the history, the tales, and the people behind the beers because as the Thinking Drinkers, we believe this is a crucial element of your drinking experience.

The beer world is spinning at an increasingly rapid pace, and there will inevitably be some beers or breweries that will change names, hands, location, or close, so no apologies for any errors of this nature. While most beers selected are easily obtainable, some are trickier to source, but due to quality they need to be mentioned regardless.

TASTING RATINGS

Symbols used in the beer listings correspond to the following definitions:

CONNOISSEUR CLASSIC Beers judged over a period of time to be of the highest quality and outstanding of their kind.

SESSION SIP Quaffable beer that won't buckle your knees but may well make your elbows ache.

SUPER STYLE Brewing blueprints that exemplify a certain style.

COOL QUENCHER Refreshing thirst-slakers that suit summer drinking.

GOOD WITH FOOD Beers that drink well at the dinner table.

THINK WHILE YOU DRINK Beers suited to slow snifter sipping and quiet contemplation.

DARK SIDE Malt-driven dark beers with a touch of sweetness.

HOP HEAD Beers that hail the hop in style.

NEW WORLD An innovative twist on a traditional beer style.

WILD, WOOD & SOUR Funky and fruity beers brewed using boisterous bacteria, wild yeasts, and wonders of wood-aging.

A LITTLE UNUSUAL Quirky beers using esoteric or exotic ingredients.

STRONG BEERS Beers with a high alcohol content. Not for those about to operate heavy machinery.

THE WORLD'S TOP-TEN BEER CITIES

1 BAMBERG

The whole of the Franconia region is fabulously fertile beer-drinking country, but Bamberg, bang in its center, is the jewel in its crown. This absurdly handsome town was first issued a license to brew beer back in 1122 and in the early 1800s was home to 65 breweries for a population of just 20,000. Today, there are 11 traditional breweries and a host of terrific taverns and inns in which to sample rauchbier, Bamberg's smoky local specialty.

RECOMMENDED BEER

Aecht Schlenkerla Rauchbier
The archetypal rauchbier.

RECOMMENDED BAR

Schlenkerla Tavern
The "limping man" is Bamberg's most famous beer bar, where getting utterly "Schlenkerlared" is a required experience for any beer tourist.

TO DO BEFORE BEER O'CLOCK

Visit the medieval town hall.

2 AMSTERDAM

It may be famed for its coffee shops peddling herbal highs, but Amsterdam has emerged as a superb city for enjoying the beverage made with cannabis's close botanical relative—the hop. Brewing influences from neighboring Belgium, America, and Scandinavia all converge here to create an expanding Dutch beer scene boasting numerous new craft-beer bars to complement the cozy, traditional brown cafés.

RECOMMENDED BEER

De Prael IPA
An awesome IPA from an inspiring brewery that works with people suffering from psychological issues.

RECOMMENDED BAR

Proeflokaal Arendsnest
Dedicated solely to independent Dutch beers, this is a great place to explore the latest developments in a beer scene considered the rising star of European craft-beer brewing.

TO DO BEFORE BEER O'CLOCK

Cruise around the canals either on foot or by boat.

3 MUNICH

There are more than 600 breweries in Bavaria, and its sun-kissed capital, Munich, reveres the beer with unbridled lederhosen-slapping gusto. The birthplace of lager and the Reinheitsgebot, Munich is home to nine breweries— including Augustiner, Hofbräu, Löwenbräu, and Paulaner— and more than 20 beautiful beer gardens in which to drink their wonderful wares. And that's before you even include the annual Oktoberfest...

RECOMMENDED BEER

Forschungsbrauerei-Pilsissimus
Not many people know about this Munich pilsner so don't tell anyone.

RECOMMENDED BAR

Augustiner Keller
Tourists go to the Hofbräuhaus. Beer drinkers go here.

TO DO BEFORE BEER O'CLOCK

Eat an enormous sausage. After all, what's the wurst that can happen?

4 LONDON

Once the envy of the brewing world back in the eighteenth century, London has rediscovered its microbrewing mojo, and there are now more than a hundred breweries within the capital—with a high proportion in Bermondsey, to the south and the hipster-heavy east. As well as the wealth of traditional pubs for whom cask ale continues to be a pillar, the rise in craft-centric beer venues has mirrored the city's brewing boom.

RECOMMENDED BEER

Meantime IPA
A classic London beer style from the brewery that kickstarted London's craft-brewing movement back when it wasn't overly fashionable to do so.

RECOMMENDED BAR

The Southampton Arms
This cozy, stripped-back boozer rocks a real fire, a decent garden, a piano, and, crucially "no crap" on its 18 taps. Cash only.

TO DO BEFORE BEER O'CLOCK

Visit the markets: Borough, Portobello, Columbia Road, etc.

5 CHICAGO

Not content with boasting more than 26 Michelin-star restaurants for a population of fewer than three million, the Windy City will also blow you away with its blinding beer scene, which has grown considerably since the last edition of this book. Chicago is ranked among North America's greatest beer cities. Beyond the beaky yellow beer taps of Goose Island, it boasts some great local breweries, taprooms, and taverns such as Revolution, Metropolitan, Half Acre, and Haymarket.

RECOMMENDED BEER

Half Acre Daisy Cutter
A perfectly poised, lush and fabulously floral pale ale.

RECOMMENDED BAR

Hop Leaf
A stalwart of Chicago's beer scene situated in the north of the city, Hopleaf's 400-strong beer list boasts a strong Belgian accent and lots of lovely local gear too.

TO DO BEFORE BEER O'CLOCK

Watch a game at Wrigley Field.

6 PORTLAND

Portland, in the top-left corner of America, is home to more than 30 breweries. Legendary beer writer Michael Jackson once described it as "Munich on the Willamette," as Portland surpasses the German city in terms of the number of breweries. While craft-beer sales account for just below four percent of the entire beer market in America, in Portland they represent a staggering 45 percent of all beer drunk.

RECOMMENDED BEER
Hair of the Dog Adam
A beautiful barley wine from one of Portland's most prestigious players that specializes in strong beer.

RECOMMENDED BAR
Horse Brass Pub
This English-style boozer played an instrumental role in Portland's brewing renaissance during the 1980s, and while certainly not hipster, its beer range remains hugely impressive.

TO DO BEFORE BEER O'CLOCK
Get on a bike. Portland is America's best cycling city.

7 PRAGUE

When the iron curtain came down in the late '80s, people flocked to Prague for pints that cost less than a dollar. While prices have gone up, so too have quality and diversity, and the city is a beguiling blend of Czech classic beer traditions and modern independents experimenting beyond bottom-fermented beers.

RECOMMENDED BEER
Kout na Šumavě 12
A lush, light-colored lager that showcases the classic Saaz hop in style.

RECOMMENDED BAR
Zlý Časy
A small and cozy bare-brick basement bar meaning Bad Times. Commands cult status among Prague's more discerning pivo drinkers, and the majority of the 25 draft taps are dedicated to Czechia's most impressive independents and lesser-known German offerings.

TO DO BEFORE BEER O'CLOCK
Take a stroll on the ornate Charles Bridge.

8 BRUSSELS

It may not look that attractive, even when you're wearing beer goggles, but those who dismiss Brussels as dull simply don't know it. Just like the lambic beers of Cantillon Brewery, a must-see while you're here, Brussels rewards patient perseverance. The Brussels beer scene is very much part of a thriving epicurean underbelly, waiting to be explored.

RECOMMENDED BEER
Taras Boulba
A sensational slaking modern saison, fermented with two yeast strains, brewed by Brasserie de la Senne.

RECOMMENDED BAR
Moeder Lambic
Modern, minimalist and rated by many as the best beer bar in the city, the modern-looking Moeder serves beers only from independent, artisan breweries and has 46 draft beers, 200 bottled beers, food, live music, and DJs.

TO DO BEFORE BEER O'CLOCK
Check out St. Catherine Square, considered the artisan "stomach" of Brussels.

9 MELBOURNE

If you're going to drink great beer Down Under then there's no better place to do so than in Melbourne. It's a city that really captures the creative craft-brewing culture, and there are some superb breweries scattered all over the city, including Mountain Goat, Moon Dog, Two Birds, Colonial, Hop Nation, and Boatrocker.

RECOMMENDED BEER
Mountain Goat Summer Ale
A lush quality quencher that's superb in the sunshine.

RECOMMENDED BAR
Forester's Hall
This sizable craft-beer mecca has an incredible beer list and knowledgeable staff, who don't get too geeky about it. Great pizzas and live music.

TO DO BEFORE BEER O'CLOCK
Run, cycle, or walk in the stunning green spaces of Melbourne before heading to St. Kilda's artisan esplanade market.

10 COPENHAGEN

Copenhagen is where modern lager brewing was born in the nineteenth century but it's now the engine room for Scandinavia's exciting artisan beer scene and home to two of Europe's most impressive beer festivals. Mikkeller, the Danish gypsy brewer and beer geek guru, is Copenhagen's beery kingpin, with several fine-looking bars and bottleshops, while the likes of Fermentoren, Nørrebro Bryghus and Taphouse won't disappoint.

RECOMMENDED BEER
Mikkeller Beer Geek Breakfast
An oatmeal stout with cult status.

RECOMMENDED BAR
Mikkeller
Sunk down below street level in the Vesterbro district, this minimalist, deftly designed venue walks the right line between cool and cozy, and its rotating beer menu celebrates the classic and the cutting edge.

TO DO BEFORE BEER O'CLOCK
Order a cup of rosehip tea and watch the city's beautiful people walk by.

BRITAIN

&

IRELAND

Above: Harvey's Royal Oak in Borough is a must-visit destination for lovers of good beer and well-preserved pub interiors.
Below: BrewDog creates a statement in its Ellon brewhouse in Scotland.

LOVE HOPS AND LIVE THE DREA

INTRODUCTION
BRITAIN & IRELAND

There was a time when Britain was the most important brewing nation in the world, exporting huge quantities of its highly respected top-fermenting brews to all four corners of its sprawling and expanding empire.

But Britain doesn't really have an empire anymore, (heck it's not even part of Europe anymore,) and its brewing scene is no longer looked upon by other nations with the same green-eyed envy. That said, after a long period in the doldrums, British beer has most definitely rediscovered its microbrewing mojo. British-born beer styles continue to drive and shape the modern global craft-brewing scene, with styles such as India pale ale, pale ale, porter, stout, and, one could possibly argue, with tongue firmly in cheek, golden lager. Without British pale malting techniques (and if they hadn't stolen yeast and beer from British brewers), who knows when European brewers would have "seen the light."

While the rest of the world's nations have made these beer styles their own, no other "style" of beer that is more essentially British than cask ale. Having been brought back from the brink by CAMRA (Campaign for Real Ale) in the 1970s, cask ale courses deep through the DNA of not just British brewing but British culture too—remaining a key pillar of the classic British pub, the number of which is dwindling every day.

When it is looked after and cared for properly from the pub cellar to the glass, by people who know what they are doing, in pubs where customers keep it flowing fresh, cask ale can be a truly inspiring drinking experience.

However, cask ale continues to be undermined by the price of a pint. It's been priced far too low for far too long, and this, in turn, gives pub landlords little incentive to invest in the people and the cellaring practices required to serve it in optimum condition.

As such, bad pints are all too common, and a growing number of breweries, both independent and regionals, are more than happy putting their beers into kegs and cans as well as, or rather than, cask and bottle.

Yet, for now at least, cask remains the cornerstone of a burgeoning British brewing movement that has been transformed over the last ten years. There are more than 2,000 breweries in the UK (and that number is rising every week), and London, home to just a handful of brewers in 2007, now boasts more than a hundred breweries within its boroughs.

Yorkshire has a similar number, while Scotland, Wales, and Ireland are all home to thriving scenes that still benefit from a small brewers' tax break introduced back in 2002. As craft started to steal share from the big players, buyouts began, and the large corporations continue to kick the tires of breweries with decent distribution.

But these are inspiring times for British beer drinkers, with the bandwidth of styles broadening well beyond classic brown bitters. It's difficult to overestimate the American hop-heavy influence, with new wave British brewers aping American-style interpretations of indigenous British beer styles such as IPAs, pale ales, porter, and stout—alongside sours, Belgian-style ales, and saisons.

But let us not forget, amid all the talk of Brett influence and barrel-aging, that what British brewers do best, yet is very difficult to do, is to produce easy drinking yet characterful beers that deliver depth at modest strength. Ideally enjoyed in the local pub.

ENGLAND

ACORN BREWERY
BARNSLEY, SOUTH YORKSHIRE
WWW.ACORNBREWERY.NET

🍺 🍴 **Barnsley Bitter** 3.8%

In 2003, Acorn rose from the ashes of the dearly departed Barnsley Brewery that dated back to the 1850s. Using the same yeast strain as its predecessor and on a ten-barrel brewery, former Barnsley employee Dave Hughes brews six or more traditional Yorkshire beers, including this award-winning, full-bodied bitter that wraps plums around your gums.

ADNAMS BREWERY
SOUTHWOLD, SUFFOLK
WWW.ADNAMS.CO.UK

🍺 🍴 **Southwold Bitter** 3.7%

Since 1872, the warming aroma of Maris Otter malt has wafted from Adnams' Sole Bay Brewery in the coastal town of Southwold, traveling over the jumbled assortment of whitewashed cottages, past the lighthouse, the picture-postcard pier, and out to sea. Its flagship bitter, showcasing the resinous charms of the hop, is a crisp, floral, and balanced beer brewed using three classic English hops.

ALLENDALE BREWERY
ALLENDALE, NORTHUMBERLAND
WWW.ALLENDALEBREWERY.COM

🍺 🍴 **Golden Plover** Golden Ale 4%

Light and easy on the palate, gentle on the nose, this ravishing-looking golden ale is an award-winning refresher that tingles with a delightful citrusiness thanks to the use of noble hop Hallertau Hersbrucker and the more assertive American variety Columbus.

ALMASTY BREWING
NEWCASTLE-UPON-TYNE
WWW.ALMASTY.CO.UK

🍃 ✓ **Almasty MK** IPA 6.1%

When drinking Almasty's beers, banish all banter about Andy Capp and Newkey Brown: this relatively young brewery is at the vanguard of the city's craft scene, a brewery driven by a restless sense of exploration, as this massively hoppy IPA (featuring Columbus, Citra, Simcoe) demonstrates.

ANSPACH & HOBDAY
BERMONDSEY, LONDON
WWW.ANSPACHANDHOBDAY.COM

🍴 🍴 **The Porter** 6.7%

Founded by Paul (Anspach) and Jack (Hobday), this lively little brewery is one of the weekend haunts of the Bermondsey Beer Mile crowd. It's then, when the taproom is open, that devotees can enjoy the freshest pours of this rich, dark, and lusty porter, the beer after all that made London such a hive of brewing industry in the first place.

ARBOR ALES
EASTON, BRISTOL
WWW.ARBORALES.CO.UK

🍴 🍴 **Breakfast Stout** 7.4%

Founded in 2007, Arbor crafts a goodly amount of well-hopped beers as well as this potent coffee and chocolate oatmeal stout, which is definitely for later in the day. It's creamy and silky in its mouthfeel and boasts plenty of chocolate, coffee, and roast barley before a big bitter finish. A proper evening beer.

ARKELL'S BREWERY
SWINDON, WILTSHIRE
WWW.ARKELLS.COM

🍴 **Kingsdown Special Ale** Bitter 5%

Queen Victoria was only just getting used to sitting on the throne when this venerable family brewery was founded in 1843. Nearly 200 years later, just like the royal family, the Arkells are still here, and this smooth and silky, bittersweet, and strong bitter is testimony to their staying power.

BAD SEED BREWERY
MALTON, NORTH YORKSHIRE
WWW.BADSEEDBREWERY.COM

🍴 🍴 **Hefeweizen** 5.1%

Open a bottle of this full-flavored weizen and put on the lederhosen or the dirndl (or even both) and you'll be mixing Bavaria with Yorkshire while breaking the Reinheitsgebot rules. It's juicy and tart, emboldened by vanilla and clove notes, and brisk in its carbonation. Prost, lad.

BATEMANS BREWERY
WAINFLEET, LINCOLNSHIRE
WWW.BATEMAN.CO.UK

XXXB Pale Ale 4.8%
Set in stunning scenery beneath an imposing windmill and steeped in heritage dating back to 1874, Batemans has remained steadfast in purveying "good honest ales," of which this classic auburn-colored bitter, all citrus and shortbread, is typical.

BATHAMS
BRIERLEY HILL, WEST MIDLANDS
WWW.BATHAMS.CO.UK

Bathams Best Bitter 4.3%
Black Country beer heroes Bathams keep things simple when it comes to beer. Two beers are brewed regularly with a strong special every Christmas. Its Best Bitter is a classic, sprightly, starting off sweet before descending to a cream-cracker dryness of a finish.

BEAVERTOWN BREWERY
see Brewery Profile pages 50 to 51
TOTTENHAM, LONDON
WWW.BEAVERTOWNBREWERY.CO.UK

Bloody 'Ell Blood Orange IPA 7.2%
Fruit IPAs can sometimes be the work of the devil, but there's nothing demonic about this powerful IPA, which has been infused with the juice of many blood oranges. It's Saharalike in its dryness, juicy, chewy, fruity, sticky, and rings with orange notes in the finish. A treat.

Lupuloid IPA 6.7%
The hop varieties Citra, Mosaic, and Equinox bring a vibrant and vital fruitiness to this irresistible IPA, which also has a solid malty backbone in support and a dry, bittersweet finish.

Smog Rocket Porter 5.4%
This gorgeous looking chestnut-brown smoked porter was an early declaration of how seriously Beavertown would take their beer. There's a creamy and smoky nose, while it's smooth and chocolatey on the palate with a bitter, slightly peppery finish.

BLACKJACK BREWERY
MANCHESTER
WWW.BLACKJACK-BEERS.COM

Aces High IPA 5.5%
The wheels on the train might go around and around above them, but snug in their railroad arch in the Green Quarter district of Manchester, Blackjack are enjoying themselves with beers such as this succulent IPA, which bustles with citrus hoppiness and juicy bittersweet character.

BLACK SHEEP BREWERY
MASHAM, NORTH YORKSHIRE
WWW.BLACKSHEEPBREWERY.COM

Black Sheep Ale Bitter 4.4%
Back in 1992, Paul Theakston famously fell out with his family and started his own brewery down the road in Masham. His two sons are now involved, keeping the family traditions going, and this richly fruity and bittersweet beer remains a company bestseller throughout the UK.

BREW BY NUMBERS
BERMONDSEY, LONDON
WWW.BREWBYNUMBERS.COM

Saison 5.5% (ABV can change)
Not content with producing an exceptional saison, Brew by Numbers makes different variations on a theme, depending on what hops they have. Sometimes it's Citra, then it might be Nelson Sauvin, or there might be other additions such as orange, cucumber, or ginger. The result is a thoroughly drinkable thoroughbred.

BRIGHTON BIER
BRIGHTON, EAST SUSSEX
WWW.BRIGHTONBIER.COM

Choccywoccybrew-Ha Stout 7%
As luxurious as a long afternoon spent in a favorite armchair and as smooth as a well-worn pebble on Brighton beach, this is a luscious chocolate stout. Brewed in collaboration with local chocolaterie Choccywoccydoodah, it should be sipped slowly and with a quiet contemplation.

BEAVERTOWN BREWERY

LONDON

WWW.BEAVERTOWNBREWERY.CO.UK

As epiphanies go, the one that made Logan Plant ditch his lot as a rock singer (after all dad, Robert, made a decent living out of it) and plunge into brewing was rather unspectacular. No blinding lights, just beer and pulled pork.

He was the singer in Sons of Albion, who had been playing a record company showcase in New York. After the gig, he'd wandered into Fetta Sau, a bar that majored in both craft beer and BBQ, and the brilliant flavors of the beer and the deep soulful resonance of the food helped make his mind up. He was going to follow a different path.

> "I had this epiphany in the bar," he says. "I can't remember the beer, but there were these flavors, the stimulus, and that was it. In a week I had left the band and got a homebrewing kit."

In December 2011, several months after Logan began homebrewing, Beavertown's beers went on sale in an eighteenth century boozer in the De Beauvoir Town district of Hackney, East London. (Beavertown was the manor's old Cockney nickname.) The pub was renamed Duke's Brew and Que and underwent an elegantly scuffed makeover, while majoring in classic ribs, juicy burgers, and Plant's beer. These included Neck Oil, Smog Rocket, and 8 Ball Rye IPA.

American craft brewing was (and remains) the primary influence on Beavertown, but as time has passed it seems as if the whole of Planet Beer is visiting the brewery, with influences from

Belgium, Germany, and Czechia emerging in its approach. There are saisons, imperial stouts, Berliner weisse, and sour beers, all of which delight the tongue with their tingle of taste. There have also been collaborations with like-minded breweries, such as Pamplona-based Naparbier and Wild Beer, while Beavertown is one of the seven brewing members of the annual Rainbow Project, which sees a British brewery produce a collaborative beer with a brewery from overseas.

The brewery's current home is on an industrial estate in Tottenham Hale, North London, a bright and busy space of a warehouse, in which a cluster of space-age stainless steel conically bottomed fermenters stands, joined by a rotund mash tun and gleaming kettle; the warehouse opposite is where the barrel-aging takes place. A canning line was installed in 2014 when Beavertown

established itself as one of the main British pioneers of so-called "craft cans."

The same year saw the recruitment of Jenn Merrick as head brewer. A native of the American West, she had worked at York Brewery, Meantime, and Dark Star prior to Beavertown and in 2015 was voted Brewer of the Year by the British Guild of Beer Writers. (She moved on in 2016.)

The story of Beavertown is one of Logan continuing to strive to improve his beers through surrounding himself with like-minded people, people he knows can follow the original vision that appeared to him, Damascene-like, on that pork-and-beer filled night in Brooklyn.

BRIGHT AND BOLDLY FLAVORED BEERS
Neck Oil was one of Beavertown's debut beers, originally based on the sweetish session ales of Logan's home in the Midlands, but it soon became a standard bearer for US hops with a zip and a zest of flavor. Other beers making the tongue touch its toes and yell yahoo include Bloody 'Ell, an IPA infused with blood orange juice, and the moody smoked porter Smog Rocket.

Opposite left: Founder of Beavertown Brewing, Logan Plant.

Opposite right: Logan talks through the brewery set up during a public tour in Tottenham, North London.

Above left: Beavertown's pump clip parade featuring designs by artist Nick Dwyer.

Above right: Logan perched atop a lot of oak, part of Beavertown's impressive barrel-aging program.

* KEY BEERS

Beavertown 8 Ball Rye IPA 6.2%
Beavertown Bloody 'Ell Blood Orange IPA 7.2%
Beavertown Gamma Ray American Pale Ale 5.4%
Beavertown Lupuloid IPA 6.7%
Beavertown Neck Oil Session IPA 4.3%
Beavertown Quelle Saison 4.1%
Beavertown Smog Rocket Smoked Porter 5.4%

BRISTOL BEER FACTORY
SOUTHVILLE, BRISTOL
WWW.BRISTOLBEERFACTORY.CO.UK

Milk Stout 4.5%
Forget elderly ladies tut-tutting over a milk stout, this is the beer that brought the much-maligned style back to life when it was first brewed in 2007. Think chocolate buttons on the nose, followed by a creamy mouthfeel and mocha with a dry, toasty finish.

Southville Hop IPA 6.5%
American-influenced IPA named after the Bristol area that BBF calls home. There are ripe peach fruit and grapefruit pith on the nose, while a big boom of tropical fruit and citrus blasts the palate, followed by a long and lingering bitter finish. This is a sturdy IPA.

BURNING SKY
FIRLE, EAST SUSSEX
WWW.BURNINGSKYBEER.COM

Easy Answers IPA 6%
Mark Tranter turns transatlantic with this high-quality quaff of an American-style IPA, which is full-bodied but light and easy to drink, while all manner of piney aromatics emerge out of the glass thanks to the dry hopping. Tropical fruit, citrus, a balance of malt, and a dry, bitter finish. A beautifully balanced beer.

Saison à la Provision 6.5%
Burning Sky's brewing supremo Mark Tranter is a whiz when it comes to producing Belgian-style beers as this exemplary saison demonstrates. It's funkier than Bootsy Collins's ripe French cheese selection, pleasantly peppery with a tingling tartness, all West Coast America and New Zealand meets zesty grapefruit, and a quenching refreshing character.

BUXTON BREWERY
BUXTON, DERBYSHIRE
WWW.BUXTONBREWERY.CO.UK

Axe Edge IPA 6.8%
You want hops? Then this powerful IPA from the Peaks' premier watering hole has plenty of them, including Amarillo, Citra, and Nelson Sauvin. This makes for a blast of tropical fruit on the nose with more fruit on the palate and a dry and boldly bitter finish. West Coast America and New Zealand meet the British Peak District in a hop explosion.

CAMDEN TOWN BREWERY
CAMDEN, LONDON
WWW.CAMDENTOWNBREWERY.COM

IHL Lager 6.2%
Lager meets IPA, and the two of them get along famously in the glass with this incredibly drinkable mash-up of the two beer styles. A delicate fruitiness (a sweet, sun-stroked bowl of tropical fruit perhaps), smooth mouthfeel, and Sahara-like dry finish.

CASTLE ROCK BREWERY
NOTTINGHAM, NOTTINGHAMSHIRE
WWW.CASTLEROCKBREWERY.COM

Harvest Pale 3.8%
This gleaming gold-colored pale ale was justly crowned Champion Beer of Britain in 2010 when the judges all but did cartwheels over its fragrant and fruity hop character, juicy citrus mouthfeel, and bracing bitter finish that left them begging for more.

CHILTERN BREWERY
TERRICK, BUCKINGHAMSHIRE
WWW.CHILTERNBREWERY.CO.UK

Bodger's Barley Wine 8.5%
Sleek and slinky chestnut-brown barley wine produced by one of the pioneering microbreweries of the 1970s. With Maris Otter in the mash and whole cone Challenger, Goldings, and Fuggles hops used in the boil, the result is a vinous, muscular, bittersweet delight, particularly in winter.

CHORLTON BREWING CO.
ARDWICK, MANCHESTER
WWW.CHORLTONBREWINGCOMPANY.COM

Amarillo Sour 5.4%
If you are hesitant at the thought of sour beers, why not perk up your petrified palate with this joyous and enthusiastic thirst-quencher, which has a friendly acidity, a gorgeous burst of grapefruit juiciness, Amarillo-led aromatics, and a refreshing tartness in the finish.

CLOUDWATER BREW
MANCHESTER
WWW.CLOUDWATERBREW.CO

DIPA
Imperial IPA % (ABV can change)

When they opened in 2015 Cloudwater immediately made waves with their range of beers that changed with the seasons, especially this Imperial IPA, which alters its hop varieties each time it is brewed—expect, however, a huge injection of citrus, tropical fruit, and a balance of malt sweetness.

Vermont ESB 6.5%
When we think of ESB, we think of Fuller's magnificent example, but Cloudwater has also harnessed this big beast using hops from America and the Southern Hemisphere alongside the peachy, citrusy fruitiness of Vermont Ale Yeast.

CONISTON BREWING CO.
CONISTON, CUMBRIA
WWW.CONISTONBREWERY.COM

Bluebird Bitter 3.6% (4.2% in bottle)
Named after the speedboat that Donald Campbell fatally crashed on Coniston Water in the Lake District in 1967, this is a bright and breezy session ale with citrus fruit, grainy malt, and a bitter peppery finish, all combining to create complete satisfaction on the palate.

CROUCH VALE BREWERY
SOUTH WOODHAM FERRERS, ESSEX
WWW.CROUCH-VALE.CO.UK

Amarillo Golden Ale 5%
Before American hops were used by everyone and their mother, Crouch Vale quietly but effectively made use of this lightly spicy and seductively orangey variety to lend heft, weight, and character to a tantalizing thirst-quencher of a tipple. It has continued to win awards and widen its loyal fan base, despite a raft of Johnny-come-lately competitors.

DARK STAR BREWERY
PARTRIDGE GREEN, WEST SUSSEX
WWW.DARKSTARBREWING.CO.UK

Hophead Bitter 3.8%
As the name suggests, hops are central to the potency of this beer on the palate. First of all, there's the nose, which is a fragrant delight of flowery and elderflower notes, and then the palate joins in with more tropical fruit and a long dry finish.

ELGOOD'S BREWERY
WISBECH, CAMBRIDGESHIRE
WWW.ELGOODS-BREWERY.CO.UK

Coolship Sour Beer 6%
One of the UK's most venerable family breweries takes a bow and shows that it too can be as hip as any start-up in a London railroad arch. Grapefruit, a suggestion of sherry, soft sweetness, and acidity all combine to create a joyful and tart-tasting sour.

EXMOOR ALES
WIVELISCOMBE, SOMERSET
WWW.EXMOORALES.CO.UK

Exmoor Gold Golden Ale 4.5%
Somerset's oldest brewery secured its place in the pages of beer history books in 1986, with the launch of what is generally regarded as the first modern golden ale. Even though contemporary beers of this ilk are much more hoppy, the original remains a floral and fruity delight of refreshment. Worth seeking out.

FIRST CHOP
MANCHESTER
WWW.FIRSTCHOP.CO.UK

Ava Golden Ale 3.5%
Now for something different: First Chop's portfolio of beers is gluten-free, a sign of how far brewing has progressed in making beers that celiacs can now enjoy. This blonde bombshell is refreshing and fruity, thanks to the use of Galaxy and Columbus hops. An easy-drinking gluten-free option.

FIVE POINTS BREWING
HACKNEY, LONDON
WWW.FIVEPOINTSBREWING.CO.UK

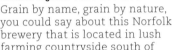

Five Points Pale Ale 4.4%

One day someone will write a thesis on the role of railroad arches in the growth of London's beer scene, and Five Points will no doubt feature. In the meantime, educate yourself with the brewery's fresh and zesty pale ale that just shimmers with hop goodness.

FOURPURE BREWING
BERMONDSEY, LONDON
WWW.FOURPURE.COM

Session IPA 4.2%

Here's that holy grail, a beer that's low in alcohol but high in flavor, in this case thanks to the liberal use of Citra, Mosaic, and Galaxy hops, all of which contribute a citrus fruitiness and a light bitter finish.

Shape Shifter IPA 6.4%

This is a West Coast IPA, the kind of beer that makes you want to grab a surfboard and head for the ocean; hazy dark orange in color, it's resinous, piney, and boldly fruity on the nose, while it swaggers on the tongue, citrus in a leather jacket perhaps, before the dry grainy finish.

FULLER'S
CHISWICK, LONDON
WWW.FULLERS.CO.UK see Brewery Profile pages 56 to 57

★ **Vintage Ale (2005)**
Barley Wine 8.5%

Every year, connoisseurs rub their hands with anticipation with the impending release of Fuller's bottle-conditioned Vintage. Golden Pride ("the Cognac of beer" according to legendary British beer writer Michael Jackson) is the foundation, but different varieties of hop or malt are often used. The result is one of the London brewery's crowning glories in a glass and a testament to the brewing prowess of John Keeling who has been leading the way there for 25 years.

GRAIN BREWERY
ALBURGH, NORFOLK
WWW.GRAINBREWERY.CO.UK

Lignum Vitae IPA 6.5%

Grain by name, grain by nature, you could say about this Norfolk brewery that is located in lush farming countryside south of Norwich. Lignum Vitae is Grain's boisterous English-style IPA, with a deep malt-edged character and plenty of hop-driven citrus notes.

Slate Porter 6%

As dark as a moonless night in the middle of the Norfolk countryside, with hints of smoke that suggest a neighbor's bonfire several fields away, this is a lubricious and lusty smoked porter with wisps of vanilla and chocolate. Enjoy it by the fire.

GREENE KING
BURY ST. EDMUNDS, SUFFOLK
WWW.GREENEKING.CO.UK

★ **Strong Suffolk** Old Ale 6%

Two beers come together as one for this mellow, well-rounded, burgundy-colored stunner. Old 5X, having been matured in oak for two years, is blended with a younger, weaker beer, and the result is a crooner of an ale featuring fruitcake, vanilla, and fall fruit notes. One of Greene King's best beers.

GREEN JACK BREWERY
LOWESTOFT, SUFFOLK
WWW.GREEN-JACK.COM

Orange Wheat Beer 4.2%

This is Green Jack's cheerful take on a Belgian witbier and includes orange peel. There is a subtle orange nose with a caramel and orange character on the palate; the flavors explode on the tongue, offering both complexity and refreshment. Orange all round.

Trawlerboys Best Bitter 4.6%

This is the kind of brawny, muscular bitter that you could imagine fishing folk diving into once they're back on dry land and the herrings have been unloaded. Featuring English whole-cone hops, it's a dazzling example of grainy malt character crisscrossed with subtle citrus before its bittersweet and dry finish.

HAMBLETON ALES
MELMERBY, NORTH YORKSHIRE
WWW.HAMBLETONALES.CO.UK

Nightmare Porter 5%

A dream of a rich and dark porter from a Yorkshire brewery that was founded by one-time headmaster Nick Stafford. Lightly roasted grain and an undercurrent of spicy hop on the nose kick off the proceedings before roast grain, chocolate, dark fruit, and a full-bodied mouthfeel join in. Truly a luscious porter for evening quaffing.

HARBOUR BREWING
BODMIN, CORNWALL
WWW.HARBOURBREWING.COM

Antipodean IPA 5%

IPA gets a dose of hops from the Southern Hemisphere, which leads to a bright and colorful beer boasting tropical fruit and resinous pine on the nose and mouth, alongside a firm backbone of malt. The finish is drier than the Australian Outback.

Pilsner 5%

From Cornwall with love comes this riff on the classic Czech beer style, with a clean and crisp mouthfeel, a gentle graininess midpalate, and a spicy bitter finish that makes you want to start drinking it all over again.

HARDKNOTT BREWERY
MILLOM, CUMBRIA
WWW.HARDKNOTT.COM

Infra-Red IPA 6.2%

Infra-red by name, self-styled "oxymoronomic IPA" by nature. Founded by ex-nuclear power engineer Dave Bailey, Hardknott is noted for its love of hops (as well as the whacky stunts from Bailey), as this rich, spirituous, citrusy, herbally inclined, and bittersweet beauty demonstrates.

HARVEY'S
LEWES, WEST SUSSEX
WWW.HARVEYS.ORG.UK

Sussex Best Bitter 4%

This is one of the great bitters of England because it demonstrates an effortless balance between rich maltiness and muscular hoppiness that a high-wire walker would be proud of. Harvey's hometown of Lewes, as well as having the brewery right in the middle of it, is a rather fine place.

HAWKSHEAD BREWERY
STAVELEY, CUMBRIA
WWW.HAWKSHEADBREWERY.CO.UK

Bitter 3.7%

This is the kind of beer hikers dream of as they traipse across the Lake District where Hawkshead is based. Not-so-active types can equally enjoy the gentle, fragrant, elderflower-like nose, a refreshing theme that continues on the palate before the crisp bitter finish.

Tonka Imperial Porter 8.5%

Hawkshead's brewers woke up one morning and decided to name their imperial porter after the sturdy toy truck. Only joking, this rich and soothing, midnight-black beer has an infusion of tonka beans and cacao nibs, which makes it as smooth as a Lycra-clad Barry White on a sled.

HOGS BACK BREWERY
TONGHAM, SURREY
WWW.HOGSBACK.CO.UK

A Over T Barley Wine 9%

This is an indulgent barley wine released every winter, and one for the fireside perhaps? Chestnut-brown in color, there're are dark fruit, caramel sweetness, and warming alcohol on the nose, while the palate is fiery, rich, and fruity, followed by a bittersweet finish.

Hogs Back TEA Bitter 4.2%

If the vicar drops by for a cup of tea, then why not offer traditional English ale instead? He or she will be delighted with the perfect balance of cookie maltiness (with hints of toffee) against a restrained hop bitterness. More TEA, vicar?

FULLER'S

THE GRIFFIN BREWERY, CHISWICK, LONDON

WWW.FULLERS.CO.UK

London was once an unrivaled brewing metropolis, its pubs and breweries the envy of the world. It was the engine room of a swaggering British Empire, and beer generously greased that empire's cogs of commerce and industry.

Behemoth brewers such as Whitbread, Watney, Ind Coope, Trumans, and Charrington smudged London's smog-smeared skyline with their bellowing brick stacks; numerous smaller, simple ventures wetted the whistles of a rapidly growing population. At its brewing peak, the city was home to more than 160 breweries.

However, by the end of the last decade, the city had only a small handful of breweries for 15 million people, most of them minor operations. London gave birth to porter, India pale ale, and stout, yet it had fewer breweries than Suffolk. Thankfully that has now changed as the amount of London breweries has rocketed, but Fuller, Smith & Turner remain the mash-led masters of all they survey in the capital.

Flanked by the river Thames on one side and one of London's main arterial roads on the other, Fuller's has been wafting malt aromas across the chimney pots of West London since 1845. More than 150 years later, Fuller's is still an

independent family brewer and one of the UK's leading regional players, with more than 360 pubs and, in London Pride, the number-one selling premium bitter in the United Kingdom.

AWARD-WINNING BEERS

Fuller's beers have won CAMRA's coveted Champion Beer of Britain not once, not twice, but thrice. The fabulously fruity and tangy London Pride, the beer on which Fuller's success has been built, scooped gold in 1979, a year after ESB, its rich mahogany-colored, spicy, strong bitter, did the same. London Pride has pepper and grassy hop notes from Challenger, Goldings, Target, and Northdown hops that are gently laid down on a bed of pale ale and Crystal malt.

In 1989, CAMRA pinned its cherished gong to the chest of Chiswick Bitter, an immensely

Above left and right: In 2017, Georgina Young became the first woman head brewer at Fuller's in Chiswick, London, where quality beers have been brewed and distributed since 1845.

aromatic "brewer's beer," dry-hopped with mellow bitter Goldings and with a depth of flavor that reaches well beyond its modest 3.5% ABV.

In 2013, Fuller's launched Frontier, their first lager since the ill-fated K2 of the 1980s. A self-styled "new wave craft lager," this is a clean and refreshing fruity kölsch-style quaff with a dry and crisp finish. The American-style pale ale Wild River and the orangey golden ale Oliver's Island have also made successful debuts.

CONNOISSEUR BREWS

The popularity and profitability of Fuller's core beers afford brewing director John Keeling the freedom to experiment with Fuller's "fine ales," which are more concerned with connoisseurs than commercial success. John, a learned and likable Mancunian, has been at Fuller's for more than 25 years and been responsible for introducing some quite outstanding elixirs.

In 2007, after years of grappling with the United Kingdom's archaic tax attitude toward aging beer in whisky barrels, he unveiled Brewer's Reserve, a blend of Fuller's 1845, its Golden Pride Barley Wine, and ESB Export, aged in 30-year-old oak whisky casks for more than 500 days. There have been several expressions since, using both brandy and different whisky casks.

Another bottle-conditioned connoisseur collectable is Vintage Ale, an annual release that always has Golden Pride Barley Wine at its foundation and as its inspiration. Each year, John gives the beer a twist in the brewing tale, be it a different variety of malt or a change of hop, the idea being that one can then behold the influence that time has on the flavor, aroma, and appearance of the beers.

Keeling has also found time to dip into Fuller's copious brewing archives and produce beers under the "Past Masters" brand.

Above left: Fuller's brewing director, John Keeling, has created some highly sought oak-aged vintage ales.

Above right: While other London brewers have fled the capital, Fuller's has refused to move from its West London home.

* KEY BEERS

Fuller's Black Stout 4.5%
Fuller's Brewer's Reserve Oak-aged Ale 7.7%
Fuller's ESB Extra Special Bitter 5.9%
Fuller's Frontier Lager 4.5%
Fuller's London Porter 5.4%
Fuller's London Pride Bitter 4.7%
Fuller's Oliver's Island Golden Ale 4.5%
Fuller's Past Masters 1926 Oatmeal Porter 7.8%
Fuller's Vintage Ale 8.5%

HOLDEN'S BREWERY
DUDLEY, WEST MIDLANDS
WWW.HOLDENSBREWERY.CO.UK

Golden Glow Golden Ale 4.4%
Gleaming gold in the glass, this Black Country classic is a deliciously dainty drop with subtle but fragrant hop aromas and a gentle daub of citrus and bittersweetness on the palate. The brewery has been in the same family since it was founded in 1915.

HOOK NORTON BREWERY
HOOK NORTON, OXFORDSHIRE
WWW.HOOKNORTONBREWERY.CO.UK

Old Hooky Premium Bitter 4.6%
Hook Norton hides itself away in the Oxfordshire Cotswolds; a divine-looking Victorian brewery that should have had a lead role in Harry Potter. Old Hooky is its leading player, an old-school bitter with a silky, mochalike maltiness, bossed about by a rich, bold, citrus fruitiness, and ending with a cookie dryness.

HOP BACK
SALISBURY, WILTSHIRE
WWW.HOPBACK.CO.UK

Summer Lightning Golden Ale 5%
This is the golden ale that turned the heads of many a lager lover when it emerged in the late 1980s. It has remained a sprightly and sparkling thirst-quencher, throwing out lively citrus shapes on both nose and palate alongside a light floral hop finish.

KELHAM ISLAND
SHEFFIELD
WWW.KELHAMISLAND.CO.UK

Pale Rider Pale Ale 5.2%
Kelham Island was founded by the sadly missed Sheffield beer legend Dave Wickett, and Pale Rider is its signature beer, fragrant pale ale with tropical fruit on the nose, which continues onto the palate alongside a sherbet softness followed by a tingling bittersweet finish.

THE KERNEL BREWERY
BERMONDSEY, LONDON
WWW.THEKERNELBREWERY.COM

Export India Porter 5.9%
Based on a recipe first developed in the days of Queen Victoria and as dark as a country lane on a moonless night, this is a lush and luxurious drop featuring chocolate, coffee, vanilla, and a bracing roastiness all wrapped up as snug as a Victorian O'Riordain, beneath a railroad arch in Bermondsey. He previously ran a specialty cheese stall at Borough Market, but on a work trip to New York he noticed the depth of flavor and complexity of aroma of the craft beers he drank.

Imperial Export Brown Stout 9.9%
Based on a recipe from 1856, this is a potent and powerful sipper of a dark beer with plenty of chocolate, molasses, mocha, and ripe dark plums on the nose. Smooth and soothing on the palate, it's equally complex and finishes with a bittersweet flourish.

LEFT HANDED GIANT BREWING CO.
ST. PHILIP'S, BRISTOL
WWW.LEFTHANDEDGIANT.COM

Duet Pale Ale 4.8%
Left Handed is one of the newest stars on the Bristol brewing scene, and Duet is its lustrous pale ale. Two American hop varieties are used, a combination that changes with each brew, making for an intriguing hop-forward experience each time.

LITTLE VALLEY BREWERY
HEBDEN BRIDGE, WEST YORKSHIRE
WWW.LITTLEVALLEYBREWERY.CO.UK

Hebden's Wheat Witbier 4.5%
Hebden's Wheat is an elegant witbier that is spicy, juicy, tart, and refreshing and brewed by Wim van der Spek, who started the organically certified brewery with Sue Cooper. The two met during their respective travels when he was cycling in Kathmandu in search of the highest brewery in the world. As you do.

THE LIVERPOOL CRAFT BEER CO.
LIVERPOOL
WWW.LIVERPOOLCRAFTBEER.COM

White Fox IPA 6.3%
On one level it's an IPA with a sweaty hop sack nose and a peppery dry finish; on another level, due to the Belgian yeast used, it throws all sorts of shapes in the glass; the kind of shapes that both perplex and delight. It's fruity (apricot/peach), spicy, dry in the finish, and there's even a hint of tartness on the edge of the palate. Blimey.

LIVERPOOL ORGANIC BREWERY
LIVERPOOL
WWW.LIVERPOOLORGANICBREWERY.COM

Liverpool Pale Ale 3.8%
As the name might suggest, these Merseyside mashers have a sustainable outlook on life with all of their beers being organic. This is their pleasing pale ale, whose blast of grapefruit on the nose sets it up for a bracing bitterness, more citrus, and a bittersweet finish.

Imperial Russian Stout 4.7%
As dark as a gravedigger's soul with a mixture of berries and licorice on the nose, this full-bodied and robust stout displays a brisk cascade of hoppy notes and ends with a coffee-bean dryness in the finish.

LOST AND GROUNDED
BRISTOL
WWW.LOSTANDGROUNDED.CO.UK

Running With Sceptres Lager 5.2%
Alex Troncoso used to be the head brewer of Camden Town Brewery, but in 2016 he and partner Annie Clements set up the Lost and Grounded brewery. This fragrant and fruity "Special Lager Beer" is the result if an IPA met a lager and had children: it's dry, bitter, crisp, and fruity and utterly delightful, even in the early evening.

LOVIBONDS
HENLEY-ON-THAMES, OXFORDSHIRE
WWW.LOVIBONDS.CO.UK

Henley Dark Porter 4.8%
Former software engineer Jeff Rosenmeier started Lovibonds in 2005 and was one of the pioneers of both craft keg and sour beers. Henley Dark has a lustrous, silky texture reminiscent of chocolate ice cream, along with some smokiness, delicate roast notes, and mocha. For those wanting to explore the beers of Lovibonds more, the brewery has a tasting room that is open most weekends.

MAD HATTER
LIVERPOOL
WWW.MADHATTERBREWING.CO.UK

Ultra One Barley Wine 11.9%
Smooth and luscious, this potent and pale-colored barley wine is a muscular calling card from the Mad Hatter brewery, which is located in Liverpool's Baltic Triangle, close to the docks; it's got malt sweetness, citrus fruitiness, a rod of bitterness running through its center, and a big boozy finish that'll have you breaking into a rendition of "The Leaving of Liverpool."

MAGIC ROCK
HUDDERSFIELD, WEST YORKSHIRE
WWW.MAGICROCKBREWING.COM

Cannonball IPA 7.4%
Think of whole American hops being fired out of a cannon with the aroma on this potent potation—a boom of passion fruit, grapefruit, and pineapple. The sensations continue on the palate, with ripe orange skin, grapefruit juice, alcohol, and a grainy, bitter limelike finish.

Salty Kiss Gose 4.1%
Huddersfield's beery heroes have a go at a Leipziger Gose with Salty Kiss, but to give it the brewery's own imprint the magnificently bearded head brewer Stuart Ross also adds gooseberries and minerally sea buckthorn. The result is a vinous, delicately sour, and lightly salty refreshing joy.

MARBLE BEERS
CHORLTON, MANCHESTER
WWW.MARBLEBEERS.COM

Marble Earl Grey IPA 6.8%

Originally brewed as a collaboration between Mancunian brewing giants Marble and Dutch brewery Emelisse, this is an intriguing IPA with tannins from the Earl Grey tea adding to the bitterness in the finish. Elsewhere there are an orange/tangerine fruitiness, a restrained sweetness, and a particularly dry and bitter finish.

Portent of Usher Imperial Stout 9%

In its original form, this unctuous and ink-black imperial stout is a deep and spirituous beer with chocolate, coffee, smoke, and caramel sweetness vying with dried fruit and a light spiciness. However, Marble has also used the beer as a base for several wood-aged experiments that are always worth keeping an eye open for.

MEANTIME
GREENWICH, LONDON
WWW.MEANTIMEBREWING.COM

India Pale Ale 7.4%

Along with porter, IPA is a beer style most identified with London (though Burton-on-Trent had its own say on it), which is what Meantime's brewmaster Alastair Hook paid tribute to when he developed this beer—stuffed full of Goldings and Fuggles hops, this is a classic English-style IPA, citrusy, earthy, and bitter, an aristocratic ale with a lot of appeal.

Yakima Red
Amber Ale 4.1%

Washington State comes to Greenwich as five hop varieties from the hop-growing heaven of Yakima Valley are used in this American-style amber ale. The result is a flurry of grapefruit and orange fruitiness engaging in a rousing dance with caramelized malts and berry fruit sweetness. This is a deservedly popular addition to the Meantime stable of consistent beers.

MONDO BREWING COMPANY
BATTERSEA, LONDON
WWW.MONDOBREWINGCOMPANY.COM

London Alt Altbier 4.8%

This London outtake on a Düsseldorf classic is copper-colored with a flurry of light caramel notes on the nose, moving slightly toward toffee. It's rich and smooth, creamy and full-bodied, with a bitter finish that stays longer than the mother-in-law.

MOOR BEER COMPANY
BRISTOL
WWW.MOORBEER.CO.UK

Hoppiness IPA 6.5%

This is a luminous marriage between barley wine and IPA that bursts with fresh zingy aromas and flavors, but it also has the kind of malt depth that stops it from being yet another one-dimensional hop bomb. A peerless example of Moor's brewing mastery.

Old Freddy Walker Old Ale 7.3%

An armchair and a favorite book are probably needed when evaluating this strong and vibrant old ale. There's vanilla, chocolate, and coffee on the nose and the palate, a silky, elegant mouthfeel (think a smooth and creamy coffee), before its dry finish with hints of chocolate.

MOORHOUSE'S
BURNLEY, LANCASHIRE
WWW.MOORHOUSES.CO.UK

Black Cat Mild 3.4%

Who says mild has to be as dull as dishwater? Not Moorhouse's, who have been brewing beer in Lancashire for 150 years. This Black Cat is a smooth, dark, and chewy mild with plenty of roast malt and chocolate flavors that are kept in check by a genial bitter finish. This beer is excellent with pizza, believe it or not.

MORDUE BREWERY
NORTH SHIELDS, TYNE & WEAR
WWW.MORDUEBREWERY.COM

Northumbrian Blonde Golden Ale 4%

As the name suggests, this is a bright golden gleaming beer from the northeast of England. It's zesty and citrusy and rings away like an unanswered telephone, with light lemon notes on the palate before the kind of dry finish that encourages you to keep on sipping.

NORTHERN MONK BREW CO.
LEEDS, YORKSHIRE
WWW.NORTHERNMONKBREWCO.COM

New World IPA 6.2%

No monks were actually involved in the making of this boldly flavored IPA—instead, when a can is opened there's a fresh celestial burst of hop aromatics (tropical fruit) thanks to the five hop varieties used, while once on the palate there are more zest and zip, a caramel sweetness, and a juicy mouthfeel. Very satisfying.

OAKHAM ALES
WOODSTON, CAMBRIDGESHIRE
WWW.OAKHAMALES.CO.UK

Citra Pale Ale 4.2%

Oakham was the first British brewery to use the magnificently fruity Citra hop and *voila!* we have this bright-gold beauty where tropical fruit aromas and flavors of leechee, papaya, and pineapple chatter away in the glass, leap out at you, and get up in your grill.

Green Devil IPA 6%

The Citra hop is the star of this robust IPA, which has been liberally garlanded with awards since being launched in 2011. Imagine a banshee note of bitterness wrapped up in a blanket of tropical fruit, ripe peach skin, mango pulp, and green earthy hop, and you're there. It has rapidly become a bit of a hop-laden classic.

OKELL & SON
DOUGLAS, ISLE OF MAN
WWW.OKELLS.CO.UK

Aile Porter Beer 4.7%

Pronounced "Isle" as in Isle of Man. Aile is the Manx word for fire. Seductively smoky and complex, with hints of licorice and Irish coffee, this peculiarly drinkable dark porter is certainly one of the best. Brewed, like all Okell ales, to the Manx Brewers Act, which forbids the use of any ingredients other than malt, water, yeast, and hops.

ORBIT BEERS
WALWORTH, LONDON
WWW.ORBITBEERS.COM

Neu Altbier 4.7%

Here's a South London take on the classic Düsseldorf *altbier*. Chestnut brown in color, it's ultra smooth in the mouthfeel, spicy and slightly peppery, with the bitterness in the finish lingering like someone unwilling to leave an enjoyable party that's about to end. The beer is named after a German band.

OTTER BREWERY
LUPPITT, DEVON
WWW.OTTERBREWERY.COM

Otter Head Old Ale 5.8%

Otter is an eco-friendly family brewery, whose Derek the Otter (a man dressed as one) pops up at halftime at Exeter Chiefs rugby matches. Presumably he saves Otter Head for later: it's a potent potation brimming with toffee, rich malt, resiny hop, and vinous fruit. This is a delightful chestnut-brown beer.

PALMERS BREWERY
BRIDPORT, DORSET
WWW.PALMERSBREWERY.COM

Tally Ho Premium Bitter 5.5%

Part of the brewery is thatched, and the same family has been in charge forever: definitely old school. On the other hand, this chestnut-brown ale reveals layers of vinous fruits, chocolate, coffee, baked banana, restrained sweetness, and a bitter, dry finish.

THE LONDON BEER BREWING SCENE

LONDON

London always used to be a beer city. Here, in the eighteenth century, porter, the first great beer of the modern era, emerged, a dark viscous liquid that was devoured with gusto by the porters who kept the city's businesses connected and supplied with goods. Later on, in the next century, porter's older and stronger sibling, stout, was a creature of London. Meanwhile, breweries — some small and almost invisible, others leviathan-like in size — supplied the citizens at the center of the British Empire. Let us not forget India pale ale. Even though its spiritual home is Burton-on-Trent, London had its role in the birth of this most iconic beer.

"The heritage is huge and it stimulated the beer world as we know it," says Logan Plant, founder of Beavertown, one of the most successful and creative of London's new wave of breweries. "The pale ales, IPAs, stouts, and porters in particular were created in and for London and its people."

However, in the twentieth century, during the postwar years as the city licked its wounds and then started swinging, it seemed as if the curtain was coming down on its grand history. Many breweries gave up the ghost and went elsewhere for cheaper sites, or they just removed themselves from brewing. Courage's Anchor Brewhouse closed in 1981 and the brewery relocated in the direction of Reading. Whitbread closed and names such as Truman, Barclay Perkins, and Charrington were just ghosts on pub facades (many of which closed). By the time of the millennium, family breweries Young's and Fuller's, along with a handful of micros, as well

as a new lager-centric brewery called Meantime were all that were left.

Fast forward to now, and, as a recent Nobel Prize laureate for literature might have written, if he had wanted to speak properly, the times have changed. At the time of writing, it is estimated that there are perhaps more than a hundred breweries in the city. True, many of them will be one man and a dog in a railroad arch making something beer-blogging wags have christened "London murky," but on the other hand there're a vitality and a vibrancy about beer in London that have catapulted it into the status of world beer city in a short time.

Breweries such as the aforementioned Beavertown, The Kernel, Camden Town (who were so successful that AB-InBev bought them), Fourpure, Anspach & Hobday, Weird Beard, and Partizan have produced a variety of great beers that are in tune with the current British beer revolution. Want a beer influenced by that great style of middle Europe Berliner weiss? Then there's Kernel's London Sour, a refreshing, tart beer with a delicate hint of lemon. There have also been versions made with raspberries

or sour cherries, and it's been blended with Kernel's saison, which was first aged in Burgundy wine barrels.

Or maybe you would prefer an IPA that will take you straight to America's West Coast, where the Pacific rollers crash in on the sands. Let's have a glass of Fourpure's Shape Shifter, a sticky, resinous, piney, flirtatiously citrus IPA. There are pale ales, saisons, imperial stouts, Baltic porters, witbiers, broody bitters, and all manner of beers being made, which all make London so special.

And let's not forget Fuller's, which has weathered the storms of three centuries and is still as important and vital to the city's beer history as ever. Ever since, Messrs. Fuller, Smith, and Turner took control of an ailing Chiswick concern in 1845, this magnificent brewery has grown to become, as the name of its bestseller declaims, London Pride. What better excuse for a pint is that?

London is calling. You'd better answer.

Opposite left: The London beer scene has blossomed in the last ten years from a handful of breweries to more than a hundred

Opposite right: London is brewing and the result is a world-class beer city.

Above left: Beavertown cans can be seen all over the capital's craft beer scene.

Above right: A bottle of London history, Anspach & Hobday's The Porter.

* KEY BEERS

Beavertown Gamma Ray 4.5%
Brew By Numbers Double IPA Citra & Ekuanot 8.5%
Camden IHL 6.2%
Four Pure Shape Shifter 6.4%
Orbit Neu 4.7%

BREW BY NUMBERS
~ BBNº ~
01|01
SAISON
CITRA
HANDCRAFTED IN LONDON
— 5.5% —

PARTIZAN BREWING

BERMONDSEY, LONDON
WWW.PARTIZANBREWING.CO.UK

Pale Ale 4.5%

Former chef Andy Smith set up Partizan in 2012 after a stint with the excellent Redemption Brew in North London, and, no doubt with his former trade in mind, this delicately fruity pale ale changes its aroma hops with each brew. However, whatever the hops (usually US), you can expect a fragrant, citrusy blast of hop goodness.

Stout 8.5%

Darker than your worst nightmares. Silky in sheen and globular of body, this especially muscular and full-bodied stout will delight with its rich complement of coffee, chocolate, roast grain, and cooked fruit notes.

PENZANCE BREWING COMPANY

PENZANCE, CORNWALL
WWW.PENZANCEBREWING.WORDPRESS.COM

Potion No. 9 Golden Ale 4%

Since taking over the Star Inn just outside Penzance, Pete Elvin has gained many awards for both the pub and the beers he brews around the back. This light gold session beer is an easy-drinking joy with a light hop character and a bittersweet finish.

POWDERKEG

WOODBURY SALTERTON, DEVON
WWW.POWDERKEGBEER.CO.UK

Cut Loose Hoppy Pilsner 4.7%

Located just over the M5 from Exeter, Powderkeg makes a nice lager-shaped noise with this juicy, fruity pilsner, which is livened up with additions of New Zealand stellar hop Moteuka. A dry, grainy finish makes you want to drink more.

PRESSURE DROP BREWING

HACKNEY, LONDON
WWW.PRESSUREDROPBREWING.CO.UK

Pale Fire Pale Ale 4.8%

Golden in color and topped with a fine white head of foam, this Hackney-born pale ale shimmers with hints of grapefruit, pineapple, and melon before finishing with a light bitterness —to make things interesting the brewery changes the aroma hops from time to time.

Wu Gang Chops the Tree Hefeweisse 3.8%

Here's a hefeweisse with a difference in that (a) it's weaker than the usual +5% and (b) the guys at the brewery have added foraged herbs to the mix. Result? A thirst-quenching beer with a throat lozenge-like herbal note, traditional cloves, and bananas.

RAMSGATE BREWERY

BROADSTAIRS, KENT
WWW.RAMSGATEBREWERY.CO.UK

No. 5 Best Bitter 4.4%

Eddie Gadd is one of the most passionate brewers around and a lover of English (specifically Kentish) hops, as can be seen in this muscular bitter. The Fuggles and Goldings used give citrusy-marmalade notes and a robust bitterness, which work like a dream alongside the grainy, cookie malt character. A classic of its kind.

REBELLION BEER CO.

MARLOW, BUCKINGHAMSHIRE
WWW.REBELLIONBEER.CO.UK

Rebellion IPA 3.7%

Pint-pot pedants will love to point out that this is not a "proper" IPA, and they will be correct. But on the other hand, let's just enjoy this copper-colored session ale's easy-drinking amiability, with its bittersweet balance of hops and malt. A quiet, traditional ale from a gastronomic Buckinghamshire town.

RED WILLOW BREWERY
MACCLESFIELD, CHESHIRE
WWW.REDWILLOWBREWERY.COM

Directionless Pale Ale 4.2%
Far from being directionless, this amber-colored beauty is a classic best bitter from a well-regarded brewery. It boasts a harmonious hum of grapefruit and lemon on the nose, more citrus on the palate alongside a frisky, grainy, malt character before a dry finish.

REDEMPTION BREWING
TOTTENHAM, LONDON
WWW.REDEMPTIONBREWING.CO.UK

Urban Dusk Bitter 4.6%
As well as the incredibly tasty pale ale Trinity, which is only 3% and drinks like a much stronger beer, Tottenham hop-stars Redemption produce this chestnut-colored bitter that has bright citrusy notes and hints of caramel on the nose, while the dry, crisp nutty palate leads to a long-lasting bitter finish. A perfectly balanced and irresistible London brew.

REDWELL BREWING
NORWICH, NORFOLK
WWW.REDWELLBREWING.COM

Kofra Coffee Stout 5.9%
This is a beer born of a collaboration between Redwell and Norwich-based indie coffee shop Kofra. Dark and topped with a cream-colored head, it's almost as if a mocha went on a road trip across the Fens in the company of a roasty stout.

ROBINSONS
STOCKPORT, LANCASHIRE
WWW.ROBINSONSBREWERY.COM

Old Tom Barley Wine 8.5%
First brewed when Queen Victoria was still (just) on the throne and gentlemen lifted their hats to ladies, this barnstormer of a barley wine is a mouthfilling and vinous beer full of toffee, caramel, chocolate, and joyful fruitiness. The smirking cat on the label is a bonus and has been part of this Manchester brewery's distinctive branding for decades.

ROOSTERS
KNARESBOROUGH, NORTH YORKSHIRE
WWW.ROOSTERS.CO.UK

Baby-Faced Assassin IPA 6.1%
One of Yorkshire's finest breweries demands your full attention with this bold, colorful, and vividly flavored IPA. The Citra hop shines through with all its glorious aromatic strength, bringing forth citrus orange, juicy mango, and passion-fruit notes against a bracing bitterness and grainy dryness.

ST. AUSTELL
ST. AUSTELL, CORNWALL
WWW.STAUSTELLBREWERY.CO.UK

Proper Job India Pale Ale 5.5%
Such a cavalcade of tropical fruit spills out of this beer that you should really drink it from a coconut shell wearing a Hawaiian shirt while wondering where you put your surf board. Leechees and ripe guava join grapefruit on the nose, while there's more tang and zest on the palate before its satisfyingly bitter finish. A true classic, this one.

SACRE BREW
WOLVERHAMPTON, WEST MIDLANDS
WWW.SACREBREW.COM

Wendigo IPA 6%
Sacre Brew might be a small outfit, but it's been making plenty of waves with its boldly flavored beers, such as this American-style IPA, which is love-bombed with plenty of Mosaic hops both during the brew and then in the dry-hopping process. The result is a juicy, fruity creation. Rumor has it that the brewery will be sold, but brewing will continue.

SALOPIAN BREWERY
SHREWSBURY, SHROPSHIRE
WWW.SALOPIANBREWERY.CO.UK

Kashmir IPA 5.5%
Passion fruit and ripe orange peel combine with the sensuous pungency of a big bag brimming with hops on the nose, while each taste reveals something akin to a deeply orangey, boozy Fanta without the sweetness, plus more tropical fruit and a lasting bitter finish. A fantastic beer from one of Shropshire's brewing legends.

SALTAIRE BREWERY
SHIPLEY, WEST YORKSHIRE
WWW.SALTAIREBREWERY.CO.UK

Cascade Pale Ale 4.8%

As the name of the beer suggests, there's more than a whisper of American hops in this much-awarded pale ale with Centennial joining the classic Cascade in the brew. The result is a refreshing, floral, and fruity thirst-quencher with an ample dry finish. A craveworthy quaffer that slips down the throat with amiable ease.

SIREN CRAFT BREW
WOKINGHAM, BERKSHIRE
WWW.SIRENCRAFTBREW.COM

Broken Dream Stout 6%

Given its strength, it's probably best to wait until lunchtime before partaking of this smooth and elegant, silky and soothing sipper of a "breakfast" stout that has coffee, chocolate, a subtle roastiness, and hints of licorice on the palate. Who would have thought such beery joy possible in Berkshire?

Soundwave IPA 5.6%

A West Coast IPA that is a hugely well-balanced affair, its resiny hoppiness combining beautifully with its juicy and fruity (imagine a sun-kissed bowl of mango, grapefruit, and ripe peach) character. The crisp dry finish provides a suitably superb crescendo. A beautiful beer for sure.

THEAKSTON
MASHAM, NORTH YORKSHIRE
WWW.THEAKSTONS.CO.UK

Old Peculier Premium Bitter 5.6%

This legendary strong Yorkshire bitter is enjoyable when sat supping by the fire in the pub and reveling in its fruity, malty, slightly smoky, and bitter character, or, as an extra treat, with a slice of fruitcake and Wensleydale cheese at the dining table. First brewed in 1890, the peculiar spelling of Peculier premium bitter refers to Masham's twelfth-century ecclesiastical court.

THORNBRIDGE BREWERY
see Brewery Profile pages 68 to 69
BAKEWELL, DERBYSHIRE
WWW.THORNBRIDGEBREWERY.CO.UK

Jaipur IPA 5.9%

This is the beer that rewrote the rules and kicked off the golden age of IPAs. First brewed in 2005 (when BrewDog's Martin Dickie was in the brewhouse), it's as fruity as a greengrocer's display, lightly honeyed, and its bitter finish is as biting as a Dorothy Parker putdown.

THREE KINGS BREWERY
NORTH SHIELDS, TYNE AND WEAR
WWW.THREEKINGSBREWERY.CO.UK

Silver Darling Pale Ale 5.6%

Bitterness and citrusy fruitiness combine to create a wonderfully characterful pale ale, with plenty of grapefruit and light orange on the nose (Cascade is liberally added as an aroma hop), followed by more citrus on the palate and a bittersweet and dry finish.

THREE KINGS BREWERY
SILVER DARLING
5.6%
PALE ALE

THWAITES
BLACKBURN, LANCASHIRE
WWW.THWAITES.CO.UK

Crafty Dan 13 Guns Pale Ale 5.5%

Until the release of 13 Guns, north-west brewing stalwart Thwaites was best known for its bitter and mild. But the release of this American-style pale ale marked a new direction, as this amber-gold beer brims with citrus and pine on both nose and palate, before its robust bitter finish.

13 GUNS
AMERICAN IPA
ALC 5.5% VOL
CRAFTY DAN

TIMOTHY TAYLOR
KEIGHLEY, WEST YORKSHIRE
WWW.TIMOTHY-TAYLOR.CO.UK

Landlord Pale Ale/Bitter 4.3%

One of the world's finest beers, Landlord is a masterpiece, an incessant award-winner and, what's more, Madonna's favorite pint. Brewed, like all Taylor's beers, entirely with a Golden Promise malt more readily associated with scotch, and soft water that runs off the Pennine hills, it's full of zing and tang, shifting effortlessly between rosemary-pine hop character and mouthfilling malt. Genius in a glass. Little wonder the chap on the label is smiling.

TITANIC BREWERY
STOKE-ON-TRENT, STAFFORDSHIRE
WWW.TITANICBREWERY.CO.UK

Titanic Stout 4.5%

Darkly seductive stout with dashes of port, chocolate, pepper, plums, hazelnuts, and coffee. A touch of smoke and a dry roasted finish. Sales of the 2004 Champion Bottle-Conditioned Beer of Britain were buoyed when it was used in a recipe for ice cream by a TV chef. That aside, it is a very good stout.

TRACK BREWING
MANCHESTER
WWW.TRACKBREWING.CO.UK

Sonoma Pale Ale 3.8%

It might be only 3.8% and the kind of beer more beefy types might sneer at, but this juicy and punchy pale ale is packed full of flavor with enough grapefruit and tropical fruit notes to make you feel that you're getting your five-a-day fruit hit.

TRING BREWERY
TRING, HERTFORDSHIRE
WWW.TRINGBREWERY.CO.UK

Tea Kettle Stout 4.7%

Lusciously dark and chewy and intensely flavored, there are plenty of molasses, fruitcake, coffee, chocolate, and a silk scarf of smoothness in this handsome stout. As for the name? Apparently Tring Brewery's home county of Hertfordshire is said to be shaped like a kettle.

TRIPLE FFF BREWING COMPANY
ALTON, HAMPSHIRE
WWW.TRIPLEFFF.COM

Alton's Pride Bitter 3.8%

Triple FFF has been going for only just over a decade, but what a success it's been, winning many awards. The beers, including a mild and a best bitter, are all structured on a Maris Otter backbone. This, the 2008 Champion Beer of Britain, is a great brusque, brunette bitter mellowed by mouthwarming malt.

TRUE NORTH BREW CO.
SHEFFIELD, SOUTH YORKSHIRE
WWW.TRUENORTHBREW.CO.UK

Red Rye Red Ale 4.7%

Founded in 2012, when the beers were brewed at Welbeck Abbey Brewery, True North got its own space in Sheffield in 2015 and goes from strength to strength, with beers like this rich ruby-colored ale which is single-hopped with the New Zealand variety Rakau. Full-bodied and richly flavored, this is an ample ale.

TRUMAN'S BREWERY
HACKNEY WICK, LONDON
WWW.TRUMANSBEER.CO.UK

Zephyr Pale Ale 4.4%

Until it closed in 1989, the Truman name was one of the greats of British brewing. It returned in 2010, and two years later Truman's beers were being made in Hackney Wick. Zephyr is a brash and juicy pale ale crammed with tropical fruit and citrus notes alongside a delicate bittersweetness.

TWICKENHAM FINE ALES
TWICKENHAM, LONDON
WWW.TWICKENHAM-FINE-ALES.CO.UK

Naked Ladies Golden Ale 4.4%

For those of you with a mucky mind, let's get one thing clear: the name of this gleaming golden beer refers to a famous statue of water nymphs in Twickenham; it's all very arty and classical. As for the beer: it's fragrant and fruity, bittersweet and full-flavored, and a delight to drink.

TWISTED BARREL ALE
COVENTRY, WEST MIDLANDS
WWW.TWISTEDBARRELALE.CO.UK

Beast Of A Midlands Mild 3.9%

Mild meets the modern world, and the result is a flurry of chocolate, sugary coffee, and a delicate nuttiness on the nose and palate, with toffee and licorice joining in the fun during the latter phase. Flat caps optional.

THORNBRIDGE BREWERY

BAKEWELL, DERBYSHIRE

WWW.THORNBRIDGEBREWERY.CO.UK

Back in the olden days, British landed gentry often had a brewery within the grounds of their country mansions, but as the world changed and the gentry cashed out, this convention dwindled. However, back in 2005, in rural Derbyshire, within the grounds of a grandiose Jacobean manor, the tradition was rekindled by Thornbridge Brewery—set in stunning scenery dominated by the Hall itself.

What not so long ago was a crumbling stately home was gradually restored to its former glory by Emma and Jim Harrison, but it was the late Dave Wickett, a friend and owner of Sheffield's Kelham Island brewery, who suggested opening a brewery in their back "garden."

In 2004 Jim invested in a second-hand ten-barrel brewing system and installed it in a derelict stonemason's shop yards from the stately home. He then turned to Stefano Cossi, a 26-year-old food scientist from Udine in northern Italy, who was initially joined by young Scotsman Martin Dickie and then, after Dickie left to found BrewDog, New Zealand brewer Kelly Ryan. This combination of Kiwi creativity and Italian flair saw Thornbridge scoop more than 75 awards in its first three years, with approximately half going to

its boldly flavored IPA Jaipur (5.9% ABV). As well as Jaipur, Thornbridge's core range included Kipling (5.2% ABV), a South Pacific pale ale brewed using Nelson Sauvin hops from New Zealand, and Wild Swan, a modest 3.5 % ABV beer swathed in spice and citrus hop aromas.

In the space of only four years, soaring demand outstripped the capability of Thornbridge's original brewery, and, in 2009, it was moved into a state-of-the-art brewery in nearby Bakewell. Since the move, Thornbridge has continued its unwavering commitment to the unusual, innovative elixirs that first thrust it into the limelight, while the old brewhouse is now a pilot brewery for more left-field liquids.

Now in its second decade of brewers with Cossi and Ryan long gone, there is a new team

of young, dynamic brewers led by head brewer Rob Lovatt, who joined from Meantime in 2010. Without the weight of history that shackles so many British ale brewers, they courageously venture into experimentation and innovation where others dare not tread. Rob Lovatt explains:

> "I am very style driven and feel that classic styles have evolved as they are because they are a proven formula that inherently works. There is nothing more satisfying than nailing a classic style. That's not to say I am adverse to experimentation and brewing beers which are a bit more left field; however, a lot of thought needs to go into making beers like these to make sure the final beer is balanced and any novel ingredients complement the other components within."

This sense of adventure is by no means new. In 2005 Thornbridge was one of the first British microbreweries to dabble in the dark, woody art of barrel-aging. Its super satin-smooth St. Petersburg Imperial Russian stout was put to sleep for 300 days in Scottish whisky barrels from distilleries, including Caol Ila and Macallan. Lovatt has followed the Flemish tradition of blending young beers with aged beers that have spent up to two years in wood. The result includes Sour Brown, a 7% grand West Flemish brown, plus two sour red ales, Love amongst the Ruins and Days of Creation. There have also been pilsners, a Scotch ale, a kölsch, a black IPA, and some imperial IPAs. This is a brewery that, like the beers it keeps in wood, can only keep improving with age.

* KEY BEERS

Thornbridge Black Raven Black IPA 6.6%
Thornbridge Bracia Dark Ale 9%
Thornbridge Halcyon Imperial IPA 7.7%
Thornbridge Jaipur IPA 5.9%
Thornbridge Otto Weizen Doppelbock 8%

Far left and center: Thanks to its enormous success, Thornbridge Brewery had to relocate from its original Jacobean manor location to a purpose-built brewery in Bakewell, Derbyshire.

Left: Under the watchful eye of head brewer Rob Lovatt, beers are carefully created and lovingly monitored to ensure consistent quality at all parts of the brewing process.

VOCATION BREWERY

HEBDEN BRIDGE, WEST YORKSHIRE
WWW.VOCATIONBREWERY.COM

Life & Death IPA 6.5%

Straight outta Hebden Bridge, this American-style IPA is the color of bruised gold and positively pulsates with vibrant hop character on both the nose and palate. Think a bowl of ripe tropical fruit, including mangoes, papaya, and passion fruit alongside a spike of grapefruit, with a full-bodied mouthfeel and big bitter finish.

Pride & Joy Pale Ale 5.3%

Hebden Bridge's hop-happy heroes have gone to town with this assertive pale ale, which positively trembles with tropical fruit notes on the nose, while in the mouth there's more fruit (passion fruit and grapefruit) alongside a resinous character before a dry finish.

WADWORTH

DEVIZES, WILTSHIRE
WWW.WADWORTH.CO.UK

Wadworth 6X Bitter 4.3%

Rewarding, friendly, and craveworthy, 6X appeals to those yearning a good malt 'n' hop balance in their bitter. With its Victorian tower brewery open coppers, shire horses, bespoke sign-painter, and a rare working cooperage, Wadworth really has been left to its own Devizes since moving into its Northgate brewery in 1885.

WEIRD BEARD BREW

BRENTFORD, LONDON
WWW.WEIRDBEARDBREWCO.COM

Black Perle Milk Stout 3.8%

An eloquent, well-spoken creaminess emerges from the nose when this coffee milk stout is poured, while sip after sip unveils a creamy coffee-like character, hints of black pepper in the background, and a roasty bitter finish. Incredibly characterful for 3.8%.

Mariana Trench Pale Ale 5.3%

American and New Zealand hops come together in this American-style pale ale to create a luminous and lustrous beer whose aromatics of passion fruit and mango bubble away on both the nose and the palate with the urgency of an underwater geyser.

WESTERHAM BREWERY

EDENBRIDGE, KENT
WWW.WESTERHAMBREWERY.CO.UK

Audit Ale Old Ale 6.2%

Westerham's learned resurrection of the strong beers that Oxbridge colleges used to brew until World War II is a tawny-copper ale with vinouslike sweetness, booze-soaked raisins and currants, a hint of chocolate, and a dry, bitter finish. Gowns and mortars optional for this multi-award-winner.

Scotney Bitter Best Bitter 4.3%

This amber-hued bitter was originally brewed for the National Trust using hops from their farm at Scotney Castle in Kent. It's now a Westerham regular, blasting forth siren calls of malt sweetness, spicy hop, and a long dry finish. It's also gluten-free.

WHITSTABLE BREWERY

WHITSTABLE, KENT
WWW.WHITSTABLEBREWERY.CO.UK

Oyster Stout 4.5%

Whitstable is noted for its oysters, so it makes complete sense for the local brewery to make a stout that is a sublime accompaniment to half-a-dozen bivalves. Silky-smooth and as dark as a moonless night, this is a superb stout that goes well with beef and game too.

WICKWAR BREWERY

WICKWAR, GLOUCESTERSHIRE
WWW.WICKWARBREWING.COM

Station Porter 6.1%

Located in the former brewhouse of the long-closed Arnold Perrett Brewery, Wickwar produces a collection of quality Cotswolds ales including this ebony ale with a blend of three malts and plenty of Fuggles hops. Pitch-black in color, it's a potent porter overflowing with notes of roast malt, chocolate, raisins, coffee, and licorice wrapped up in a smooth mouthfeel. Seriously velvety.

THE WILD BEER CO.
WESTCOMBE, SOMERSET
WWW.WILDBEERCO.COM

Modus Operandi Old Ale 7%
Wild Beer is the Somerset-based king of sour and wood-aged beers, and their debut beer is first brewed as an old ale and then aged in bourbon barrels, which brings forth a lush, generous beer featuring a sexy earthiness, as well as chocolate, cherry, and soft vanilla notes with a generous bitter finish.

Ninkasi Saison 9%
Named after the ancient Sumerian goddess of beer, this is an equally divine Belgian-style saison made with Southern Hemisphere hops, wild yeast, and local apple juice which is then refermentated in the bottle with Champagne yeast. Complex and cultivated, it's spritzy and refreshing and a superb sub for fizz.

Pogo Pale Ale 4.1%
A boing-ing pale ale infused with passion fruit, orange, and guava. Naturally it's fruity, but it's also juicy and bittersweet and the ideal companion for a hot summer's day. One of the best examples of the contentious and much-debated fruit-flavored pale ale genre.

WINDSOR & ETON BREWERY
WINDSOR, BERKSHIRE
WWW.WEBREW.CO.UK

Conqueror 1075 Black IPA 7.4%
Black IPA, dark India ale, black bitter? Who cares what niche this beer from the Royal Borough of Windsor falls into? It's damn fine and is named after the year in which William the Conqueror built Windsor Castle, and there's much to enjoy in its fabulous flurries of toffee, smoke, burned toast, chocolate orange, and hints of vanilla alongside a dry and assertive finish. The deserved winner of several Society of Independent Brewers (SIBA) awards.

WIPER AND TRUE
ST. WERBURGHS, BRISTOL
WWW.WIPERANDTRUE.COM

Milk Stout Milk Shake 5.6%
This modern milk stout is as smooth as a crooner and as deep as a philosophy lecture at the Sorbonne, with chocolate, vanilla, and coffee notes ringing away on both nose and palate.

Quintet IPA 6.2%
Five different varieties of hops go into Quintet (geddit!) every time a batch of this boldly flavored IPA is brewed. Expect hophead heroes such as Mosaic, Citra, and Columbus alongside new cones on the block such as the Australian Ella.

WOODFORDE'S BREWERY
WOODBASTWICK, NORFOLK
WWW.WOODFORDES.CO.UK

Wherry Bitter 3.8%
This awesome award-winning ale is hard to resist for a repeat visit once tasted. One of a bunch of brilliant beers from a brewery named after Parson Woodforde, a well-known eighteenth-century Norfolk clergyman and beer-drinking epicurean.

WORTHINGTON'S BREWERY
BURTON-ON-TRENT, STAFFORDSHIRE
WWW.WORTHINGTONS-WHITESHIELD.COM

Worthington's White Shield India Pale Ale 5.6%
A legendary beer that is making the biggest and most unexpected comeback since Bobby Ewing stepped out of the shower in *Dallas*. One of the five bottle-conditioned beers that was around in 1971, WWS courted extinction before drinkers were reawoken to its estery effervescence, superb balance, gentle bitterness, and thick-cut marmalade and apricot flavors.

WYLAM BREWERY
NEWCASTLE-UPON-TYNE
WWW.WYLAMBREWERY.CO.UK

Jakehead IPA 6.3%
Formerly best known as brewers of unadventurous beers, Wylam now has a bold portfolio, with this self-styled "super-charged" IPA leading the pack. Waves of American hops emerge from the glass and its bittersweet hop furnace will have you going back for more.

SCOTLAND

ALECHEMY BREWING
LIVINGSTON, SCOTLAND
WWW.ALECHEMY.BEER

Rye O'Rye Red Rye Pale Ale 5.6%
Former chemist James Davies founded Alechemy in 2012, eager to recreate and recalibrate some of the US beers he'd tasted and enjoyed on his travels. Since then, Alechemy has become known for a whole series of beers (some hop bombs, others not), such as this amber ale spiced with rye, which gives a warming, crunchy, and crisp mouthfeel, with plenty of citrus to keep the balance. Available in cask, bottle, and keg.

BELHAVEN BREWERY
DUNBAR, EAST LOTHIAN, SCOTLAND
WWW.BELHAVEN.CO.UK

80/- Bitter 4.2%
A russet-red classic Scottish shilling ale once described by an Austrian emperor as "the Burgundy of Scotland." Massively malty, dried fruits, and a touch of bitterness, with Challenger, Fuggles, and Goldings hops courtesy of Scotland's biggest and oldest regional brewer, now owned by the British brewer Greene King.

BLACK WOLF BREWERY
STIRLING, SCOTLAND
WWW.BLACKWOLFBREWERY.COM

Lomond Gold Golden Ale 5%
Originally called Traditional Scottish Ales, Black Wolf was rebranded under its current name in 2014. Lomond Gold, as the name suggests, gleams golden in color, while citrus fruit and a light barley touch enhance its drinkability.

BREWDOG
FRASERBURGH, SCOTLAND
WWW.BREWDOG.COM

Born to Die Imperial IPA 8.5%
Heavily hopped Imperial India Pale Ale, which is released only twice, once in April and then again in November. Its intensity of tropical fruit, savoriness, and pungent hoppiness is stunning. Its name is a reference to the fact that it should be consumed within a month of being bought if you want to experience the vivid and vibrant freshness of its hop zinginess.

BREWDOG
BORN TO DIE
31.08.2016

Punk IPA 5.6%
This is the beer that made BrewDog and, along with Thornbridge, influenced a new generation of brewers. An American-style IPA ringing with peach and ripe apricot skin on the nose, while leechees, papaya and mangos trip off tongue alongside a gentle touch of white pepper in the dry and grainy finish.

CAIRNGORM BREWERY COMPANY
AVIEMORE, SCOTLAND
WWW.CAIRNGORMBREWERY.COM

Trade Winds Spiced/Herb Beer 4.3%
CAMRA's Champion Specialty Beer of Britain in 2004, 2005, and 2006 mixes elderflower together with Perle hops and a weighty dose of wheat. Delicate, floral, and smooth, this is a luscious beer both at home on the dining table and the bar top.

CROMARTY BREWING CO.
DAVIDSTON, CROMARTY, SCOTLAND
WWW.CROMARTYBREWING.COM

Red Rocker Rye IPA 5%
This is just one of the excellent beers brewed by this family brewery in the Highlands, whose beers started being brewed at the end of 2011. Reddish brown in color, it is a brilliant marriage of American and New Zealand hops with a malt bill that includes the spiciness of rye. It's grainy, citrusy, resiny, and spicy with an appetizingly bitter and dry finish.

DRYGATE BREWING CO.
GLASGOW, SCOTLAND
WWW.DRYGATE.COM

Bearface Lager 4.4%
Drygate is a joint venture between the owners of Tennents lager and the Williams Bros brewery in Glasgow. The outfit also includes a bar and a restaurant. Bearface is a crisp and well-hopped lager that reaches the parts other beers fail to. As well as a core range of ales, there is also a "studio" selection of well-flavored beer in cans.

FYNE ALES
ACHADUNAN, SCOTLAND
WWW.FYNEALES.COM

Jarl Golden Ale 3.8%

The northern end of Loch Fyne is home to this eponymous family-owned brewery founded in 2001 on a farm. Jarl is the beer that brought Fyne to national promience, a honeyed, hoppy golden ale that uses one hop to make its statement. The hop is Citra, though, the poster boy for the American hop revolution.

Superior IPA 7.1%

Hops. As all good IPAs should be, this is all about the hops, in this case Citra and Cascade, oodles of which are added at four points during brewing. The result is a greengrocer's barrel of fruit (apricot, peaches, grapefruit) on both nose and palate, with a long bittersweet finish that makes you want to dive into the glass and lingers there like a contemporary beer-loving Esther Williams.

HARVIESTOUN
ALVA, SCOTLAND
WWW.HARVIESTOUN.COM

Bitter & Twisted Blond Beer 4.2%

The mantel at Harviestoun's brewery sags under the weight of beer awards —many of which have been pinned to the chest of this zesty, refreshing light ale full of pear drop, lemon, and grapefruit flavors.

Ola Dubh Oak Aged Ale 8%

This gloriously gloopy collaboration between Harviestoun and Highland Park whisky distillery looks like the viscous liquid usually seen on sorry-looking oil-spill seabirds. A porterlike old ale matured in casks that have previously housed Highland Park 30-year-old whisky. Big but not brutal, it oozes chocolate, espresso, and vanilla bean.

Schiehallion Cask Conditioned Lager 4.8%

Named after a nearby mountain, this rare example of a cask-conditioned lager is a balletic balance of sturdy cookie malt and snappy citrus hop. Flowery yet with a big barley backbone.

INNIS & GUNN
EDINBURGH, SCOTLAND
WWW.INNISANDGUNN.COM

Innis & Gunn Rum Finish Oak Aged Beer 6.8%

After the initial success of Innis & Gunn's wood-aged Original, a liquid love-child of Scottish distilling and brewing, there followed many other barrel-aged treats. This is the rum version, which quickly switched from the Limited Edition range to become a core beer for the brewery. It's spicy, fruity, and mellow in its finish.

THE ORKNEY BREWERY
QUOYLOO, ORKNEY, SCOTLAND
WWW.ORKNEYBREWERY.CO.UK

Dark Island Premium Bitter 4.6%

Twice Champion Beer of Scotland, this bitter bestows melodious mocha and molasses in the mouth, sharpened at the back of the throat by First Gold and Goldings hop bitterness. Its fruity finish clamors for the cheeseboard.

Red Macgregor Strong Ale 5%

An awesome, intensely ecologically aware brewery nestled in the far north of Scotland. This convivial, cozy ruby beer, with toffee and plum flavors and a touch of leechee, is magical with a red-meat roast.

SIX DEGREES NORTH
STONEHAVEN, ABERDEENSHIRE, SCOTLAND
WWW.SIXDNORTH.CO.UK

Tripel 9%

Based north of Aberdeen, Six° North produces a variety of intriguing beers with a strong Belgian influence such as this lustrous Tripel. Pear and peach tremble on the nose, while hints of bananas and ripe peach plus a trace of pepperiness sooth the palate; the finish is honeyed and bittersweet.

TEMPEST BREWING CO.
GALASHIELS, SCOTLAND
WWW.TEMPESTBREWCO.COM

Long White Cloud Pale Ale 5.6%

Scotsman Gavin Meiklejohn was a chef in New Zealand with a sideline in homebrewing, but in 2010 he came home and Tempest was born, with a remit to brew boldly flavored beers. Long White Cloud is one such beer, being one of Tempest's first beers, a zesty, tangy pale ale packed with New Zealand hops.

TRAQUAIR HOUSE BREWERY
INNERLEITHEN, SCOTLAND
WWW.TRAQUAIR.CO.UK

Traquair House Ale Scotch Ale 7.2%
A brooding, boozy, and beguiling blend of wood notes, figs, plums, and mulled wine brewed in the grounds of Traquair House, a stunning Scottish castle that isn't far from the English border. Now the oldest inhabited house in Scotland, the site was a place of brewing as early as 1566 but was revived from a long slumber by Peter Maxwell Stuart, 20th Laird of Traquair, in 1965. Under the stewardship of his daughter Catherine, its beers are still fermented in oak and exported all over the world. This is a must-visit place if you find yourself in Scotland.

Jacobite Ale
Strong Ale/Barley Wine 8%
A sensational strong ale seasoned with coriander to enhance its heavy hop character. Voluptuous, rich, and vinous, with a touch of spicy chocolate.

VALHALLA BREWERY
UNST, SHETLAND, SCOTLAND
WWW.VALHALLABREWERY.CO.UK

White Wife Golden Ale 4.5%
If you want a brewery that's so north it's probably closer to the Arctic than London, then Valhalla is it. Based on Unst since 1997, White Wife is one of its bestsellers, a luscious dark-golden ale bursting with juicy citrus, crisp cookie malt, and a dry finish. Its name refers to a local tale of the ghost of an elderly woman.

WEST
GLASGOW, SCOTLAND
WWW.WESTBEER.COM

St. Mungo Helles 4.9%
West is a brewpub with attached restaurant based in Glasgow in a former nineteenth-century factory; it was founded by Bavarian Petra Wetzel in 2006. Lagers and wheat beers make up the mainstay of production, with this dark golden helles as West's bestseller. Crisp on the palate and blessed with a dry bitter finish.

WILLIAMS BROS BREWING CO.
ALLOA, SCOTLAND
WWW.WILLIAMSBROSBREW.COM

Double Joker Imperial IPA 8.3%
Originally called Heather Ales on its foundation in the 1990s and well-known for its heather ale Fraoch, Bruce and Scott Williams now oversee a diverse range of historic ales and their modern counterparts, such as this bittersweet, citrus-loving, tangy, and palate taming blow-your-socks-off imperial IPA.

Profanity Stout 7%
Deeply dark and full of complex flavors that boom like a never-ending peal of giant church bells, this is a riot of roast, malt, and chocolate with a floral, fruity bouquet thanks to some Nelson Sauvin hops.

WALES

BRAINS
CARDIFF, WALES
WWW.SABRAIN.COM

Brains Black Stout 4.1%
Launched in Cardiff on St. David's Day in 2010, you could argue that this is the Welsh brewery's attempt to match a certain Irish stout. By all accounts it does well, perhaps due to its creamy, espresso-colored foam, smooth mocha character, and easy finish.

LINES BREW CO.
CAERPHILLY, WALES
WWW.LINESBREWCO.COM

Farmhouse IPA 6.1%
Eco-conscious brewery, which is the brainchild of Tom Newman, formerly of Celt. It's not a pint of your usual either, as this barrel-aged IPA demonstrates: Burgundy oak provides the woodiness, while the addition of wild yeast adds an earthiness that mingles with the hops in the background.

PURPLE MOOSE BREWERY
PORTHMADOG, WALES
WWW.PURPLEMOOSE.CO.UK

Dark Side of the Moose
Old Ale/Mild 4.6%
A delicious, fruity dark ale from this diminutive yet discerning brewery born out of Lawrence Washington's homebrew hobby. Sweet and roasty.

TINY REBEL
NEWPORT, WALES
WWW.TINYREBEL.CO.UK

Cwtch Welsh Red Ale 4.6%

Not long after it was founded in 2012, Tiny Rebel began to shake up Wales's brewing scene as award after award came its way. This culminated in 2015 with Cwtch winning the coveted CAMRA Champion Beer of Britain, and what a drop of joy in the glass this is. Called a "Welsh red ale," it's amber in color and brimming with tangy and aromatic hoppy goodness, which is balanced against the deep caramel notes of the malt. As for Cwtch, it means a cuddle, which seems about right.

Dirty Stop Out Stout 5%

This smoked-oat stout has a creamy mouthfeel and plenty of mocha, licorice, and smoke aromatics, while chocolate, coffee, and cola claim the palate before the dry, lightly smoked finish.

NORTHERN IRELAND

BOUNDARY BREWING
BELFAST, NORTHERN IRELAND
WWW.BOUNDARYBREWING.COOP

Export Stout 7%

Complex, rich stout from one of the leading lights in the Northern Irish beer scene, which is organized along the lines of a cooperative. Chocolate liqueur, vanilla, and ripe dark plums on the nose give way to a creamy, chocolatey, soothing presence on the tongue before a bitter finish. Boundary also brews a 9.1% stout.

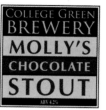

HILDEN BREWERY
LISBURN, CO. ANTRIM, NORTHERN IRELAND
WWW.HILDENBREWERY.CO.UK

Molly's Chocolate Stout 4.2%

In 2006, Northern Ireland's oldest independent brewery celebrated its 25th year of real reverence. The pick of its Anglo-Irish ales is a rich, coffee-capped dark stout brewed with malted oats, chocolate barley, and Northdown and First Gold hops. Each year, owners Seamus and Ann Scullion host a lively beer festival with more *craic* than a natural fault line.

IRELAND

CARLOW BREWING COMPANY
CARLOW, CO. CARLOW, IRELAND
WWW.CARLOWBREWING.COM

O'Hara's Irish Red 4.3%

A small craft brewery set up in 1998. In recent decades, Irish Reds have been more popular in Mediterranean markets than in their homeland. Fruity and aromatic, sprinkled with notes of coffee, and with a hop bitterness and sizable mouthfeel owing to plenty of roasted barley. Overall, an incredibly smooth ale.

O'Hara's Irish Stout 4.3%

Carlow specializes in Celtic beer styles from yesteryear and is located about 50 miles from Dublin in the Barrow Valley region, which was once Ireland's hop-growing heartland. This splendid brew won the Gold Medal at the Millennium Brewing Industry Awards for its dark black, dry, and marvelously minerally Irish stout. Look out for it.

GALWAY BAY BREWERY
GALWAY, CO. GALWAY, IRELAND
WWW.GALWAYBAYBREWERY.COM

Stormy Port Irish Porter 5.5%

Galway Bay started off as the in-house brewery at the Oslo bar in Salthill. Now it's a stand-alone brewery (though the Oslo is very much part of Galway's setup, along with several other bars) and one of the most highly regarded in the Irish craft beer movement. This is its rich and velvety porter with a harmony of chocolate, creaminess, roastiness, and a subtle sweetness.

THE PORTERHOUSE BREWING COMPANY
DUBLIN, CO. DUBLIN, IRELAND
WWW.PORTERHOUSEBREWCO.COM

Oyster Stout 4.8%

Hugely successful chain of brewpubs with outlets in London and Dublin, it proudly shuns the ubiquitous Guinness in favor of its own silky stouts. This award-winning beer is smooth and viscous, with a lovely, minerally mouthfeel thanks to Galena, Nugget, and East Kent Goldings hops.

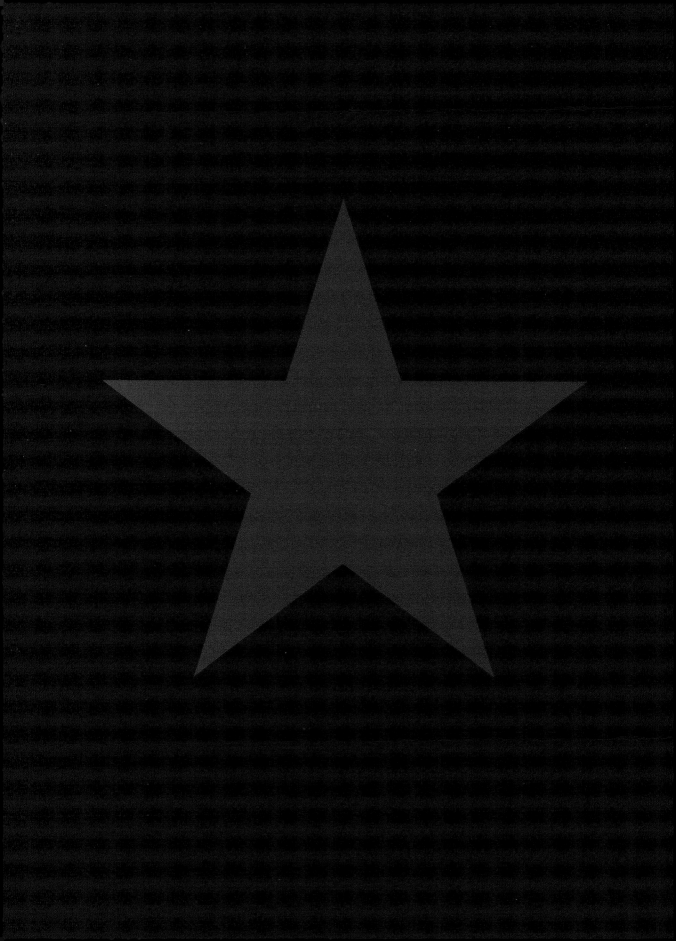

THE WORLD OF BEER

EUROPE

Above: The Orval monastery in Villiers-devant-Orval has been producing superlative Trappist ale since 1931.
Below: At Cantillon's fascinating brewery in Brussels, the magical alchemy of yeast is a joy to behold.

INTRODUCTION
BELGIUM

I n both its beer and its being, Belgium is Europe's baffling state–run by a crazy dictator wearing a hardly thought-out hat. Some dismiss Belgium as being boring. They're wrong.

It's been invaded so often that the Belgians deliberately try to make their country look as dull as possible in the hope that prospective invaders choose somewhere more exciting to plunder.

It's got a town called Silly and a town called Dave, and it's only been around officially since 1830, but it's not really a country at all—more an uneasy union of two distinct regions: the Dutch-speaking Flanders to the north and the French-speaking Wallonia to the south.

They live in a loveless marriage in which both are desperate to divorce, but, having looked at the finances, both know they can't afford to split up. Neither recognizes any kind of national narrative whatsoever, and the dividing lines run beyond language into ideology, politics, wealth, education, and media—even the "national" soccer team is alleged to have been riven by regional tensions in the past.

The one thing that brings the two regions together, however, is a mutual passion for beer. Belgium is brewing's holy land, home to more indigenous beer styles than any other country on the planet. Belgium's love of beer even stretches to its most famous (and somewhat underwhelming) monument—a bronze statue of a boy urinating into a basin.

In Belgium, beer is worshipped and given a level of rich reverence more readily associated with fine wine. Forget BrewDog, the Belgians were the original punks of brewing, anarchic advocates of esoteric ales who, throughout history, have refused to be straitjacketed by purity laws.

Much like the country itself, Belgian beer is steeped in a turbulent history of war and religion.

It's highly idiosyncratic, initially impenetrable to those who are unfamiliar, cand impossible to clearly categorize in terms of national identity.

Flanders is famous for its Flemish reds and lambic beers, and Wallonia, the more rustic region, is synonymous with saison, wheat beers, and farmhouse ales, while monastic beers are dotted on both sides of the divide.

Yet the current bipolar nature of Belgium's beer scene has less to do with regional identity and more to do with ideology.

In one corner, there's the established, old guard; the founding fathers of Belgian beer, upholders of tradition, and pioneers of the past. These include both the Trappists and abbey ales as well as independent iconic family brewers such as Duvel, Palm, Dupont, De Koninck, and St. Feuillien to name but a few.

In the other corner, there are Belgium's young Turk brewers like de La Senne, De Ranke, Beersel, Bastogne, and Jandrain-Jandrenouille, who, disillusioned with strength, sweetness, and spice, are eclipsing their older counterparts and making some of the best beer not just in Belgium but the wider world too.

Shaped by a healthy respect for their own country's brewing past (but absolutely no intention of getting stuck there), Belgium's newer independents are not blinded by pomp or pride and have freely embraced influences from abroad.

They're twisting on Belgian traditions too, and whether it's an American-style IPA or a native saison, it's being done with the kind of carefree derring-do that percolates right through Belgium's brewing past.

ABBAYE DES ROCS
MONTIGNIES-SUR-ROC, HAINAUT
WWW.ABBAYE-DES-ROCS.COM

Blanche des Honnelles Witbier 6%
Named after the river that once supplied the brewing water, this dry beer pulls back the reins on the spice and the full-on fruit. Beneath the light-golden veneer, there are hints of oranges and lemons, boiled candy, and a touch of Chartreuse. It feels like it's doing you good, so hopefully it is.

Grand Cru Strong Strong Ale 9.5%
A dainty Walloon brewery that has grown from a tiny, tumbledown outfit in 1979 into one of Belgium's most impressive modern breweries. Its brewing processes draw on a dazzling array of spices, grains, and malts and this beauty of a beer is rich and rambunctious, in its fruitiness (think cherries and other dried fruit), caramel-like sweetness, and cuddles of chocolate.

ACHEL
HAMONT-ACHEL, LIMBURG
WWW.ACHELSEKLUIS.ORG

Achel 5 Blond Blonde Ale 5%
Unlike most Trappist beers, which feel as though they could put hair back on a thinning pate, this herbaceous, nutty golden ale is modest in strength. You will taste pink grapefruit, pear, and a touch of cream soda.

Achel Extra Bruin Trappist Ale 9.5%
Achel began commercial brewing again in 1999 to raise much-needed funds for the abbey, and since then it has become a firm favorite among those with a taste for trappist ales. Burnished brown in color, its complex nose boasts chocolate, light spice, dark fruit, and vanilla, while the palate continues in this theme with a bitter finish. A classic Belgian Trappist ale.

ACHOUFFE
BRUSSELS
WWW.ACHOUFFE.BE

Houblon Dobbelen IPA Tripel 9%
An imperial, highly aggressive India pale ale that wears its radioactive resins, stewed bitterness, and deep-orange marmalade notes on its dark golden sleeve.

N'ice Chouffe Barley Wine 10%
A real winter warmer, this is a rarely sighted, richly endowed beer best enjoyed by the fireside with the wind howling and the rain coming down like hail on a winter's night. This beer, unlike the elves and gnomes that feature on the brewery's labels, is rather immense.

AFFLIGEM
OPWIJK, FLEMISH BRABANT
WWW.AFFLIGEMBEER.BE

Tripel 8.5%
There is evidence of Affligem beers being brewed as far back as the sixteenth century. The monastery once owned hop gardens in both Belgium and Kent, England, but is now under the global wing of Heineken. Despite this, the ale's sophistication has not been sacrificed. This terrific tripel leads with an awesome orange aroma, its body bolstered by peppery fruit sweetness before dropping away as dry and whiskey-warm.

ALVINNE
MOEN, WEST FLANDERS
WWW.ACBF.BE

Morpheus Extra RA
Belgian Ale 7.1%
Eclecticism is the name of the game with Alvinne, whose sour beers, wood-aged ales, and IPAs excite the beer buffs. Morpheus Extra RA is a rare regular whose tangy, grassy nose has an undercurrent of grapefruit, while jaunty citrus, resiny hop, and an effervescent mouthfeel create fireworks on the palate.

ANKER
MECHELEN, ANTWERP
WWW.HETANKER.BE

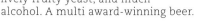 **Gouden Carolus** Classic Brown Ale 8.5%

Dating from the fourteenth century, the "anchor" is a contender for the oldest brewery in Belgium. "Golden Charlie," named after a coin and first racked up in the 1960s, is a brandy-colored beer made with pale and dark malt, brimming with nutmeg, spice, Curaçao, peppery Belgian hops, lively fruity yeast, and much alcohol. A multi award-winning beer.

BELLEVAUX
BELLEVAUX, LIEGE
WWW.BRASSERIEDEBELLEVAUX.BE

Black Old Ale 6.3%

Bellevaux is a family-owned brewery based just outside Malmedy in the Ardennes. This cola-colored ale is a rich and exceptionally assured creature with flurries of chocolate, coffee, and toffee notes before it finishes with an assured bitterness and appetizing dryness. Good with chocolate.

BLAUGIES
DOUR, HAINAUT
WWW.BRASSERIEDEBLAUGIES.COM

La Moneuse Amber Ale 8%

An anarchic amber ale that flips between tartness and subtle sweetness with the capricious whimsy of a moody toddler. One of many beers to look out for from a clever craft brewery that has carved itself a revered reputation for its eclectic yet often excellent ales.

DU BOCQ
PURNODE, NAMUR
WWW.BOCQ.BE

Blanche de Namur Witbier 4.5%

Founded in 1858 by farmer Martin Belot, Du Bocq is a big, family-owned, niche player that has retained craft brewing traditions yet thinks nothing of sharing its space with other breweries looking for a contract brewer. Their Blanche de Namur is a wheat-led whirlwind of spice, sweetness, and fruit.

BOELENS
BELSELE, EAST FLANDERS
WWW.BROUWERIJBOELENS.BE

Waas Lander Belgian Ale 6%

The Boelens family have been involved in maltings and brewing since 1864, but this particular incarnation has been been running since 1993. Boelens made its name producing honey beers, but recent years have seen it branch out with beers such as this gold-colored bottle-conditioned brew with a citrus-sweet nose and palate, creamy texture, and a dry finish.

BOON
LEMBEEK, PAYOTTENDLAND (FLEMISH BRABANT)
WWW.BOON.BE

Geuze Mariage Parfait Gueuze 8%

In 1977, when lambics were really not popular, Frank Boon purchased De Vits and brought the brewery back from the brink. This "perfect marriage" gueuze offers a fine fusion of fizzy fruit, a pungent hop character, and the trademark Brettanomyces "horse-blanket" aroma. Pure gueuze.

Oude Kriek Boon 6.5%

If you've yet to test your palate with kriek, then this traditional tart version of the style, brimming with cherries, may be a bit much. But if fruit, bone-dry acidity, and face-contorting sharpness are your things, then this Brettanomyces-based beauty is one to reach for.

BRUSSELS BEER PROJECT
BRUSSELS
WWW.BEERPROJECT.BE

Dark Sister Black IPA 6.6%

The Project began as a gypsy brewery, but it now has its home in Brussels thanks to the marvels of crowdfunding. US beers are a big influence, as this expressive Black IPA demonstrates with its swagger of orange, grapefruit, and chocolate alongside a grainy dry finish and a short burst of sweetness.

CANTILLON
see Brewery Profile pages 84 to 85
BRUSSELS
WWW.CANTILLON.BE

★ 🏷 🍺 **Cantillon Grand Cru Bruocsella**
Lambic 5%

Set within a fusty shed in a
run-down part of Brussels
that is conveniently close
to the Eurostar train
terminal, Cantillon brews
fiercely authentic and
magical lambic beers. This
marvelously musty and
mildewed three-year-old
sherrylike ale is not for
learners, but for learned
Lambic lovers.

★ 🍺 🍽 **Cantillon Iris**
Lambic 6.5%

CANTILLON

Grand Cru Bruocsella
1996

Lambics traditionally make use of only aged
hops, which are used for their preservative purposes.
However, with Iris Cantillon, dry hops are also used
before bottling, with the result being a complex
lambic-ale crossover.

★ 🏷 🍺 🍽 **Cantillon Kriek Lambic** 5.5%

At least 1 cup of sour cherries goes into 4 cups of
this elegant-looking blush-red lambic that positively
takes you to the orchard when it's young, while time
sees the lambic tartness and sourness taking the
upper hand. A connoisseur's classic, ideal too for
quenching thirst and at the dining table.

CANTILLON

Kriek 100% Lambic

"Let us drink for the replenishment
of our strength, not for our sorrow."
—CICERO
PHILOSOPHER & ORATOR 106–43 BC

CARACOLE
FALMIGNOUL, NAMUR
WWW.BRASSERIE-CARACOLE.BE

Caracole

Alc. 7,5 % vol.

🏷 🍽 **Ambrée** Amber Ale 7.5%

Francois Tonglet and Jean-Pierre Debras founded
Caracole in 1994 in the tiny village of Falmignoul.
The brewery produces quirkily packaged,
idiosyncratic Wallonian ales like this soothing,
smooth amber ale, crammed with caramel and a
flicker of fiery chile.

🍺 🏷 🍽 **Nostradamus** Strong Brown Ale 9.5%

Caracole's strongest brew made with five different
malts is a delectable, fruity brown ale furnished
with figs, prune, and sweet caramel flavors.

🍺 🥛 🍽 **Troublette** Witbier 5%

It may have a snail on the label, but there's nothing
sluggish about this zesty, moderately spiced wit.
Deliciously dry and very drinkable.

CAZEAU
TEMPLEUVE, HAINAUT
WWW.BRASSERIEDECAZEAU.BE

🏷 🏷 **Tournay Noire** Stout 7.6%

Home for this delightful little outfit is a bunch of
old farm buildings a short distance from the French
border. (The father of brewery founder, Laurent,
used to make beer here until the 1960s.) This
handsome dark beer manages to bring
together vanilla, coffee, and milk chocolate
in one luxurious embrace.

CHIMAY
BAILEUX, HAINAUT
WWW.CHIMAY.BE

⭐ Chimay Cinq Cents
Trappist Golden Ale 8%

A drier, hoppier beer than the Bleue, introduced in the 1960s. Gloriously golden in color, with vanilla and almonds on the nose, a voluptuous body-full of orange blossom, and apricot resinous tones. Pine on the finish.

⭐ Chimay Grande Réserve Bleue
Trappist Abbey Ale 9%

Within connoisseur circles, Chimay has come under fire for perceived cutting of corners in the brewing process. But the world's best-known Trappist brewery, with the biggest sales, is still home to some first-class ales. Chimay Bleue, or Grand Reserve, in a 75cl bottle, is a deep, mahogany-colored classic whose spicy, amazingly aromatic, portlike complexity intensifies in the bottle. Best consumed a couple of years after brewing, ideally with blue cheese. No discernible cutting of corners in this Trappist classic.

CNUDDE
EINE-OUDENAARDE, EAST FLANDERS
NO WEB ADDRESS

Cnudde Oudenaards Bruin
Brown Ale 4.7%

This unusual, acidic, and slightly sour aged brown ale is a rare example of an East Flanders specialty. Until it was bottled in 2009, it was available only in a handful of bars around the brewery, which dates back to the end of World War I.

CONTRERAS
GAVERE, EAST FLANDERS
WWW.CONTRERAS.BE

Tonneke Amber Ale 5%

Contreras has been brewing in East Flanders for nearly 200 years, but it's only recently that marketing has become a consideration. Plain brown bottles with no labels, distinguishable only by their caps, have been replaced by more interesting affairs, and the beer has been enhanced too. An appetizing, slightly effervescent amber ale available from the barrel and in bottles. Bittersweet flavor, with a soft mouthfeel.

DE BRABANDERE
BAVIKHOE, WEST FLANDERS
WWW.PETRUSSOURBEER.COM

Petrus Aged Pale 7.3%

This family-owned brewery has been blazing a trail in the US with its oak-aged pale ale that, until 2000, was brewed solely as an ingredient in the brewery's sour brown ales. Aged in huge oak barrels, this hazy-yellow ale has a massively complex and slightly unhinged character. Sherrylike musk, cider apple, and woody notes, astringent acidity, and a finish that oscillates between dry and sweet. Unusual but appealing.

DE CAM
GOOIK, FLEMISH BRABANT
WWW.DECAM.BE

⭐ De Cam Oude Gueuze 6.5%

Karel Goddeau is the go-to guy for gueuze from Gooik. In 1997, he revived the age-old tradition of buying lambics from elsewhere and merging them together in a utopian union. He produces some of the finest, most fiercely traditional, lambic beers in Belgium. The Oude Geuze is a hazy-yellow mishmash of tart ripe fruit: melon, pineapple, and dried apricots underpinned by "horse blanket" and musty wood.

⭐ De Cam Oude Kriek Fruit Lambic 6.5%

Using antique barrels that once housed Pilsner Urquell from Czechia, De Cam steeps cherries with their pits for a fuller, more rounded almond flavor. Not as tart as other cherry lambics, this is softly sour, with tons of tannins and a dry, vinous mouthfeel. Hard to resist a second one.

CANTILLON

For those familiar with modern beer, first impressions of Cantillon's left-field liquids can daunt and dumbfound. However, don't be downhearted if you don't get them on the first or indeed second sip, as debut drinkers seldom do. Lambics reward patient perseverance in ways that no other beer style can.

If you're going to learn to love lambic, then there's no better aphrodisiac than a visit to Cantillon, a brewery-cum-working museum a short walk from the Brussels Eurostar terminal. The brewery, which has been here since 1900, is a terrific time warp; big, frothing oak barrels soar high into the musty rafters, fusty fumes fill the nostrils, while sacks of grains and crates crammed with cherries are heaped atop bags of moldy hops; pipes drip, hoses trip, and decrepit nineteenth-century copper vessels and wooden tuns clunk, churn, and creak to create a beer whose main characteristic is that of horse sweat.

Unlike other breweries that source their specific yeast from a laboratory, leashing it tight like an obedient, docile dog, Cantillon's head brewer Jean Van Roy, relies on wild, unpredictable, naturally occurring airborne yeast and bacteria to romp about the place like a flock of cheeky chimpanzees.

The Cooling Room, high up in the brewery rafters, is where the anarchic alchemy takes place; here, on a whim and a waft, the undomesticated yeast and bacteria weave their inoculating magic. During winter, when conditions are cold enough, each brew sees around 11,980 gallons of sterile wort poured into a shallow red copper to ensure maximum exposure. Once the ideal temperature is reached more than 80 different types of wild yeast, wee beasties, and bacteria wage war on the wort in an unpredictable manner.

Natural brewing yeasts (such as Brettanomyces) are like an airborne infantry. Their mission is to clear the wort of sugar and oxygen, excrete a flavor, alcohol, and carbon dioxide, and flatten the pH level in preparation for the bacteria, foot soldiers if you will, to march in and sweep up whatever remains in the arid, acidic, and worty wasteland bereft of sugar and oxygen.

When the beer is decanted into oak or chestnut barrels that in a previous life housed French wine, port, and sherry, frenzied fermentation continues for three or four days, sending foam billowing from the bunghole all over the barrels. When the wild yeast wanes, slow fermentation in the barrel begins and lambic is born, staying put for one to three years.

Jean monitors each cask, periodically tasting the contents to determine how long it should sleep. The younger lambic is slender, spritzy, and softer on the palate; older lambic is firmer, more complex, and tongue-twistingly sour. But no two casks are the same, and the tall task facing Jean each spring is to blend the lambic and achieve harmony.

> "Before you taste lambic, you need to cast all conceptions of beer from your mind," says Jean. "It's totally flat, very acidic, and is more comparable to a wine than a beer. Lambic is a white wine, while Gueuze is a Champagne."

Opposite left: Schaarbeek cherries are added to lambic after three years of barrel aging, then left to macerate for another few months, during which time the beer dissolves the fruit.

Opposite right Jean van Roy is a legendary brewer who allows wild yeasts to tramel through this historic brewery-cum-working museum in the heart of Brussels to create lambic and gueuze beers that taste more like wine than ale.

With Gueuze, using the *méthode Champenoise*, he blends one-, two-, and three-year-old lambics, and the mixture of old and new sparks a second, wondrous fermentation in the bottle.

Then there are Cantillon's phenomenal fruit lambics, which make use of whole Schaarbeek cherries (Kriek), French apricots (Fou'foune), raspberries (Rose de Gambrinus), Italian muscat grapes (Cantillon Gueuze Vigneronne), and Bordeaux Merlot grapes (Saint-Lamvinus). Using 10½ ounces of fruit for each quart of beer, maceration takes at least three months, during which time the beer dissolves the fruit (even the seeds) and wrings out its flavors, color, and sugars. Then, one-third of young lambic—which supplies sugar for fermentation—is added, and the beer, a fruity yet still acutely acidic brew, is bottled and corked. Elegant and eloquent, this is beer as you've rarely had before. It's a taste worth acquiring.

* KEY BEERS

Cantillon Bruocsella Grand Cru Lambic 5%
Cantillon Vigneronne Grape Lambic 6%
Cantillon Kriek Lambic Fruit Lambic 5%

DE DOLLE BROUWERS
ESEN, WEST FLANDERS
WWW.DEDOLLEBROUWERS.BE

De Dolle Extra Export Stout 9%

Head brewer and former artist Kris Herteleer has painted this after-dinner ale blacker than Darth Vader's helmet. With nods to the Irish and British stouts of yore, there are cooking chocolate, astringent ground coffee, and a flurry of burned toffee on the finish. Hugely popular in the USA.

Oerbier Strong Brown Ale 9%

Meaning "beer from the original source," this terrific twist on the local bruin beer was the liquid that launched De Dolle. A yeast akin to that being used by Rodenbach, three kinds of fresh Belgian hop flowers, and half a dozen malts produce a strong, sharp-tasting brown ale that veers into lambic territory before making a last-minute turn for Belgian/scotch ale country.

De Dolle Stille Nacht
Barley Wine 12%

Highly innovative, slightly subversive, and still at the forefront of Belgium's new wave of craft brewing, the "mad" brewers are not mad at all, they know exactly what they're doing: brewing some very special, often brilliant, bottle-conditioned beers. This dark orange, outrageously complex barley wine is brewed for Christmas. It's stewed in pale malt, Nugget hops, and candy sugar. Bittersweet, it has an enormous depth of flavor, melodic notes of caramel, and sugared grapefruit. Seriously strong but subtle, it's not just for Christmas and is best laid down for a few years to mature and intensify.

DE HALVE MAAN
BRUGES, WEST FLANDERS
WWW.HALVEMAAN.BE

Straffe Hendrik
Quadrupel 11%

This is a luxuriously languid, strong and dark ale that is full-bodied and fruity, warming, and well-endowed with its own sense of malt richness and complex layers of sensuousness. It is made in the sole brewery in Bruges, which in 2016 made headlines when it installed a two-mile pipeline from the brewery leading to an out-of-town bottling plant.

DE KONINCK
ANTWERP
WWW.DEKONINCK.BE

De Koninck APA Flemish Ale 5%

An iconic brewery that is now owned by Duvel Moortgat. A fine example of a Flemish pale ale, its flagship beer is a beautifully balanced melange of pale malts, fruity esters, and peppery hops. Best served in a bolleke glass.

Wild Jo Blond 5.6%

Yes it's a blond beer, which Belgian breweries produce in their dizzy droves, but what makes this one stand out is the addition of Brettanomyces. The funkiness provided by the wild yeast melds into the fruity, honeyed sweetness of a blond.

DE KROON
NEERIJSE, FLEMISH BRABANT
WWW.BROUWERIJDEKROON.BE

Super Kroon Pale Ale 6.5%

The use of the word "super" suggests the kind of beverage consumed in the park by those who call the bench home, but in fact it's an amber-flecked pale ale with crisp carbonation, cuddly citrus, delicate toffeelike sweetness, and a dry finish that's as assertive as a sergeant-major on the parade ground.

DE RANKE
DOTTIGNIES, HAINAUT
WWW.DERANKE.BE

Cuvée De Ranke Sour Beer 7%
De Ranke are best known for XX, which put bitterness into Belgian beer in 1996, but those with a penchant for sourness head for this curvaceous Cuvée, which is a mixture of their own barrel-aged beer and one-year-old lambic from Girardin. The result is a frisky and fulsome sour with a tart finish.

XX Bitter 6%
You'd be forgiven for thinking this intensely hoppy ale hails from the northwest of America, not Belgium, but De Ranke is renowned for doing things a little differently. Brewers Nino Bacelle and Guido Devos brew boisterous beers with balance and boast a dedicated cult following both at home and abroad. Resinous, herbaceous, and with an IBU of 65, it's proper hoppy, folks.

DE RYCK
HERZELE, EAST FLANDERS
WWW.DERYCKBREWERY.BE

Arend Tripel 8%
1886 was when the first beers emerged from de Ryck, and the family is still in charge, with Anna de Ryck as head brewer. This silky, hoppy, delicately malty, gently fruity tripel is a joy in the glass and ideal as an apéritif.

3 (DRIE) FONTEINEN
BEERSEL, PAYOTTENLAND
WWW.3FONTEINEN.BE

Faro Lambic 5.5%
A more approachable but no less impressive lambic available on tap at the fantastic Drie Fonteinen restaurant that's right next door to the brewery. It's sweeter and less tart than some of the other lambics, with lemongrass and leechees, melon, and a background of acidic grapefruit. This is lambic's version of a fine single-malt whiskey with a light splash of water.

Oude Geuze 6%
Regarded as the godfather of Gueuze (whichever way it is spelled), all hail the spritzy lemon and grapefruit flavors, the teeth chattering tartness, the blue-cheese aroma, the bone-dry finish, and the magical art of masterful blending. A classic.

Oude Kriek Fruit Kriek 6%
If you're a lambic lover, this is not just Payottenland, it's more like the Promised Land. The De Belder family have been crafting classics using outside lambics since 1953. Brothers Armand and Guido branched out into brewing their own kriek in 1999 by ripening cherries (flesh and seeds) in young lambic for a period of 6 to 8 months. The result provides a sublime sip, a huge frisson of fruit on the nose, archetypal dry and cidery lambic notes, and a sharp, biting bitter finish. Simply incredible.

DUBUISSON
PIPAIX-LEUZE, HAINAUT
WWW.BR-DUBUISSON.COM

Bush Prestige
Wood-aged Beer/Vintage Ale 13%
An incredibly elusive oak-aged version of the Ambrée, an upstanding 75cl bottle of greatness with vanilla, apricots, wood, sweet cookie and a bitter, tannic finish. Quite rare, so if you see it, buy it. Then drink it slowly and enjoy the sensation.

Scaldis (Bush Ambrée)
Barley Wine 12%
A family-owned farm brewery since 1769, the Dubuisson family dropped the farming side of the business in the 1930s and now ploughs a flavorsome furrow in the field of big and rather brilliant beers. This elegant, amber-hued Belgian take on an English barley wine is the most well-known and rightly rated. It is dry and hoppy, with a slightly sweet and rustic Armagnac feel on the finish. Also known as Bush Ambrée in the USA.

BRASSERIE DUPONT
TOURPES, HAINAUT
WWW.BRASSERIE-DUPONT.COM

Avec les Bons Voeux
Barley Wine 9.5%

An unusual Christmas ale, this is fruity, slightly oily, and leathery, with some citric sharpness and no small amount of kinetic spice sensations jumping on the tongue. Interesting.

Moinette Blonde Ale 8.5%

Bucolic farmyard brewer celebrated for its sensational saisons and, more recently, organic ales. Moinette, Dupont's biggest Belgian seller, is subtly spiced with an underlying, snappy hop bitterness.

Saison Dupont Saison 6.5%

A legendary, hazy-golden liquid hailed by many as the world's best saison. A piquant, peppery hop bitterness is rounded out by green apple, sugared grapefruit, and an unyielding yeast character. One not to miss on your beer travels.

DUVEL-MOORTGAT
BREENDONK-PURS, ANTWERP
WWW.DUVEL.BE

Duvel Belgian Strong Golden Ale 8.5%

Iconic, bottle-conditioned blonde abbey ale first brewed in 1923. Its shimmering lemon coloring and mischievous drinkability makes for a devilish disguise. It's satin smooth, strong, and fruity with heady herbal hop aromas and a gorgeous white head. Delicious with seafood.

Maredsous 8 Brune Abbey Ale 8%

A luxurious dark abbey ale that is rich with caramel on the nose and burned toffee, dark chocolate, and ripe plums on the palate.

Maredsous 10 Tripel 10%

This terrific tripel has a seductive sparkle in its eye. Sour and sweet do battle on a bitter grapefruit background for a balanced finish.

Vedett Extra White Witbier 4.7%

A delicious, refreshing, and surprisingly crisp "wit" punctuated with coriander and orange peel milled at the brewery. Launched in 2008 after Duvel Moortgaat ended its relationship with Steendonk beer, it is unfiltered, bottle-conditioned, and has a funky bottle.

ELLEZELLOISE (BRASSERIE DES LÉGENDES)
ELLEZELLES, HAINAUT
WWW.BRASSERIEDESLEGENDES.BE

Hercule Stout 9%

Hercule is named after Agatha Christie's detective Hercule Poirot. (Belgium's most famous fictional sleuth supposedly hailed from Ellezelles.) A slick, velvet-jacketed stout, as black as night, that's spicy, astringent, and very dry.

Saisis Wheat Beer 6.2%

This wheat beer has a hardened citrus hop character, with notes of coriander, pine needles, and Curaçao. Eschewing the use of spices and supplementary sugars, the brewery coaxes magic from just the malt, hops, and distinctive yeast to craft five first-class beers in total, matured in German oak casks. The name is pronounced "el-zel-was."

GÉANTS (BRASSERIE DES LÉGENDES)
IRCHONWETZ, HAINAUT
WWW.BRASSERIEDESLEGENDES.BE

Gouyasse Tripel 9%

A "Goliath" of a beer with a sizable footprint of piney hops, sweet shortbread, and a dessert-wine finish. A very impressive tripel.

Saison Voisin 5%

A more hoppy, fruity, and less spicy take on a saison, the Voisin is generously fruity with a cookie-rich maltiness, a smattering of sweetness, and a balanced bitterness on the finish.

Urchon Brown Ale 7.5%

This dark-copper ale has an inquisitive-looking hedgehog on the label; a caramel and toffee-apple tingly effervescence on the tongue, and a bitter, cheek-contracting finish.

GIRARDIN
SINT-ULRIKS-KAPELLE, SENNE VALLEY
WWW.SPECIALITYBEER.COM

Girardin Kriek 5%

A big cherry bouquet, slightly dry with a sweeter signature. Sharpness soothed by full-on fruit and a gentle almond character. Best drunk as an apéritif, a dessert beer, or with succulent duck.

Girardin Gueuze 1882 (Black Label) 5%

The jewel in the crown of Belgium's biggest lambic and gueuze specialist. A tremendous, tartaric, keenly citrus scented, and musky masterpiece that epitomizes the inexplicable art of lambic blending. A balmy balance of lemongrass, grapefruit, wine vinegar, ripening pear, honeysuckle, orange zest, and much more.

GLAZEN TOREN
ERPE-MERE, EAST FLANDERS
WWW.GLAZENTOREN.BE

Jan de Lichte Witbier 7%

Journalist-turned-brewmaster Jef van den Steen has earned himself a reputation for innovative ales since he began brewing out of a garage next to his house back in 2004. A mouth-filling, weighty wheat beer endowed with spice and cedar flavors, a dry backbone of bitterness, and a crisp, sharp finish.

HANSSENS ARTISANAL
DWORP, PAYOTTENLAND (FLEMISH BRABANT)
NO WEBSITE

Oude Kriek 5.8%

Hanssens is heralded for its leftfield lambic blends. Don't be fooled by the farmyard fragrance, this top-quality kriek is a dry kaleidoscope of tart red fruit, marzipan, and cream soda.

HOF TEN DORMAAL
TILDONK
WWW.HOFTENDORMAAL.COM

Saison 7.5%

Here's that rarity on a par with a panda in the wild, a Flemish saison brewed on a farm north of Leuven. It's pale and winsome in the glass with a fine showing of classic saison leanness, brisk carbonation, hints of lemon citrus, pepper, and sourness before the long, dry finish.

HOPPERD
WESTMEERBEEK, ANTWERP
USERS.TELENET.BE/DENHOPPERD

Kameleon Tripel 8.5%

This is a brewery named after the old Dutch word for hopped wort, specializing in eccentric eco-warrior ales and fronted by Bart Desaeger, a former student from the brewing schools of Ghent. Packaged in a bottle adorned with a cartoon chameleon, the beer pours golden and clear, while estery wheat-beer-like aromas waft forth before a spicy finish.

BRASSERIE DE JANDRAIN-JANDRENOUILLE
JANDRAIN-JANDRENOUILLE, WALLONIAN BRABANT
WWW.BRASSERIEDEJANDRAINJANDRENOUILLE.COM

IV Saison 6.5%

Old and new come together in this archetypal saison from a brewery that was founded in 2007. Unfiltered and unpasteurized, with a spicy hop signature, this beer  is the nearest the Belgians get to a US West Coast hop-monster. Try it with meat, cheese, and seafood.

VI Wheat 6%

Hazy orange in color, with a tart citrus on the nose, this is an earthy and refreshing wheat ale (rather than witbier or weiss) that bursts with an orange-like sweetness and light pepper on the palate before a long, dry finish that makes you want to keep sipping. A refreshing beer.

KERKOM
KERKOM-SINT-TRUIDEN, LIMBURG
WWW.BROUWERIJKERKOM.BE

Adelardus Tripel 9%

This top-class tripel, named after a do-gooder local abbot, is seasoned with "sweet gale," a 10-strong herb and spice mixture from the region. Ideally drunk on draft in the incredibly cozy and welcoming café next to the brewery.

Bink Blond Blonde Ale 5.5%

The stock of this modest-size microbrewery museum in south Limburg has risen ever since Marc Limet and Marina Siongers took over in 1999, but its history dates back to 1878. Bink Blonde, meaning "blond guy," is a lightly tanned, perfumed pale ale propped up by some serious hells-a-poppin' hops, California style.

LEROY
WATOU, WEST FLANDERS
WWW.BROUWERIJHETSAS.BE

Christmas Leroy
Scotch Ale 7.5%

Murky, dark, and complex bottle-conditioned Scotch ale with rich roasted malts, fruit cake flavor, spicy chocolate bitterness, orange peel, and a fading fruit finish.

Hommel Bier
Blonde Ale 7.5%

Produced with the Leroy brewery, Van Eecke's most celebrated ale translates as "hop beer" and has a fine floral presence. Bottle-conditioned, dry-hopped, and buttressed by a trio of malt varieties, this popular golden-hued brew has a heightened citrusy and spicy hop character, consisting of maple syrup, ripe pears, and a dry, hoppy finish.

Kapittel Abt Tripel
Barley Wine 10%

Van Eecke has been family-owned from the 1840s. Working in partnership with the neighboring Leroy brewery, it produces a fine and flavorsome line of weighty ales that improve with age. The Kapittel range is revered among aficionados, not least this orange-toned tripel with its notes of pear candy, citrus, and slight spice before a dry bitter finish.

LIEFMANS
OUDENAARDE, EAST FLANDERS
WWW.LIEFMANS.BE

Liefmans Goudenband
Brown Ale 8%

From the family-run brewery based in Oudenaard and overlooking the river Schelde, this is an archetypal oude bruin (old brown ale) that leapt from local to world fame when its strength was increased and its signature sourness subdued. Full-bodied and rich, it has thankfully retained a high level of tart complexity and a rich, roast malt flavor.

LINDEMANS
ST. PIETERS LEEUW-VLEZENBEEK, FLEMISH BRABANT
WWW.LINDEMANS.BE

Cuvée René Kriek 7%

All hail this gorgeous cherry kriek, which is produced by a family brewery that has been making spontaneously fermented beers since before Belgium became independent in 1830. Cherries are fermented in big oak vats in a lambic that is at least six months old. Next it's bottled and a spontaneous second fermentation occurs in the bottle.

MALHEUR
BUGGENHOUT, EAST FLANDERS
WWW.MALHEUR.BE

Malheur 6
Blonde Ale 6%

A fragrant, floral, and spicy bottle-conditioned ale brewed using a trio of flowered hops and a mix of specialty malts. Aimed squarely at everyday appreciation, its faintly acidic, bitter finish entices you to opt for one more.

Malheur Bière Brut
Champagne Beer 11%

A superior Champagne beer from a brewery brought back to life in 1997 after nearly 60 years of hibernation. At the forefront when it comes to marketing and creative, cultured brewing, Malheur uncorked the concept of Champagne beers with this brisk and balanced bubbly beauty, based on its Malheur 10 ale. Champagne yeast is called upon for secondary fermentation. The beer undergoes riddling and disgorging and, when decanted from a Champagne bottle, delivers a lemon-hued feast of fruit, a crisp bitter bite, and a winelike alcohol warmth. For weddings, it's an ideal "I do" brew and is significantly more affordable than Champagne.

Malheur Dark Brut Noir Champage
Brown Ale 12%

This dark-brown ale, adorned with the Malheur "superhero" logo, is difficult to define. Is it a beer? Is it a Champagne? No, it's a Champagne beer that differs from its bubbly brethren by being aged in young, specially charred American casks to give a nutty and fruity flavor. Its aroma is complex and includes sherry, Madeira, vanilla, and wood, together with coffee notes from the roasted malt. To appreciate it at its best, serve in a coupe.

THE MUSKETEERS
URSEL, EAST FLANDERS
WWW.THEMUSKETEERS.BE

Troubadour Obscura
Stout 8.2%

A strapping sweet stout that resembles an Irish coffee in both looks and aroma. Mouth-filling and stacked with layers of mocha, roast chestnuts, and dark caramel, it is the brainchild of the four "musketeers," a clever quartet of former home brewers who ply their hobby at the Proef brewery (though their own brewery is expected to be built by 2018) and export to an admiring American audience. A mild and tasty stout.

Troubadour Westkust Black IPA 8.5%
Another beery joy from the dashing musketeers, this is dark chestnut in color and has a complex nose of licorice, molasses, and a drawer where spices are kept; it's Dubbel-like in its maltiness alongside ripe plums and chocolate liqueur before its fruity, bitter finish.

ORVAL
VILLERS-DEVANT-ORVAL, LUXEMBOURG
WWW.ORVAL.BE

Orval Pale Ale 6.2%
Beer doesn't get much better than this. In a superb and picturesque setting, the good monks of Orval have been performing ale alchemy since 1931. Founded in 1132, the Orval abbey was ruined by Napoléon and fully rebuilt only in 1926, but five years later, with the builder's bills dropping on the doormat, the monks began making beer. Unlike other Trappist breweries, it makes only one beer (though the monks have a weaker version of the original for themselves)—but what a beautiful, intensely aromatic, and uniquely intricate beer it is. Brewed with bespoke specialist malt, the beer is dry-hopped with intensely aromatic whole Hallertau, Strisselspalt, and Styrian Goldings hops and lagered in a long and languid fashion. Prior to its induction into the iconic bowling-pin bottle, it is tapped with the Brettanomyces wand of secondary fermentation. The greatest pale ale on the planet and worthy of its saintly standing among beer buffs.

OUD BEERSEL
BEERSEL, FLEMISH BRABANT
WWW.OUDBEERSEL.COM

Oud Beersel Oude Geuze Oude Gueuze 6%
Founded in 1882 and then closed in 2002, this family-owned lambic brewery was reopened in 2005 by Gert Christiaens and his father. This gorgeous and eloquent gueuze has grapefruit on the nose and palate with an edge-of-palate sourness that adds to its refreshing quality.

PALM
STEENHUFFEL, FLEMISH BRABANT
WWW.PALMBREWERIES.COM

Palm Spéciale Pale Ale 5.2%
Palm is an enigmatic beer-maker that teeters on the tightrope of pleasing both the connoisseur and the common man. With more launches than NASA, it sometimes disappoints, courtesy of some crass commercial ale; however, the eighteenth-century brewery is also renowned for producing some gems. Palm Spéciale, a grand old golden Belgian ale with a touch of blood orange tang, is the bestselling beer of the bunch.

"Ale, man, ale's the stuff to drink for fellows whom it hurts to think."
—A.E. HOUSMAN
ENGLISH POET 1859–1936

"Beauty is in the eye of the beer holder."
—ANONYMOUS

PROEF

LOCHRISTI, EAST FLANDERS
WWW.PROEFBROUWERIJ.COM

Boerken
Strong Ale 9.5%

A hedonistically hoppy, amber-hued ale full of deep fruit flavor, alcoholic ardor, and a spicy send-off. All grounded on a good, wholesome grainy core and stored in a stylish bottle.

Reinaert Grand Cru
Belgian Strong Ale 9.5%

When they're not busy brewing beers for others, Proef do their own, which includes this grandmaster ale. As ruddy-faced in color as the most choleric of farmers, it has swirling spices and a bittersweet finish.

Reinaert Tripel 9%

Dark-brown in color, Proef's tripel is a well-balanced and complex riff on the style, with a restrained sweetness, delicate tropical fruitiness, and a warm and bittersweet finish.

Zoetzuur Flemish Reserve Ale 7%

Proef offers advice, equipment, and brewing expertise to orphaned ale producers from all over Belgium and the world, executing their instructions with deadly accuracy. Zoetzuur, a copper-colored face-contorting beer, measures high on the sour scale of Flemish reds. Dry and rather delicious.

ROCHEFORT

ROCHEFORT, NAMUR
WWW.TRAPPISTES-ROCHEFORT.COM

Rochefort 8 Belgian Strong Ale 9.2%

The residents of the abbey, which dates back to 1230 and began brewing in 1899, are allowed one bottle of beer a day but rarely reach for it except on days of celebration. It is hard to know how they resist this fino sherry nose and full-bodied fruit-cake character, silky molasses texture, and dry, cider-apple finish.

Rochefort 10 Quadrupel 11.3%

A must-drink beer from the notoriously introverted monks at the Abbaye Notre-Dame de Saint-Remy, who produce cultured, complex tawny Trappist ales that light up beer lovers' faces the world over. A burnished bottle-conditioned, Burgundy-colored beer from two hops, two malts, two yeasts, and plenty of monk-led magic. Lay a bottle down in the knowledge that the port-like body will bulge, that the chocolate, figgy pudding and pine flavors will intensify, and when you finally drink it, all will be well in the world.

RODENBACH

ROESELARE, WEST FLANDERS
WWW.RODENBACH.BE

Rodenbach Foederbier
Flemish Red Ale 6%

Rodenbach is all about the wood. After the first and second fermentations in stainless-steel tanks, the beer is decanted into close to 300 enormous oak barrels known as "foeders." Weighing 20 tons when full and with some dating back 150 years, each foeder endows the beer with a particular flavor and acidic character. The skill of the Rodenbach brewers is to achieve consistency and perfection through blending. Foederbier, the canvas on which all other Rodenbach beers are painted, is a balance of beer sourced from three to five foeders, with an average age of two years' maturation. Amber and oaky with a bone-dry Riesling acidity, its tremendous tartness is a rite of passage for any ambitious beer drinker. Difficult to drink and difficult to find, this is one of the very few Holy Grail ales.

Rodenbach Grand Cru Flemish Red Ale 6%

The Rodenbach family had a significant presence in nineteenth-century Flanders. They began brewing in 1820, and their phenomenal, sour Flemish oak-aged red ales, now owned by Palm, are rightly rated as brewing grand masters. Rodenbach ales source their outstanding fruit aromas, and distinct, refined tartness, and sharp tannin from wood aging, a mixed yeast culture, and the art of aged beer blending. This is genius in a bottle. A Belgian beer tour would not be complete without a visit to this historic site with its vast oak vats in West Flanders.

"If you ever reach total enlightenment while drinking beer, I bet it makes beer shoot out of your nose."
—JACK HANDEY,
AMERICAN COMEDIAN 1949-

LA RULLES
RULLES-HABAY, LUXEMBOURG
WWW.LARULLES.BE

La Rulles Blonde 7%

When Gregory Verhelst opened his brewery in 2000, this hoppy, strapping, and tasty blonde caused ripples among locals. Several years later, La Rulles is riding the crest of Belgian new-wave brewing, courtesy of esoteric ales admired both in Belgium and the United States. The labels are great too.

La Rulles Tripel 8.4%

This is the macho Jean-Claude van Damme of boutique Belgian beer: a strapping, bronze muscular Belgian tripel with an American hop accent. Dried apricots, tropical fruit, and spice, with a sweet malt finish.

ST. BERNARDUS
WATOU, WEST FLANDERS
WWW.SINTBERNARDUS.BE

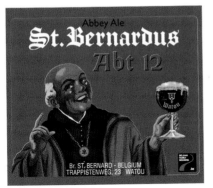

St. Bernardus Abt 12 Quadrupel 10%

Set up immediately after World War II, this cheese dairy turned Flemish brewery contract-brewed St. Sixtus ales until introducing its own quartet of beers in the 1990s, including this complex, dark, tawny quadrupel full of chocolate raisin, almonds, and fruit character. Definitely one of the world's best beers.

St. Bernardus Prior 8 Dubbel 8%

Styrian hops and lengthy, languid lagering lend this full-bodied, deep-purple dubbel its drinkability; a perfect balance of sweet, bitter, and malt notes. No wonder the monk on the bottle label is smiling.

SAINT FEUILLIEN
LE ROEULX, HAINAUT
WWW.ST-FEUILLIEN.COM

St. Feuillien Brune Réserve
Brown Ale 7.5%

Apart from an 11-year break that ended in 1988, the Friart family has been brewing beer on this site since 1873. In the last ten years, the company has carried out significant investments, including the building of a new brew house. This chestnut-brown brew has a sweet toffee complexity, full-bodied fig flavor, and warming alcohol in the finish.

St. Feuillien Triple 8.5%

Despite its extensive distribution, this piquant, aromatic ale, full of fruit and citrus spice, has stayed in the leading pack of the best tripels in the world of beer. For an extra treat, help yourself to one of the 50-ounce bottles, which continue to shine when laid down and left to develop to their own delicious devices.

SAINT-MONON
AMBLY, LUXEMBOURG
WWW.SAINTMONON.BE

La Saint-Monon Brune Dubbel 7.5%

Award-winning dubbel from a Wallonian microbrewery set up in 1996. Dark-brown color, roasty malt spine, fall fruit aroma, seriously spicy, and a finish whose sourness flirts with a Flanders brown ale.

SCHELDE BROUWERIJ
HOOGSTRATEN, ANTWERP
WWW.SCHELDEBROUWERIJ.COM

Strandgaper Blonde 6.2%

"Beach yawner" is the best recognized beer brewed by this traditional brewer that has relocated from the coastal town of Gravenolder in Zeelander, Netherlands, to Hoogstraten in Belgium. The clean, spicy Saaz and Halltertau hops shake up the mellow malt. This beer is a perfect match for mussels.

BRASSERIE DE LA SENNE
BRUSSELS
WWW.BRASSERIEDELASENNE.BE

Stouterik Stout 4.5%
In the last few years iconoclastic brewers Bernard Leboucq and Yvan de Baets have kicked away the crutch of conformity on which so many other Belgian brewers lean. Originally brewing their beers at De Ranke, they got their own brewery in 2011 and brewed beers that eschew the Belgian spice obsession and embraced a wide gamut of international beer styles. This stout is big and black, silky sweet, and slightly scorched, tainted with tobacco, licorices, raw grassy hop character, and earthy aromas.

Taras Boulba Pale Ale 4.5%
If you thought Belgian beer was all about power and strength, then try this lovely pear-colored, heartily hopped pale ale. A deliciously dry departure from all the big high-alcohol content Belgian brain-fuddlers.

Zinnebir Bitter 6%
A slightly Anglo-centric ale named after "Zinneke"—a pejorative term for stray dogs and those of mixed Flemish/French parentage associated with the poorer parts of Brussels. Slightly pungent, with a cookie sweetness and a crisp, dry hop finish.

SILENRIEUX
SILENRIEUX, NAMUR
WWW.BRASSERIEDESILENRIEUX.BE

Joseph Belgian Ale 5.4%
A Wallonian barn turned brewery renowned for eco-ales and the use of esoteric grains. Joseph, a rich golden ale with Flemish sour undertones, gets its sweetness from the use of spelt in the mash. The beer appears cloudy in the glass due to a secondary fermentation that takes place in the bottle.

SILLY
SILLY, HAINAUT
WWW.SILLY-BEER.COM

Scotch Silly Scotch Ale 8%
Once known as the Meynsbrugen brewery, Silly dates back to 1850. With the original family name a bit of a mouthful and the village name a marketer's dream, it was no surprise when the Silly label was taken up. The yeasty, spicy brews with lots of fruit flavor are well hopped and bottle-conditioned. Scotch Silly was launched in 1920 and named after Payne, a big-drinking Scottish soldier who was stationed in Silly after World War I. Toffee, vanilla, banana, chocolate, and caramel are all present in this marvelously smooth beer.

SLAGHMUYLDER
NINOVE, EAST FLANDERS
WWW.SLAGHMUYLDER.BE

Slaghmuylder Passbier Lager 5.2%
More Bavarian than Belgian, this is a clean, crisp, and crazily quaffable seasonal lager with zesty, herbal hops sprung from a bready malt base. It puts the mainstream nonsense to shame.

Witkap Stimulo Blonde Ale 6%
First brewed under the auspices of former owner and Westmalle brewer Henrik Verlinden, this voluptuous blonde ale is brewed by a slightly enigmatic Flemish family brewery that, despite more than 150 years of brewing heritage, has kept the brilliance of its brewing recipes under its beret.

SMISJE
OUDENAARDE, EAST FLANDERS
WWW.SMISJE.BE

Nature Ale Belgian Ale 7%
Originally based in Bruges with a brewery called Regenboog, Johan Brandt moved to Oudenaarde in 2011, while also cutting down on the amount of beers he produced. This amber-hued ale has herbal hints on the nose, while on the palate it's crisp in its carbonation and has a delicate malt sweetness, spice, and fruit with a bitter finish.

Winter Belgian Strong Ale 11%
One for when the weather turns bad and you want some comfort in a glass. Dark brown in color, caramel richness on the nose, and a slice of fruitcake alongside raisin, bittersweetness, and a cherry finish.

STRUBBE
ICHTEGEM, WEST FLANDERS
WWW.BROUWERIJ-STRUBBE.BE

Strubbe Pils Pilsner 5%
When Norbert Strubbe took hold of the brewery reins in 2008, he was the seventh generation of his family to do so. Founded in 1830, it specialized initially in modest-strength beers, and, more recently, it has provided shelter for local ales orphaned by breweries that have closed. The Strubbe Pils is crisp, medium-bodied, and deftly hopped, with a glorious mousse head. Definitely pale and interesting.

Vlaskop Witbier 5.5%
Energetic, enigmatic wheat beer which takes a sour slant on the traditional and nicely balanced mix of coriander, orange, and lemon. Citrus and spice tones, with a long, dry finish.

STRUISE
OOSTVLETEREN, WEST FLANDERS
WWW.STRUISE.COM

Aardmonnik Flemish Red Ale 8%
Originally, the "sturdy" brewers—Carlo, Peter, Phil, and Urbain—did not possess a brewhouse of their own. They borrowed space and equipment from other breweries, mostly at the Deca Brewery in Woesten-Vleterenfind. However, in 2013 they opened their own brewhouse in a former schoolhouse. Their modern interpretations of classic world beer styles, have earned enormous admiration around the globe. Their beers are hard to find but worth the search. This cherry-colored ale has sourness and a dry finish.

Black Albert Imperial Stout 13%
While De Struise were still gypsy brewers they had the freedom to create small-batch bespoke brews, hence this sublime Royal Belgian stout. Illusory in its alcoholic strength, it has immense character and was brewed specifically for the Ebenezer pub in Maine. It has a dark chocolate, coffee-like fragrance underpinned by dried apricots and dried plums, and a robust hop accent at the end.

Pannepot Grand Reserva Wood-aged Ale 10%
An oak-aged version of Pannepot, this is Struise's spearhead beer, full of spice and dried fruit flavors, and a modern twist on a late nineteenth-century Flemish fisherman's ale. Matured in wine barrels for 14 months and then Calvados casks for 10, it's a refined yet rich rampage of oaky tannins, dried plums, vanilla, fennel, sour cherry, and a firm bite of bitterness on the back end. Simply stunning.

TILQUIN
REBECQ-ROGNON, WALLONIAN BRABANT
WWW.GUEUZERIETILQUIN.BE

Gueuze Tilquin à l'Ancienne
Lambic 4%
One of the new kids on the lambic block, Pierre Tilquin buys worts from breweries such as Boon, Lindemans, Girardin, and Cantillon and then ferments and matures them before getting the blending going. This has a Champagne-like spritziness, a grapefruit-like sauciness, and a dry and quenching finish.

VAN DEN BOSSCHE
SINT-LIEVENS-ESSE, EAST FLANDERS
WWW.BROUWERIJVANDENBOSSCHE.BE

Buffalo 1907 Stout 6.5%
This opaque ale straddles the world of stout and dunkel in style. It is mocha-tinged and toffee-ish, with a touch of roast malt. Easy to sip, the Buffalo brand (there is also a 9% version) is what this family-owned brewery, a blend of tradition and technology, has been built on.

VANDER GHINSTE
BELLEGEM, WEST FLANDERS
WWW.OMERVANDERGHINSTE.BE

Omer Blonde 8%
As well as making spontaneously fermented wood-aged classics, Vander Ghinste go golden and gorgeous with this fruity and silky bestseller, which entrances with its delicate Moussec-like mouthfeel and a hint of white pepper in the finish.

Vander Ghinste Oud Bruin
Flemish Old Brown 5%
Founded in 1892 and named Bockor between 1977 and 2014, this family-owned brewery is one of the few still making a traditional oud bruin, a tantalizingly tart mix of new and old beer, with the latter having spent 18 months in wooden foeders.

VAN HONSEBROUCK
INGELMUNSTER, WEST FLANDERS
WWW.VANHONSEBROUCK.BE

St. Louis Fond Tradition Gueuze 5%
Van Honsebrouck is not based in the
regions where Lambic is traditionally
produced, but that didn't stop it
experimenting with the style in 1968.
Brewing purists might not like what they
have done, but this is a beer beauty.

VAN STEENBERGE
ERTVELDE, EAST FLANDERS
WWW.VANSTEENBERGE.COM

Gulden Draak Barley Wine 10.5%
Dating back to the nineteenth century, this
impressive family-owned brewery has
willingly embraced modern technology. Its
Gulden Draak (Golden Dragon) Barley Wine/
Dark Tripel is housed in an iconic white
bottle and is a chewy, toffee-tainted dark
tripel-style brew, with a sweet medicinal
body spruced by herbaceous hop flavors.

Piraat Golden Ale 10.5%
Floral Flemish golden ale that owes
its spark and spice to Saaz hops. Dry,
assertive, and appetizing, with a touch
of brandy butter.

VAPEUR
PIPAIX-LEUZE, HAINAUT
WWW.VAPEUR.COM

Saison de Pipaix Saison 6%
A fabulous example of a saison from a steam-
powered brewery that was brought back to life by two
teachers in 1985. The brewery produces a traditional
Wallonian saison beer that was first brewed back in
1785 (though it's probably changed over time). Dry,
gently hopped, and mashed until a little acidic, the
result is a sharp, spicy blend of black pepper, ginger,
sweet orange peel, curaçao, and star anise.

VERHAEGHE
VICHTE, WEST FLANDERS
WWW.BROUWERIJVERHAEGHE.BE

Duchesse de Bourgogne
Wood-aged Ale 6.2%
In this Burgundy-colored blend of new and old, beer
that's been laid down in oak barrels for 18 months
is married with an eight-month-old version before
being bottled and, preferably, laid down again in a
cellar to develop further. Spicy and sweet, Duchesse
has a red, glowing allure.

Echt Kriekenbier Cherry Beer 6.8%
Almond-tasting ale made with real cherries merged
with the Vichtenaar. A chocolate and cherry
character conjures a Black Forest gâteau.

Vichtenaar Flemish Brown Ale 5.1%
This family-owned brewery has been around since
1880, and ales aged in oak is what it does best. This
archetypal oud bruin (brown ale) has earned a strong
following, with its sharply spiked sweetness and
cinnamon-slanted mulled wine flavors.

WESTMALLE
MALLE, ANTWERP
WWW.TRAPPISTWESTMALLE.BE

Westmalle Dubbel 7.5%
Westmalle is the largest of the Trappist
breweries, dating back to 1836. This
quality, dark, and fruity classic, with a
port-like appearance, has flavors that
include raisins, bitter chocolate, and
burned toast, plus a peppery prickle and
a finish of almond liqueur.

Westmalle Tripel 9.5%
A tremendous tripel from the long-
established Abbey of Westmalle, one of
the most revered of Trappist breweries.
Its color approaches that of a honeyed-
golden glow, while the bittersweet taste bops you on
the palate, then follows up with jabs of herbal elixirs,
grainy malt, macadamia nut, and an almost minty
pine finish. This is truly an unmissable connoisseur
classic if ever there was one.

WESTVLETEREN
WESTVLETEREN, WEST FLANDERS
SINTSIXTUS.BE

Westvleteren 12
Quadrupel 10.2%
Westvleteren is the tiniest
and most secretive of
Trappist brewers, producing only 11,000 gallons of
beer every year. The scarcity of its beers, packaged
in plain, label-free bottles, may have inflated their
perceived excellence, but even so they're hugely
impressive ales. None more so than this deliciously
decadent quadrupel that delivers a potent aroma;
soothing dark rum character, chocolate-covered
raisins, leather, and heather on the palate; and an
astonishing finish of port and petits fours.

Westvleteren Blonde Belgian Ale 5.8%
First released by the Sint Sixtus abbey in 2000.
Beneath its green cap, there's an enchanting,
golden-colored cornucopia of resinous, heady yet
remarkably refined hop flavors. A marvelous bit of
magic that is quite incredible with cheese.

TRAPPIST BEERS

"Beer is proof that God loves us and wants us to be happy."
—BENJAMIN FRANKLIN

This quote can be seen emblazoned across T-shirts at beer festivals, adorning pub walls, and quoted ad infinitum in books such as this one. Thing is, Benjamin Franklin never said it. He wrote something similar about wine but at some point it was purloined by beer drinkers and proliferated on the worldwide web along with other fake news.

But like George said to Jerry in an episode of *Seinfeld*, "It's not a lie if you believe it" and Trappists and abbey ales are all the evidence you need to know that God is most definitely a beer guy.

Christianity and brewing have been getting it on since AD 612, when a bishop called Arnulf of Metz halted a plague by plunging a crucifix into a beer kettle and telling everyone in his parish to stop drinking water and start drinking beer instead. No one argued with him.

But it wasn't until the Benedictine Movement emerged in the sixth century that monasteries and abbeys became centers of altruistic ale-making. Mashfork-wielding monks not only saved the local community and pilgrims from the dangers of disease-ridden water, they also made money that went toward maintaining the monasteries and funding local good causes—and it was also great papal PR.

However, centuries of reformations, revolutions, and Europe-wide iconoclasm dropped monastic brewing to its knees. Brewing slipped into secular hands, and it wasn't until 1836, when the abbey of Westmalle fired up its kettle again, that the monks rediscovered their brewing mojo.

Today, the beers with the closest link to godliness are those endorsed by the Cistercian Order of the Strict Observance, also known as the Trappists. Renowned for their rigorous religious obedience, sustained silence, and strict adherence to self-sufficiency, the Trappists have six abbey breweries in Belgium (Achel, Chimay, Orval, Rochefort, Westmalle, and Westvleteren), two in the Netherlands (La Trappe/De Koningshoeven & Zundert), and one each in Austria (Stift Engelszell), Italy (Tre Fontaine), and the USA (Spencer).

By law, these are the only producers allowed to brew Trappist beer, and to be deemed an "Authentic Trappist Product" the beer must adhere to three key rules:

Monks must make or oversee its production.

It must be made within the confines of the Trappist abbey.

Any profit made must be used for social or charitable work.

Trappist beer is less a style and more of a status, but Trappist ales are associated with strength, sustenance, and a celestial serve.

Most monasteries make a dubbel, a strong brown ale that gets its color from a mixture of malts and candy sugar, and a tripel, a lighter yet more intoxicating, fruity golden beer of which Westmalle is arguably the most iconic.

The "Authentic Trappist Product" is widely acknowledged as a badge of quality, and some Trappist beers, Westvleteren and Orval in particular, are rightly rated as being among the best beers in the world. Similar to their secular counterparts, Trappist brewers are prone to dips in form and the commercially driven cutting of corners on quality. While it's tempting to conjure up romantic images of balding men in robes studiously stirring wort, monks tend to fulfill a "supervisory" role, with the actual brewing done by lay brewers.

Above: The Festweisse is an annual six-day beer festival put on by the Erdinger brewery in Bavaria.
Below: The Althstadthof brewery is also a brewpub, bakery, and distillery.

INTRODUCTION
GERMANY

On the surface, one might simply celebrate the Germans for lager and tradition. And why not? Lager has an impressive claim to fame when considering around 90 percent of the beer enjoyed around the world is inspired by lager. Meanwhile, tradition remains a crucial part of that story and is respected in earnest. But labeling Germany as the land of lager falls painfully short of the entire story, and when it comes to tradition a new wave of brewers is gently rocking *das boot*.

Germany's influence on beer, brewing, and beer-drinking culture is extraordinarily far reaching, and even in this new golden age, it is a country with more pedigree than almost any other.

The success of the lager style doesn't do the Germans justice, bastardized as it has been in so many lazy and lackluster forms. But the Germans can laugh at the wider mundanity of the mass-produced lagers, since in its homeland it is showcased across a glorious spectrum of expressions. Presented in an abundance of hues and furnished with a wealth of grain and hop-driven flavors, Germany's lager family includes helles, märzens, and rauchbier, or bocks, doppelbocks, maibocks, schwarzbier, and more. The first golden lagers were Bohemian, while Germany blondes didn't appear until later in the nineteenth century.

Unlike many European neighbors, Germany has preserved these native styles and their traditional techniques, remaining relatively unscathed by the insidious creep of global consolidation and international mergers. Many attribute this to the fact that, historically, the Reinheitsgebot has prevented foreign imports from gaining a foothold. The order stipulated beer should be brewed using only malted barley and wheat, yeast, hops, and water, and even though it was revoked in the 1980s as a "restraint of trade," the brews from abroad still failed to sway a drinking public fiercely loyal to their native liquid.

The loyalty runs local, and there are very few ubiquitous beer brands in Germany. In Bavaria, where there are hundreds of different breweries, people drink Bavarian beers such as weissbier and dunkels; in Cologne you're served kölsch without asking, and the same happens with alt in Düsseldorf. Franconia is where you'll find kellerbiers and the smoky rauchier and märzens of Bamberg; Dortmund keeps blue-collar beer drinkers refreshed in the industrial north with bottom-fermented Dortmunder; Berlin has its challenging Berliner weisse beer style, and Munich is famous for its Oktoberfest beer, consumed in huge quantities by many thousands of people at the biggest beer festival in the world.

With all this heritage and success, it's hard to imagine anyone grumbling about the state of beer in Germany. Even so, some have courted the global craft revolution, and in a country passionate about beer it is fitting that there is a potent new batch of brewers. Taking inspiration from America, these "radicals" are moving away from purity and embracing innovation across nonnative styles. The likes of the Bavarian Camba Hop Gun brown ale and the Haffner pale ale from Baden-Wurttemburg, respectfully, hint at rebellion. Many more are emerging, but what is exciting is that the traditional brewing ethos that made the country great is being incorporated into a brewing movement that blends tradition with influences from beyond German borders.

ALE-MANIA
BONN, NORTH RHINE-WESTPHALIA
WWW.ALE-MANIA.DE

Imperial Red Ale 9.2%

Like many a new brewer in the past few years, Fritz Wülfing began his beery antics as a home brewer, but in 2010 he went pro, initially using other breweries to produce his assertively tasting beers. (He now has his own facility.) Packed with Centennial, Cascade, Amarillo, and Simcoe, Imperial Red Ale is robust and highly hopped, with tropical fruit and caramel sweetness strolling along without a care in the world.

ALTSTADTHOF
NÜRNBERG, BAVARIA
WWW.ALTSTADTHOF.DE

Rotbier Vienna Lager 5.2%

Rot as in red, rather than how most of us feel after a few beers. Caramelized malts lead the way, ushering in a fruity-sweet palate plus a certain bracing crispness in the mouthfeel; the finish is bittersweet.

Schwarzbier 4.8%

This is a Nuremburg brewpub, bakery, and distillery that has been confidently riding the new wave of German microbrewing since opening in 1984. Techniques and equipment of yore are used to produce half a dozen unfiltered beers ranging from a terrific helles to this mauve-tinted black lager, whose tantalizing flavor profile is underpinned by roasted coffee beans and crème brûlée flavors.

AND UNION
MUNICH, BAVARIA
WWW.ANDUNION.COM

Friday IPA 6.5%

Now here's something completely different: And Union is a father, son, and business colleague operation that works with a small group of Bavarian family breweries to produce a variety of beers. This is an amber-orange IPA boasting a creamy collar of foam (do dive in); the mouthfeel is soft and slightly chewy, and there are hints of toffee and orange marmalade before the assertive bitter finish.

ANDECHS
ANDECHS, UPPER BAVARIA
WWW.ANDECHS.DE

Andechs Doppelbock Dunkel 7.1%

Chocolate raisins, dried plums, bitter coffee beans, and a peppery twang all feature in this archetypal maroon-colored triple-decocted doppelbock from a monastic brewery located at the foot of the "Holy Mountain," south of Munich. Benedictine monks have been brewing here since 1455, yet they are anything but cloistered in their modern and forward-thinking brewing techniques.

Andechs Hell Helles 4.8%

A sensational, gorgeously golden sip, delicate, and dry with a heightened hop presence on the finish.

AUGUSTINER
MUNICH, BAVARIA
WWW.AUGUSTINER-BRAEU.DE

Edelstoff Oktoberfest/Märzen 5.6%

Founded in 1328 by Augustine monks, Augustiner is Munich's oldest brewery, one of the "big six" Oktoberfest breweries, and still in German hands. It also owns one of the city's biggest and most boisterous beer halls and has never dabbled in the vulgar black art of advertising, preferring instead to let its eight beers do the talking. A golden helles-pils hybrid, Edelstoff has an easy balance of sweet malt and citrus hops with a clipped finish.

Maximator Doppelbock 7.5%

A lush, rich, and colossal dark copper-colored doppelbock with a superb nuanced sweetness, rated by many as a world-beater. This is a classic Bavarian doppelbock.

AYINGER
MUNICH, BAVARIA
WWW.AYINGER.DE

Altbairisch Dunkel 5%

On the outskirts of Munich, in the tiny town of Aying, beer has been brewed since 1878, the year the town was founded by Johann Liebhard. The beers are more traditional and forceful than most other beers brewed in Bavaria, hence this sweet, fruity dunkel laced with espresso and licorice overtones.

★ ☑ **Celebrator** Doppelbock 7.2%

In 1999, the brewery moved to a state-of-the-art site, its exterior draped in ivy, from where one in ten beers is exported to the rest of Europe or the United States. Several of its beers are often serial World Beer Cup medal winners. This silky-smooth, deep, darkly rich doppelbock, with a complex Christmas-cake character, boasts smoky tones and a substantial Stateside following.

BAYERISCHER BAHNHOF

see Brewery Profile pages 102 to 103
LEIPZIG, SAXONY
WWW.BAYERISCHER-BAHNHOF.DE

★ ☑ **Original Leipziger Gose** 4.6%

Gose, Germany's answer to the lambic beers of Belgium, originated in the East German town of Goslar as far back as AD 1000 yet later, in the mid-eighteenth century, became linked to Leipzig. By the 1960s, gose was gone thanks to the rise of lagers and dwindling Eastern Bloc interest. In 2000, Thomas Schneider (no relation to the wheat-beer brewing family) revived gose at the Bayerischer Bahnhof, a large

brewpub housed in a disused train station. This tart, quirky, top-fermenting wheat beer is brewed using salt, coriander, and lactic acid added to the boil.

☑ ★ **Schaffner Naturtrübes Pils** Pilsner 5%

As well as a gose, Bayerischer makes several other beers, including this cloudy yellow pils, which is fresh and spritzy and has a dry and bitter finish.

BERGBRAUEREI ULRICH ZIMMERMAN

BERG, NORTH RHINE-WESTPHALIA
WWW.BERGBIER.DE

★ ☑ **Ulrichsbier** Vienna Lager 5%

It's been more than 250 years since the Zimmerman family took control of this boutique brewery, but it continues to innovate with ingredients, extended lagering times, and alternative interpretations of German beer styles. Hazelnut, caramel, apple, and sweet cream-soda flavors spring forth with glorious enthusiasm.

BITBURGER

BITBURG, RHINELAND-PALATINATE
WWW.BITBURGER.DE

☑ ☑ **Bitburger Premium Pils** Pilsner 4.8%

One of Germany's biggest breweries that is still family-owned, Bitburger was founded in 1817 and was the first pioneering purveyor of pilsner back in 1883. Aided initially by the reach of the railroads and later by its iconic "Bitte Ein Bit" (A Bit, Please) advertising slogan, Bitburger Premium Pils has become one of Germany's most popular beers. Yet size hasn't sacrificed style on the altar of short-termism, and it remains a gloriously golden accord of soft, sweet malt and brusque, lingering hop bitterness.

BOLTEN

KORSCHENBROICH, NORTH RHINE-WESTPHALIA
WWW.BOLTEN-BRAUEREI.DE

☑ ☑ ☑ **Ur-Alt Bier** Altbier 4.8%

While not as widely distributed as Diebels nor as well known, Bolten's "original" Altbier is the grand daddy (and granddaddy) of the beer style, having been first brewed back in 1266. Brewed 16 miles outside Düsseldorf, it glows a deep red with a slight, subdued sparkle. Sweet and malty with a touch of vanilla on the nose, spice and astringent bitterness follow, with an alcoholic accented end. However, it's the mellow malt that calls the tune.

☑ **Landbier** 5.4%

An unfiltered, light-colored, crisp, and drinkable beer that, were it not for those Cologne-based sticklers for tradition and German law, could, and should, be called a kölsch. Lemon, grapefruit, and a touch of chamomile.

BREWBAKER

BERLIN
WWW.BREWBAKER.DE

☑ ☑ **Indigo Pale Ale** 5%

BrewBaker began in 2005, one of the first signs that Berlin might be ready for beer beyond the usual pils that most people seemed to drink. This is its American-style pale ale, which skips, hops, and jumps out of the glass like a beer gazelle, trailing clouds of citrus, malt sweetness, and pine in its wake.

BAYERISCHER BAHNHOF

KG BAYRISCHER PLATZ 1, 04103 LEIPZIG, SAXONY

WWW.BAYERISCHER-BAHNHOF.DE

Opening its doors in 2000, Bayerischer Bahnhof is a lively brewpub situated in the oldest railroad terminus in the world. The terminus closed in 2002, but the interior of the bar and restaurant is a reminder of the past, cozy and comfortable like an old-style station waiting room, while railroad lamps hang over the tables. Up above the diners and drinkers, the brewing kit gleams, unique in that this is one of the few breweries in Germany where a Leipziger gose is brewed. This is a tart sour beer long linked to Leipzig, a beer with salt and coriander in the mix and with a heritage that apparently goes back centuries. (Its original home town was Goslar.)

Gose is a bit of a survivor. This is a beer that died out in the 1960s, before being resurrected in East Germany two decades later. Now every craft brewery and its mother (especially in the USA) seems to be making a gose, all too often with added spices, fruits, and even dark malts. Gose is perhaps one of the on-trend beer styles in the global craft beer movement, but at Bayerischer Bahnhof devotees of this singular beer style can enjoy it untroubled and unchanged.

Gose is also a beer that seems to enchant and inspire people. Take brewery owner Thomas Schneider, for instance. In the late 1990s he happened to meet a drinks wholesaler who was keen on getting gose brewed in Leipzig again. (At the time, the two breweries making gose were based elsewhere.) Schneider first produced a gose at his own brewery and then, in 2000, opened Bayerischer Bahnhof, and gose was back in Leipzig once again.

Matthias Richter has been the brewmaster since 2003, and he says, "I brew the gose like a wheat beer, with malted barley and wheat, salt, coriander, and lactic acid. The latter is produced separately, and part of the wort is fermented with it and then added to the other part of the wort."

Right: The classic sitar-shaped gose bottle.

Far right: Brewery owner Thomas Schneider, who got gose going again in Leipzig back in 2000.

Opposite above left: Brewmaster Matthias Richter, who has been with the brewery since 2003.

Opposite above right: The boisterous Bayerischer Bahnhof situated in the oldest railroad terminus in the world.

Only one hop is used, though when asked about the amount of salt used, Richter gives nothing away: "It's my secret."

On the nose there is a flurry of salty, spicy, fresh ozonelike notes; the palate is spicy and delicately salty, with the latter condiment seemingly adding to the body of the mouthfeel (there's a tingle of salt but it's out there on the edge of the known universe of taste); a lemon-flavored hard candy character also takes a bow. The end contains more boiled lemon sweetness, alongside a saltiness and the spice of coriander. It is damned refreshing and one of those glasses of beer at which those that taste it for the first time cannot but help make eyes and ask: "Where have you been all my life?"

Richter also makes the robust and bittersweet Schaffner Pils, which has a rasping dry finish reminiscent of Jever Pils, plus Heizer Schwarzbier —for the latter, think schwarzbier, porter, and dunkel all rolled into one big creamy, chocolaty, orangey, spirituous glass of goodness. Meanwhile, a further project of his involved a glass of Berliner weiss into which Brettanomyces has been added. This had an earthy barnyard nose while bananas hovered in the background—it was a great Mexican standoff, if you like, between sweetness and sourness.

If you make it to Bayerischer Bahnhof, while you're studying your glass of gose, don't forget that it makes a heavenly beer and food combination when matched with a crispy leg of pork and potato dumplings. Or you could do what some locals do: drink it with a drop of kummel (caraway spirit) in it. This is known as an "umbrella" and packs a fair punch, so it might not be for the lily-livered.

* KEY BEERS

Heizer Schwarzbier 5.3%
Original Leipziger Gose 4.6%
Schaffner Naturtrübes Pils 5%

CAMBA BAVARIA
TRUCHTLACHING, BAVARIA
WWW.CAMBABAVARIA.COM

Hop Gun Brown Ale 6.4%

When it opened its doors in 2008, Camba was meant as a pilot plant for brewing-kit makers BrauKon GmbH. Since then it has become known as a pioneer of a variety of beer styles, many outside the German brewing canon, such as this full-bodied American-style brown ale, with its luscious love-in of tropical fruitiness, crisp caramel, and light bitterness.

CREW REPUBLIC
MUNICH, BAVARIA
WWW.CREWREPUBLIC.DE

7:45 Escalation Imperial IPA 8.3%

As well as being a center of traditional beer, Munich is also home to this self-assured young craft brewery, whose 7:45 Escalation is a self-confident Imperial IPA featuring Columbus, Simcoe, Amarillo, and Chinook. The result is a veritable explosion of flavor. "Craft beer is not a crime" is the brewery's slogan. Indeed.

DIEBELS
ISSUM, NORTH RHINE-WESTPHALIA
WWW.DIEBELS.DE

Diebels Alt Altbier 4.9%

Like a particularly friendly and diligent Darth Vader, Diebels has been fighting the fight for the dark side against a wave of blonde upstarts for quite some time now. Diebels is the biggest brewer of altbier in the world, and, until AB-InBev opened its wallet in 2001, had been family-owned since 1878. Peaking in the 1960s, when Diebels was selling more than 440,0000 gallons a year, this seriously smooth, chocolate-cookie altbier is brewed with a double-decoction mash, Perle and Hallertau hops, and dark, caramelish malt.

DOM
COLOGNE, NORTH RHINE-WESTPHALIA
WWW.DOM-KOELSCH.DE

Dom Kölsch 4.8%

The "cathedral" kölsch is a particularly fragrant, floral, and fresh example of the kölsch style. It's best drunk in its very own bustling beer halls, where it's served by men in blue aprons, often with impressive facial hair. Clean, crisp, and clipped in its hoppy finish. See pages 110 to 111 for a profile of kölsch beers from Cologne.

DREI KRONEN MEMMELSDORF
BAMBERG, BAVARIA
WWW.DREI-KRONEN-MEMMELSDORF.DE

Stöffla Rauchbier/Kellerbier 4.5%

Highly, and rightly, rated hybrid beer dovetailing the smoky smoothness of a rauchbier with the robust, unpasteurized aromatic hop signature of a kellerbier. Brewed by a brewery-cum-fancy hotel located just a few miles outside Bamberg that was originally founded in 1457.

EINBECKER
EINBECK, LOWER SAXONY
WWW.EINBECKER-BRAUHAUS.DE

Ur-Bock Dunkel Bock 6.5%

Classic and original, this ocher-brown beer is to bock beer what Pilsner Urquell is to pils. It was first brewed back in 1378 and purportedly boasts the fifteenth-century Protestant door vandal Martin Luther as one of its biggest fans. It was originally designed to withstand long journeys across Germany. Massive malt and huge hop content make this the kingpin of bocks.

ERDINGER
ERDING, BAVARIA
WWW.ERDINGER.COM

Erdinger Urweisse Weissbier 5.6%

Released in 2008 as an authentic replica of the wheat beers that were drunk back in the day. This is more robust, fruitier, and spicier and brewed with more muscular malt than the world-famous Erdinger beer. Raises the bar for the weissbier aficionados.

ESCHENBRÄU
BERLIN
WWW.ESCHENBRAEU.DE

🔳🍺 **Panke Gold Pale Ale** 5.2%

Aromatics reminiscent of an unsweetened lemon meringue continue onto the palate alongside a grainy breakfast cereal character, while a stern bitter backbone keeps all in order. Best drunk at the brewpub's popular tree-lined beer garden in the Wedding district of Berlin.

J B FALTER
REGEN, BAVARIA
WWW.PRIVATBRAUEREI-JB-FALTER.DE/START.HTM

🔳✓ **Regenator Doppelbock** 7.3%

This is the style of beer that monks allegedly lived on when they were fasting during Lent, and you can't do any worse than this plumy, nutty, moderately malt concoction, which finishes lightly toasty. Monks weren't fools.

FORSCHUNGS BRAUEREI
MUNICH, BAVARIA
WWW.FORSCHUNGSBRAUEREI.DE

✓ **Forschungs-Pilsissimus** 5.2%

Scarcely heard of amid the noise made by the big Bavarian breweries is this traditional tinkering brewpub and beer garden founded in the 1920s as an experimental brewery for local breweries. Now a well-kept secret among beer buffs and closed during the winter months, it brews two beers, one of which is this heavenly and hoppy helles-cum-pilsner, medium-bodied, crisp in the mouthfeel, and bittersweet in the finish. A must if you're in Munich.

Pilsissimus
Hell Export
alc. 5,2 % vol.

FORSCHUNGS-BRAUEREI
MÜNCHEN
BRAUEREI-ABFÜLLUNG
Bier   Mindestens haltbar bei Sicht Kundendatum   Inh. 0,5 l

FRÜH
COLOGNE, NORTH RHINE-WESTPHALIA
WWW.FRUEH.DE

⭐✓🍺 **Früh Kölsch** 4.8%

Opposite the striking cathedral, the enormous Früh am Dom is Cologne's most famous and most frequently visited brewpub. Downstairs is where the serious drinking seems to be going on. to be going on. Saying Früh is fruity isn't merely indulgent alliteration; it really is. Enjoy the taste of a fruity, crisp hoppiness and a smooth malty mouthfeel as you enjoy the architectural views.

Früh
KÖLSCH
SEIT 1904

GAFFEL
COLOGNE, NORTH RHINE-WESTPHALIA
WWW.GAFFEL-HAUS.DE

🍺 **Gaffel Kölsch** 4.8%

A floral, aromatic hop-led kölsch ideally drunk outside the traditional Gaffel-Haus tavern in Cologne, tucked behind the railroad station on Alter Markt, one of the city's cutest squares and a must-visit destination in Cologne.

GÖLLER
ZEIL AM MAIN, LOWER FRANCONIA
WWW.BRAUEREI-GOELLER.DE

⭐🍺🍴 **Göller Kellerbier** 4.9%

The Franconian town of Zeil am Main, 16 miles north of Bamberg, is renowned as much for its wine as its beer, and is home to a picturesque brewery and restaurant with a lovely beer garden. Bought by the Göller family in 1908, it specializes in traditional German beer styles, of which this cloudy, amber-colored cellar beer is a hop-laden highlight.

⭐🔳✓ **Göller Rauchbier** 5.2%

Göller's take on Bamberg's specialty beer is lighter, less smoky, slightly sweeter, and easier to drink than more famous interpretations such as Schlenkerla. It's always good with food and especially great with smoked cheese, smoked meats, and chargrilled dishes.

GOSLAR
GOSLAR, LOWER SAXONY
WWW.BRAUHAUS-GOSLAR.DE

⭐🍺 **Gose Helle Gose** 4.8%

The town of Goslar was the original home of gose beer back in the sixteenth century, though its popularity in Leipzig led to it being claimed by the city in the 1800s. So it's good to see it's being brewed in its home town. Coriander spice, salt, and citrus dance off the nose; it's tart, crisp, and delicately fruity to drink.

GUTMANN
TITTING, BAVARIA
WWW.BRAUEREI-GUTMANN.DE

✓🍴 **Gutmann Weizenbock** 7.2%

Family-owned Bavarian wheat beer specialist founded in 1707. Amber-colored weizen that turbo-boosts the bubblegum, banana, and pear candy flavors. A perfect summer season beer with a strength that slowly sneaks up on you.

HACKER-PSCHORR
MUNICH, BAVARIA
WWW.HACKER-PSCHORR.DE

★ ▣ Hacker-Pschorr Animator Doppelbock 8.1%
Sensational, seriously strong, and slightly syrupy. Spicy with soothing alcohol like a thinking man's mulled wine, there are dark rum molasses, toffee, caramel, and raisins too. Signs off with plenty of sweet malt and alcohol.

★ ☑ Hacker-Pschorr Oktoberfest-Märzen 5.8%
The Hacker brewery, founded in 1417, earned its double-barreled title in 1793, when Joseph Pschorr married Therese Hacker and took over her family business. In the 1970s, it joined forces with fellow Munich brewer Paulaner, before being taken under the wing of Heineken. Hacker-Pschorr's 16-strong range of beers is now brewed at the Paulaner brewery. Archetypal strong, copper-colored full-bodied Munich märzen with a marvelous mince-pie finish from one of the original Oktoberfest brewers.

HÄFFNER
BAD RAPPENAU, BADEN-WÜRTTEMBERG
WWW.BRAUEREI-HAEFFNER.DE

▣ ▣ ▣ Hopfenstopfer Citra Ale
Pale Ale 5.1%
Häffner Brau is in the southern German town of Bad Rappenau and is an old family brewery producing traditional beers; however, several years ago its head brewer Thomas Wachno branched out to brew beers under the Hopfenstopfer brand. Citra Ale features plenty of the fabulously fragrant American hop in the mix with a bracing bitter backbone to make a great pale ale.

HEIDENPETERS
BERLIN
WWW.HEIDENPETERS.DE

▣ ▣ Pale Ale 5.3%
Go to the foodie paradise of Markthalle in the Berlin district of Kreuzberg and, after ordering a hot beef brisket sandwich, wander along to the bar that this small brewery keeps in a corner. The Pale Ale is an ideal accompaniment: floral, fruity, bitter, and refreshing. Order another.

HERTL BRAUMANUFAKTUR
SCHLÜSSELFELD, BAVARIA
WWW.SHOP.BRAUMANUFAKTUR-HERTL.DE

▣ ▣ Frankonian Straight Whiskeydoppelbock 10.6%
As the name might suggest, this is a classic German doppelbock produced by the smallest brewery in Franconia. The beer has spent some time in whiskey barrels, a process that has created a rich light amber-colored beer with coffee, fruit, smoke, peat, and vanilla all making their presence felt.

HIRSCH BRAUEREI HONER
WURMLINGEN, BAVARIA
WWW.HIRSCHBRAUEREI.DE

☑ ▣ Hirsch Hefe-Weisse Hefeweizen 5.2%
Major regional brewery dating back to the 1780s that blends eighteenth-century old tradition with the shiniest of new brewing technology on a site to the east of the Black Forest in southwest Germany. Standout beers include an awesome aromatic zwicklbier and this cloudy, clove-tastic conglomeration of spice, tropical fruit aromas, and a flourish of vanilla on the finish.

HOEPFNER
KARLSRUHE, BADEN-WÜRTTEMBERG
WWW.HOEPFNER.DE

☑ ▣ Hoepfner Pilsner 4.8%
A hundred years after a priest began brewing its beers in 1798, Hoepfner moved into a new, rather fancy fortress in the eastern part of Karlsruhe, a vibrant university town in the southern part of the Rhine. It's a charming spot to sip, or indeed sink, this terse, totally ace golden lager that calls upon the aromatic armory of four hop varieties. Given that the Hoepfner family name originates from "hop farmer," the full-on fragrance is a fitting one.

▣ ▣ Hoepfner Porter 4.9%
Unlike other German breweries of its age and more akin to an American micro, Hoepfner veers off-piste when it comes to traditional beer styles and is boosted by running its own maltings. In 1998 this spectacular black beer from the edge of the Black Forest was reintroduced. Ink-black in color, with a singed molasses sweetness and a smidgen of smoke. It's a rare German take on an old, classic English style—Vorsprung durch Technik, as they say around these parts.

HOFBRÄUHAUS
MUNICH, BAVARIA
WWW.HOFBRAEU-MUENCHEN.DE

 **Hofbräu München** Maibock 7.2%

The Hofbräu brewery, its origins dating back to 1589, is synonymous with the Hofbräuhaus—the most famous pub in the world and not just because it was here, in 1920, that Adolf Hitler announced the 25 theses of the National Socialist German Workers' Party. Regardless of the day of the year, the state-owned Hofbräuhaus is a thigh-slapping, whip-cracking, pretzel-munching, stein-swaying, feet-stomping, oompah-playing, sausage-stuffing shrine to golden lager-driven good times. While the helles holds forth as Hofbräu's world-famous beer, the best time to don your lederhosen is in the last week of April, when the first barrel of maibock is tapped. Munich's oldest bock, dating back to 1614, it is strong yet medium-bodied, citrus-scented, with a bright, zesty vibrancy on the palate. All together now … "oans, zwoa, g'suffa."

HUMMEL
MEMMELSDORF-MERKENDORF, BAMBERG, BAVARIA
WWW.BRAUEREI-HUMMEL.DE

Raucherator Doppelbock Rauchbier/Doppelbock 8.1%

It sounds like a medieval torture mechanism, and, as with all rauchbiers, there's no smoke without fire among some beer drinkers. But for fans of peat and lean bacon flavors, this potent and peaty liquid is well worth the short bus ride out of Bamberg. A brewery tour of this region is, in any case, a Holy Grail for serious beer fans.

HÜTT
BAUNATAL, HESSE
WWW.HUETT.DE

Schwarzes Gold
Dark Lager 4.9%

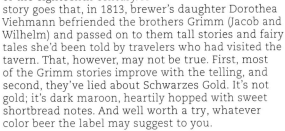

A family-owned north German brewery and restaurant dating back to the middle of the eighteenth century. A story goes that, in 1813, brewer's daughter Dorothea Viehmann befriended the brothers Grimm (Jacob and Wilhelm) and passed on to them tall stories and fairy tales she'd been told by travelers who had visited the tavern. That, however, may not be true. First, most of the Grimm stories improve with the telling, and second, they've lied about Schwarzes Gold. It's not gold; it's dark maroon, heartily hopped with sweet shortbread notes. And well worth a try, whatever color beer the label may suggest to you.

ISERLOHNER
OBERGRUNE, NORTH RHINE-WESTPHALIA
WWW.ISERLOHNER.DE

Iserlohner 1899 Dunkel 4.9%

Iserlohn, situated on the northernmost border of the Sauerland in the North Rhine-Westphalia region of Germany, is the capital of German ice hockey. After a hard day of giving a flying puck far too much attention and brandishing a stick, this warming, dark, extremely nutty dunkel does the trick.

JEVER
JEVER, LOWER SAXONY
WWW.JEVER.DE

Jever Pilsener 5%

Not just the occupier of the biggest building in the coastal town of Jever, Friesland, but also one of Germany's leading purveyors of Pilsner, Jever has had a tumultuous history since being formed in 1848 but now finds itself in the safe hands of corporate cash. Pilsners don't come much more Germanic than this: biting hop flavors, floral aromas, and underscored with a faint malt base. Serve chilled.

KALTENBERG
KALTENBERG, BAVARIA
WWW.KALTENBERG.DE

König Ludwig Dunkel 5.1%

The members of the Wittelsbach royal family, which ruled Bavaria from the twelfth century until World War I, loved their beer. They helped establish the Beer Purity Law, the Reinheitsgebot, in 1516, founded the Hofbräuhaus, and invented the Munich Oktoberfest. In 1976, descendant Prince Luitpold, the great-grandson of Ludwig III, took over Kaltenberg and blazed a trail with a distinctive, dry-hopped dark lager. The delicious Dunkel is decked in dark malt, mocha coffee, and dried fruit flavors.

König Ludwig Weissbier Hell 5.5%

A well-regarded, hugely popular golden wheat beer, which displays a haze of yeasty goodness. Well-balanced bitterness with malty overtones, an applelike aroma, and a banana skin sign-off. Hugely refreshing and ideally consumed in July, when the castle hosts a medieval tournament with jousting, jesters, drinking, gluttony, music, drinking, falconry, more jousting, and then more drinking again.

KARG
MURNAU, BAVARIA
WWW.BRAUEREI-KARG.DE

 **Karg Dunkels Hefe-Weisbier**
Dunkelweizen 5.2%

A 50-year-old weissbier specialist based at the base of the Bavarian Alps.The brewery and restaurant tap are beloved by wheat beer drinkers, who talk of this dunkel-weizen in hushed and excited tones. Akin to putting banoffee pie in a blender, the huge yeast presence gives it the look of a lackluster Lava Lamp.

KETTERER
HOMBERG, BAVARIA
WWW.KETTERERBIER.DE

Schützen-Bock 7.5%

Deep in the woods of the Black Forest, close to the town of Hornberg, lies a modest family-owned microbrewery famed for its esoteric ales. The most remarkable is this opaque, barrel-aged, blackish brown stout with sweet chocolate on the nose, rich red wine notes (Château Musar), and a vanilla finish.

KLOSTERBRÄU
BAMBERG, BAVARIA
WWW.KLOSTERBRAEU.DE

Klosterbräu Schwarzla Dark Lager 4.9%

Melodious matte-black beer from the oldest brewery in Bamberg, founded in 1533 and once owned by the prince bishops who ruled the region. It's a sweet-toothed sipper, with chocolate raisins, coffee, and anise on the finish.

KLOSTERBRAUEREI ETTAL
ETTAL, BAVARIA
WWW.KLOSTERBRAUEREI-ETTAL.DE

Ettaller Kloster Curator Doppelbock 9%

Founded in 1333, Ettal is one of very few genuine monastic breweries remaining in Germany today. The brewery distributes both locally and to the USA. A delightful doppelbock, its Christmas-cake flavors include dark navy rum, molasses, and maraschino cherries, and a dry roast finish.

Ettaler Kloster Dunkel 5%

Complex, reddish brown dunkel brewed with Vienna, Pilsner, and Munich malt. Bitter chocolate and a dry-roasted finish.

KNEITINGER
REGENSBURG, BAVARIA
WWW.KNEITINGER.DE

★ **Kneitinger Bock** 6.4%

Kneitinger, as the rather inquisitive-looking goat on its bottle label suggests, is renowned for a quite brilliant seasonal bock, rich, dark, and chocolaty. Attached to the brewery is a Michelin Guide restaurant where terrific dumplings, sauerkraut, and other Bavarian specialties are best digested with the brewery's very own bock-based schnapps. Every year, the first cask of bock is tapped on the first Thursday in October.

Kneitinger Dunkel 5.2%

Regensburg, located at the most northerly point of the Danube, boasts a marvelous Old Town, with labyrinthine streets and UNESCO World Heritage status. Kneitinger, one of five breweries in Regensburg, began brewing here in 1530 and is run by a charitable foundation. The brewery's Dunkel is nutty, sweet, bready, and smooth.

KÖSTRITZER SCHWARZBIERBRAUEREI
BAD KROSTRITZ, THURINGEN
WWW.KOESTRITZER.DE

★ **Köstritzer Schwarzbier** 4.8%

Köstritzer is to German schwarzbier what Michael Jordan is to slam-dunking. Dating back to 1543, it has steadfastly championed the black stuff, first as a healthy drink, then as a delicious and different one, throughout Communist rule. Spiked with chocolate, roasted nut, and coffee flavors, this balanced bitter black-cherry-colored beer claims to have been Goethe's favorite and, now owned by Bitburger, represents more than half of all the Schwarzbier in Germany. As for marketing, it's regarded as Germany's version of Guinness.

KROSTITZER
KROSTITZ, BAVARIA
WWW.UR-KROSTITZER.DE

Schwarzes Schwarzbier 4.8%

A sizable regional brewery near Leipzig owned by the ompnipotent Oetker group, Krostitzer's dark lager is very often confused with the market-leading Köstritzer beer. No bad thing if one does, though, for this slightly smoky schwarzbier is every bit as impressive, with a melodic malty mix of bitter chocolate, dried plums, and black pepper. The color does not, as the name may suggest, have a ruby red shimmer to it.

KULMBACHER
KULMBACH, BAMBERG, BAVARIA
WWW.KULMBACHER.DE

★ 🍷 🍺 **Eku 28 Strong Lager** Eisbock 11%
In the past two decades, Kulmbacher
has munched its way through Franconia,
gobbling up other breweries, to
become the region's biggest brewery.
When it acquired the EKU brewery, it
inherited this—one of the strongest
lagers in the world. First brewed in
the 1950s according to the purity law,
Reinheitsgebot, it stacks the mash with
masses of malt and, before throwing
it in, lets the yeast know it has nine
months of cold fermentation to work its
way through the sugar. Citrusy, estery,
and acutely alcoholic, Eku 28 has vied
with Samichlaus in the quest to become
the world's strongest continually brewed
lager. Not for the fainthearted.

★ 🍷 🍺 **Kulmbacher Eisbock** 9.2%
Not to be confused with insipid American "ice" beers
that were once touted as the latest thing in beer, this
classic lager was the original Eisbock first brewed
by the Reichelbrau brewery, which, in 1996, was
bought up by Kulmbacher. Legend has it that a barrel
of bockbier, accidentally left in the old Reichelbrau
brewery yard midwinter, froze and snapped open.
When the ice was chipped away, a denser, more
intense, more clean-cut, and, with less dilution, far
stronger beer was discovered.

🍽 🍺 **Monschof Kapuziner Schwarze Hefeweizen** 5.4%
Take the juicy, fruity, and yeasty wheat tang of a
Bavarian hefeweizen, blend it with the deep, dark
cocoa bitterness and roasted malt flavor of a black
lager, and hey presto, you've got yourself an ace,
rather unusual unfiltered hybrid.

LOWENBRÄU-BUTTENHEIM
BUTTENHEIM, BAVARIA
WWW.LOEWENBRAEU-BUTTENHEIM.DE

🍴 🍺 **Lowen-Bräu Ungespundetes Lagerbier** Kellerbier 4.8%
Buttenheim, a market town in
Bamberg, has two claims to fame.
The first is that jean guru Levi
Strauss was born here. The second,
and more important, is beer—lots
of lovely beer. Not to be mixed
up with its mainstream Munich
namesake, Lowenbräu is the
smaller of the two Buttenheim

breweries (see St. Georgen on page 114) and was
established in 1880. Distribution rarely roams
beyond 31 miles outside Buttenheim, but its beer
gardens and restaurant make for charming spots
to sip this tasty, tangy, unfiltered lager. Another
recommended pit stop for any Bavarian beer tour.

MAHR'S BRÄU
BAMBERG, BAVARIA
WWW.MAHRS.DE

★ 🍺 🍷 **Der Weisse Bock** 7.2%
For many, Mahr's seventeenth-century
brewery tap in Bamberg is the best place
in the world to drink beer. Unparalleled
in its comfy coziness during the winter,
Mahr also has a chestnut-tree-lined beer
garden—a solar-powered, stein-swaying
shrine to cheery summertime swigging
of seriously sublime small-batch beers.
Originally brewed by the abbey's monks
for Lent, this decadent dark wheat beer
conjures up chocolate-covered poached
pears. It's eminently quaffable.

★ 🍷 🍺 **Mahrs Bräu Ungespundet Hefetrüb** Kellerbier 5.2%
A twist on the zwicklbier and kellerbier styles,
"Ungespundet" means unbunged and refers to the way
in which the beer eschews closed conditions in favor
of being left exposed to the elements. The result,
after eight weeks of lagering, is less effervescent,
more acidic, and hugely refreshing.

🍷 **Mahrs Weiss Bräu** Weissbier 5.2%
Wonderful yeast-inspired wheat beer that defies its
modest strength with a cornucopia of fruit flavors:
leechee, kiwi, banana, vanilla, and a sweet caramel
base. Hazy on the eyes, zesty on the nose, and tingle-
tastic on the tongue.

MAISEL
BAYREUTH, BAVARIA
WWW.MAISEL.COM

★ 🍷 **Maisel's Weisse Original** Wheat Beer 5.4%
A Bavarian brewery renowned for its
wonderful wheat beers. The old brewing
site, dating back to 1887, was turned
into a chin-scratching brewery in the
1970s, when the brewery expanded into
bigger premises capable of meeting
the heightened demand of the weisse
renaissance. Darker and fruitier than
most Bavarian wheat ales, Maisel is
toffee, cookie, and banana—like a
beautifully blended banoffee pie that's
been poured into a glass.

🍺 🍴 **Maisel & Friends HopfenReiter** Double IPA 8.5%
This brewery-within-a-brewery was set up at
Maisel in 2012 and allowed fourth-generation
family member Jeff Maisel to experiment with
different styles of beer (some
that, because of the constraints
of the Reinheitsgebot, the parent
brewery cannot do). This has an
array of tropical fruit on the nose,
sweet citrus and malt midpalate,
and a bittersweet finish.

KÖLSCH

Cologne is a wonderful city, but you wouldn't want to
kiss it – even if you're wearing beer goggles.

What once stood regal on the Rhine was reduced to rubble in World War II, when
Allied air forces unleashed their thousand bombs on that notorious night. The only
reminder of the city's handsome past is the magnificent cathedral which, having
taken more than 600 years to build, was in no mood to buckle under the mainly
British bombardment. But even the cathedral's undoubted Gothic splendor can't
disguise the fact that Cologne most definitely fell out of the ugly tree and hit every
branch on the way down.

A lack of an esthetic charm is one of the reasons
that Cologne lags behind other cities in most
people's pecking order of great German beer-
drinking destinations. Another reason that
Cologne is overlooked by beer buffs is its local
specialty: kölschbier. Kölschbier, the most fragrant
and delicate of beer styles, tends not to be worn
as a badge of honor among hardcore, in-the-
know imbibers—too accessible to be regarded as
unique and too clean, crisp, and quaffable to be
considered a classic among connoisseurs.

That is, of course, nonsense. Beer snobs may
disagree, often via the medium of indignant
spluttering, but they're wrong.

Drinking kölsch in Cologne is beer tourism at
its best. Brewed like blonde ale yet conditioned
like a lager, kölsch was introduced at the
beginning of the twentieth century by Cologne's
brewing community, who were concerned by the

meteoric rise of pilsner—
with which it shares some
similarities.

Shimmering a brilliant
gold and softer than a
mattress stuffed with
sheep, it boasts both the
parch-slaying powers of a
light pilsner yet the fruity
roundedness and dryness
of a top fermenting beer
—but with an immaculate

aftertaste shorn of yeasty awkwardness. The hop
bitterness is provided by Hallertau and Tettnang,
mellowed by small amounts of wheat.

Brisk and convivial, it embodies the city's
terrific beer-drinking culture. Kölsch is more
than just a beer style; it's the local dialect and a
philosophy—a relaxed way of being, a shoulder-
shrugging acceptance that "Hatte noch immer jot
jejange" (It will be all right in the end).

This all-embracing attitude makes Cologne the
perfect place for a pub crawl. The breweries are
mostly small taverns and brewpubs, all clustered
within walking distance of one another, while the
beers are served in a small, narrow, and session-
friendly 7-ounce glass called a "stange."

Cologne's kölsch bars are governed by kobes,
dry-witted waiters clad in blue aprons, who are
both rude yet welcoming and tear about their
traditional wood-clad taverns, "alu-kranz" (trays)
in hand, plonking kölsch on tables before you've
asked for it. The beer, often decanted straight
from the barrel, will keep coming until you leave
your glass half full or place a beer mat over the
top. It's marvelous.

One word of warning: don't, under any
circumstances, mention the beer from Düsseldorf.

Left Sion Kölsch is served at its eponymous bräuhaus, a basic but
welcoming place where the walls are furnished with old beer taps
and wooden barrels.
Opposite Crisp, creamy, and refreshing, Gaffel can be found at the
Gaffel-Haus, close to the Alter Markt, in Cologne, and the perfect
spot to sit and people-watch.

WHERE TO FIND KÖLSCH

GAFFEL-HAUS
WWW.GAFFEL-HAUS.DE

Old, affable kölsch tavern at the back of the Alter Markt. Its creamy yet crisp köslch is best drunk while sitting at the alfresco tables during the summer months with not a care in the world.

SION
WWW.BRAUHAUS-SION.DE

Sion speaks with a hoppier accent than most. A basic, busy drinking den with old beer taps on the wall and wooden barrels on the bar. Outside drinking and a big dining area.

FRÜH AM DOM
WWW.FRUEH.DE

Vast and very popular, this is the daddy of kölsch taverns, located at the base of the cathedral. Spread across three floors and littered with tiny alcoves—the serious drinking seems to be done downstairs.

PÄFFGEN
WWW.PAEFFGEN-KOELSCH.DE

A lively and grandiose beer hall decked out with chandeliers, etched glass, and black wooden beams. Beer, laced with interesting spice and fruit tones, is served straight from the barrel.

MALZMUHLE
WWW.MUEHLEN-KOELSCH.DE

A terrific, staunchly traditional brewpub near the Heumarkt, serving its soft, creamy Mühlen kölsch.

MALZMUHLE
COLOGNE, NORTH RHINE-WESTPHALIA
WWW.MUEHLENKOELSCH.DE

☑ ☑ **Mühlen Kölsch** 4.8%

A cracking kölsch from one of Cologne's most traditional brewhouses, which is situated in the city's Haymarket area. Adorned with wood paneling and frequented by pork-knuckle guzzling locals, it's a vibrant and lively shrine to sophisticated sipping. Very delicate, mellow in malt, and with measured hop content, it has an ever-so-slightly sweet, fruity finish.

MEUSEL
BUTTENHEIM-DREUSCHENDORF, BAVARIA
WWW. MUEHLEN-KOELSCH.DE

▢ ★ **Bamberger Landrauchbier,** 5.4%

Small family-owned brewhouse in one of the most vibrant brewing areas of Upper Franconia. Rauchbier is one of the local specialties, and this is a good opener to what can be a rather challenging beer style with a moderate smokiness on the nose and palate alongside malt sweetness.

NEUHAUS
OBERPFÄLZ, UPPER PALATINATE
WWW.ZOIGLBIER.DE

★ ☑ **Zoigl Beer** 5.2%

The Oberpfälz Wald (Palatinate Forest) region, near the border with Czechia, is home to the old-fashioned zoigl beer style. It's a funky farmhouse lager that's similar to kellerbier, but with the musty barnyard flavors more readily associated with wild yeast beers. It undergoes short primary fermentation and lagers for about three weeks at around 45 to 46 degrees Fahrenheit before being released to "zoigl houses" in only five towns in the region: Eslarn, Falkenberg, Neuhaus, Mitterteich, and Windischeschenbach. Brewmasters hang a brewer's star, known as a zoigl, outside their house when the beer is ready.

PÄFFGEN
COLOGNE, NORTH RHINE-WESTPHALIA
WWW.PAEFFGEN-KOELSCH.DE

☑ ☑ **Päffgen Kölsch** 4.8%

Down-to-earth kölsch that's spicy and a little more estery than its Cologne counterparts. Pockmarked with musty, slightly lactic, woody notes from the barrel and a bitter bite at the back, this is a refreshing beer that hits all the right notes.

PAULANER
MUNICH, BAVARIA
WWW.PAULANER.COM

★ ☑ **Original Münchner** Munich Lager 5.5%

It's the world's biggest-selling Munich lager, and some would argue the finest. Unlike its Bohemian rival pilsner, there's continuing conjecture and confusion as to which Munich brewery originally pioneered the city's helles. Certainly Paulaner has always been hot when it comes to refrigeration and, in the early twentieth century, hailed the helles more than most.

★ ☑ ☑ ☑ **Salvator Doppelbock** 7.5%

When friars from the Order of Saint Francis of Paula arrived in Munich from Italy in 1627, they brewed the first-ever strong beer, designed to tide them over through Lent. The "liquid bread" beer was so good that they sent it off to Rome for a papal blessing for fear that they may be accused of overindulgence during a period of abstention. Luckily, the long, hot journey completely ruined the beer, and the pope, unimpressed and unaware of the beer's true glory, confirmed it bad enough to drink by way of penance and mortification. If you've been a really bad person—and you really have—then don a hair shirt and seek solace in the forgiving, amber-colored bosom of this legendary liquid. Majestically malty, nutty with a deliciously dry finish.

PETERS BRÄUHAUS
COLOGNE, NORTH RHINE-WESTPHALIA
WWW.PETERS-KOELSCH.INFO

☑ ☑ **Peters Kölsch** 4.8%

An eminently easy-drinking kölsch that is pale straw in color, full and creamy in the mouth, and with a citrus hop bitterness that jumps out of nowhere. Available in bottles but best swigged from small glasses in the ornate yet rather rowdy eponymous brewhouse in Cologne.

PINKUS MULLER
MÜNSTER, NORTH RHINE-WESTPHALIA
WWW.PINKUS.DE

Pinkus Münstersch Alt Altbier 5.1%
Born a tiny brewery and bakery in 1816, Pinkus emerged more recently as a pioneering proponent of biobrewing and claims to be the world's first certified organic brewery. This golden alt interpretation is lighter, fruitier, and more vinous than those associated with Düsseldorf. Pinkus's Altbier Bowl is a legendary summer brew.

Pinkus Pils Pilsner 5.2%
Under the impressive auspices of the Muller family, Pinkus has outlived more than a hundred breweries in Münster, a university town in the nation's north and known as the "other" altbier town. Pinkus has grown into a big, bustling brewery tap where students drink this flowery, fragrant pilsner—nearer to Bohemia than Bavaria in style—in quantities that make it seem as if they don't have to get up in the morning.

REISSDORF
COLOGNE, NORTH RHINE-WESTPHALIA
WWW.REISSDORF.DE

Reissdorf Kölsch 4.8%
Fluffy and soft on the palate with sweet touches of vanilla, anise, and fresh pine bitterness, it's served in its brewhouse direct from mini wooden casks hauled up from the cellar via a dumb waiter. Formed in 1894 and still family-run, Reissdorf was bombed seven times during World War II but recovered to produce Germany's bestselling kölsch.

RITTERGUTS GOSE
BORNA, SAXONY
WWW.LEIPZIGER-GOSE.COM

Original Ritterguts Gose 4.7%
Even though it's produced under license by the Reichenbrand brewery in Chemnitz, many connoisseurs think that this gose is closest in style to the beer that Leipzig calls its own—it's lean and lemony sour, refreshing, slightly salty, and has a quenching finish. Definitely worth checking out to compare with the new wave of sour beers being produced elsewhere in the world.

ROSTOCKER
ROSTOCK, MECKLENBURG-VORPOMMERN
WWW.ROSTOCKER.DE

Bock Hell 6.9%
A big-bodied bitter bock that veers into double IPA/barley wine territory. Molasses, toffee, dried apricots, and butterscotch all drop in to say hello, and it doesn't overstay its welcome.

Pilsener 4.9%
Formed in 1878 by two engineers, Rostocker thrived until the beginning of World War II, when equipment was shifted to the Soviet Union and the brewery was nationalized. Today, it's under the private ownership of Oetker, and it's this forceful golden pilsner—which pulls no punches in terms of bitterness—that's the town's default drop.

ROTHAUS
ROTHAUS, BADEN WÜRTTEMBERG
WWW.ROTHAUS.DE

Rothaus Hefeweizen 5.4%
Nestled in the hills of the Black Forest and at 328 feet above sea level, Rothaus is Germany's highest brewery and, it claims, draws upon seven mountain springs to produce its trio of beers. This is a fiercely fruity, effervescent wheat beer complete with all the cloves, coriander, and bubblegum notes you'd expect. Founded in 1791, the brewery is 100 percent owned by the state of Baden-Württemberg.

ROTHENBACH
AUFSESS, BAVARIA
WWW.AUFSESSER.DE

Aufsesser Bock Bier 6.5%
A rich, malty, and dry Bavarian bock that pours from a swing-top bottle and is brewed by a family-owned brewpub located on the "Beer Road" in Franconian Switzerland. Its hometown, Aufsess, currently holds the Guinness world record for the most breweries per capita—a population of 1,500 boasts an amazing four brewhouses.

ST. GEORGEN
BUTTENHEIM, FRANCONIA, BAVARIA
WWW.KELLERBIER.DE

Keller Bier 4.9%

Word of this tangy kellerbier has broadened well beyond the small Franconian village of Buttenheim to the other side of the Atlantic. The St. Georgen Brewery, situated to the south of Bamberg, has been in the same family since 1624, and it still ignores the advent of refrigeration by continuing to age its beer in durable unbunged oak casks placed deep down in chilly, dark, rock caverns on the village outskirts.

St. Georgen Pils Pilsner 4.9%

Medium-bodied perfumed pilsner; grainy maltiness with substantial hop character in the balance. A slight medicinal bitterness on the finish.

SCHLENKERLA
BAMBERG, BAVARIA
WWW.SCHLENKERLA.DE

Aecht Schlenkerla Rauchbier 5.2%

An archetypal rauchbier from a boutique, family-owned Bamburg brewery begun in 1405. So smoky it's like drinking a beechwood campfire through a barbecued cured fish that's been swimming in lapsang souchong tea all its life. It is to German beer what Laphroaig is to Scotch whisky, dividing opinion in the same way.

Schlenkerla Lentbeer Smoked Beer 5.5%

If you're in Bamberg during Lent, then make your way to the Schlenkerla tavern, where this slice of smoky heaven is available on tap. However, for those preferring to slumber in their armchairs, it's also available in bottled form.

SCHLOSSBRAUEREI HERRNGIERSDORF
HERRNGIERSDORF, BAVARIA
WWW.SCHLOSSBRAUEREI-HERRNGIERSDORF.DE

Trausnitz Pils Pilsner 5.2%

A perfumed pilsner, this delicious drop, defined with a lovely cookie malt and pine-forest aroma at its crux, is brewed in Bavaria. The castle after which it is named, situated nearby, was home to the Wittelsbach dynasty and was built in 1204. This tiny microbrewery, however, is even older, having been formed in 1131, which makes it, as far as anyone can tell, the oldest independent brewery in the world.

SCHLÜSSEL
DÜSSELDORF
WWW.ZUMSCHLUESSEL.DE

Schlüssel Alt Altbier 5%

Altbier experiences don't come much more authentic than this. The Zum Schlüssel brewery and tap has resided in the old town of Düsseldorf since 1850 and was inherited by the Gatzweilers, a brewing family since the fourteenth century. Its brewery tap is altbier utopia, with Schlüssel served from the barrel.

SCHNEIDER WEISSE
KELHEIM, BAVARIA
WWW.SCHNEIDER-WEISSE.DE

Schneider Aventinus
Weissbock 8.2%

A truly wondrous wheat beer fully deserving of its world-classic status and first brewed by Georg Schneider in 1907 as a reaction to the rise of barley-based doppelbocks. Its spicy, banana-scented fruit salad notes and malty chocolate, dark rum, and fig flavors are effervescent and slightly acidic.

Brooklyner-Schneider Hopfen-Weisse Weissbock IPA 8.2%

Hard to find yet hailed in hallowed terms on both sides of the Atlantic, this pale weissbock is a joint creation of head brewer Hans-Peter Drexler and Garrett Oliver of the Brooklyn Brewery. Hoppy and zesty, it deftly bestrides a balanced American IPA and a fruity, aromatic wheat beer.

Schneider Weisse Weissbier 5.5%

A fabulous, fragrant flag-bearer for the Bavarian style. While other brewers have blown hot and cold with regards to wheat beer, the Schneider family has been proudly brewing nothing else since 1855, when Georg Schneider I began brewing in Munich on behalf of the Royal Court. In 1872, he bought his own brewery and the rights to brew wheat beer from the King Ludwig II brewhouse in Kelheim. The signature burst of bubblegum, bananas, and cloves has often been imitated but never improved upon.

SCHÖFFERHOFER
FRANKFURT, HESSE
WWW.BINDING.DE

Schöfferhofer Hefeweizen 5%

Well-balanced, refreshing, hazy amber wheat beer from an enormous Frankfurt brewery better known for its popular nonalcoholic Clausthaler brands. Bready notes, leechee, and ripe banana, with a spicy nutmeg finish. Now owned by the Radeberger group.

SCHÖNRAM
SCHÖNRAM, BAVARIA
WWW.BRAUEREI-SCHOENRAM.DE

Imperial Stout 9.5%

Sometimes called Bavaria's best imperial stout, this is once again proof of Eric Toft's genius in the brewhouse. As dark as a murderer's thoughts on a moonless night, it's got molasses, marzipan, and coffee liqueur springing out of the glass, while on the palate it's all mocha, cocoa, bittersweetness, and vanilla. A magnificent beer.

Schönramer Pils Pilsner 5.4%

Brewmaster Eric Toft, the man currently working the mash-fork magic at this eighteenth-century brewhouse, doesn't hail from Bavaria, but from Wyoming. In Germany, he's continued the Schönram legacy of brewing seriously smooth and swiggable beers. Using a bespoke variety of barley, and hops for their aromatic rather than bittering powers, the pils is regarded by many as one of Germany's finest. A brainy blonde lager with a zesty lemon aroma, glorious grainy undertones, and a tinglesome, tight finish. This is a truly delicious example of a German pils.

SCHUMACHER
DÜSSELDORF, NORTH RHINE-WESTPHALIA
WWW.BRAUEREI-SCHUMACHER.DE

Schumacher Alt Altbier 4.6%

A dark-tanned, especially fruity altbier mellowed out with masses of malt and perked up with piney hops at the finish. Slightly smoky too. Comes courtesy of Düsseldorf's oldest brewery, dating back to 1838 and it's remained independent ever since.

SCHWABEN
STUTTGART, BADEN WÜRTTENBERG
WWW.DS-AG.DE

Das Schwarze Schwarzbier 4.9%

A sensational schwarzbier from the Schwaben brewery in Stuttgart. This classic brew is black and a little bit briny, with caramel, molasses, herbal hop notes, and anise at the end.

SCHWERTER
MEISSNER, HESSE
WWW.SCHWERTER-BRAUEREI.DE

German Porter 6.5%

The picturesque town of Meissen, in the Saxon Elbe valley, is great if you're a fan of porcelain because it's home to the world-renowned Meissener Porzellan factory. This town is even better if you're a fan of porter because Schwerter, a brewery first mentioned in the fifteenth century, makes a glorious German interpretation of the industrial black English ale. Sharp, roasty, and—at 6.5% ABV—stouter than its British brethren. While it may be authentic to do so, try to avoid operating heavy machinery or canal boats after drinking this particular tipple.

SION BRÄUHAUS
COLOGNE, NORTH RHINE-WESTPHALIA
WWW.BRAUHAUS-SION.DE

Sion Kölsch 4.8%

Sion's brewhouse, a cozy drinking den with old beer taps bedecking the walls and stained-glassed windows, has lived in the shadow of Cologne cathedral since 1318. Its creamy kölsch, cut short with a bitter finish, makes for a fine, floral friend to watch people with, possibly in the company of a currywurst or two from the brewhouse's kitchen.

SPATEN-FRANZISKANER
MUNICH, BAVARIA
WWW.SPATENBRAEU.DE

Spaten Oktoberfestbier
Oktoberfest/Märzen 5.9%

Peerless in its pursuit of brewing excellence, Spaten was the first to use refrigeration and steam engines in the brewing process, the first to export its beers by airplane, and one of the earliest advocates of light-colored lagers. Its spade logo, assumed in 1884, was a groundbreaking marketing move too. When its Oktoberfest lager was launched in the 1870s, it was a lot darker than it is now, but the muted malt sweetness and smooth, rounded body have been retained. Ideally drunk under a big tent in the company of pretzels, sausages, and ladies in dirndls—in other words, the biggest beer festival in the world.

SPEZIAL
BAMBERG, BAVARIA
WWW.BRAUEREI-SPEZIAL.DE

Lagerbier 4.6%
Spezial is the oldest rauchbier
brewery in Bamberg, and its smoked
beers are brewed using grain from
its own maltings and smoked on site
using beechwood logs. Considerably
less smoky than Schlenkerla.

Märzen Rauchbier 5.3%
Despite the presence of 70 percent smoked malt, the
smoke flavors are gently wafted away by a fruity
yeast character and hop bitterness. The subdued
smokiness and complexity will suit those beer
drinkers who find other rauchbiers a bit too much.

SPITALBRAUEREI
REGENSBURG, BAVARIA
WWW.SPITALBRAUEREI.DE

Spital Pils Pilsner 5.5%
Founded in 1266, it's the oldest brewery
in Regensburg and was once a hospital
brewery, where patients were given beer as
a soporific nightcap. Spital's philanthropy
remains, with profits from beer sales
funding the adjacent retirement home.
Charitable deeds don't come much more
enjoyable than sipping this perfumed
pilsner in the brewery's gorgeous beer
garden, with a view of the River Danube.

TUCHER BRÄU
FÜRTH, NUREMBERG, BAVARIA
WWW.TUCHER.DE

Tucher Bajuvator Doppelbock 7.2%
Tucher christened its coppers back in 1672, making
it one of the world's constantly active breweries. A
definite must-try for doppelbock devotees, its chief
calling card is this mellow, malty mouth-filler, now
owned by the Radeberger Group.

UNERTL BREWERY
HAAG, BAVARIA
WWW.UNERTL.DE

Unertl Weissbier 4.8%
The rather grandiose-sounding Alois III is the latest
member of the Unertl family to run things at this
medium-sized Bavarian wheat-beer brewery, not to
be confused with the Unertl brewery in Muhldorf,
although they also produce great wheat beers. This
traditional weissbier stays steadfastly between the
tracks of tangy fruit, citrus, and cloves.

VELTINS
MESCHEDE, NORTH RHINE-WESTPHALIA
WWW.VELTINS.DE

Veltins Pilsner 4.8%
Like lager? You'll love this.
A classic, clean, and crisp well-
constructed pilsner from northern
Germany. Steadfastly autonomous,
the family-owned brewery is a major player on the
home front and has the clout and capacity to commit
beyond Germany's borders.

WALDHAUS
WALDHAUS, BADEN-WÜRTTEMBERG
WWW.VELTINS.DE

Waldhaus Diplom Pils Pilsner 4.9%
Waldhaus, buried deep inside the Black
Forest, has been brewing since 1833.
Its pilsner, like all its beers, is acutely
aromatic, hails the hop with unashamed
enthusiasm, and is lagered long and
languid for maximum mouthfeel and
yeast-flavor yield. The unfiltered lager, at
5.6%, is special too, a quality that has won
it a few brewing awards.

WARSTEINER
WARSTEIN, NORTH RHINE-WESTPHALIA
WWW.WARSTEINER.DE

Warsteiner Premium Dunkel 4.9%
While everyone in Germany is familiar
with Warsteiner's clean, crisp flagship
lager, there is no reason to miss the
warming allure of its mahogany brown
dunkel, which is lesser known. Coffee,
nuts, bitter chocolate, a little licorice,
and vanilla are all present in this
complex ale. Seek it out if you can.
You won't regret it.

WEIHENSTEPHANER
FREISING, BAVARIA
WWW.WEIHENSTEPHANER.DE

Hefe-Weiss 5.4%
The brewery has withstood all manner of religious
and political tumult, not to mention secularization
in 1803, to become an esteemed center of brewing
education without rival. In 1852, Weihenstephan
was affiliated with the university, and it's
been responsible for some of the world's most
accomplished master brewers. Not many, however,
will be able to better this heavenly unfiltered wheat
beer, with its big bready base, banana, toffee, and
tropical fruit.

⭐🍺🍷 Hefeweissbier Dunkel 5.3%

Despite a history that's nearly a thousand years old, Weihenstephan's state-owned brewery is at the diamond-cutting edge of technology. It sources Hallertau hops, Bavarian malt, and soft local water for its beers, and still matures them for 30 days in cellars 49 feet underneath the monastery garden. On the nose it's slightly toasty, with chocolate and banana notes; there are nuts and cloves on the palate and a fruity finish.

⭐🍺🍷 Korbinian Doppelbock 7.4%

The legendary brewery at Weihenstephan is the oldest in the world. Situated on a hill in the Bavarian town of Freising, the brewery site has been home to a monastery since 725, and there are records showing a hop garden here since 768. While it was likely that the "Holy Stephen" Benedictine monks brewed previously, it was in 1040 when Weihenstephan was granted a license to brew officially. Korbinian is a deliciously dark brown double bock that's nutty, full of dark fruit, and with a pronounced but not overly malt signature. Another German classic.

WELTENBURGER KLOSTER
KELHEIM, BAVARIA
WWW.WELTENBURGER.DE

⭐🍺🍺 Urtyp Hell Helles 4.9%

A hell from brewing heaven. Weltenburger is the oldest abbey brewery in the world and arguably the most picturesque too. Founded in 1050 by a couple of monks named Agilus and Eustasius, it's perched on a bucolic bend on the River Danube, next to the Weltenburger castle, in the shadow of huge white cliffs and chestnut trees. A sublime spot to sip on this pale, luscious, medium-bodied lager brewed with Hallertau hops and lagered 131 feet beneath the brewery. Only the beers labeled "Weltenburger Kloster" are brewed here, the rest at Bischofshof.

WÜRZBURGER
WÜRZBURG, BAVARIA
WWW.WUERZBURGER-HOFBRAEU.DE

🍺🍷 Hofbräu Schwarzbier 4.8%

Dark lager that bleeds black into deep maroon. A cacao aroma followed by roasted chestnuts, molasses, and a hint of cream soda on the palate. When chilled, it matches marvelously with pretty much anything you care to cook on the barbecue, especially meat and fish.

⭐🍺🍷 Hofbräu Sympator Doppelbock 7.9%

The surrounding countryside may have more vineyards than it does barley fields, but Würzburg hails the grain as much as the grape. Würzburger is housed in a nineteenth-century town-center site with a brewing history dating back to 1643. It's a boozy, breast-beating seasonal beer, big on fruit, cake flavors, tobacco, and Cognac on the nose, and a toffee-tinged finish.

ZEHENDNER
MÖNCHSAMBACH, BAVARIA
WWW.BRAUEREI-ZEHENDNER.DE

🍺 Mönchsambacher Lagerbier 5.5%

On the label there's a cheeky-looking monk giving a rather smug wink. It's little wonder he's looking so happy with himself, for this unfiltered lager is simply phenomenal. Brewed by a dinky little farmhouse brewery in a tiny, rustic town 16 miles outside Bamberg, it is gently sweet, grainy, and perfectly poised. Terrific.

ZUM UERIGE
DÜSSELDORF, NORTH RHINE-WESTPHALIA
WWW.UERIGE.DE

⭐🍺 Uerige Alt Altbier 4.5%

Zum Uerige is the preeminent Düsseldorf brewpub. It serves a classic altbier, and in the opinion of many, the finest. Very aromatic, bright and coppery, and bursting with both malt and hops in the bouquet, this very assertive beer would be too bitter for some were it not for the rich, dark malt platform to offset the hops. Smooth, deep, and savory, the hops linger forever, a constant reminder of what is to come. The label proudly refers to its beer as "dat leckere Dröppke," the delicious drop. The brewpub is nestled in the heart of the Altstadt and is the quintessential altbier experience.

⭐🍺🍽 Uerige Sticke Alt 6.5%

This is a stronger version of the famous Uerige Alt, produced twice a year—firstly for the pre-Lenten carnival of late winter and secondly for late fall. Robust, roasty, and fruity, it's the perfect tipple to help you take a celebratory part in any festivities wherever you are but preferably best imbibed in Düsseldorf itself.

Above: The distinctive neo-renaissance double-arched gates, entrance to Plzensky Prazdroj, Pilsner Urquell's historic brewery.
Below: Kocour Brewery, one of a number of new-wave Czech breweries experimenting with styles different from the lager tradition.

INTRODUCTION
CZECHIA

Since it split from wine-supping Slovakia, Czechia can lay claim to being the greatest beer-drinking country in the world, where they drink more beer than any other nation. Every citizen, on average, sinks a staggering 31+ gallons a year, some of it enjoyed upside down during the annual Headstand Beer Drinking contest in Opava. True story.

It's easy to see why they have such a thirst for it. Czechia can call upon not only a rich brewing heritage but with it a wealth of natural brewing resources. The world's most sought-after hop variety, the spicy Saaz, is grown in the northwest region of Žatec, while barley hailing from the Hana plateau along the River Moravia is floor malted and affords Czech beer its signature smoothness. Then there's the natural water, softer than anywhere else in Europe.

All these indigenous ingredients dovetailed together to magnificent effect in the fall of 1842 when, in Pilsen, the first golden lager was born. As well as inventing the first pilsner, Czechia was brewing Budweiser beers in the town of České Budějovice long before the Anheuser family began producing its "king" beer.

While Communist rule stifled growth and investment here, it also inadvertently froze traditional, time-honored brewing techniques and spared smaller breweries from the clutches of corporate conglomeration. This changed dramatically when the 1989 Velvet Revolution laid out a red carpet for foreign investors. Many breweries were bought by outsiders, with the new boys demanding efficiency at the cost of patience in production, and while Budvar remained resolute in its approach, elsewhere the venerable values were overlooked.

But in the nooks and crannies of the nation the purists hunkered down and stabbed at this new substandard beer with pitchforks.

These stalwarts successfully preserved their praiseworthy practices, and now Czech beer is being rediscovered. From 100 breweries in the '90s, to around 400 today, there has been a bold revival in the roots of production and style.

As with all the newly urgent brewing nations around the world, there are some that are putting enthusiasm ahead of quality, but a restored devotion to triple decoction mashing and unhurried cold-conditioning has seen demand for quality světlý ležáks (pale lagers) met.

Some of the cutting-edge crews are following the respected traditionalists down the heritage path, new and old now helping the various shades of beer come back into the limelight. Darker malty ambers like the Polotmavý or the tmave (dark) and cerne (black) ležák are all demanding glass time. Meanwhile, the cult of the American revolution is making itself known with IPAs and porters muscling onto menus. The best brewers can confidently combine old with new: Pivovar Matuška prides itself on the classics but has enjoyed success with modern marvels like its Hellcat Imperial India Pale Ale.

A creaking distribution system restricts reach even domestically, and the adage that the best of a nation's beer needs to be drunk on location is rarely truer than in Czechia. Pick one of the ripest fruits of labor, the excellent Únětický pivovar, and we can see them starting to travel, but to enjoy the best, you should go to the source, as much of it is still reserved for the taps.

ALBRECHTICKÝ
KARVINA, MORAVIAN-SILESIAN
WWW.ALBRECHTICKYPIVOVAR.CZ

 **Pačan 12°** Pilsner 4.7%

Small brewery on the Polish border that was founded in 2015. Well-made and fresh tasting pilsners are its forte (though there's also a stab at oddness with a pumpkin beer). This classic 12° pilsner is golden in color with a light bitterness.

ANTOŠ
SLANÝ, CENTRAL BOHEMIA
WWW.PIVOVARANTOS.CZ

Antošův Ležák Pilsner 5%

Likable brewpub in a small town 15 miles northwest of Prague. Many beers are produced, including cask ones, but this is one of its bestsellers; a crisp, refreshing, and bittersweet beer to be drunk in the company of friends, and gulped rather than studied.

Fat Bat Rye IPA 6.7%

No bats were harmed in the making of this rich and grainy beer. Instead, it has malted rye added to the mixture, which, along with the addition of four American hops, makes for a citrusy and tropically fruity drop, while the rye shines midpalate with a hint of caramel and a malt-loaf like richness.

BAD FLASH
PRAGUE
WWW.BADFLASH.CZ

Hop Wings Pale Ale 5.2%

No, not something you order in a Tex-Mex restaurant with a side of beer, but an amply flavorsome American-style pale ale with a crisp and fruity mood on the palate and a gentle dry finish. Bad Flash, though based in Prague, terms itself a flying brewery, as its beers are often brewed at other concerns.

BERNARD
HUMPOLEC, VYSOČINA
WWW.BERNARD.CZ

Bohemian Ale
Belgian Strong Ale 8.2%

This beer may be strong, but there're a subtlety in the taste and an elegance that make you want to keep sipping. It's spicy and sensuous, fresh and fruity, and warm in the finish. A Czech classic that's worth seeking out.

Dark Lager 5.1%

When in 1991 a trio of investors led by Stanislav Bernard breathed life back into a sixteenth-century brewery, he lent his name to a superlative selection of full-flavored, unpasteurized beers. Five types of succulent malt, all sourced from the brewery's own maltings, conspire to create a slighty spicy and superbly smooth ebony-hued lager that is remarkably refreshing.

U BIZONA ČIŽICE
ŠTĚNOVICE, PLZEŇ
WWW.UBIZONA.EU

 Karolína Světlá 13° Pilsner 5.1%

Lilliputian brewery that started out in 2011 making 24-gallons of beer per batch; the outfit has grown since and now makes 88 gallons of each brew. This is its slightly stronger pilsner (some call it a Special), which makes a medium-bodied bittersweet quaff.

BŘEVNOVSKÝ KLÁŠTERNÍ PIVOVAR
PRAGUE, BOHEMIA
WWW.BREVNOVSKYPIVOVAR.CZ

Monastic IPA 6%

Established in 2011 in the grounds of a monastery in north Prague, this neat little brewery produces a godly range of good beers. This is its gold-flecked IPA with a hymnal of tropical fruit on the nose, and more fruit alongside a caramel-like cookieness leading to its long dry finish. Simply heavenly.

Russian Imperial Stout 8.5%

This big brawny beer bellows its boisterousness to the world with a swirl of chocolate, roast grain, and coffee aromatics, as if to tempt the most saintly of us, while it has a full-bodied mouthfeel with more roast, chocolate, caramel, and coffee and an assertive bitter finish.

BŘEZŇÁK
VELKÉ BŘEZNO, ÚSTÍ NAD LABEM
WWW.BREZNAK.CZ

Březňák Svetle Výčepní 14 Golden Lager 6.5%

Extensive and extravagant lagering times and open fermentation are what the Březňák brewery is known for. This glorious golden lager gets its gloop and acute alcohol accent from four months of aging.

BROUMOV
BROUMOV, HRADEC KRÁLOVÉ
WWW.PIVOVARBROUMOV.CZ

Opat Bitter Extra Chmelené Plvo Pilsner 4.2%

There's been a brewery in the town of Broumov since the Middle Ages, when it was attached to the Benedictine monastery. Now, it's situated just outside of town, where its range of Opat beers features pale lagers flavored with all manner of things. This, however, just has Saaz hops, producing a fragrant nose, a gentle malt sweetness, and a refreshing finish.

BUDWEISER BUDVAR
CĚSKÉ BUDĚJOVICE, SOUTH BOHEMIA
WWW.ORIGINAL-BUDWEISER.CZ

Historically, České Budějovice is as significant a beer town as Pilsen, Munich, and Burton-on-Trent. In the fifteenth century, it was home to 44 breweries and the Royal Court brewery of Bohemia. Its beers were known as Budweisers and, due to the royal connection, as the "beer of kings." Alas, like Pilsen, České Budějovice neglected to trademark the name of its flagship beer, and in 1876 American brewer Anheuser-Busch was able to choose Budweiser as the name of its new, bland-tasting yellow lager. Twenty years later, the Budějovice Brewery was founded, began brewing Budvar, and exported it under the name Budweiser Budvar. This miffed those in Missouri, and, more than a hundred years later and nearly as many lawsuits, the two breweries are still arguing over the Budweiser brand name. Even though Anheuser-Busch can claim its beer preceded Budvar's by two decades, the Czechs cite geographical significance and also the fact that Budweiser beer had been exported by Samson, the other surviving brewery in České Budějovice, long before the Americans adopted exactly the same beer name. Differing legal decisions have meant that both beers have had to adopt pseudonyms in countries that have ruled against them (Budvar is known as Czechvar in America).

B:Special 5%

Once rarely encountered outside the Czechia, but now more common, this golden krausened lager delivers a fuller flavor and heightened hop character thanks to the extra addition of yeast before bottling—affording a softer, less sparkling mouthfeel.

B:Dark Dark Lager 4.7%

A dark brunette lager launched in 1994 and brewed using Munich, Crystal, and roasted malt. Coffee and chocolate character with a touch of chicory and spice on the full-bodied finish.

B: Original Premium Lager 5%

Cynics may suggest that the Czech brewery has benefited from exposure as the underdog in a global "David versus Goliath" battle, but that would be an injustice to one of the world's great beers. Clever-clogs lawyers may be able to argue that Anheuser-Busch's beer was first, but there's no courtroom on the planet that can say it is better. Fermented in open vessels and cold-conditioned for three months, Budvar sets succulent cookie malt off against a flourish of floral Žatec (Saaz) hop. Beautifully balanced.

CHODOVAR
CHODOVAR PLANA, PILSEN
WWW.CHODOVAR.CZ

Chodovar President 5%

The family-owned Chodovar brewery dates back to 1573 and is renowned for its labyrinth of rock cellars. In recent years, it has championed beer's health-giving properties with its famous beer spa, where one's mind, body, and soul are enhanced with a bath featuring brewing yeast, hops, and herbs. The brewery also lends its name to beer shampoo and beer cosmetics, but the beer will make you feel and, if you drink enough, look better too. A golden, grandiose lager that intertwines a southern Bohemian malt signature with a pilsner-esque hop character.

CHOTĚBOŘ
CHOTĚBOŘ, VYSOČIN
WWW.PIVOVARCHOTEBOR.CZ

 Original Pilsner 4.1%

Sometimes all you need with a beer is a sense of refreshment, a dance of malt sweetness and hop spiciness, and a boost of bitterness in the finish, which is why this light golden beer from a brewery in the heartlands of southern Bohemia is such a first-class slurper.

CLOCK
POTŠTEJN, RYCHNOV NAD KNĚŽNOU
WWW.PIVOVARCLOCK.CZ

American Pale Ale 5%

Time flies when you're enjoying good beer, and the exceptional beers from this young brewery (opened in 2014) certainly melt away the minutes and hours once they keep being poured. Their APA is a delight of citrus and pine, balanced by subtle malt sweetness before the dry bittersweet finish. The robot-themed bottle labels and branding are also pretty cool.

DŮM
PRAGUE, BOHEMIA
WWW.PIVOVARSKYDUM.COM

Pšeničné pivo Wheat Beer 4%

Bohemia tends not to take on Bavaria and Belgium in the wheat beer arena, but this fruity and clove-wielding contender could hold its own.

Štěpán Český Klasický Ležák Světlý Pale Lager 4%

As you'd expect from a brewpub situated below the Czech Research Institute of Malt and Brewing, Pivovarský Dům is keen on experimentation, dabbling with innovative ingredients in its seasonal beers. While these funky forays are fun, it's the traditional Czech beers, such as this grassy, grainy golden lager, that pull in the beer-loving punters.

DVŮR LIPAN
DRAŽÍČ, SOUTH BOHEMIA
WWW.PIVOVAR-LIPAN.CZ

Nefiltrovany Světlý Ležák Lager 5.3%

If you're ever down in the south Bohemian town of Dražíč then beat a path to the door of this brilliant brewpub and distillery offering a bed and breakfast, big portions, a bevy of fruit brandies, and—best of all—lots of lovely yeast-laden beer. Sparkling and soft, light and fruity on the nose, bread and butter on the palate, and sweet on the finish.

FALKON
ZATEC, ÚSTÍ NAD LABEM
WWW.PIVOFALKON.CZ

Nightstalker
Black IPA 6.7%

Most of the beer world might call a beer hopped like an IPA but as dark as your mother's well-burned treacle pudding a Black IPA, but Jakub Veselý goes for the occasionally controversial label such as Cascadian dark ale. Whatever it's called, this is a bracing, roasty, hoppy drop of etymologically confused beer goodness.

Superfly Saison 6.2%

Jakub started homebrewing when he was a 12-year-old whippersnapper, but it wasn't until 2012, after he'd gained a degree in brewing technology, that he started to brew professionally. Even though short of money, he rented space in various breweries and got to work on his new career. He's still a gypsy brewer, but his beers have gained several accolades among Czech beer connoisseurs. Superfly is his luscious yet lean mash-up of a saison and a Belgian IPA. This is a truly tasty beer.

HEROLD
BŘEZNICE, CENTRAL BOHEMIA
WWW.PIVOVAR-HEROLD.CZ

Czech Black Lager Dark Lager 5.3%

This luscious drop is lagered for ten weeks and brewed using a quartet of dark malts. Dark mahogany brown verging on black, and shaped by a sturdy malt backbone. Creamy vanilla, bitter chocolate, and a long, cedary, dry smoky finish.

Traditional Czech Lager 4.1%

A crisp and clean "working person's workhorse Czech lager" from a sixteenth-century castle brewery, located 40 miles south of Prague. Following the Velvet Revolution, its beer flourished under a new Herold name and ownership of the Research Institute of Malt and Brewing. In 1998, it was bought by American investors, who have retained the traditional brewing techniques such as the hand turning of its own malt and the use of Saaz hops and well water from the park on the estate.

JIHLAVA
JIHLAVA VYSOČINA
WWW.PIVOVAR-JIHLAVA.CZ

Jihlavský Grand 8.1%

This is a heavily hopped, honey-colored, muscular malt-accented jewel in the crown of a thoroughly modernized brewery located in a town whose breweries back in the sixteenth century graced the beer glasses of Austrian royalty. Nowadays the brewery is part of the Lobkowicz group, which owns several breweries throughout Bohemia and Moravia, including Černá Hora, Protivín, and Rychtář. This is an ideal beer to sip contemplatively or perhaps to accompany a ripe blue cheese.

KOCOUR
VARNSDORF, ÚSTÍ NAD LABEM
WWW.PIVOVAR-KOCOUR.CZ

Gypsy Porter Baltic Porter 7.1%

A luxurious and potent Baltic porter that was brewed in collaboration with now-defunct English brewery Steel City and Prague-based beer writer Max Bahnson. It's a brawny, sleeves-rolled-up kind of beer, make no mistake about it, but the use of Citra adds a tropical fruity lightness to the chocolate, coffee, and licorice notes.

IPA Samuraj 5.1%

Founded in 2008, Kocour were one of the first Czech breweries to look beyond traditional Czech brewing world of pilsner and instead be influenced by all manner of world beer styles. Amber-orange in color, Samuraj has a leafy, sweet orange effervescent sparkle on the palate, followed by an appetizing bitterness. An appealing ale, for sure.

KOUT NA ŠUMAVĚ
KOUT NA SUMAVE, PILSEN
WWW.PIVOVARKOUT.CZ

Světlý Ležák Pilsner 5%

What many Czech beer cognoscenti regard as the most impressive and underrated pilsner in the country and thus the world. Soft and spritzy with fruity yeast, a boundary-breaking bitterness, and a voluptuous, velvety malt mouthfeel. Find it if you can. Drink it. Then drink some more. A golden gift from the gods and worth a special trip to Czechia.

Tmavý Speciál 18°
Doppelbock 9%

Here's a big boy, a mighty doppelbock with its origins in Bohemia rather than Bavaria. Dark brown in color, it has a swirl of cocoa, cookie, nuts, and gently toasted malt on the nose, while it slips down like the nectar of winter (when it's best drunk) with a bittersweet finish.

Tmavý Super Special
Dark Lager 9%

Much to the delight of right-drinking beer lovers, Kout burst back into life in 2006 after nearly 20 years of hibernation, and this delicious, deeply drinkable dark lager is both super and special.

KRUŠOVICE
KRUŠOVICE, CENTRAL BOHEMIA
WWW.KRUSOVICE.CZ

Dark Dark Lager 3.8%

Czechia's biggest-selling dark beer with a mild hop bitterness, sweet caramel, and a hint of blackberry, reminiscent of a British mild. Ambitious drinkers can indulge in the tradition of layering Krušovice Dark on top of the Imperial.

Imperial Premium Lager 5.5%

Krušovice beers have been brewed at the Imperial Brewery, 31 miles west of Prague, since 1517. In 1583 the brewery was bought by the Holy Roman Emperor Rudolf II, but now it's under the control of the Oetker Brewing Group and has become the fifth largest brewery in Czechia. This is a full-bodied, bitter hoppy lager whose popularity hasn't weakened its allure.

LOBEČ
LOBEČ, CENTRAL BOHEMIA
WWW.LOBEC.CZ

Lobeč Tripel 9.1%

Yes, you read correctly, that's Tripel, as in the gleaming, glossy beer that Belgians love to serenade about as they lift chalices of the stuff. Belgium is a long way from central Bohemia, but that hasn't stopped these young guns from having a go, and the result is a fulsome and fruity riff on the classic style.

LOBKOWICZ
VYSOKÝ CHLUMEC
WWW.LOBKOWICZ.CZ

Lobkowicz Baron Dark Lager 4.7%

While other small breweries have disappeared, Lobkowicz has thrived by remaining steadfast in its commitment to open fermentation, lengthy lagering below the brewhouse, and the use of its own water and environmentally friendly malt. The darker grains coming to play here provide a flavor that is earthy and nutty, with a smoldering sweetness.

LUCKY BASTARD
BRNO, MORAVIA
WWW.LUCKY-BASTARD.CZ

India IPA 6.7%

There's a suaveness about the brandings of this Brno brewery, but anyone fearing style triumphing over content when it comes to the beer will be perfectly assured once they start to quaff this iridescent IPA. Citrus, tropical fruit, pine, and a fine malt sweetness rock the palate until the long dry finish.

MATUŠKA
see Brewery Profile pages 126 to 127
BROUMY, CENTRAL BOHEMIA
WWW.PIVOVARMATUSKA.CZ

Raptor IPA 6.3%

Even though he's not yet reached 30, Adam Matuška is seen as one of the leading brewing lights on the Czech scene. (He has even judged at the Great American Beer Festival.) His beers cross a whole range of styles, with Raptor being his classic IPA: ripe peach aromatic, a juicy, bittersweet mouth feel, and a dry bitter finish, with more fruit joining in the fun.

NOMÁD
PRAGUE
WWW.PIVOVAR-NOMAD.CZ

Karel Česká IPA 7.6%

Sometimes it's not that hard to get an IPA right, as this beauty reveals with its aromatics of grapefruit, mandarin, and pine, then by a bittersweet construction of grapefruit and orange on the palate alongside a grainy dryness followed by a bitter finish. Nomád is a gypsy brewer collaborating across Czechia.

NYMBURK
NYMBURK, PRAGUE METROPOLITAN
WWW.POSTRIZINY.CZ

Francinův Ležák Pilsner 5%

Brewing since 1895, Nymburk proves that you can never have too much of a well-made Czech-style pilsner as one (or maybe three) sips of this beauty demonstrates. It rings and chimes like an old clock with sweet malt and lemony hops, while the finish is clean with a welcome bounty of bittersweetness.

PIVOVAR PARDUBICE
PARDUBICE, PARDUBICE
WWW.PERNSTEJN.CZ

Pardubický Porter 8%

There was a time when Baltic porters blessed many Czech breweries, but then golden lagers came along and the dark beers got lost in their shadow. This peppery, suede-colored, and espresso-accented porter made its name during the nineteenth century and hasn't lost any of its allure. Worth seeking out.

PILSNER URQUELL/GAMBRINUS
PILSEN
WWW.PILSNERURQUELL.COM

Kvasnicový Pilsner Urquell
Unfiltered Pilsner 4.4%

A hazy, hallowed, unpasteurized, and unfiltered version of the original pilsner spruced up with a dose of young beer. Available only at the brewery (and a select few bars), it is drawn from the barrel straight into the glasses of excited, privileged pilsner drinkers.

Pilsner Urquell Pilsner 4.4%

Before this was brewed in 1842, golden lager simply wasn't a thing. Here, Saaz hops, succulent Moravian malt, triple decoction, and long lagering times combine to produce the gentle, golden, and velvet-smooth giant on whose shoulders all other lagers and pilsners stand.

POUTNÍK
PELHŘIMOV, VYSOČINA
WWW.PIVOVARPOUTNIK.CZ

🍺 Poutník Speciál 14 Pilsner 5.8%
State-owned until 2001, the "Pilgrim" brewery has a turbulent history dating from the sixteenth century. Since 2003, new owners have secured a return to traditional Czech brewing practices with their unpasteurized beer. This seasonal beer, produced twice a year, at Easter and Christmas, is an amber-colored, sweet, softly sparkling special lager, accented with almonds, cookie, and traces of cotton candy.

PRAGER LAFFE
PRAGUE
WWW.PRAGERLAFFE.CZ

🍴 Smokie Smoked Beer 5.2%
Yet another brewery without a home and yet another interesting beer. This one, as the name might suggest, is smoky, though it doesn't go for the full inferno of rauchbier. Instead, it's lightly smoked bacon or a campfire in the next field, alongside caramel sweetness and a dry appetizing finish.

PRIMÁTOR NÁCHOD
NÁCHOD, HRADEC KRÁLOVÉ
WWW.PRIMATOR.CZ

🍴 Primátor Stout 4.7%
Located in the charming northeastern town of Náchod, Primator is one for the purists and the past. It hasn't strayed far from traditional techniques (it uses open fermenters, for instance), though it also hasn't ignored what's going on in the rest of the world as this bitter, dry, and roasty stout demonstrates (the brewery also produces an IPA and a pale ale).

🍺 Primátor Weizenbier 4.8%
This Bohemian weizen is a lazy Sunday conglomeration of cloves, zesty wheat, and hints of banana on the nose, before its brisk mouthfeel and Saaz bitterness turn up the volume a bit to a finale that presents a balanced and tasty wheat beer.

RAVEN
PILSEN, WESTERN BOHEMIA
WWW.PIVOVAR-RAVEN.CZ

🍺 White IPA 6.3%
You've got to admire the nerve of Raven. Even though they are Lilliputian in size, they opened their brewery in Pilsen, one of the world's most famous beer cities, where Pilsner Urquell rules the roost. This is deep orange in color, with tropical fruit on the nose, and a juicy fruitiness on the palate before its dry bitter finish. For a small brewery, they are most definitely not insignificant.

REBEL
HAVLÍČKŮV BROD, VYSOČINA
WWW.HBREBEL.CZ

Cerný Rebel
Dark Lager 4.7%
Since the descendants of the founding family took over the brewery in 1995 (with the original foundation being 1834) and administered some technical tender loving care, Rebel's beers have conformed in terms of consistency. Matured for 50 days, this is a dark brown craveworthy drop, with strongly stewed coffee and scorched caramel on the palate.

REGENT
TŘEBOŇ, SOUTH BOHEMIA
WWW.PIVOVAR-REGENT.CZ

Bohemia Regent Dark Lager 4.4%
Founded in 1379, the Regent brewery is one of the oldest in the world and is named after Jakub Křín, who began life as a Rosenberg accountant and then rose to become not just regent of the large dominion of Vilem, but also the uncrowned king of the entire Bohemian kingdom. Almost as impressive is this delicious garnet-colored, spicy hop creamy lager with a licorice and almond finish. A fine example of a classic Czech dark lager.

MATUŠKA

U RADNICE 115, 267 42 BROUMY, CENTRAL BOHEMIA
WWW.PIVOVARMATUSKA.CZ

Drinking beer in Czechia, especially in Pilsen, home of the original golden lager, must be close to number one on most beer connoisseurs' bucket lists. This is a country where beer takes pride of place similar to wine and food in France. Its beer lovers tend to think about beer in the same way as the ancient Roman philosophers did as they tried to make sense of the world, though without having to wear togas. In a perceptive essay, "Pivo at the Heart of Europe," Timothy O'Hall starts off with a quote: "A Czech never says that he's going out to have a few beers, and he never counts the beers while he's having them. You go out for a beer."

Of course, when we think about beer in Czechia, it's the golden glow of the Pilsen-style beers (světlý ležák) that comes to mind, alongside a brooding selection of dark lagers (tmavý ležák). However, the past few years have seen an infusion of energy, brewing exploration, and sheer revolution added to the Czech beer scene as new breweries have emerged, not content to plow the same brewing furrow as those that have gone before them, though they haven't completely dumped on the past and continue to make tantalizing pilsners.

Pivovar Matuška is one of the leading lights of this movement, a small and productive family-owned brewery based in a village to the west of Prague. It was founded in 2009 by Martin Matuška, who had learned to brew at Prague's famous brewpub U Fleků and then went onto brew around the world before coming home. After working at Prague Strahov, he began his eponymous brewery.

He's still there, but now his son Adam is at the helm, and he has definitely learned from his well-traveled father. Adam is seen as one of the most accomplished brewers in the country and had the accolade of judging at the Great American Beer Festival in his early 20s.

"I studied fermentation at college in Prague," says the baseball-playing brewer, "and I was the first guy in the school to use dry hopping. I'd heard my father talking about it, so I wanted to do it. What I want from my beer is that it must be of a perfect quality and it must be fresh. This is very important to me because, if a customer has one bad experience with our beer, he will never try it again."

The beers he makes cover a variety of styles, including the bright and sunny hop-ridden pale

Above: If you like pictures of conical fermentation tanks and a ladder, then feast your eyes on these bad boys.

California, the intensely bitter Raptor IPA (influenced by the first time he drank Sierra Nevada's Torpedo in New York), and the full bodied, robust, and punchy Pilsner Speciální Světlé. "I want to call it pilsner, but you can't," he says.

> "We also always try to brew some new kinds of beer, and we experiment in combining US, UK, and Australian hops with Czech decoction brewing style and other things."

He also makes a saison, which is unspiced, a witbier with orange peel and coriander, and even an ESB, which uses the English hop varieties Fuggles and Bramling Cross with Moravian malt. There are also plans for barrel aging and some time in the future playing around with Brettanomyces.

As for what's going on in the Czech brewing scene, Matuška isn't completely sure whether it's right to call it a revolution. "Everywhere in the western world craft brewing is very popular because it has already had some time to evolve. In Czechia it would also have become more popular earlier if it could have been possible. But we have had a small delay because of the Communist times when it was impossible for anyone to own and run a small brewery."

"Despite the emergence of craft breweries, we still have drinkers who say that IPA is not a beer because they dislike its fruity and citrusy aromas. The only reason they say this is that they didn't have a chance to try this beer style before, and they say they will never accept it and never drink this nontraditional beer. Fortunately, there are fewer people like this nowadays."

* KEY BEERS

California 5.3%
Černá Raketa 6.9%
Raptor IPA 6.3%
Weizenbock 6.8%

Bohemia Regent Jedenáctka Pilsner 4.6%

When the Velvet Curtain left in 1989, Regent's beers were among the first to shine on the international stage, and, despite murmurs among purists regarding the sacrifice of traditional techniques, they are still regarded as some of the best in south Bohemia. With grassy notes and a grainy base, this barely carbonated beer is a much more worthy effort than the brewery's popular flagship Bohemia lager.

RICHTER BREWERY
PRAGUE
WWW.PIVOVARUBULOVKY.CZ

Richter Ležák Lager 5%

A new-wave Prague brewpub which opened in 2004 to huge acclaim. In a marked departure from his Czech counterparts, highly skilled head brewer František Richter embraces a dazzling array of European influences, including stouts, porters, bocks, and alts. Championing the Czech tradition is this delicious deep copper-colored lager full of floral fragrance and with a superb malty body.

STRAHOV MONASTIC BREWERY
PRAGUE
WWW.KLASTERNI-PIVOVAR.CZ

Svatý Norbert IPA 6.3%

A Prague brewpub in prime position near to the castle on the site of the Strahov Monastery founded in 1140. The brewery was closed in 1907 but revived in 2000 as a modern brewpub and is now doing a nice bit of monk-y business courtesy of some rather impressive unfiltered lagers, sought-after seasonals, and this fresh and fruity IPA.

Svatý Norbert Tmavý Dark Lager 5.5%

A brown-to-black beer with Munich roots, yet drier and bitter than a Bavarian dark beer. Attenuated with whole malts and heaps of hops, it comes up with caramel, honey, and toffee-apple tones. At the brewpub, it makes a perfect beer and food combination when drunk with beef tenderloin, goose liver, and bacon.

SVATOVÁCLAVSKÝ PIVOVAR
OLOMOUC, OLOMOUC
WWW.SVATOVACLAVSKY-PIVOVAR.CZ

Pšeničné Wheat Beer 5.9%

Since 2006, the Svatováclavský brewpub has been brewing some new-wave Czech beers with a difference in the Moravian student town of Olomouc and in the shadow of the famous Holy Trinity Column. Brandishing Bavarian-style bananas and bubblegum aromas, it's solid and spicy, with a wonderfully wispy white head.

PIVOVAR SVIJANY
SVIJANY, LIBEREC
WWW.PIVOVARSVIJANY.CZ

Svijany Kníže Lager 5.6%

Dating from 1564, the Svijany brewery has changed hands more often than a "jazz cigarette" at a Grateful Dead concert. Following nationalization, it settled down under private ownership in 1998 and has excelled with unpasteurized beers brewed by traditional means. All the beers are worth investigating, but if you like your lagers heady of hop and moreish of malt, then this is the one for you.

U FLEKŮ
PRAGUE
WWW.UFLEKU.CZ

Flekovský Tmavý ležák Dark Lager 4.6%

No right-thinking beer drinker worth his malt should visit Prague without taking in the Gothic grandeur of the legendary U Fleků pub, the world's oldest brewpub dating back to 1499. It's a stylish stained-glass shrine to one of the world's finest dark beers. Behind the ink-black sheen and beneath the wonderful frothy head hides licorice, creamy mocha, dark bitter chocolate, and the peppery, piquant presence of hops. So sublime you won't notice the tourists or the oompah band.

U MEDVÍDKŮ

PRAGUE
WWW.UMEDVIDKU.CZ

 X33

Wood-Aged Beer 12.6%

From this gigantic Gothic and grandiose brewpub dating back to 1466 comes this superb, sensuous shape-shifter of a beer. Following a languid lagering period in traditional oak barrels for around seven months, it flirts with a feast of different flavors. On a vinous background there are vanilla, tobacco, and woody resins and a lingering finish. A true sipper.

ÚNĚTICKÝ

ÚNĚTICE
WWW.UNETICKYPIVOVAR.CZ

Pivo 10° Pilsner 4.9%

Únětický makes only two regular beers (though it occasionally dabbles with others), and this session-strength pilsner is a golden delight on the tongue as it murmurs away with tales of fields of Moravian malt and Saaz hops.

VALÁŠEK

VSETÍN, ZLÍN
WWW.MINIPIVOVAR.COM

IPA Saison 6.4%

Belgian yeast throws crazy shapes in the glass, combined with the aromatic smoothness of Belgian and Czech hops, and good local water, these produce a creamy, spicy, fruity IPA saison. Rather pleasing.

VELKÉ POPEVICE

VELKÉ POPEVICE, CENTRAL BOHEMIA
WWW.KOZEL.CZ

Kozel Premium 5%

Kozel means "goat" in Czech, and a comical image of one clutching a frothing tankard, designed by a French artist, adorns the brewery logo. Historically, the goat symbolizes strength and power and is traditionally associated in Germany and Bavaria with bocks, but this fantastically floral Bohemian lager is well worth locking horns with. A very popular beer from a brewery now owned by Asahi.

VELKORYBNICKÝ HASTRMAN

HROZNĚTÍN, KARLOVY VARY
WWW.PIVOHASTRMAN.CZ

Alt 5.5%

Here's that rare beast, the special beer of Düsseldorf brewed not only outside the city limits but also of Germany. Purists shouldn't worry though, as this small brewery and restaurant make a fine job of the beer, which is lip-smacking refreshing and has the bracing graining and light hopping that connoisseurs would expect from alt.

ŽATEC

ŽATEC, ÚSTÍ NAD LABEM
WWW.ZATEC-BREWERY.COM

Celia Dark Gluten-free 5.7%

Here's a treat for those unlucky celiac folk who cannot enjoy a regular beer. This is one of two gluten-free beers that Žatec produces. (The other one is blonde, naturally.) It's dark brown in color with notes of toffee and malt on the nose, followed by further richness on the smooth palate. A perfectly acceptable gluten-free beer.

ZHŮŘÁK

ZHŮŘ, PLZEŇ REGION
WWW.PIVOVARZHURAK.CZ

Asfalt Extreme Stout 7.4%

Even though it's very much a small-scale, part-time operation, US expat Chris Baerwaldt founded his brewery in 2013 in a village 16 miles south of Pilsen and has built up a sizable reputation for his beers. This is a rich and roasty imperial stout, which is brewed annually and aged for eight months before release. Others to look out for include Total Eclipse Black Ale.

ZVIKOV

ZVÍKOVSKÉ PODHRADÍ, SOUTH BOHEMIA
WWW.PIVOVAR-ZVIKOV.CZ

Zlata Labut Svetlé Kvasnicové Pivoo Pilsner 4.7%

This bucolic brewpub, located at the confluence of the Vlatva and Oltava rivers in south Bohemia, has some lovely, lovely lagers. Small and skilled in the science of brewing, it replicates the beers made by a brewery that was once housed in the nearby Zvikov castle, using hops from its own hop field. This is an aromatic and hazy yeast beer with a touch of banana to balance out the pronounced crisp bitterness. A perfectly balanced pilsner from the heart of Bohemia.

Above: At Grado Plato in Chieri, Sergio Omea, who founded the brewery in 2003, personally attends to the brewing process.
Below: Craft beer bars are an increasingly common phenomenon in Italy.

INTRODUCTION
ITALY

Of all the up-and-coming brewing nations in the world, Italy is still the one to watch. Having lived for so long in the brewing shadow of its more northerly neighbors, Italy now finds itself at the diamond-cutting edge of new-wave brewing.

It arrived a little later to the craft beer party, but it did arrive fashionably dressed like a dream before coolly tossing a set of Ferrari keys onto the table. Until the appreciation of all things epicurean got the better of it, Italy had remained relatively immune to the microbrewing bug, but a craft-brewing craze that started in the early 1990s, with a few homebrewers opening brewpubs, has mushroomed into a pioneering movement that's young, energetic, and aiming squarely at the top end of the market—well away from the Euro-fizz peddled by Italy's big brewers. Such is its allure that some Italian brewers are regulars on the collaboration brewing scene in the UK and the USA.

The movement strengthened in 1998 with the creation of Unionbirrai, a craft-brewing union designed to raise awareness that Italy is now home to some insanely inventive unpasteurized ale. (The Union also organizes the competition Birra dell'Anno, which is held annually in the glitzy surroundings of Rimini.) In the past 20 years, the likes of Teo Musso at Baladin and Agostino Arioli at Birrificio Italiano have taken the common perception of Italian beer to a different level. Other champions include Lambrate, Panil, BrewFist, and Birra del Borgo, although the list could go on and on. So potent is the appeal that AB-Inbev snapped up Birra del Borgo in 2016, a mere 11 years after the brewery had opened. The move upset a few of their craft peers, but it should enable the newly expanded brewery to get more brilliant beer out there. Fingers crossed.

But one of the most staggering elements of the beer reformation has been the move from vertical beer drinking at the bar to drinking while dining. This seems an unlikely victory up against a well-worn wine culture, but it has been a carefully considered approach by the brewers. While the rest of Europe has had to shoehorn the virtues of beer and food onto restaurant menus, with various mixtures of success and failure, the Italian consumers have seen the pairings slip on effortlessly, like a precious pair of soft and roomy Ferragamo shoes.

Unsurprisingly, the brewers have achieved this by considering aesthetics, wooing fashion-conscious consumers with stylish bottles and glassware to ensure beer is not the ugly duckling on a dinner table. But this isn't merely a beer-and-pizza or spaghetti-and-suds project, and by working in close association with Italy's Slow Food movement, the country's craft brewers have taken collaborations across a range of local boutique artisan producers. Brewers are not only mixing in with top chefs but are also bringing a new flavor direction to their beers, bunging unusual botanicals into the beer itself to deliver concepts in the glass that are as dynamic as those on the plate. It comes as no surprise to learn that one of the innovative new styles emerging from Italy is grape ale, where grapes or grape must is added during fermentation; the result is a ringing and chiming beer hybrid that makes the best of the grape and the grain.

It's a vibrant and unavoidable scene, and the swerve on flavor and passion is helping the global geek think beyond hops. This is helping inspire not only the Italians but also the rest of the world.

ALMOND '22
PESCARA, ABRUZZI
WWW.BIRRAALMOND.COM

 Torbata Barley Wine 8.5%

Chestnut honey, orange peel, and cane sugar join peated smoked malt to create a superb bottle-conditioned smoked ale from a microbrewery in the green hills of Pescara in the Abruzzi region. The brewery's name refers to the year, 1922, when a legion of elderly women worked in the same building as the brewery, peeling almonds to produce the world-famous confetti of Sulmona.

AMARCORD
RIMINI, EMILIA-ROMAGNA
WWW.BIRRAAMARCORD.IT

Tabachéra Belgian Strong Ale 9%

Rimini-based brewery whose branding has the kind of style and eloquence you'd associate with the city's favorite son, Fellini. This is a powerful Belgian-style ale that veers toward the malty and caramelly side of things, while the finish is dry and bittersweet.

BABB
MANERBIO, LOMBARDIA
WWW.BABB.IT

Omnia Pilsner 5.5%

Funky, forward-thinking microbrewery and brewpub-cum-restaurant near Brescia that warms up its sparse and stark interior with minimalist art, a gleaming brewery that looks as if it's been built in 2099, and a range of unusual yet first-rate beers boasting both style and substance. A Bohemia-leaning pilsner, this golden sipper leads with brown bready notes and a spiky, sharp hop finish.

BALADIN
see Brewery Profile pages 134 to 135
PIOZZO, PIEDMONT
WWW.BALADIN.IT

POP Pale Ale 5%

There are four different multicolored designs for the contemporary cans that hold this lively and likable pale ale. Whatever can you get, you can be sure that the luscious liquid inside has a spicy, citrusy character before finishing dry and bittersweet.

⭐ Super Baladin
Strong Belgian Ale 8%

Super indeed. Widely regarded as the jewel in Baladin's multi-festooned crown. Influenced by Belgian monastic beers and akin to a tripel, it veers off-piste with the inclusion of English yeast and is fermented a second time in the bottle. Richly perfumed with touches of tropical fruit esters, the palate is dry and long and warmed up with a rum-like alcohol.

DEL BORGO
BORGOROSE, LAZIO
WWW.BIRRADELBORGO.IT

⭐ **Ke To Reporter** Porter 5.2%

In May 2005, former college brewer and biochemist Leonardo di Vincenzo set up del Borgo in Lazio to the northwest of Rome. His brewing approach is shaped primarily by the brewing traditions of England and Belgium, and he places unusual ingredients and food compatibility at the forefront of much of what he does. This remarkable elixir is a smoky porter infused with tobacco. Acquired by Ab InBev in 2016.

My Antonia Imperial Pils 7.5%

This exceptionally creative brewery north of Rome has collaborated with several US breweries including Dogfish Head, with whom it created My Antonia. Golden in color and brisk beneath a white head of foam, this has grass, citrus, and plenty of hop character before its dry finish.

BREWFIST
CODOGNO, LODI
NEW.BREWFIST.COM

Spaceman IPA 7%

BrewFist began brewing in 2010 and looks to the USA for inspiration. Spaceman is a raucous IPA with tropical fruit aromas, while the palate features tropical fruit notes and a furnace blast of hoppiness balanced by a malt sweetness before a bitter finish.

Spaghetti Western Imperial Stout 8.7%

For this potent imperial stout, BrewFist went to Oklahoma to work with Prairie Artisan Ales. The result is richly flavored beer, with the addition of coffee and cocoa nibs adding depth and extra complexity. Potent, yes, though the smooth mouth-feel makes it dangerously drinkable.

CR/AK
CAMPODARSEGO, VENETO
WWW.CRAKBREWERY.COM

Guerrilla IPA 5.8%

2015 saw the arrival of this brewery, and a year later Guerrilla had taken first place in the IPA category at the presitigious Birra dell'Anno in Rimini. It's a well-integrated beer with plenty of tropical fruit contrasting well against the sweet, cookie maltiness, and dry finish.

CROCE DI MALTO
TRECATE, PIEDMONT
WWW.CROCEDIMALTO.IT

Temporis Saison 6.8%

Spring is the time when this intensely golden beer appears, a harbinger of warmer weather to come. It's a saison and an award-winner at the World Beer Cup in 2014 (as well as elsewhere). An elegant and tangy quaff with citrus and spice on the nose and palate, finishing dry. A refreshing sip.

DADA
CORREGGIO, EMILIA-ROMAGNA
WWW.BIRRIFICIODADA.IT

Knock Out IPA 6.1%

Originally entitled Ghost Batch #2 on its first release in 2012, this then became Knock Out and is a fine example of an IPA in which American hops provide citrus, pine, and tropical fruit character alongside a bracing cookie malt backbone.

DOPPIO MALTO
ERBA, LOMBARDY
WWW.DOPPIOMALTO.IT

Oak Pils Pilsner 4.8%

Golden yellow in color, this Czech-style pilsner has an elegant bready and grassy nose, while on the palate it is fine and subtle, before finishing with a bracing bout of bitterness. Worth seeking.

DEL DUCATO
SORAGNA, PALMA
WWW.BIRRIFICIODELDUCATO.IT

New Morning
(Nuova Mattina in the USA)
Saison 5.8%

Hazy golden orange in color, this saison is peppery, flinty, fruity (as in hard candies), tart, and dry in the finish, while there's almost a hint of vermouth midpalate. It's a sign of how global beer has become that such a lynchpin of Wallonian brewing can be attempted in northern Italy and come out smiling.

VIÆMILIA Pilsner 5%

Giovanni Campari founded del Ducato in 2007 in Verdi's home village of La Roncole, and one of his first beers was this elegant and floral pilsner, which is also the brewery's bestseller. Crisp and aromatic.

EXTRAOMNES
MARNATE, LOMBARDY
WWW.EXTRAOMNES.COM

Zest Belgian Ale 5.3%

Based in a small town not far from Milan, Extraomnes looks to Belgian brewing traditions for its beers, such as this spicy and hoppy take on Belgian ale. A delicate orange in color, it's spicy, citrusy, bittersweet, and herbal, before finishing dry.

BALADIN

PIAZZA 5 LUGLIO, 12060 PIOZZO, PIEDMONT

WWW.BALADIN.IT

Teo Musso (along with Birrificio Italiano's Agostino Arioli) is a pioneer of the Italian craft beer scene, having founded his brewery in 1996, ten years after opening a Belgian beer bar of the same name in his home village of Piozzo, south of Turin. He is regarded as something of a rock star brewer and is an eloquent advocate of his eclectic and intriguing beers.

Among his beers are several made with specialty grains, spices, chocolate, coffee beans, even myrrh, while top-fermenting yeast is joined by strains more usually found in whiskey or wine.

They are also complex and packaged in elegant wine-like bottles, and, most important, they taste pretty fine. Xyauyù was (and remains) the star, a dark potent ale that spends 18 months sitting

outside in a container in the brewery courtyard. Viscous and limpid in the glass, it is warming and sherry-like.

Eight years on from its inception, the contents of a glass of the same beer have now spent time in wood for five years. This deep slumber had given it a port-like character with notes of chocolate, golden raisin, and toffee alongside a creamy and smooth mouthfeel.

A lot has changed for Baladin and Musso. Now there are Baladin bars in Italy and elsewhere in the world, and his beers are recognized as some of the best in Europe. However, perhaps the biggest change is the opening of an impressive new brewery in 17 acres of grounds off the main road below the village.

There is a flamboyant air about Musso rarely seen in other brewers. As he leads a group of visitors around the light and airy brewhouse, the space seems to be an extension of his personality. The olive green walls are painted with bold words declaring the function of each section (fermentation here, mashing there). The gantry above the brewing area has samples of hops, malts, and spices dotted about, and, finally, before descending to see a collection of newly made oak wooden barrels, we watch a short movie that features a young Musso (played by a child actor) sitting in a field of barley, and then the adult Musso (played by the brewer) appears sitting beneath a tree in the middle of the same barley field. The message is about provenance, though some might think it a vain step too far.

However, all this showmanship would be useless without exceptional beers, and Musso rarely fails to deliver. Unlike other Italian new-wave breweries, he has avoided going down the IPA route, black, imperial, or otherwise—and so the stars of his beery firmament include the dry and chewy Belgian-style ale Super and Rock'n'Roll, a bittersweet pale ale with pepper in the mix. However, a concession to the hop craziness affecting craft beer is the pale ale POP, which is packaged in six different garishly colored cans. This is a dry hopped pale ale with rich malt, spicy Saaz character, and a dry finish.

The Italian spirit of adventure and inspiration that drove the likes of Marco Polo and da Vinci is very much alive in Teo Musso.

> "Every week I think in my head of a new beer, and every two months I try and brew one," he said in 2008. "A new taste is like a new way of communicating with people. My beers try to communicate new flavors and aromas to people. I never get bored with brewing. I am like a volcano spewing out new ideas. I could never be a wine producer because there I could only expect to be creative once a year, while in beer you can be creative all the time."

He hasn't changed that much.

* KEY BEERS

Isaac Witbier 5%
POP Pale Ale 5%
Rock'n'Roll Pale Ale 7.5%
Super Baladin Strong Belgian Ale 8%
Xyauyù Barley Wine 14%

Opposite: Teo Musso with cans of his pale ale POP, which is packaged in half-a-dozen different colors.

FORST
FORST, SOUTH TYROL
WWW.FORST.IT

 **Sixtus** Bock 6.5%

Venerable brewery that was founded in the nineteenth century and is based in an area close to the Austrian border, hence its lager traditions. This beautiful-looking bock is dark chestnut in color and palpitates with chocolate, roasted grains, sweetness, mocha, and a succulent nuttiness.

GRADO PLATO
CHIERI, PIEDMONT
WWW.GRADOPLATO.IT

Chocarrubica Oatmeal Stout 7%

This is a voluptuous, big-boned, black beer filled out with an enormous amount of oats in the grist. The addition of Venezuelan cocoa beans sourced through Sicily gives the beer its silky and chocolaty character.

ITALIANO
LURAGO MARINONE, LOMBARDY
WWW.BIRRIFICIO.IT

Bibock Heller Bock 6.2%

Amber-orange in color and blessed with a gorgeous head of foam, this is creamy, fruity, hoppy, and finishes dry and bitter. It's a big-hearted bittersweet "heller bock" that is just as good at the bar or on the table with a risotto.

Tipopils Pilsner 5.2%

If you like your pilsners with a hardened hop character, then you'll no doubt lap up this wonderfully bitter and dry, bottom-fermented beauty. An exquisitely constructed interpretation of traditional pilsner, this delicate and refreshing drop rekindles one's faith in a much mistreated and maligned beer style.

Vùdù Dunkelweizen 5.5%

Chestnut-brown in color with crimson tints on the edge, this is a robust and delicious take on a Bavarian classic, with bananas, roast malt, sweet cookie, and ripe fruit making their presences known on both nose and the palate, while the finish is bready with a subtle sweetness to it.

LAMBRATE
MILAN, LOMBARDY
WWW.BIRRIFICIOLAMBRATE.COM

Ghisa Smoked Stout 5%

Milan's most eminent brewpub was founded in 1996 in a railroad station, and is home to eight excellent ales, of which this jet-black beer, dry like an Irish stout with the smokiness of a gentle German rauchbier, is the most intriguing. Fabulous with smoked cheese and fish—not at the same time, though.

LOVERBEER
TURIN
WWW.LOVERBEER.COM

BeerBera Wine-Beer 8%

Given Italy's reputation as a wine country, it makes sense to marry the juice of the grain with that of the grape. With BeerBera, freshly pressed Barbera grape juice along with the skins is added during fermentation before maturation in oak vats. The result is a complex and refreshingly sour beer with hints of wine on the palate.

Madamin Sour Beer 5.7%

Once this beer is brewed, off it goes to spend time in oak vats, where it ages elegantly and gracefully to produce an Italian craft riff on Flemish red ales. It's tart and fruity (as in cherries), and there's a balsamic note before its light sour finish.

MONTEGIOCO
MONTEGIOCO, PIEDMONT
WWW.BIRRIFICIOMONTEGIOCO.COM

★ ⬛ ⬛ ⬛ Dolii Raptor
Strong Barrel-Aged Beer 8.5%

This dark ale is aged in Barbera wine barrels for more than half a year and given added gusto with the addition of wine yeast. Dark amber in color, its nose gives off dried plums, apricot, and sweet hazelnut.

★ ⬛ ⬛ Montegioco Draco
Barley Wine 11%

The sensational malt-accented beers of Montegioco are all packaged attractively in tissue paper à la Liefmans in Belgium. Draco is the brewery's particularly potent barley wine, brewed with fresh blueberries, a variety of barley and wheat malt, and fermented not once, not twice, but thrice. Aromas of honey, toffee, and fall fruit, with a peppery hop bitter finish, all contribute to this stunning brew. The blueberry influence is restrained.

L'OLMAIA
MONTEPULCIANO, TUSCANY
WWW.BIRRIFICIOOLMAIA.COM

⬛ ⬛ La 5 Golden Ale 5.5%

Named after a farmhouse where brewing began in 2004, this lively little micro is now close to Montepulciano, where it produces a series of beautiful beers. La 5 is its bestseller, a straw-colored quaffer with a good bitter finish.

OPPERBACCO
NOTARESCO, ABRUZZA
WWW.OPPERBACCO.IT

⬛ ⬛ Triplipa Belgian-Style Tripel 7.8%

Here's a conundrum: is this lustrously gold beer an IPA or a hoppy tripel? There's citrus on the nose and palate, which belongs to the school of IPAs, but there's also a honeyed sweetness and spiciness that point to Belgium. Whatever the answer (and let's root for a hoppy tripel), this is a sensual beast of a sipper and one of Italy's finest new-wave interpretations of a classic Belgian beer style.

PANIL
TORRECHIARA-PARMA, EMILIA-ROMAGNA
WWW.PANILBEER.IT

⬛ ⬛ ⬛ Barriquée
Sour Red Ale 8%

A marvelous microbrewery in Provincia di Parma— "the larder of Italy" and home to some of the finest food and drink in the world. Son of a winemaker and biology buff, Renzo Lossi began brewing at his father's winery in 2000, and much of what he does with beer is garnered from grape-based techniques, such as wood-barrel-aging and the use of sparkling wine yeast. Barriquée is delicious, sherry-like, and aged in oak for a period of more than 16 weeks.

★ ⬛ ⬛ Panil Enhanced
Strong Belgian Ale 9%

A lovely light blond liquid with an enlivening effervescence and dry fruity esters, courtesy of the "spumante" wine yeast. Smoke on the nose, burned marshmallow malty in the mouth, and earthy, grassy bitterness brought to the finish by English whole hop flowers. Truly delicate and finely balanced, worth seeking when in Italy.

PONTINO
LATINA, LAZIO
WWW.BIRRIFICIOPONTINO.COM

⬛ ⬛ Runner Ale Pale Ale 4.8%

Founded in 2012 and at that time brewing in a garage, this is a masterful micro with a passion for creating all manner of beers. Runner is the American-style pale ale, the beer with which Pontino announced itself to the world. A fresh and tantalizingly tangy drop of joy.

REVELATION CAT
ROME
NO WEB ADDRESS

⬛ ⬛ ⬛ Black Knight Imperial Stout 14%

Here's a monster of a dark beer, pulsating like a star deep out in space, ready to explode on the tongue with chocolate, tobacco, dark fruit, and smoke, along with a dry and virtuous finish. Starting off as a gypsy brewery, Revelation Cat is now based in Rome and is yet another reason to visit the Eternal City.

Above:-The Nogne Ø Brewery in Norway is a trailblazer for Norwegian craft beers.
*Below:*At the brewhouse of Nogne Ø you can almost smell the wood-aging within.

INTRODUCTION
SCANDINAVIA

Here is a region that endures or enjoys (depending on your affection for sunlight) cold and dark winters. Such conditions demand the periodic dipping into a drinking den, since, if nothing else, a decent beer helps pass the time. Perhaps consequently, the natives display a deft devotion to brewing.

Note all the d's in that last sentence, so let's start with Denmark. Probably the best-known Danish brewery in the world is Carlsberg, but beyond its vast commercial reach the company has made a worthy contribution to brewing heritage. Here in 1883 lab-coated Emil Hansen cultivated *Saccharomyces pastorianus*, one of the first "pure" bottom-fermenting yeasts, and thus industrial brewing was born. Scientists from the Carlsberg labs also invented the pH scale, the concept of protein structures, and the characterization of enzymes for good measure, so you might argue that a brewery is responsible for the scientific marvels that have changed the world. Certainly we would.

That said, Carlsberg's success, along with that of Tuborg, did mean that from the early twentieth century to 2002, pale lagers were the Danes' predominant pint. Then, from 2002 to 2008, the country went from 19 breweries to more than 100 as the natives found a little extra cash in their pockets and started searching for more artisanal and luxurious food and drink experiences. Craft beer arrived, and the kids that kick-started it earned instant superstar status first at home, then garnering international acclaim.

Mikkeller deserves the first nod, and while the great Dane might not revel in the same level of adulation as Carlsberg, he's getting there. In 2006, Mikkel Borg Bjergsø, then a teacher, stopped grading homework and established his brand without even owning a brewery. After popularizing the term "gypsy brewer," he proceeded to brew award-winning creations and collaborations around the world.

His success inspired the launch of another gypsy operation, Evil Twin, led by his twin brother Jeppe Jarnit-Bjergsø. Then came two of his school pals, who opened

the outstanding To Øl. The list is growing, with Amager, Ugly Duck brewery, and Hornbeer, to name three more, also featured in this chapter.

All are dovetailing with an intrepid Danish dining scene, and obsessive Michelin-starred chefs who have foraged for indigenous ingredients are influencing brewers, with bog myrtle, juniper, and local berries now making it into beers.

Scandinavia's success reaches further, though, and Sweden is equally impressive in its embrace of beer with flavor. Its laws on beers above 3.5% ABV restrict advertising and confine retail to the state-owned Systembolaget liquor stores, but innovative brewers are turning heads with lower ABV beer. Nils Oscar's Imperial Stout at 7% ABV doesn't fit this mold, nor does Jämtlands Heaven schwarzbier, but both are examples of beer that have the geeks squawking with pleasure.

In Norway there might be one or two who can remember the inhumane prohibition that took place between 1919 and 1926, but they can at least enjoy the winter of their years with a choice of tasty beer. Again, 2002 was a watershed here; the brewery Nøgne Ø opened and was responsible for stemming the tide of tiresome pale lagers, and in the decade that followed nearly 70 new breweries popped up.

Even in countries that consider themselves less Scandinavian, we see shoots of creativity. Iceland, where it was illegal to sell beer over 2.25% ABV until 1989, has produced players such as the excellent Ölvisholt. While in Finland (yet another country from this region that endured prohibition) there is acclaim for the darker beers, not least Plevan's Siperia Imperial stout.

While the region might suffer more than its fair share of winter darkness, the brewers can see the light.

DENMARK

ABELGREN & RAMVAD
RISTINGE, LANGELAND, SYDDANMARK
WWW.ARBREW.DK

No. 7 Imperial Rye Stout 9.5%
The island of Langeland is home to this small brewery, which is keen on experimenting with different ingredients. Each brew is numbered and does change. This is a midnight-black potent sipper with a creamy mouthfeel and chocolate, coffee, malt softness, and a light roastiness making appearances in the brew.

ALEFARM
KØGE, SJÆLLAND
WWW.FACEBOOK.COM/ALEFARMBREWING

Funk Orchard Saison 7%
Yes, as the name says, this brewery is based on a farm, and it also specializes in both farmhouse-style beers and the kind of sours that deliver a pucker-shock to the mouth. This is a juicy, tart, fruity, and funky saison that is dry hopped with Citra.

AMAGER
KASTRUP, SJÆLLAND
WWW.AMAGERBRYGHUS.DK

The Amager Bryghus has been instrumental in transforming Denmark's brewing landscape. Having caught the brewing bug in the early 1990s as part of a college project, the Amager team vowed to create their own brewery. Life, however, got in the way, and it wasn't until 2002 that the dream was rudimentarily realized in the shape of a homemade hand-brewing plant in a cellar. Unfettered experimentation followed, and, in 2005, Amager found itself on the podium at the Danish Homebrewing Championships. Inspired by drinkers' delight, a foray into full-time brewing was made. Inspired by the US craft beer scene, Amager is now a byword for adventurous, big, bombastic yet balanced beers that take no prisoners.

Bandini, Wait Until Spring Saison 6%
Single-hopped seasonal saison (Mosaic hops), which is yellow gold in the glass and has delicate wafts of grapefruit, melon, and freshly cut grass on the nose. It's a juicy-tasting saison with plenty of citrus, a frisky sense of carbonation, and a dry finish.

Imperial Stout 10%
Warning. This is not a drill. Unless you are a seasoned extreme beer enthusiast with an unhealthy infatuation for IBUs and blisteringly radioactive roasted bitterness, put this beer down and step away.

Rugporter Porter 8.5%
Just to be absolutely clear, this is not a porter with carpet fibers in it. Rug in Danish means rye, so this pitch-black beer has an underlying spiciness and an appetizing hint of acidity that combines with coffee and chocolate notes before its bittersweet and dry finish.

BEER HERE
TEJN, HOVEDSTADEN
WWW.BEERHERE.DK

Glupulus Pale Ale 4.7%
Founded in 2008, Beer Here is based on the island of Bornholm, which sits in the Baltic Sea, possibly the easternmost part of Denmark. However, the islanders can take heart in the excellent beers of Beer Here, especially this refreshing American-style pale ale with its tropical fruit and citrus character able to light up most days.

BØGEDAL
VEJLE, SYDDANMARK
WWW.BOEGEDAL.COM

Bøgedal No Various %
Brewer Casper Vorting, who makes some of the most expensive beers in Denmark, oversees Scandinavia's sole all-gravity brewhouse and is renowned for championing "Goodbeer," Denmark's rather aptly named traditional beer style. All Casper's beers are brewed to the same formula, but the vagaries of the process mean that no two beers are the same and are distinguished using a numbering system that renders tasting notes obsolete. If you see it, make sure you drink it—that's all you need to know.

BRUS
COPENHAGEN, HOVESTADEN
WWW.TAPPERIETBRUS.DK

Saving Private Sammy Black IPA 7.5%

A former iron foundry is home to this lively little brewpub, which is a collaboration between TO Øl and Mikropolis bar. The modernist bar is the place to sample the brews, especially this big lad of a black IPA with its cavalcade of slight roastiness, earthy hop, fruit, and long dry finish.

DJÆVLEBRYG
COPENHAGEN, HOVEDSTADEN
WWW.DJAEVLEBRYG.DK

Son of Nekron Porter 6.5 %

The "Devil's Brewery" began in 2002 as a hobby, but after gaining plaudits among the discerning Danish homebrew crowd, the Devil went to work professionally in 2006. Anything but sweetness and light, Djævlebryg's drops are lords of darkness, bitterness, and smoke. Peaty porter brewed with peat-smoked malt, roasted malts, and dark brown sugar, and swathed in chocolate, coffee, and chipotle.

DRY AND BITTER
GØRLØSE, HOVEDSTADEN
WWW.DRYBITTER.COM

Christian Bale Ale Session IPA 4.6%

Given some of the Hollywood actor's meaty roles, you'd think that a beer named after him would be big and bombastic, but this slightly hazy session IPA has a gentler kind of role in mind, with a citrus fruitiness lacing its way through both aroma and taste before the dry and bitter finish.

EBELTOFT
EBELTOFT, MIDTJYLLAND
WWW.EBELTOFTGAARDBRYGGERI.DK

Le Sacre Bière de Garde 6.7%

It's a long way from the old port town of Ebeltoft on Denmark's east coast to the spiritual home of bière de garde in northern France, but Le Sacre demonstrates that distance is no object when making good beer. Yellow-gold in color, this is fruity, slightly tart, and blessed with a bittersweet finish.

FANØ
NORDBY, SYDDANMARK
WWW.FANOEBRYGHUS.DK

Vestkyst Pale Ale 5.7%

Highly rated small brewery that initially opened in 2006 only to close a couple of years later, but since reopening in 2009 its reputation has grown, especially as it has brewed beers for Evil Twin and Mikkeller. This is a fruity and bittersweet American-style IPA with a light and bitter finish. Tasty.

FERMENTOREN
COPENHAGEN, HOVEDSTADEN
WWW.FERMENTOREN.COM

Yippie IPA 6.3%

Fermentoren is a series of craft beer bars dotted through Denmark, and as well as having an excellent choice of beers, they also have beers brewed for them under their name. This is a fresh and flowery IPA, which is brewed under license at Ølkollektivet.

GYPSY INC
COPENHAGEN, HOVEDSTADEN
WWW.GYPSYINC.DK

Tipsy Gypsy Pilsner 4.7%

You don't need a degree to work out that Gypsy Inc is one of those breweries that gets its beer brewed elsewhere, in this case De Proefbrouwerij. This is a delightful German-style pils with American hops giving vibrant color and flavor alongside a dry finish.

HANCOCK
SKIVE, MIDTJYLLAND
WWW.HANCOCK.DK

Old Gambrinus Dark Doppelbock 9.5%

A small, independent brewery that is enamored of Bohemia's bottom-fermented beers and specializes in lovely lagers. Hancock's beers are brewed at low gravity with long lagering times (between seven weeks and a year) at extremely low temperatures, and showcase the Saaz hop in style. A rich, dark, and plum-like doppelbock brewed with lager malt.

HERSLEV
HERSLEV, SJÆLLAND
WWW.HERSLEVBRYGHUS.DK

Herslev Pilsner 5.5%

Family-owned farmhouse brewery situated in the small village of Herslev, near Roskilde, and founded in 2004. Malt and hops from Bavaria give a distinctively Germanic flavor to this crisp, bitter pilsner. All the full malt and bitter hops you'd hope for.

HORNBEER
HYLLINGE, SJÆLLAND
WWW.HORNBEER.DK

The Fundamental Blackthorn Imperial Stout 10%

It's difficult to decide what is more impressive: Jørgen Fogh Rasmussen's huge range of incredibly innovative ales or the wonderful labels, designed by his artist wife, Gunhild, that adorn them. Either way, having burst onto the burgeoning Danish brewing scene in 2008, Hornbeer is well worth checking out. This midnight-black imperial stout has honey and walnuts added to it, making for a wonderfully complex beer pulsating with licorice, coffee, and plenty of honey notes.

Top Hop IPA 4.7%

This is more of a session IPA than a full-blown monster coming from the West Coast, though the addition of American hop varieties Centennial, Simcoe, Cascade, and Amarillo creates plenty of citrus, tropical fruit, and pine-like notes, which work well alongside a caramel sweetness.

HOWLING MONKEY
ODENSE, SYDDANMARK
WWW.HOWLINGMONKEY.DK

Nationen! Pale Ale 4.6%

We all need the odd howling monkey in our life, especially when it comes in the shape of this medium-bodied, fetchingly fruity, and dinkily dry American-style pale ale, whose production is outsourced to the Ølkollektivet brewery.

JACOBSEN
COPENHAGEN, HOVEDSTADEN
WWW.JACOBSENBRYG.DK

Abbey Ale Dubbel 7.3%

Carlsberg has a microbrewery onsite in Copenhagen and it brews some mighty fine beers, such as this take on the classic Belgian beer style. Roast malt, dried fruit, and a delicate caramel sweetness all mingle like guests at a party before a striking dry finish.

KRAGELUND
SILKEBORG, MIDTJYLLAND
WWW.BRYGHUSETKRAGELUND.DK

Kragelund Natmand Havre Stout 6%

A black, flint-dry, all-grain stout that is unashamed in its deep, dark malt signature. Mouth-filling oats and chocolate malt make for a "thinking man's" milkshake.

DET LILLE BRYGGERI
BRINGSTRUP, SJÆLLAND
WWW.DETLILLEBRYGGERI.DK

Columbus Ale IPA 7.8%
Founded in 2005 and in its current home since 2009, this Lilliputian brewery has a salivating selection of boldly flavored beers, including this potent IPA, into which a lot of Columbus hops are stuffed. The result? Like putting your nose in a big bag of hops and staying there. An enjoyable experience.

MIKKELLER
see Brewery Profile pages 144 to 145
COPENHAGEN, HOVEDSTADEN   WWW.MIKKELLER.DK

Beer Geek Breakfast Brunch Weasel
Imperial Stout 10.9%
Plenty of coffee brewed with weasel droppings (yep), ratcheted up to make a powerful imperial stout.

Hallo Ich Bin Berliner Weisse 3.7%
Mikkeller's take on the classic beer of Berlin is a tart and sweetly sour sip with brisk carbonation and a great sense of its own refreshment.

Simcoe Single Hop IPA 7.3%
As the name suggests, Simcoe is the sole hop used here, producing fruity and piney aromatics, which blend in well with the caramel sweetness. The finish brings forth more fruitiness in one of Mikkeller's many and popular beers.

NØRREBRO BRYGHUS
COPENHAGEN, HOVEDSTADEN
WWW.NOERREBROBRYGHUS.DK

Böhmer Pilsner 5.2%
A beautifully balanced beer, created in the Bohemian mold, from a brilliant Copenhagen brewpub founded in 2003. Brewer Anders Kissmeyer is widely recognized for the quality and quirkiness of his beer.

North Bridge Extreme Imperial India Pale Ale 9.5%
Hugely hoppy American-style IPA with a nose-bleeding IBU count. Best drunk after you've tried everything else. It'll knock out your taste buds, so they won't be getting up anytime soon.

Old Odense Ale Sour Ale 7.5%
Brewed in conjunction with Sam Calagione of the Dogfish Head Brewery in Delaware. Seasoned with milfoil, star anise, short lip, and woodruff, it has a tartness that will tilt your head sideways.

Pacific Summer Ale

Pacific Summer Ale Pale Ale 5.6%
Brewed in association with Brooklyn Brewery's Garrett Oliver, this pale ale showcases aromatic North American hops in style. Crisp, spicy, and fairly bitter, with a long-lasting finish of pine needles.

Skargaards Porter 6%
A proper porter brewed in association with Nynäshamns brewery. Smooth and elegant, with a palate of chocolate and creamy coffee.

ØLSNEDKEREN
COPENHAGEN, HOVEDSTADEN
WWW.OLSNEDKEREN.DK

Amerikaner Stout 5.6%
Smart and modernistic brewpub, which has been making its own beers since 2012. This is its self-titled American-style stout, where—invariably—hops lead the way alongside the dry roastiness of the stout. Brewed with yeast that originates from Edinburgh, this stout is boldly flavored with a memorably dry finish.

MIKKELLER

VESTERBROGADE 20 1 TH, COPENHAGEN, HOVEDSTADEN

WWW.MIKKELLER.DK

When Mikkeller started making beers, you could argue that it was only when an Indonesian weasel called a luwak entered the scene that people really woke up and smelled the coffee, so to speak.

Otherwise known as a civet or a musang, the luwak is a small, wild, nocturnal mammal much like a mongoose. Thanks to a noxious odor excreted from its scent glands, situated near its anus, and bearing an uncanny resemblance to testes, many people associate it closely with the skunk species on stinkiness alone. Expert climbers, which spend their lives in trees, these animals eat small vertebrates, insects, ripe fruits, seeds, and palm sap, but a fondness for coffee berries is responsible for luwaks making a rare cameo appearance in a book on beer.

While the outer fruit of the berries is digested, the coffee beans are passed through the luwak's digestive tract untouched and excreted as part of the animal's droppings. The caffeine-carrying excrement is then collected by farmers before the resulting cleaned green beans are roasted, sold for a lot of loot, and—this is the crucial bit—used to brew one of the world's strangest and yet most sought beers.

Danish brewer Mikkel Borg Bjergsø, the man behind the marvelously idiosyncratic Mikkeller beers, used 15 pounds of Kopi Luwak coffee beans in every 880 gallons of an awe-inspiring imperial oatmeal stout called Beer Geek Breakfast (Weasel). He brewed the coffee in pots and poured it into the beer the day before it was bottled; the resulting beer wasn't cheap, but it became a sensation and put Mikkeller on the world beer map.

Since then, this gypsy brewer has become a symbol of maverick brewing, showing that he is unafraid to experiment with unusual ingredients such as gooseberries, Merlot grapes, hemp, poppies, and nettles to create outrageous, out-there beers. Hops are also on his radar as well.

He was one of the first not to have his own brewery and is otherwise known as a gypsy brewer. A former homebrewer, , Mikkel chose to trot the globe like a hedonistic hobo, collaborating with the cream of craft brewing and borrowing their brains and equipment to create his unique beers.

"What I find is that I can make a range of different styles by going to the breweries that have a strength in that style," he says. "I rent the equipment and have a good relationship with the whole of the brewing community. I don't have to brew beer that sells well. I just brew beer that I like, as there's very little financial risk. I can think of flavor rather than customers. It's a huge freedom."

Mikkeller's small-batch output has increased over the years. Collaborating with some of the world's greatest brewers has been key to its appeal, with classic names such as Cantillon, Jester King, BrewDog, Stone, and AleSmith getting involved. As well as these collaborations, there has been a flood of different beers. For instance, in 2013 it was estimated that more than 120 different beers were being produced, many instantly snapped up by Mikkeller's legion of fans.

And the beers? Inspired by the eclectic approach of American breweries, Mikkeller runs a huge gamut of styles, including Californian-style Belgian tripels, chile-infused imperial stouts, Lambics, beers aged in Calvados barrels, smoked ales, and single-hop IPAs. His beers are now sent all over the world, and he is consistently rated as one of the best brewers globally. If that's not enough, there are Mikkeller bars in places as diverse as Copenhagen, San Francisco, and Stockholm, to name but a few. That weasel has a lot to answer for.

Above: Mikkel tastes one of his brews at the Norrrebro brewhouse in Copenhagen, where some of his beers are prepared.

Left: Mikkeller's beers are audacious, award-winning adventures in brewing.

* KEY BEERS

Please note not all Mikkeller beers are always regularly available.

American Dream Lager 4.5%
Beer Geek Breakfast Espresso Stout 7.5%
Black Imperial Stout 15.7%
Monk's Brew Quadrupel Belgian Ale 10%
Spontanmango Sour 7.7%
Stateside IPA 7%

ØRBÆK
ØRBÆK, SOUTHERN DENMARK
WWW.OERBAEK-BRYGGERI.NU

Ørbæk's Porter 7%

Lovely old brewery that was founded in 1906 and went through a series of owners until bought and renovated by the current owners in 1996. All the beers are organically produced, including this rich, chocolaty, and creamy porter.

RANDERS
RANDERS, MIDTJYLLAND
WWW.RANDERSBRYGHUS.DK

Cascade IPA 5.5%

Small brewery that was founded in 2008 but merged with Raasted Brewery in 2012. (Raasted's beers are also produced here.) This IPA is hopped with a lot of Cascade, which gives it plenty of grapefruit and pine on the nose, while the hop character merges superbly with a grainy, bittersweetness on the palate.

SKAGEN
SKAGEN, NORDJYLLAND
WWW.SKAGENBRYGHUS.DK

Skagen Vaeltepeter Doppelbock 7.5%

A sweet, creamy, and strong malty doppelbock with a touch of smoke and tar that's reminiscient of the whiff of fishermen's nets in Skagen Harbor. This dark brown doppelbock is better than chewing tobacco or a pinch of snuff, with its aroma of malt syrups and roast chestnuts, a sweet, medium-long body, and a long-lasting moderate to light bitter finish.

SKANDS
BRØNDBY, HOVEDSTADEN
WWW.BRYGGERIET-SKANDS.DK

Bla Chimpanse Belgian Ale 6.5%

A boutique brewery from Brøndby that has kept things small-scale and manageable. This Belgian-style beer has a malt sweetness and a funky, fruity aroma, with a low hop bitterness, allowing sweetness and dried fruit to shine.

Elmegade IPA 6.2%

A softly spoken and subtle American-style IPA with Maris Otter malt hopped with Northern Brewer and Cascade. Unfiltered and unpasteurized.

SKOVLYST
VÆRLØSE, HOVESTADEN
WWW.BRYGGERISKOVLYST.DK

Skovlyst Skovm Aerkebryg Spice Ale 5%

Set in the heart of the woodlands of Hareskoven, this bucolic brewery is distinguished from others by the way it sources many of its ingredients from the neighboring forest—whether herbs, spices, or plants. Only lightly filtered, this delicate, spicy ale features natural forest honey and Hareskoven's hand-picked woodruff flowers.

STEVNS
HÅRLEV, SJÆLLAND
WWW.STEVNSBRYGHUS.DK

Klintekongens Stout 7.5%

A full-bodied, very fruity, and smoky stout from a prolific micro that's on a mission to return craft beer to the head of the Danish dining table. Hopped with Northern Brewer and Centennial and boosted on the palate with barley and oats.

SVANEKE
SVANEKE, HOVEDSTADEN
WWW.AMAGERBRYGHUS.DK

Mørk Guld Dunkel 5.7%

Lively brewery on the eastern side of Bornholm Island, which began making its beers in 2000. This is its take on a German dunkel. Malt and caramel lead the way on the nose, while caramel, nuts, and dried fruit are present and correct on the palate. Bittersweet finish.

THISTED
THISTED, NORDJYLLAND
WWW.THISTED-BRYGHUS.DK

Limfjords Porter 7.9%
Thisted has brewed beer in the eponymous town since 1902, but it's only since it started making organic beers in 1995 that those beyond a regional radius of the brewery have been able to access its excellent ales. Baltic porter, known locally as the "gentleman of beers," was introduced in 1989 after seven years of experimentation. Smoked malt and licorice make an upstanding pillar of a porter.

TO ØL
COPENHAGEN, HOVEDSTADEN
WWW.TO-OL.DK

Goliat Imperial Coffee Stout 10.1%
Tobias Emil Jensen and Tore Gynther are the two guys behind this well-regarded gypsy brewery, a duo whose imaginations and passion for beer come up with all manner of creations, many of which can be found at their stylish bar in Copenhagen. (They also share a bar with Mikkeller in the Danish capital, as well as in Reykjavik.) This is their gigantic-tasting imperial stout, which also has coffee in the mix. It's not for the fainthearted.

Liquid Confidential Imperial Stout 12.3%
Hold onto your hats when approaching this beast of a beer. It is a stout that also has ancho, guajillo, and smoked chipotle chiles added, all of which take your palate on the kind of adventure that only used to happen to explorers in search of lost cities. Other versions are aged in wine and Cognac barrels.

Sur Amarillo Sour Ale 7.5%
Even if this beer was just dry-hopped with the Amarillo variety, it would make for an intriguing liquid lushness, but to make things a bit more interesting To Øl sours things up, all of which makes for a tart, quenching, slightly sour, fruity, and refreshing beer that will perform cartwheels of joy in your mouth.

UGLY DUCK BREWING
FUNEN, SOUTH DENMARK
WWW.UGLYDUCKBREWING.DK

Imperial Vanilla Coffee Porter 9.5%
Ugly Duck is part of the venerable Indslev brewery, a kind of experimental play pit if you like. For this pitch-black beer, 22-plus gallons of Costa Rican coffee go into each brew. The result is a dense, smooth, and full-bodied dessert of a beer, rampant with coffee, chocolate, and vanilla.

WARPIGS
COPENHAGEN, HOVEDSTADEN
WWW.WARPIGS.DK

Lazurite IPA 7.4%
Warpigs is a brewpub and a joint collaboration between Three Floyd and Mikkeller. The joint rocks with loud music, and aromatics of smoked BBQ float on the ether. For a beer? Try this hazy orange IPA with its mixture of pine and peaches on the nose and a rush of grapefruit, caramel, and more peaches on the palate. Serve with beef brisket.

WINTERCOAT
SABRO, MIDTJYLLAND
WWW.WINTERCOAT.DK

India Gold IPA 6.3%
Small, family-owned brewery based on a farm where bottle-conditioned English-style beers are produced. Unlike other breweries' IPA, WinterCoat turns its back on American hops and the result is a fruity, juicy, full-bodied beer with a bittersweet finish.

SWEDEN

BEERBLIOTEK
GÖTEBORG, VÄSTERGÖTLAND
WWW.BEERBLIOTEK.COM

 **Black IPA Cascade & Columbus** 6.9%
Lively young brewery based in central Göteborg, with a good track record of brewing modern classics. Cascade and Columbus hop varieties provide fresh fruit and pine, which works well with delicate roastiness and a bitter finish.

BREKERIET
LANDSKRONA, SKÅNE
WWW.BREKERIET.WORDPRESS.COM

Barrique Ambrée Sour Beer 6.5%
Spontaneous fermentation is the name of the brewing game for the Ek brothers, Fredrik, Christian, and André, who set up Brekeriet in 2012. Wild yeast and various bugs are encouraged, and fruit is often used to induce a secondary fermentation. Barrique Ambrée is a beer that's tart, funky, delicately fruity, and above all refreshing and quenching.

BREWSKI
HELSINGBORG, SCANIA
WWW.BREWSKI.SE

Mangofeber DIPA Imperial IPA 8%
There's an amiable drinkability about this well-hopped imperial IPA, with the hops giving plenty of tropical fruits and citrus on the nose and palate, with a contrast of pine and light caramel before the bracing bitter finish.

DUGGES
LANDVETTER, VÄSTERGÖTLAND
WWW.DUGGES.SE

Boxed Idjit
Wood-Aged Imperial Stout 12.1%
Idjit is this young brewery's imperial stout, but this is a beer after it's spent time slumbering in whiskey barrels. The result is rich and spirituous, with a depth of flavor that compares with falling down a bottomless well.

JÄMTLANDS
PILGRIMSTAD, JÄMTLAND
WWW.JAMTLANDSBRYGGERI.SE

Pilgrim Pale Ale 4.5%
English pale ale with an American accent in which tangy, resiny hops outwit the caramel cookie base. Leechees and lime on the nose that mellow on the palate.

MALMÖ BREWING CO.
MALMÖ, SCANIA
WWW.MALMOBREWING.COM

Canned Wheat IPA 7%
This is a brewpub that likes to experiment with its beers, though this fruity IPA is a seasonal regular. With 50 percent wheat in the mash, there's a lightness about the mouth-feel, which enables the sweet and juicy hop character to shine through, followed by a mildly bitter finish.

NÄRKE KULTURBRYGGERI
ÖREBRO, NÄRKE
WWW.KULTURBRYGGERI.SE

Kaggen Stormaktsporter Börb'nåhallon
Imperial Stout 9%
Since coming into being in 2003, Närke has pricked up the ears of beer lovers with some seriously adventurous ales, such as this imperial stout that has been stored in oak with raspberries. Alongside regulation chocolate, licorice, and mocha there's a lovely pass of berry fruit on the palate.

NILS OSCAR
NYKÖPING, SÖDERMANLAND
WWW.NILSOSCAR.SE

 India Ale IPA 5.3%

The Nils Oscar microbrewery/distillery was established in 1996, founded by Swedish entrepreneur Karl-David Sundberg. He named the business after his grandfather, Nils Oscar, who farmed in the same rolling landscape less than an hour's drive from Stockholm. With its own maltings and barley fields, it brews a range of 13 beers many of them award-winning, and distills both aquavit and vodka. As the location of Nils Oscar is too far north to grow hops, it calls in heaps of American Amarillo to give this enormously aromatic West Coast IPA its citrusy sensuality.

NYA CARNEGIEBRYGGERIET
STOCKHOLM
WWW.NYACARNEGIEBRYGGERIET.SE

Kellerbier 5.9%

This city-center brewpub is the result of a collaboration between Brooklyn Brewery and Carlsberg. (Its name is a nod to the latter's Carnegie Porter.) The kellerbier is a lushly hoppy take on the classic German beer style.

OCEANBRYGGERIET
GÖTEBORG, VÄSTERGÖTLAND
WWW.OCEANBRYGGERIET.SE

India Pale Ale 5.4%

Who knows what a modern IPA constitutes these days? Ocean has its own answer by using both American and English hops, plus a pinch of Vienna and Munich malts. The result is an amber-hued brew that combines citrus, juicy malt, and a dry, bitter finish.

OMNIPOLLO
STOCKHOLM
WWW.OMNIPOLLO.COM

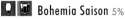 Noa Pecan Mud Cake

Imperial Stout 11%

Here's a beer for dessert if ever there was one. Created by gypsy brewers Omnipollo (and brewed at Dugges), it's a luxurious beer with lots of chocolate, vanilla, and hazelnut on the nose; on the palate there's more, and, yes, it does taste of pecan mud cake. The finish is bittersweet and dry.

O/O BREWING
GÖTEBORG, VÄSTERGÖTLAND
WWW.OOBREWING.COM

Bohemia Saison 5%

Yet another example of how Swedish craft brewers know no boundaries when it comes to creating their own individual beers. This easy-drinking saison is crisp and lively in its carbonation, but it's the spicy and floral Saaz hop notes on nose and palate that really lift things.

OPPIGÅRDS
HEDEMORA, DALARNA
WWW.OPPIGÅRDS.COM

Indian Tribute IPA 6.6%

An American-style IPA enriched by Centennial and Cascade hops, this is a rich amber color, medium-bodied with some floral and grapefruit notes on the nose, leading to some bitterness in the finish. Well worth a try.

"Few things are more pleasant than a village graced with a good church, a good priest, and a good pub."
—JOHN HILLABY *ENGLISH WRITER AND WALKER 1917–1996*

ÖREBRO BRYGGHUS
ÖREBRO
WWW.OREBROBRYGGHUS.SE

Saison des Brasseurs Saison 5.7%

Even though it opened only in 2016, this ambitious brewery has been gaining fans with its meticulously made beers. This is its saison, a tribute to the farmhouse ales of Wallonia, with spicy, peppery, and citrus notes on the nose and a subtly sweet, fruity, and spicy palate before its dry finish.

POPPELS BRYGGERI
JONSERED, VÄSTERGÖTLAND
WWW.POPPELS.SE

DIPA Double IPA 8%

Young brewery that is undoubtedly influenced by the US craft beer revolution as this decidedly delicious DIPA demonstrates. It's big and bold in its flavors as citrus, dried orange peel, pine, and a perfect malt balance strut their funky stuff.

ST. ERIKS BRYGGERI
ARLANDASTAD, SIGTUNA, STOCKHOLM COUNTY
WWW.STERIKSBRYGGERI.SE

Pilsner 5.3%

St. Eriks was originally founded in the mid-nineteenth century and was a major player in the Swedish brewing scene. After it closed, the brand was relaunched with the emphasis on craft beer in 2010. This is its hop-forward pilsner, with plenty of citrus on the nose and palate, before it finishes dry.

SAHTIPAJA
SÄTILA, VÄSTERGÖTLAND
WWW.FACEBOOK.COM/SAHTIPAJA

Rött men inte Sött Berliner Weisse 4.4%

When it comes to brewing, Sahtipaja's founder and brewmaster, Timo Krjukoff, is as eclectic as they come. As well as trying his hand at various beer styles, he also makes mead and cider (and has a day job in IT). This Berliner weisse has additions of raspberries, which make for a tart, berry-licious kind of beer.

SLOTTSKÄLLENS BRYGGERI
UPPSALA, UPPSALA
WWW.SLOTTSKÄLLEN.SE

Slottskällens Imperial Stout 9%

In 1997 former duty-free salesman Hans Finell opened Slottskällens after an enlightening beer-drinking trip to the West Coast of America at the height of the microbrewing boom. Based in the university town of Uppsala, 50 miles north of Stockholm, Slottskällens crafts unpasteurized classic beer styles with a twist. If you're looking for rich roasted coffee notes, chicory, molasses, and port, then you can't go wrong here.

STIGBERGETS BRYGGERI
GÖTEBORG, VÄSTERGÖTLAND
WWW.STIGBERGETSBRYGGERI.SE

West Coast IPA 6.5%

There's a fruit bowl emerging from this beer, with passion fruit, grapefruit, and mango all jostling to make their mark. There're also pine, grass, juicy malt, and a bitter finish. Take a sip and imagine you're by the Pacific.

NORWAY

7 FJELL BRYGGERI
BERGEN, WESTERN NORWAY
WWW.7FJELLBRYGGERI.COM

Ulriken Double IPA Imperial IPA 8.5%
Brewmaster Gahr Smith-Gahrsen is seen as one of the founding fathers of Norwegian craft brewing, so you're in safe hands when you try one of 7 Fjell's beers. Ulriken shimmers with tropical fruit and hop character, ending with an assertive, lengthy bitterness on the palate.

AASS BRYGGERI
DRAMMEN, EASTERN NORWAY
WWW.AASS.NO

Aass Bock 6.5%
Aass (pronounced "orse") is the oldest brewery in Norway and still brews using traditional methods. This dark, sweet, floral, beefy bock benefits from double decoction, an extended boil, and months of maturation.

ÆGIR BRYGGERI
FLÅM, WESTERN NORWAY
WWW.FLAMSBRYGGA.NO

Natt Imperial Porter 10%
Lively brewpub in the popular tourist destination of Flåm (sadly, not twinned with Flim), with a goodly range of American-influenced beers. This is its complex imperial porter, as dark as the darkest night; Lynchburg Natt was a limited edition, aged in Jack Daniels barrels—if you see it, snap it up.

AUSTMANN BRYGGERI
TRONDHEIM, SØR-TRØNDELAG
WWW.AUSTMANN.NO

Sjokolade & Kirsebærporter
Imperial Porter 7.5%
This is a chocolate and cherry porter. Each sip of it gladdens the soul and heart. It's rich and luscious, though the chocolate and cherry notes are light, while freshly ground coffee beans, roast grains, and a hint of vanilla add to the bibulous fun.

HAAND BRYGGERIET
DRAMMEN, EASTERN NORWAY
WWW.HAANDBRYGGERIET.NET

Norwegian Wood Smoked/Spiced Ale 6.5%
Innovation knows no bounds at this eccentric, forward-thinking operation run by four dedicated amateur brewers who dabble in wild yeast, barrel aging, high IBUs, and unusual indigenous ingredients.

KINN BRYGGERI
FLORØ, WESTERN NORWAY
WWW.KINNBRYGGERI.NO

Vestkyst IPA 7%
Given that Vestkyst translates as West Coast, you don't have to be a Nobel Prize winner to guess the influence of this ardent IPA. Grapefruit and pine dominate the aromatics, while more citrus, pine, and light malt on the palate lead to a bittersweet finish.

LERVIG AKTIEBRYGGERI
STAVANGER, WESTERN NORWAY
WWW.LERVIG.NO

Brewers Reserve Rye IPA 8.5%
Malted rye makes up to 20 percent of the mash for this rock-solid rye IPA, adding a spicy, slightly peppery note to the fruit-laden cavalcade of American hops. The long bitter finish suggests you might want to keep on drinking, a neat little trick that Lervig manages to do with all its beers.

LITTLE BROTHER
OSLO, EASTERN NORWAY
WWW.LITTLEBROTHERBREWERY.COM

 Epic Venture IPA 6.5%

Small brewery situated in the Norwegian capital since 2013, which was founded by brothers (and avid homebrewers) Cameron and Andrew Manson. Epic Venture is a dry-hopped IPA with New World superstars Centennial, Citra, and Galaxy in the mix. It's fruity, juicy, and bittersweet in the finish.

NØGNE Ø
GRIMSTAD, SOUTHERN NORWAY
WWW.NOGNE-O.COM

Imperial Stout 9%

Awards have been showered like beery confetti on this dark destroyer of an imperial stout, with chocolate, mocha coffee, a hint of vanilla, and a bracing roastiness, making it a meal in a glass.

"The church is near
but the road is icy,
the bar is far away,
but I will walk carefully."
—RUSSIAN PROVERB

FINLAND

FINLANDIA SAHTI
SASTAMALA, WESTERN FINLAND
WWW.FINLANDIASAHTI.FI

Finlandia Sahti 8%

Beer doesn't come much more traditional than sahti. Brewed using a variety of grain, mostly rye and oats, it's flavored, filtered, and often heated using juniper branches and berries. Once the exclusive domain of quirky homebrewers, sahti is now being produced by several Finnish brewers as well as some American craft breweries. Fans of hefeweizen will appreciate its hazy amber misty hue and fruity banana-like yeast esters. Refreshing and strong.

KOSKIPANIMO
TAMPERE, PIRKANMAA
WWW.PLEVNA.FI

Plevnan Severin Extra IPA 5.9%

Brewpub that was set up in the mid-1990s on the site of old cotton mills built in the early nineteenth century. First brewed in 2007, this IPA pulsates with the aromatics of Amarillo, Nugget, and Tomahawk hops, while there's a solid bitterness in the finish.

LAMMIN SAHTI OY
LAMMI, SOUTHERN FINLAND
WWW.SAHTI.FI

Lammin Sahti 7.7%

This sahti started the revival. It's still brewed in open wooden mash tuns and troughlike strainers known as kuurnas, where the juniper acts as the main preservative. Present in the palate are banana, clove, spearmint, and caramel, with notes of anise on the nose and juniper notes in the finish.

Ruisrääkkä Rye Beer 7%

Rye is the specialty grain added to this full-bodied strong ale, an ingredient that gives the beer a bready, spicy note, which works like a particularly nice dream with the beer's toffee and dark fruit notes.

MAKU
TUUSULA, UUSIMAA
WWW.MAKUBREWING.COM

India Pale Ale 7.3%

Even though Maku was founded in 2014, it's been making waves in Finnish beer circles with its thoroughly modern beers. India Pale Ale is orange-gold in color, with citrus, tropical fruit, and a hint of caramel on the nose, while the palate is more fruit with caramel, followed by a dry finish.

PANIMO HIISI
JYVÄSKYLÄ, CENTRAL FINLAND
WWW.PANIMOHIISI.FI

Humulus Lupus Double IPA 9%

Lively brewery that was founded in 2013 with the declared aim of wanting to make beers that its brewers would like to drink. They like hops, as this dynamic DIPA demonstrates: it has more mangos than a mango tree, while its finish is bittersweet and juicily citrusy.

SINEBRYCHOFF BREWERY
KERAVA, SOUTHERN FINLAND
WWW.SINEBRYCHOFF.FI

Sinebrychoff Porter 7.2%

Now internationally owned, Sinebrychoff was founded to the north of Helsinki by a Russian called Nikolai Sinebrychoff on October 13, 1819, and, apart from a brief period when it wasn't allowed, it's been brewing a toasty porter ever since. It slides down on a soothing cushion of chocolate, coffee, and graham cracker.

ICELAND

BORG
REYKJAVÍK, CAPITAL REGION
WWW.BORGBRUGGHUS.IS

Garún Icelandic Stout Nr. 19 Imperial Stout 11.5%

Small brewery owned by the much larger Egill Skallagrímsson, but which brews its own take on modern craft beer. This is rich and dark and brimming with chocolate, licorice, and coffee. The Nr. 19.1 reboot of the beer is stronger still at 12.5% ABV.

EINSTÖK ÖLGERÐ
AKUREYRI, NORTHEASTERN REGION
WWW.EINSTOKBEER.COM

Icelandic Toasted Porter 6%

Einstök is located just 60 miles from the Arctic Circle and claims to use some of the purest water around for its brewing. This smooth and soothing porter caresses the palate with the softest strokes of espresso, chocolate, and delicate toastiness.

ÖLVISHOLT
SELFOSS, ÁRBORG
WWW.BRUGGHUS.IS

Ölvisholt Lava Imperial Stout 9.4%

Smoked imperial stout that was originally brewed as an experiment, but such was the positive response at a beer expo in Sweden that it has become a regular. Chocolate, coffee, and smoke all work together to produce a delectable drop, which also ages well.

Above: Cofounders of Les Brasseurs du Grand Paris, Fabrice Le Goff (left) and Anthony Baraff.
Below: Deck & Donohue, another Parisian brewery, set up by Americans Thomas Deck and Mike Donohue in 2014.

INTRODUCTION
FRANCE

France may be a nation more readily associated with the grape than the grain, but if, like us, you've read the Asterix books, then you'll know that the ancient Gauls have been brewing for centuries.

More recently, much like its European neighbors, France caught the craft-brewing bug, and at the moment microbreweries are mushrooming into view all over "l'Hexagon."

Where once, in the early twentieth century, there were just 50 breweries in France, now the Gallic beer scene numbers just short of 900 breweries, with the majority of these having fired up their mash tuns only in the last decade or so.

What's more, the movement is not merely rooted in the two traditional French brewing areas of Alsace and Nord-Pas-de-Calais. On the one side, there's the lager-loving Alsace region to the east, where the Germanic influence is evident in the clean, crisp, bottom-fermented blonde beers—of which Kronenbourg 1664 is the most ubiquitous.

Farther north is Nord-Pas-de-Calais, a regional département synonymous with the famous French farmhouse ale known as bière-de-garde —with Duyck Jenlain Ambrée being perhaps the most classic example.

But France's beer map is becoming much less polarized these days, with breweries popping up all over the place—and as far south as Corsica, where Brasserie Pietra has been at the forefront of the French beer scene since 1996

The Rhône-Alpes region to the southeast, home to the city of Lyon and renowned as the gastronomic capital of France, is where a lot of the new-wave brewing noise is being made.

A population of just six million is served by more than a hundred breweries, while pockets of envelope-pushing ale making can be discovered elsewhere, including in Languedoc-Roussillon, Aquitaine, and, of course, Paris.

The French capital's beer scene has improved immensely thanks in no small part to the influence of an innovative and influential expatatriate community that has introduced American and European beer styles, which, a few years ago, simply wouldn't have been part of a Parisian's drinking repertoire.

Micros are dusting down brewing tomes and reawakening traditional French beer styles to broaden their brewing bandwidth beyond only blonde and brown beers. They are becoming better at telling the beer's tale from grain to glass and rooting their beers more deeply in their respective regions.

Brittany is a case in point. France's most northwestern nook has a bountiful brewing past dating back to the seventeenth century and currently boasts a handful of independent micros breathing life back into the Breton tradition of brewing with buckwheat (blé noir)—and adding other left-field local and foraged ingredients such as seaweed, elderberries, and honey.

Most of the new French brewers are content to simply furnish their surrounding areas with their beer and allow the wider market to still remain in the hands of the big brewers—especially in the bars and cafés.

But if the rate of growth continues as it has over the last few years, then don't be surprised if people begin to hail it as a potential "grand fromage" of the European beer scene.

FRANCE

D'ANNOEULLIN
ANNOEULLIN, NORD
NO WEB ADDRESS

L'Angelus Wheat Beer 7%
Located between Lille and Lens
in a village of the same name, the rustic and rather
rudimentary Annoeullin brewery has been in the
hands of the Lepers family since the 1880s. As well as
producing a gently hopped bière de garde, Annoeullin
is well known for waking up the French wheat beer
tradition in the late 1980s. L'Angelus is strong and
spicy, and gets its syrupy substance from
the use of 30 percent unmalted wheat.

AU BARON (BALLEUX)
GUSSIGNIES, NORD
WWW.BRASSERIEAUBARON.COM

Cuvée des Jonquilles Bière de Garde 7%
Jonquilles translates as daffodils, but no
flowers are used in this full-flavored
cult beer, brewed at a small restaurant-
brewpub a popped cork's distance from
the Belgian border. Blond in color, it has
a spice and herbal nose, and a zing of
tropical fruit on the palate before an
assertive bitter finish.

BOURGANEL
VALS-LES-BAINS, ARDÈCHE
WWW.BIERES-BOURGANEL.FR

Miel de Châtaignier Honey Beer 5%
Founded in 2000, this is a brewery
keen on using the products of the local
Ardèche area, which is why there are
beers made with blueberries, verbena,
and chestnuts. This slinky little sipper
has local chestnut honey in the mix,
making for a refreshing, not-too-sweet
brew, which is ideal at the dining table as
well as on the bar-top.

DE BRETAGNE
TRÉGUNC, BRITTANY
WWW.BRITT.FR

Gwiniz Du Strong Ale 5.4%
Founded in 1998, de Bretagne is one of the more
venerable of French microbreweries. This dark and
roasty beer is brewed with buckwheat and qualifies
as the Breton beer style bière au blé noir. It's light
in its bitterness, adrift with caramel, grain, and
roastiness, before finishing dry and bittersweet.

CASTELAIN
BÉNIFONTAINE, NORD-PAS-DE-CALAIS
WWW.CHTI.COM

Ch'ti Blonde 6.4%
Much like its English equivalent,
northern French brewing history is
heavily entwined with the region's
rich industrial heritage. While the coal
mining has waned, the brewing goes
on, and Castelain, brewing since 1926,
is a big producer of bière de garde. This
sweet, slightly bitter herbal blonde is
made with four types of hop.

Ch'ti Triple 7.5%
Launched in 1997, this is Castelain's
strongest calling card. A feverishly
fruity and forceful abbey-style beer,
it borrows some of the medicinal,
Chartreuse-style notes from its
bière-de-garde brethren. Packaged
in a rather smart corked-and-caged
champagne bottle.

LA CHOULETTE
HORDAIN, NORD-PAS-DE-CALAIS
WWW.LACHOULETTE.COM

La Choulette Ambrée Tripel 8%
Cookie-base, mousse-like white head, and
shimmering gold in color. Toffee, dried plums,
and a deep, lingering warm alcohol finish.

COREFF
CARHAIX, BRITTANY
WWW.COREFF.COM

Coreff Ambrée Brown Ale 5%
Not content with berets, lovely cider, and clichéd
stripy sweaters, Brittany is also home to one of
France's finest microbreweries. It was founded in
1985, when it was the first new artisanal brewhouse
in France for 30 years and the first Breton brewery
for more than 50. Spicy and warm, with a dry,
lingering, malty, brown sugar finish.

> "God has a brown voice
> as soft and full as beer."
> —ANNE SEXTON AMERICAN POET 1928–1974

CRAIG ALLAN
PLESSIS-DE-ROYE, OISE
WWW.CRAIGALLAN.FR

Agent Provocateur Belgian Ale 6.5%

British-born Craig Allan worked in breweries in the UK before moving to the French countryside about an hour's drive north of Paris. His three beers are brewed at De Proef over the border in Belgium with Agent Provocateur being a spicy, aromatic sipper that is a showcase for Allan's use of American hops.

LA DÉBAUCHE
ANGOULÊME,
NO WEB ADDRESS

Demi Mondaine Imperial Stout 11%

Ambitious microbrewery influenced by global beer styles. This is its belter of an imperial stout, which also has coffee beans and chocolate added. Unsurprisingly, it's rich and tempting, a collaboration of beery notes, chocolate, coffee, cola, and a lingering finish with roast notes.

DECK & DONOHUE
MONTREUIL, PARIS
WWW.DECK-DONOHUE.COM

Indigo IPA 6.5%

Americans Thomas Deck and Mike Donohue founded their brewery in 2014 and have gained a reputation for producing flavorsome beers that are both food-friendly and a joy at the bar. This US-style IPA uses Alsatian-grown American Nugget hops that impart gorgeous tropical fruit notes to a distinctive beer.

DUYCK
JENLAIN, NORD-PAS-DE-CALAIS
WWW.DUYCK.COM

Jenlain Ambrée Bière de Garde 6.5%

Duyck is the second largest independent brewer in France and almost single-handedly revived the bière-de-garde style. Imperiously packaged in Champagne bottles, Jenlain is one of France's most recognizable and revered beers, and is still in the hands of the Duyck family, who hail originally from the Belgian side of Flanders. A distinguished, dark amber dinner companion.

DE L'ETRE
PARIS
WWW.FACEBOOK.COM/BRASSERIEDELETRE

Cerberus Tripel 7.5%

This is a recent addition to the growing Paris craft beer scene and won RateBeer's best new brewery in France award in 2016. With beers named after mythical creatures, this is its bittersweet and honeyed take on the great Belgian Abbey beer style.

GALIBIER
VALLOIRE, SAVOIE
WWW.BIERE-GALIBIER.COM

Alpine American Pale Ale 4.8%

At an altitude of 4,757 feet, this is the highest craft brewery in France, which means that its beers are in peak condition. This is an aromatic, refreshingly hoppy, American-style pale ale with a dry finish.

DES GARRIGUES
SOMMIÈRES, GARD
WWW.BRASSERIEDESGARRIGUES.FR

La Frappadingue IPA 7.5%

And now for something different—an IPA from southwestern France. Founded in 2008, this go-ahead microbrewery has gained a name for its boldly flavored beers, such as this intuitive IPA, which has plenty of tropical fruit, citrus, and light malt all wrapped up in a full body before its fruity and bitter finish. Tasty indeed.

PARISIAN CRAFT BREWERS

For all too long, beer in Paris played second fiddle to wine and apéritifs, with bar after bar selling ubiquitous mass-produced lagers, sometimes leavened with bière de garde from northern France or Belgian imports.

However, things are changing, and a growing number of breweries and brewpubs are emerging in the company of intriguing beers (and savvy beer stores). It's as if Paris's beery soul has rediscovered itself—after all, there were up to 60 breweries in the city during the nineteenth century. (Something refreshing had to quench the thirst after a good riot, perhaps?)

Names to drop, if you're so inclined, include The Triangle, which is a restaurant and brewery. Based in the 10th arrondissement, its beers include a porter, an American-style pale ale, and (demonstrating that, if nothing else, its brewers know what's going on in the outer world) a New England-style IPA. Then there's Brasserie de la Goutte d'Or, which is seen as the first craft brewery in the city (founded in 2012).

Les Brasseurs du Grand Paris is another up-and-coming beery name to let fall out of your hands. It started as a gypsy brewery, but in 2017 it began brewing with its own kit in the northern suburb of Saint-Denis. Anthony Baraff is the cofounder, an American who, when he moved with his French wife to Paris in 2011, was slightly concerned about a life without hoppy beers.

"We had made a number of trips to visit her family here in France in the preceding years, and I always did what I could to try and find good beer," he says. "Grocery stores and bars always had the same boring lineups of industrially made flavorless lager and overly sweet Belgian beers, and I had no luck finding the hoppy American-style beers that I loved. Fearing a life spent without hoppy beer, I learned to brew while still living in New York City. As soon as I could reliably reproduce the hoppy IPAs and APAs that I loved, I gave the go-ahead for our move to France."

He cites his IPA Citra Galactique as the sort of beer that he knew he couldn't live without: "tropical fruit aroma, a bracing bitterness, and a dry finish that makes the beer easy to drink. It's the reason that I learned to brew and the reason I've left my job of 15 years in IT and finance to start a brewery."

Another of the brewery's standouts is Porter Gourmande, whose origin Baraff puts down to a childhood love of drinking chocolate milk.

"We always had a bottle of Hershey's chocolate syrup in the refrigerator," he recalls. "It was a special treat when we were getting to the bottom of the plastic gallon jug of milk, because rather than pouring the milk into the glass and stirring in the syrup, I would just add the chocolate directly to the jug, replace the cap, and give it a good shake. The resulting

chocolate milk was foamy and always seemed to taste that much better. Porter Gourmande is a bit about my trying to re-create that experience, only in beer form."

Deck & Donohue is another transatlantic collaboration, with old friends Thomas Deck (who is from Alsace) and American Mike Donohue setting up their kit in 2013 in east Paris. One of their bestsellers is Indigo IPA.

"The idea behind this beer," says Deck, "was to bring a classic IPA to the French public. Historically, French people tend to classify beer by color only. Since IPA is such a different style, and defining the beer as "blonde" or "amber" would not really help the drinker identify what we try to do here, we decided to name this beer Indigo, which originally means "from India." Even though the beer is obviously not blue, it is our way of trying to put into question simplistic classifications of beer.

> "As a Franco-American team brewing in France, we decided to use Alsatian-grown American Nugget hops for this recipe, as a local tribute to the IPA resurrection by American brewers over the last 30 years."

Paris. City of light, city of gastronomy, city of fine wine, and now, it seems, city of craft beer.

Above: A tantalizing range of Parisian craft beer from Les Brasseurs du Grand Paris.
Left: Mike Donohue and Thomas Deck of the eponymous brewery, one of whose bestsellers is Indigo IPA.

* KEY BEERS

LES BRASSEURS DU GRAND PARIS
IPA Citra Galactique 6.5%
Porter Gourmande 5.9%

DECK & DONOHUE
Indigo IPA 6.5%

GOUTTE D'OR
L'Assommoir Imperial Barbessian Stout 9.7%

LES BRASSEURS DE GAYANT
DOUAI, NORD
WWW.BRASSEURS-GAYANT.COM

🍴 **La Goudale** Bière de Garde 7.2%
Gayant is one of the biggest breweries in northern France and was founded in the aftermath of World War I in 1919. This is its bestseller, an easily accessible blonde bière de garde with malt, toffee, caramel, and pepper on the palate, while the finish is dry and citrusy.

GOUTTE D'OR
PARIS
WWW.BRASSERIELAGOUTTEDOR.COM

⚙ **Ernestine** IPA 7%
When this opened in 2012 in the eighteenth arrondissement, it was generally seen as the first craft brewery in the City of Light, and its bold branding and equally confident beers have kept it in the spotlight. This irresistible IPA has oodles of Chinook, Centennial, and Columbus hops thrown into the brewing kettle, producing tropical fruit and grapefruit notes that work well with a firm cookie body.

LES BRASSEURS DU GRAND PARIS
PARIS
WWW.BGP.PARIS

⚙ **IPA Citra Galactique** IPA 6.5%
When it comes to starting a brewery, it's a simple story. A couple of beer lovers get together, one an American, the other from Brittany, and start a brewery. They're gypsies until 2017. This audacious US-style IPA explodes with tropical fruit and juicy citrus, before finishing dry and bitter.

BRASSERIE DU HAUT BUËCH
LUS-LA-CROIX-HAUTE, DRÔME
WWW.BHBBRASSERIEARTISANALE.BLOGSPOT.CO.UK

▢ ⚒ **Teckel Bull** Baltic Porter 9.5%
Big and boisterous Baltic porter that is as dark as the bottom of a well; it has licorice, chocolate, roasted malt, and berry fruit running around in the glass, all of which are wrapped up in a bitter finish.

LANCELOT
LE ROC SAINT ANDRÉ, BRITTANY
WWW.BRASSERIE-LANCELOT.BZH

⚙ ▢ **XI.I Samhain** Barley Wine 11.1%
You could see Lancelot as the godfathers of modern Breton brewing, having opened in 1990. This is their luscious and luxurious barley wine that is brewed once a year over the Celtic festival of Samhain. Dark brown in color, it has vanilla, mocha, and chocolate on the nose and palate, while the finish is dry.

MONT BLANC
CHAMBÉRY, SAVOIE
WWW.BRASSERIE-MONTBLANC.COM

▢ ✓ **La Blanche** Witbier 4.7%
This well-established brewery has a water catchment on nearby Mont Blanc, with the liquid being brought to the brewery to be used in brewing. It obviously works, as awards are showered on its beers, including this tangy and refreshing witbier, with its perfect balance of spice and orange fruitiness.

BRASSERIE DU PAYS FLAMAND
BLARINGHEM, NORD
WWW.BRASSERIEDUPAYSFLAMAND.COM

▢ ⚒ **Anosteké Blonde** 8%
As you might guess from the name, this is a blonde-colored beer, sparkling and golden in the glass. There're citrus and a touch of peach on the nose, while citrus, hops, and an elegant bitterness make themselves at home on the palate alongside a bittersweet finish.

> "Beer, it's the best damn drink in the world."
> —JACK NICHOLSON
> AMERICAN ACTOR, 1937–

PIETRA BREWERY
FURIANI, CORSICA
WWW.BRASSERIEPIETRA.COM

Pietra Amber Lager 6%

When husband-and-wife team Dominique and Armelle Sialelli opened the Pietra microbrewery in 1996, it was the first commercial brewery to set foot on the gorgeous Mediterranean island of Corsica. Indigenous chestnuts are used in the brewing of Pietra's eponymous flagship beer. Crushed into flour and added to the grist, they afford the amber-colored lager a dry and voluptuous mouthfeel, and a certain amount of spice on the finish. The nutty malt sweetness is designed to give just the right amount of hop bitterness.

PLEINE LUNE
CHABEUIL, DRÔME
WWW.BRASSERIE-PLEINELUNE.FR

Gens de la Lune Lager 4.9%

This is a bright and brisk lager, golden in the glass, flavorsome on the palate, with fruit, subtle bitterness, a hint of grassiness, and a dry finish wrapping things up.

ST. RIEUL
TRUMILLY, SENLIS
WWW.ST-RIEUL.COM

Brune Brown Ale 8%

Set in the middle of a family-run farm, this brewery was founded in 1998 and looked to near neighbors for inspiration for its beers. With hints of coffee on the nose, this chestnut Belgian-style brown ale is probably best as a tasty lunchtime quaff, while hints of coffee, caramel, and dark fruit swirl out of the glass before its bittersweet finish.

SAINTE CRUCIENE
COLMAR, HAUT-RHIN
WWW.SAINTE-CRU.COM

Antisociale Black IPA 7.2%

Passionate brewery that was founded in 2012 and which loves to use American hops, such as in this boldly flavored Black IPA, where Columbus, Citra, Amarillo, and Simcoe combine with a judiciously planned malt background for a beer that is fruity, citrusy, lightly roasty, and bright and appetizing in its finish.

ST. SYLVESTRE
ST. SYLVESTRE, NORD-PAS-DE-CALAIS
WWW.BRASSERIE-ST-SYLVESTRE.COM

3 Monts Bière de Garde 8.5%

The "three mountains" name is a bit of an inside joke in this hop-growing part of northern France. The landscape is flatter than a superskinny stingray and the hills are more mound than mountain. Corked like a bottle of wine, it's fairly vinous too, with undulating flavors of dry apricot, grapefruit, toffee, and sherry. Not surprising given the location where it's produced, it's highly hoppy too.

Gavroche Strong Amber Ale 8.5%

A sweet, generously hopped, copper-colored, and bottle-conditioned ale, brewed with a variety of malt and a showboating yeast given free, fruity rein. Named after the rebellious Parisian urchin in the Victor Hugo novel *Les Misérables*.

THEILLIER
BAVAY, NORD-PAS-DE-CALAIS
NO WEB ADDRESS

La Bavaisienne Bière de Garde 7%

Only a few miles from the border with Belgium, in the little town of Bavay, the Theillier family has been making some rather beautiful bières de garde for generations. The charming brewery is part of the seventeenth-century family home. Dark amber with a dense head, this beer is hearty, malty, and spicy, with a minty fresh finish.

DE THIRIEZ
ESQUELBECQ,
NORD-PAS-DE-CALAIS
WWW.IFRANCE.COM/BRASSERIETHIRIEZ

La Blonde d'Esquelbecq Blonde Ale 5.8%

This was the first beer Daniel Thiriez produced when he set up his brewery in an old farm building in the small town of Esquelbecq, near Dunkirk. It is the brew that was responsible for establishing his reputation as a brewer of note, and this zesty blonde has not lost its lively orange-peel appeal. The Belgian influence is clearly discernible here.

AUSTRIA

7 STERN BRÄU
WIEN, VIENNA
WWW.7STERN.AT

Winterrauchbock Lager 6.2%
A sensational, sweet, strong, and smoky lager from a long-running Viennese brewpub that attaches electrodes to the nether regions of long-neglected beer styles and gives them an almighty jolt. Also produces a chile beer and a hemp ale if you're feeling adventurous.

1516
VIENNA
WWW.1516BREWINGCOMPANY.COM

Slipper Pale Ale 6.2%
Busy and popular brewpub that makes a wide variety of beer, especially ones that feature aromatic and palate-pounding selections of boldly flavored hops from around the world. This pleasing pale ale has Sorachi Ace, Citra, and Galaxy, all of which offer peachy, lemony, and tropical notes against a broad backbone of malt.

ALEFRIED BEER
GRAZ, STYRIA
WWW.ALEFRIED.COM

Fladerant Farmhouse Ale Saison 6.5%
Artisanal is the way to go for this forward-thinking young brewery that plies its trade in the second largest city in Austria. This Styrian take on a saison is tart and full-bodied, spicy and succulent, and well worth a swig or three.

BIEROL
SCHWOICH, TYROL
WWW.BIEROL.AT

Padawan Pale Ale 5.6%
Bierol is run by three self-styled beer anarchists, and their beers have been stirring up interest since 2014. Padawan is an assertive American-style pale ale, a shout-out especially for Citra and Mosaic. Padawan, by the way, got its name after brewery fans voted on Facebook for Pale Ale Doing Alright Without A Name.

BIERSCHMIEDE
STEINBACH AM ATTERSEE, NIEDERÖSTERREICH
WWW.BIERSCHMIEDE.AT

Amboss Imperial Stout 9.5%
Another new entrant to the growing Austrian craft beer sector. Amboss is an insatiably dark Imperial stout with plenty of roastiness, coffee goodness, and chocolate seduction, alongside a full body and a bittersweet finish. Deeply, darkly good.

BRAUWERK WEIN
VIENNA
WWW.BRAUWERK.WIEN

Haus Marke 2 Session IPA 4.3%
Microbrewery that has links with Ottakringer (and opened on its site in 2014). Beers are influenced by world brewing trends. (There's a Flemish red and a porter, for instance.) This is a celebration of American hops, with grapefruit and mango aromatics and a bracing bitterness.

BREW AGE
VIENNA
WWW.BREWAGE.AT

Eisknacker Barley Wine 12.2%
The words "be careful" spring to mind when considering this potent potentate of an "iced" barley wine. It's silky in the way sweet malt slides on the tongue, which is then joined by brown sugar, dried fruit, vanilla, and cherries before finishing with a gentle bitterness.

EGGENBERG
VORCHDORF, NIEDERÖSTERREICH
WWW.SCHLOSS-EGGENBERG.AT

★ **Urbock 23** Doppelbock 9.6%
Mention Austrian beer to any beer lover worth their malt, and it won't be long before there's talk of this delicious doppelbock. The "23" refers to the Plato degrees, but everything gets mellowed during a nine-month maturation period. A seriously strong beer disguised under a cloak of cotton candy, pear, cloves, pumpkin pie spice, orange, grapefruit, and melon.

"From man's sweat and God's love, beer came into the world."
—ST. ARNULF OF METZ *AUSTRIAN BISHOP AND PATRON SAINT OF BREWERS, 580–640*

FORSTNER
KALSDORF BEI GRAZ, STEIERMARK
WWW.FORSTNER-BIERE.AT

🅰️ 🍺 **Styrian Ale** Brown Ale 6.6%

A modern-thinking brewpub that takes a different tack from the older, more traditional breweries in Austria. Gerhard Forstner draws inspiration from off-center American ales and Belgian beers for his hard-to-pigeonhole liquids, such as this russet-brown drop that skips between a hoppy Californian pale ale and a Belgian dubbel.

GÖSSER BRAUEREI
LEOBEN, STEIERMARK
WWW.GOESSER.AT

⭐ ✅ **Gösser Märzen** 5.2%

Gösser is part of the vast Heineken group and boasts an enormous following among Austrian beer lovers, especially for its malty, mellow märzen—the most popular beer style in Austria, where it is typically lower in alcohol than its German namesake.

HIRTER BRAUEREI
MICHELDORF, KÄRNTEN
WWW.HIRTERBIER.AT

🍺 🍻 **Morchl** Dunkel 5%

Sumptuous and silky dark beer that purrs on the palate like a contented cat, though there's a tiger in the tank in the subtly bitter finish. The brewery recommends this with game dishes or creamy desserts.

🍺 🍺 🍺 **Privat Pils** Pilsner 5.2%

An excellent unpasteurized, straw-colored, Bohemian-style pilsner from Austria's oldest brewer, whose origins date from 1270. A grassy hop aroma with a long, soft butter and caramel velvety body, followed by a delicate and gentle short, dry bitter finish courtesy of Saaz Hallertau hops.

HOFBRÄU KALTENHAUSEN
HALLEIN, SALZBURG
WWW.EDELWEISSBIER.AT

🍺 🍽️ **Gamsbock** Weissbier 7.1%

Nestled in the bosom of the Austrian Alps, Edelweiss first began brewing in 1475 but began making weissbier only in the 1980s. It still cold-conditions and ferments its beers naturally in mountain-embedded caves. In this Gamsbock, there is lots of boozy brawn plus some sweet banoffee pie flavors and a deceptively dry finish.

SCHREMSER BREWERY
SCHREMS, NIEDERÖSTERREICH
WWW.SCHREMSER.AT

⭐ ✅ 🎖️ **Roggen** Rye Beer 5.2%

Small independent brewery created in 1410 in one of the most bucolic regions of Austria. The modern set up, in Trojan family hands since 1838, has revived the long-forgotten and once-forbidden brewing of rye beer. Light brown, fruity, pithy, and dry.

STIEGL BREWERY
SALZBURG
WWW.STIEGL.AT

🍺 **Stiegl-Goldbräu** Premium Lager 4.9%

This is Austria's biggest private brewery, based in Salzburg, and once a favorite of the composer Wolfang Amadeus Mozart. When in Austria, you can't miss the red-and-white Stiegl (Steps) logo, although the beer's ubiquity is by no means a byword for bland. Crisp, clean, and with a clipped bitterness.

STIFT ENGELSZELL
ENGELHARTSZELL AN DER DONAU, NIEDERÖSTERREICH
WWW.STIFT-ENGELSZELL.AT

🍺 🍺 **Gregorius Trappistenbier** Tripel 10.5%

This temptation of a Trappist beer is vinous, rummy, raisiny, and slightly ashy (in a good way), while a background caramel sweetness takes prayer with dry toasty notes. First produced by the monks of Engelszell in 2012, it was the first of its kind to be brewed outside Belgium or the Netherlands.

TRUMER
SALZBURG, SALZBURG
WWW.TRUMER.AT

🍺 ✅ **Trumer Pils** 4.9%

When the pilsner bandwagon first began rolling in the mid-nineteenth century, Trumer was quick to clamber aboard and shift the focus toward the new golden beer and away from the traditional Bavarian bottom-fermented beers it had been brewing since 1601. Steadfast adherence to open-fermenting and lagering times is still maintained, and the brewery dabbles in seasonals and the occasional wheat beer.

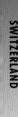

SWITZERLAND

DOPPELLEU BRAUWERKSTATT
WINTERTHUR, ZÜRICH
WWW.DOPPELLEU.CH

Single Hop Black Ale Schwarzbier 7%
The great beer style of Thuringia
and Saxony receives a modern craft
makeover with the use of one hop: the
fruity Australian variety Galaxy. This all
makes for a pleasing contrast between
the coffee and roast notes and a peachy
fruitiness before its dry finish.

FRANCHES-MONTAGNES
SAIGNELÉGIER, JURA
WWW.BRASSERIEBFM.CH

Abbaye de Saint Bon-Chien
Wood-Aged Beer circa 11%
Based in the Jura mountains, BFM is
the microbrewery that kick-started the
microbrewing revolution in Switzerland
and, in turn, this beer put Switzerland
back on the world beer map.

Cuvée Alex le Rouge
Imperial Stout 10.27%
A "Jurassian Imperial stout" with
Russian tea, Sarawak pepper, and other
idiosyncrasies. A contemplative and
incredibly complex dark beer.

La Saison 225 Saison 6%
Tart, funky, and aged in oak barrels for several
months, this is BFM's declaration of intent that
saisons don't have to be high in alcohol or full of
such oddities as shrimp, seaweed, or stale bread.

BRAUEREI LOCHER AG
APPENZELL, APPENZELL INNERRHODEN
WWW. APPENZELLERBIER.CH

Schwarzer Kristall
Black Lager 6.3%
A lovely yet rather unorthodox
schwarzbier: black, malty, rather mouth-
filling, with a solid chocolaty roast malt
backbone, almost saline notes, decent
hopping, and a nice dash of smoked malt
in it. Very pleasant, rich yet not too heavy.

Weizenbier 5.2%
Swiss take on the classic Bavarian beer
style that pulsates with banana and clove aromatics
and flavors, has a brisk carbonation, is refreshing
on the palate, and a real quencher after you've been
cutting the lawn or something similarly frenetic.

LA NÉBULEUSE
LAUSANNE, VAUD
WWW.LANEBULEUSE.CH

Malt Capone Porter 7%
American-style porter that is infused with
bourbon and vanilla sticks. The result is a
creamy, luxurious drop of goodness that
also has a gentle roastiness and hints of
chocolate and mocha alongside a subtle
fruitiness and long bittersweet finish.

Stirling California Common 5.3%
The beers of this thriving and go-ahead
brewery, founded by four friends in 2014,
have made many friends among the Swiss
craft beer scene. Stirling's genesis is the
result of a journey to the West Coast of the
US, and an appreciation of the California
common beer style. Citrusy and clean, refreshing and
eager to please on the palate, it's a wow all alone or
with Mediterranean cuisine.

STORM & ANCHOR
WINTERTHUR, ZÜRICH
WWW.STORMANDANCHOR.COM

No Country for Old Grain Wheat Ale 6.6%
Founded in 2011, on a farm
site but came to an end in
2014. Since then, the brewer
Tom Strickler has operated
as a gypsy brewer. This wheat
ale, which is brewed at the
Doppelleu Brauwerkstatt
brewery, is bready and grainy,
medium-bodied, and blessed
with light citrus and tropical
fruit notes before a dry finish.

TROIS DAMES
SAINTE-CROIX, VAUD
WWW.BRASSERIE3DAMES.CH

IPA 6.5%
This Californian IPA, brewed using Chinook,
Simcoe, and Columbus hops, is a floral,
aromatic, and beautifully bitter example
of Trois Dames' successful Anglo-American
brews. A truly tasty beer.

La Semeuse Espresso Stout 7.5%
A solid chocolaty imperial stout with a
wonderful wakey-wakey espresso coffee
edge courtesy of coffee beans from Vietnam,
Ethiopia, and Brazil. Like all Trois Dames'
beers, it comes packaged in a terrific-
looking bottle.

BRAUEREI LOCHER AG

APPENZELL

WWW.APPENZELLERBIER.CH

If Switzerland were noon on a cuckoo clock or a rather expensive watch face, then Appenzell could be found at about half past one. Appenzell is about as Swiss as you can get: surrounded by *The Sound of Music* hills and chocolate-box pretty houses, with heart-shaped shutters.

Appenzell is the butt of Swiss urbanite jokes because it is situated in the least populated region of Switzerland, where cows outnumber people (15,000 to 1) and where women were given the regional vote only in 1991.

The local brewer is unashamed in proudly circumventing convention. The Locher family has been brewing at its eponymous brewery since 1886, but Karl, the fifth generation of the family to run it, wears the weight of history lightly by doing some fairly extraordinary things with his beer.

Locher's flagship beer, Vollmond, meaning "Full Moon," is a quirky case in point. Borrowing biodynamic techniques more readily associated with winemaking, Karl brews the clean and crisp pilsner only when the moon is at its most rotund. "People in this region believe the moon has supernatural powers and that it determines much more than you think," says Karl with the wide-eyed,

infectious zeal of a mad professor. "If winemakers can use biodynamics, why can't we do something similar with beer? Some people say it is mumbo-jumbo, but all I know is that when this beer is brewed at full moon, it simply tastes better."

But it's not just in the brewhouse where Locher does things differently. A few years ago, Karl teamed up with Appenzell's Hotel Hof Weissbad spa resort to extol beer's many health-giving benefits. There are beer jacuzzis where yeast and wheat germ oil swirl around you on powerful liquid jets; there's an all-over body cleansing using malt mash and beer residue that leaves your backside baby-smooth; there's a hop massage that soothes the mind, body, and soul with soporific powers; and you can even get a hair-care treatment and scalp massage using Ninkasi Beer, a low-alcohol lager that tastes better than antidandruff lotions.

Beer, it's nothing if not versatile.

Left: Taking a sample of the beer to check that everything is as it should be.

Above: Sharp, refeshing, and in a glass of its own, Holzfass amber ale lager is one of Locher's key brews.

* KEY BEERS

Castégna 5%
Hanfblüte 5.2%
Holzfass-Bier 5.5%
Schwarzer Kristall 6.3%
Vollmond Bier 5.2%

Above: De Molen is based in the town of Bodegrave, where it hosts one of Europe's best beer festivals each year.
Below: Oproer, borne of Utrecht brewers Rooie Dop and Ruig, is one of the new breweries driving a dynamic Dutch beer scene.

INTRODUCTION
NETHERLANDS

It can't be easy living next door to Belgium and Germany, two of the world's most prestigious brewing nations.

But the Netherlands has, over the last decade or so, defiantly stepped out of the shadow of both Belgium and Germany to become a discerning beer-drinking destination in its own right, leaving its postwar pils-popping past behind it.

One can draw parallels between the craft-brewing movement in the Netherlands with that of America, borne out of desperation in the 1980s. Having once boasted more than 700 breweries in the mid-fifteenth century, Dutch beer found itself scraping the bottom of the barrel in 1980.

During the 1960s and '70s, Heineken had gone on a rampage, snapping up breweries, closing them down, and lending bar-owners money in return for long-term exclusive listings. When it finally closed its check book, there were just 14 Dutch breweries left, knocking out fewer than 10 beer styles between them, and 99 percent of the beer sold in the country was taste-alike pilsner.

Dutch beer lovers couldn't take it anymore. Inspired by the Campaign for Real Ale (CAMRA) across the English Channel, not to mention the neighboring Belgian and German beer scenes, a group of "right-drinking" beer lovers embarked on a craft beer crusade aimed at preserving proper Dutch beer.

It was called Vereniging Promotie Informatie Traditioneel Bier (PINT), and it fired the starting pistol for a Dutch beer renaissance which, initially and unsurprisingly, began with the brewing of Belgian-style beers, but its influences have since broadened beyond its immediate borders.

Their geographic position has helped the Dutch develop a diverse beer scene. Their ports are often the entry points into Europe for exports from both America and the UK, while further inspiration drips down from the thriving Scandinavian scene to the north.

The result is a booming and rather unique Dutch beer scene, with more than 450 breweries scattered all over the country, with the cities of Amsterdam, Utrecht, and also Gronigen leading the charge, with Nijmegen, The Hague, Rotterdam, and Haarlem not far behind.

The depth and breadth of the Dutch beer experience can best be discovered at Proeflokaal Arendsnest, a traditional Amsterdam bar that stocks beer brewed only in the Netherlands. The rotating menu regularly features the traditional players, such as Gulpener, Hertog Jan, and La Trappe, as well as the Netherlands' "New World" brewers such as Oproer, Emelisse, De Molen, Oedipus, and Jopen, a lovely Haarlem-based brewer that has revived Dutch beer styles.

Despite rapid growth since the 1980s, the vast majority of the emerging Dutch beer craft brewers remain modest operations that seldom sell beyond their local neighborhoods, let alone to other countries.

As such, the big brewers have yet to smell blood. All that has happened so far is that De Molen entered a distribution partnership with Bavaria in 2016 to increase availability in the notoriously difficult Dutch market.

A similar deal was brokered between Duvel Moortgat and the Amsterdam brewery, t'IJ, a year before. Both they and De Molen claim these collaborations come at no cost to the beer quality and hopefully as the Dutch beer scene continues along its steep trajectory, the dark days of rampant consolidation of the 1960s and 1970s won't repeat themselves.

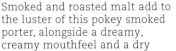

THE NETHERLANDS

BAXBIER
GRONINGEN, GRONINGEN
WWW.BAXBIER.COM

 Kond Vuur Porter 6.3%

Smoked and roasted malt add to
the luster of this pokey smoked
porter, alongside a dreamy,
creamy mouthfeel and a dry
finish. This beer is perfect for sinking in front of the
campfire with, or enjoy it in the depths of the winter.

DUITS & LAURET
EVERDINGEN, UTRECHT
WWW.DUITSLAURET.COM

 Extra Blonde
Belgian Strong Ale 8.5%

How's this for a brewery
home? Duits & Lauret is
based in a historic fort from
which emerges a righteous bombardment of great
beers. This hefty and happy blonde is a mixture of
spice, citrus, and a weight of alcohol, with a pleasing
bitterness in the finish.

EMELISSE
KAMPERLAND, ZEELAND
WWW.EMELISSE.NL

Oostende Dubbel Slot 7%

Chestnut-brown in color, this variant on an
abbey beer, from one of the Netherlands'
leading craft breweries, has a grainy
and fruity nose, with a hint of spice in
the background. Alongside the fruit are
delicate swipes of caramel and a tempting
spiciness, before a bitter finish.

GRUTTE PIER
LEEUWARDEN, FRIESLAND
WWW.GRUTTEPIERBROUWERIJ.COM

Tripel 8%

Award-winning brewery named after
a freedom fighter who stood up for
Friesland in the sixteenth century.
Belgium is the influence, though, for this
luminous and spicy, citrus-honeyed tripel,
with a brisk carbonation and bitter finish.

GULPENER BIER BROUWERIJ
GULPEN, LIMBURG
WWW.GULPENER.NL

Korenwolf Wheat Beer 5%

A multigrain, unpasteurized
Dutch witbier. It was first
brewed to raise aid for a
dwindling local population
of korenwolf (field hamsters)
until it was discovered that,
rather than dwindling, they
had merely moved across
the border.

GULZIGE GANS
COEVORDEN, DRENTHE
WWW.DEGULZIGEGANS.NL

Waggel Tripel 9%

Translated as the greedy goose, this energetic
microbrewery makes a selection of frisky beers.
This one (Waddle in English) is a bright and breezy,
unfiltered, and unpasteurized tripel with plenty of
fruit, spice, and alcohol.

DE HEMEL
NIJMEGEN, GELDERLAND
WWW.BROUWERIJDEHEMEL.NL

Nieuw Ligt Grand Cru Barley Wine 10%

The delightfully named Herm Hegger is a veteran
of the Dutch brewing scene, having set up the Raaf
microbrewery in 1983, where he introduced the first
Dutch wheat beer. Having sold it to Oranjeboom
brewery, he started De Hemel (Heaven) in a splendid
twelfth-century cloister in the town of Nijmegen.
Here, in addition to the mighty fine ales, they also
produce vinegar, mustard, gin, and brandy. Matured
for more than a year in cellars, the Nieuw Ligt Grand
Cru is a firm-bodied, vinous barley wine, with stewed
hop resin aroma, a mellow touch of malt vinegar, and
an everlasting arid endgame.

HERTOG JAN
ARCEN, LIMBURG
WWW.HERTOGJAN.NL

Grand Prestige Barley Wine 10%

This strong, vinous Dutch barley wine
is one of a number of intriguing ales
from an old Arcen-based brewery that's
had more comebacks than a boomerang.
Expect a fusion of pears, plums, dried
apricot, and warm alcoholic tones
of spiced dark rum.

JOPEN
HAARLEM, NORTH HOLLAND
WWW.JOPEN.NL

⭐ 🍺 **Bokbier** 6.5%

Jopen, located in the lovely town of Haarlem, just a half-hour outside Amsterdam, revels in re-creating the Dutch beer styles of yesteryear and has received critical acclaim for doing so. An authentic interpretation of an indigenous, once-ubiquitous Dutch brown beer: smoky and spicy with a sharp tongue of licorice.

KEES
MIDDELBURG, ZEELAND
WWW.BROUWERIJKEES.NL

🍺🍺🍺 **Peated Imperial Stout** 11.2%

Kees Bubberman was famously known as the best homebrewer in the Netherlands before becoming head brewer at Emelisse. In 2014, he set off on his own, and his journey of great beers has continued ever since. This intensely flavored dark beer is smoky and peaty but also soothing and succulent.

KLEIN DUIMPJE
HILLEGOM, SOUTH HOLLAND
WWW.KLEINDUIMPJE.NL

🍺🍺🍺🍺 **Blue Tram** Tripel 7.5%

Klein Duimpje, which translates as Tom Thumb in Dutch, is a small yet incredibly prolific brewery. Drawing inspiration from all over the world, former hedonistic homebrewer Erik Bouman doesn't let diversity dilute the character of his small-batch beers. This jauntily angled tripel flashes elements of pear, clove, tropical fruit, and shortbread.

KOMPAAN BIER
DEN HAAG
WWW.KOMPAANBIER.NL

🍺🍺 **No 39 Bloed Broeder** Imperial Stout 9%

First there was the bar where beer was celebrated and contemplated with consummate ease; then came the brewery with a fine selection of beers such as this port-infused imperial stout, which is rich, deep in flavor, and as memorable as a kiss from a loved one.

DE LECKERE
DE MEERN, UTRECHT
WWW.DELECKERE.NL

🍺🍺 **Organic Pilsner** 5%

Here is a positive veteran of the Dutch craft beer scene, having opened its doors in 1997. Belgian beer seems to be the brewery's center of the universe, but there is also this fresh and bittersweet Czech-style pilsner, whenever you're in need of urgent refreshment.

MAXIMUS
UTRECHT, UTRECHT
WWW.BROUWERIJMAXIMUS.NL

🍺🍺🍺 **Saison** 5%

There's a tasting bar onsite at this young and thrusting brewery, whose founders say they want to make beers that they want to drink. This Wallonian-style classic is blonde in color, brisk, spicy, and fresh on the palate with a bitter finish.

DE MOLEN
BODEGRAVEN, SOUTH HOLLAND
WWW.BROUWERIJDEMOLEN.NL

🍺🍺🍺 **Mout & Mocca**
Imperial Stout 11.6%

Ever since it began brewing in 2004, De Molen is one of the superstars of the Dutch brewing scene, throwing out all manner of stupendous beers, sometimes in collaboration with breweries from all over the world. This is an intensely endowed imperial stout, which just happens to have coffee in the mix. There's a velvety richness, a cuddly roastiness, and plenty of coffee character alongside chocolate and a bittersweet finish.

⭐🍺🍺 **Rasputin** Imperial Stout 10.4%

Brewing small-batch beers in a modestly sized brewhouse which uses former dairy equipment, brewmasters Menno Olivier and John Brus are proponents of big interpretations of traditional global beer styles. Rasputin is a limited-edition imperial stout, loaded with warming molasses, rich roasted coffee notes, and a touch of vanilla and spice. This beer is brewed only once or twice a year, so make sure to grab it if you see it.

NOORDT
ROTTERDAM, SOUTH HOLLAND
WWW.BROUWERIJNOORDT.NL

Bok 7%

There has long been a tradition of seasonal bok beers in the Netherlands, and yet these are beers whose taste profiles could be assumed to be closer to their Bavarian counterparts, especially when it comes to the malt profile. This young brewery's version is full-bodied, gently bitter, and soft, with hints of malt.

OEDIPUS BREWING
AMSTERDAM
WWW.OEDIPUS.COM

MAMA Pale Ale 5%

This lively and ambitious brewery (which also has a popular bar) insists the beer's name has nothing to do with the mother-fixated Freudian complex but is instead a representation of the easy-going and reliable nature of a mother. Whatever the shrink's couch implications, it's fun to enjoy this beer's hoppy nature (courtesy of Centennial hops), dryness, gentle bitterness, and long finish.

OERSOEP
NIJMEGEN, GELDERLAND
WWW.OERSOEPBROUWERIJ.NL

Sergeant Pepper Saison 7%

All you need is love or, in the case of this sensual sipper from a brewery founded in 2012, some saison yeast to impart that jazzy, spicy, angular character alongside a peppery quality and citrus notes. All together now …

OPROER
UTRECHT, UTRECHT
WWW.OPROERBROUWERIJ.NL

Oproer Imperial Oatmeal Stout 9.5%

Two breweries, Rooie Dop and RUIG Bier, got together, and Oproer was born, along with a popular bar and award-winning vegan restaurant. The brewers are constantly on the lookout for interesting flavors, and the Oatmeal Stout is one of the results of this quest, matching the promise of its starkly dark appearance. It is chock full of rich bitter chocolate and complex dark coffee flavors.

DE PELGRIM
ROTTERDAM, SOUTH HOLLAND
WWW.PELGRIMBIER.NL

Mayflower Tripel 7.2%

A terrific brewpub and restaurant located on the historic Delfshaven harbor, just a few doors down from the church where the Pilgrims last said prayers before setting sail for America in 1620. Opened in 1996, De Pelgrim brews beers inspired by Belgium and also uses the beer in the recipes for its in-house produce such as cheese, butter, chocolate, and mustard. Mayflower Tripel, named after the ship sailed by the pilgrims, bobs up and down pleasantly on an aromatic golden sea of flavor derived from orange zest, coriander, and herbal hop.

BROUWERIJ DE PRAEL
AMSTERDAM, NORTH HOLLAND
WWW.DEPRAEL.NL

Quadrupel 11.5%

Cofounders Fer Kok and Arno Kooy set up this small, ramshackle brewery in Amsterdam after working in a rehabilitation center helping recovering psychiatric patients to look for work. They created De Prael using government funding and employed their former clients. This is a dark blend of dark malt and peppery hop.

PRAGHT
DRONTEN, FLEVOLAND
WWW.BROUWERIJPRAGHT.NL

Extra Stout 8%

Like De Prael in Amsterdam, Praght is a brewery with a social conscience, with many of its employees living with various mental health issues. Extra Stout is a ravishingly dark beer with plenty of chocolate, hints of raspberry, and a roastiness and dryness wrapped up in an all embracing silkiness.

RAMSES BIER
HOOGE ZWALUWE, NORTH BRABANT
WWW.RAMSESBIER.NL

Mamba Porter 6.2%

The Ramses brewery started out in 2010 using other breweries to produce its beers, but it now has its own facility and is growing steadily. As its name suggests, the beers are on the dark side of the spectrum, where chocolate, light milky coffee, and caramel roam across the palate in the company of an assertive hoppiness.

SINT CHRISTOFFEL

BREDA, NORTH BRABANT
WWW.CHRISTOFFELBIEREN.COM

Christoffel Blond Pilsner 5.4%

Dutch diktat has it that if you want to drink delightful lagers, then you should choose Christoffel. Set up in 1986 in the former coal mining town of Roermond, it closed for a while but is now based in Breda and uses other breweries to make its beers. There is no denying the hop character here—peppery tones of marmalade, fennel, and cut grass, all expressed in unfiltered form.

STICHTING NOORDHOLLANDSE ALTERNATIEVE BIERBROUWERS (SNAB)

PURMEREND, NORTH HOLLAND
WWW.SNAB.NL

SNAB Pale Ale 6.3%

Founded in 1991, SNAB develops its beers in its own pilot-brewing plant. When it's happy with them, they get brewed in a Belgian brewery. This sort of gypsy approach seems to work, as SNAB's beers are serial international award winners. A case in point is this truly superb American-style pale ale, brewed with Cascade hops and yeast from Oregon.

TEXELSE BIERBROUWERIJ

OUDESCHILD, TEXEL, NORTH HOLLAND
WWW.SPECIAALBIER.COM

Wit Wheat Beer 5%

Recognizable by its Lighthouse logo, Texelse has endured a rocky time since it was formed in 1994 but now, under secure ownership, is conjuring up some quality craft ales on the Friesian island of Texel. This is a tasty wit that ticks all the right ingredients boxes of spice and fruit, resulting in a parch-reducing drinkability.

BROUWERIJ 'TIJ

AMSTERDAM
WWW.BROUWERIJHETIJ.NL

Columbus Belgium Strong Ale 9%

The ostrich and egg emblem on the bottles is a play on the fact that "ij" sounds like the Dutch word for "egg." In Dutch, "to find the egg of Columbus" means "I've done something rather clever" and 'tIJ has certainly done so with this copper-toned ale, imbued with heaps of hops and a bright, zesty bitterness. A heavyweight beer that caresses rather than clobbers.

TOMMIE SIEF WILD ALES

DEN HELDER, NORTH HOLLAND
WWW.TSWILDALES.COM

Cassis-Braam Sour Beer 5%

Wild hearts run free with this young brewery that was set up in 2015. More specifically, wild beers and wood-aged sours are its modus operandi (organic where possible). Cassis-Braam has blackberries and black currants in the mix, producing a tart, well-berried, funky, and dry beer.

Wild Ales

LA TRAPPE (DE KONINGSHOEVEN)

BERKEL-ENSCHOT, NORTH BRABANT
WWW.LATRAPPE.NL

La Trappe Tripel 8%

Once the only Trappist brewer outside Belgium, but now they have popped up in several other countries. In 1999, it was stripped of its Trappist status after the monks relinquished their brewing responsibilities, but, after an almighty fuss with its Belgian brethren, it was allowed back in under the condition that the monastery got back into the habit of at least overseeing the brewing. Subsequently, the beers have improved immensely, especially the Tripel.

UILTJE

HAARLEM, NORTH HOLLAND
WWW.UILTJECRAFTBEER.COM

Big Fat 5 Double IPA 8%

Originally created to celebrate the fifth anniversary of Amsterdam's Beer Temple (five hops were used in the making of it), this is a ferociously hoppy DIPA that has since become a regular—it's West Coast USA in style, so expect enough fruit to stock a greengrocer's barrel.

VOLENDAM

VOLENDAM, NORTH HOLLAND
WWW.BIERBROUWERIJVOLENDAM.NL

West Vølen/Pijtje Barley Wine 10.5%

There's a gentle nod to the Trappist tradition (West Vølen anyone?) with the name of this luxurious and lithe beer; its Samson-like strength might also help in making that connection. Whatever the speculation, though, its bittersweet, dark fruitiness and citrus character, followed by a dry boozy finish, make it a beer to be reckoned with.

Above: Barcelona is one of the emerging beer cities in Spain, with several adventurous craft beer breweries gaining worldwide attention.
Below: The Barcelona Brewing Museum displays gleaming coppers that help explain the brewing process to visitors.

INTRODUCTION
SPAIN

Spain can be very hot in the summer. This is neither the time nor place for a weather report, particularly since a climate update on Spain is not news, but in the context of a beer book, it does at least explain the triumph of mass-produced domestic lager brands such as San Miguel or Cruzcampo.

Basking in the sunburn-inducing heat of the South, you want something ice cold, sometimes so chilled in fact, that flavor is a minor consideration in your overall experience. Such beers still flourish, consumers spending hundreds of millions of euros on the stuff every year, and they will always have a place. But Spain's beer choices are becoming more diverse. The country has not been immune to the influence of the American movement, and a fledgling scene is starting to meet an evolving demand for beer with more flavor.

Alhambra provides an interesting starting point, with its Reserva 1925 imperial pils style that adapts an increasingly bland canvas and amps up the elements—more malt, alcohol, and hop profile—which starts to make the conversation a little more interesting.

But as we move away from the topic of lagers, the conversation starts to focus on styles that have not previously been successful in Spain. Madrid, for example, has been busting out some brilliant food and beer festivals in recent times and is becoming a testing ground for new boundaries in brewing—not to mention some superb specialist beer venues, such as Irreale, where the cream of Spain's craft brewing scene can be discovered alongside some terrific tapas. Cibeles breweryhas its balanced IPA, La Virgen is bestowing brown ales and breakfast stouts on the bar scene, and Henares has been properly daring with its porters. All three breweries are worth keeping an eye on in the coming years, and more are set to follow.

Then there are the pioneers who are not only aping the great new American standards but bringing a little Spanish swagger to *cerveza*. Take Domus, where they have brewed a beer called Greco, using saffron, almond, lemon, and cinnamon. In Mallorca, the Boscana brewery experiments with local chile in its IPA and at Sullerica brews a porter with cocoa and local orange blossom and a 1561 IPA with green olives. Olives *in* the beer, not in a bowl on the side.

Then there's Catalonia, perhaps the most densely populated craft beer region in the country (boasting as many as 150 breweries at the last count). Barcelona, its capital, is emerging as one of Europe's most exciting new beer cities, with the likes of BrewDog, Naparbier, and Mikkeller all opening beer bars or brewpubs in recent years. Every Spring, the city also hosts the BBF (Barcelona Beer Festival), a seriously superb celebration of Spain's beer scene and beyond, attracting more than 30,000 attendees with the likes of Edge, Garage, BeerCat, Masia Agullons, and Bocanada Cerveza Artesana all making noise.

Spain has not been as quick to flex its creative beer muscles as many other European nations, which is a little surprising given its extraordinary approach to food, but the slow approach is definitely picking up speed, and after years of gradual growth, craft beer is reigning in Spain and its beer can no longer be considered plain.

SPAIN

ALES AGULLONS
SANT JOAN DE MEDIONA, CATALONIA
WWW.MASIA-AGULLONS.COM

Setembre Sour Beer 5.5%

As the name of the beer might suggest, this is an annual release, and yes it comes out in September. This energetic Catalan brewery does take a couple of years to produce it, with the beer spending time first in wood and then in the bottle. The result is a tart and tempting sour that is ideal with tapas.

CERVEZAS ALHAMBRA
GRANADA, ANDALUSIA
WWW.CERVEZASALHAMBRA.COM

Alhambra Reserva 1925
Premium Lager 6.4%

Two brewers, Carlos Bouvard and Antonio Knorr, founded the brewery in Granada in 1925 and named it after the city's impressive Alhambra Palace. It is situated on the outskirts of Granada at the base of the imposing Sierra Nevada from which it sources its water. Presented in a terrific old-style green bottle, 1925 has caramel and toasted grain on the nose. The palate is grainy and slightly fiery thanks to the alcoholic strength, with a bittersweet finish. Try it with paella.

CERVECERA ARTESANA
NALDA, LA RIOJA
WWW.CERVEZACERIUX.COM

Ceriux Rubia Wine-Beer 5.4%

A young brewery whose Ceriux range of beers makes use of concentrated grape must in the brewing process. Rubia is its sumptuous blonde-colored beer, which also has spices as well as grape must in the mix. There're citrus and spice on the nose and the palate, then a light fruitiness before the subtle bitter finish.

BASQUELAND BREWING PROJECT
HERNANI, BASQUE COUNTRY
WWW.BASQUEBEER.COM

Imparable IPA 6.8%

Founded in 2013, this is a thrusting microbrewery with a tempting range of excellent beers, including this voraciously hopped IPA, which is pale gold in color and buzzes with tropical fruit, pine resin, and a bracing bitterness.

BIIR
BARCELONA, CATALONIA
WWW.BIIR.CAT

4B Oude Gueuze 5.5%

This "Barca" gypsy brewery demonstrates that you don't have to be around Brussels when it comes to making a lambic (though it does help that it was brewed at Belgium's De Troch). There are four different ages of lambic blended together here, and the result is a fabulously funky, tantalizingly tart, and well-balanced gueuze.

CERVEZA DOUGALL'S
LA VEGA, CANTABRIA
WWW.DOUGALLS.ES

942 Pale Ale 4.2%

Dougall's is one of the shining stars of the Spanish craft beer revolution. Founded by Englishman Andrew Dougall, its beers are a joy to drink, none more so than this glistening, gleaming American pale ale, which rings in the glass with its bold hop aromatics, and a juiciness that would put a mere orange to shame.

EDGE BREWING
BARCELONA, CATALONIA
WWW.EDGEBREWING.COM

Hoptimista IPA 6.6%

American-style craft beer is at the heart of what Edge does, which is not surprising given that it was founded by a couple of Americans in 2013. The plaudits shower down on this brewery, especially for its West Coast IPA, which is dry hopped twice and pulsates with tropical fruit, citrus, and pine character.

CERVESA ESPIGA
SANT LLORENÇ D'HORTONS, CATALONIA
WWW.ESPIGA.CAT

Espiga Black IPA 8.5%
A brewery founded by a couple of biologists in 2014, its beers have already been winning fans and accolades. One of the award winners is this brutal beast of a black IPA. Full-bodied, as black as the darkest night, and imbued with a rich, roast hop character.

GARAGE
BARCELONA, CATALONIA
WWW.GARAGEBEER.CO

Blacksmith Imperial Stout 8%
Barcelona has a thriving craft beer scene, of which Garage is a part. Originally set up as a brewpub, it is known for its boldly flavored beers (some of which are dispensed cask-conditioned). This is a rich and dark imperial stout, full of coffee, chocolate, and licorice—the brewery calls it a session Imperial stout.

CERVESA GUINEU
VALLS DE TORROELLA, CATALONIA
WWW.GUINEUBEER.COM

Riner Session IPA 2.5%
Here is the miracle of modern craft brewing an intensely flavorful beer that is low in alcohol. Classed as a "Half American Pale Ale" by the brewery, a lot of its aromatics and flavor comes from the use of a single hop, Amarillo, which produces light orange citrus and tropical fruit notes. A sensible sipper.

LAUGAR BREWERY
GORDEXOLA, BASQUE COUNTRY
WWW.LAUGARBREWERY.COM

Aupa Tovarisch
Imperial Stout 11.3%
Young brewery with the motto "brewing in the name of malt and hop," an intention carried over into their exemplary beers that ululate with flavor. This is a potent imperial stout that has plenty of chocolate, mocha, wood, vanilla, and roast grain on the nose and palate.

MATEO & BARNABÉ
LOGROÑO, LA RIOJA
WWW.MATEOYBERNABE.COM

Araña Riojan Porter 8.1%
Founded in 2012 by homebrewer Alberto Pacheco, this is an imaginative micro with stylish branding and, more importantly, equally stylish beers. This brew is released under the name of Little Bichos, which incorporates both regulars and limited releases. Brewed as a strong porter, it then sits for up to 12 months in Rioja wine barrels, with the result being an intriguing and complex quaffer.

CERVESA DEL MONTSENY
SEVA, CATALONIA
WWW.CERVESAMONTSENY.CAT

Mala Vida Bourbon
Imperial Stout 11%
Founded in 2007, Montseny was one of the first breweries in Spain to start making beers that were different from those made by the big brewers. It has continued on the same path, as this bourbon barrel-aged imperial stout demonstrates. Robust, potent, and full-bodied in its mouthfeel, it has molasses, chocolate, coffee, and bourbon making their mark all the way down the throat.

"You foam within our glasses, you lusty golden brew, whoever imbibes takes fire from you. The young and the old sing your praises; here's to beer, here's to cheer, here's to beer."
—BEDŘICH SMETANA *CZECH COMPOSER 1824–1884*

NAPARBIER
NOÁIN, NAVARRE
WWW.NAPARBIER.COM

Back in Black Black IPA 8.5%

Naparbier is another reason that beer connoisseurs are starting to turn their eyes (and palates) toward Spain and whispering that this could be the next Italy. Naparbier has an incredibly accomplished range of brews, including this seductive and explosive black IPA, which is dry, roasty, orangey, and smooth all at once. If you want more, the brewery has a brewpub in Barcelona.

CERVESES LA PIRATA
SÚRIA, CATALONIA
WWW.CERVESALAPIRATA.COM

Black Bock Imperial Stout 11.2%

Drink too much of this imperious imperial stout and you'll be walking the plank. Take it easy instead, and savor the swirls of chocolate, mocha, earthiness, roastiness, licorice, and a creamy and smooth mouthfeel.

REPTILIAN
SANT VICENÇ DE CALDERS, TARRAGONA
WWW.REPTILIANBREWERY.COM

Apokalypse Imperial Stout 11.5%

A suitably dramatic name for an intensely flavored imperial stout which is packed with roasted grain, sweet caramel, milk chocolate, the lushness of vanilla, the light acidity of espresso, and a long, luxurious finish.

PORTUGAL

MEAN SARDINE
MAFRA, LISBON
MEANSARDINE.TUMBLR.COM

Amura Pale Ale 6%

Great name, equally great beer. This small lively brewery has an impressive range of beers and has also taken part in brewing collaborations with To Øl, De Molen, and Passarola. This is its American pale ale, with a bright, bold hoppiness in the glass.

PASSAROLA
LISBON
WWW.PASSAROLA.PT

Passarola Double Oatmeal Stout Imperial Stout 8%

Creamy and soothing, this extremely dark chestnut Imperial stout has a lively and aromatic charge of coffee, chocolate, licorice, and malt sweetness, while chattering away with more coffee and an oatlike smoothness in the mouthfeel and hops in the finish.

"Sometimes when I reflect back on all the beer I drink I feel ashamed—then I look into the glass and think about the workers in the brewery and all of their hopes and dreams. If I didn't drink this beer, they might be out of work and their dreams would be shattered. Then I say to myself, 'It is better that I drink this beer and let their dreams come true than be selfish and worry about my liver.'"

—JACK HANDEY US COMEDIAN, 1949–

POLAND

ALEBROWAR
LEBORK, POMERANIAN
WWW.ALEBROWAR.PL

Black Hope Black IPA 6.2%

Cutting-edge craft gypsy brewers with a growing chain of beer bars and a big and bold selection of beers. This is a midnight-black-hued IPA, in which citrus and pine vie for attention, among hints of roast, coffee, and subtle chocolate.

BROWAR AMBER
BIELKÓWKO, POMERANIAN
WWW.BROWAR-AMBER.PL

Amber Koźlak Dunkel Bock 6.5%

With a demonic-looking ram on the label and an intense toffee-nose, this dunkel has sweet tones of licorice, plums, and dates on the palate. A port-colored beer, it's brewed by a well established, medium-size brewery near Gdansk that proudly uses local ingredients.

ARTEZAN
BŁONIE, MASOVIAN
WWW.ARTEZAN.PL

Pacific Pale Ale 5%

Based close to Warsaw, Artezan is yet another example of the emerging Polish craft beer scene. Among its standouts, this IPA is brewed with wheat, coriander, and orange peel, while it has also revived the ancient Grodziskie beer style. Pacific Pale Ale is its bestseller, a stellar swig of citrus and tropical fruit, finishing dry.

KORMORAN
OLSZTYN, WARMIAN-MASURIAN
WWW.BROWARKORMORAN.PL

Porter Warminski Baltic Porter 9%

Top-notch Baltic porter from a brewery that started plying its trade back in 2003. Chocolate, caramel, dried plums, and coffee rush out of the glass, joined by hints of rum and roast grain. It's bitter and full-bodied, subtly sweet, fruity, and chocolaty on the palate, before a bittersweet and roasty finish.

BROWAR PINTA
WROCŁAW, POLAND
WWW.BROWARPINTA.PL

Vermont IPA 6.1%

Juicy, fruity, bitter, and full-bodied, this is PINTA's take on the latest IPA fad/style out of the USA, making use of a yeast strain developed in Vermont which produces a much fruitier IPA than its West Coast counterpart. (Think Heady Topper in the Baltic and you might be getting warm.)

PRACOWNIA PIWA
MODLNICZKA, LESSER POLAND
WWW.PRACOWNIAPIWA.PL

Dwa Smoki IPA 5.8%

Even though the name of the beer might suggest something smoked, it's in fact a harmonic happiness of an IPA with Belgian-style wit. It's full-bodied and smooth in its mouth-feel, generous in its citrus, while coriander and chamomile add an eloquent spiciness.

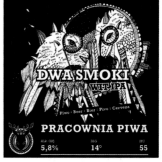

STU MOSTÓW
WROCŁAW, LOWER SILESIAN
WWW.100MOSTOW.PL

WRCLW Rye RIS Imperial Stout 10.2%

This is a rapturous and stylishly branded imperial stout from a newish brewery in the historic city of Wrocław; it's dense in its darkness, aromatically adventurous (chocolate, umami, dried fruit, hazelnut, roastiness) and plunges the palate into an intense sense of joy as the aromatics continue. The long finish is bitter.

WĄSOSZ
KONOPISKA, SILESIAN
WWW.BROWARWASOSZ.PL

Terrence American IPA 6%

Even though it was founded in 1994, Wąsosz is no stick-in-the-mud when it comes to the beers it sends out into the world. This is its generously (some might even say insanely) hopped IPA, where Citra and Amarillo send great gusts of tropical fruit and citrus alongside appetizing caramel and a bracing bitter finish. A totally convincing IPA.

ŻYWIEC
ŻYWIEC, SILESIAN
WWW.ZYWIEC.COM.PL

Żywiec Porter Baltic Porter 9.5%

A meze of dark malts makes up the sweet, buttery backbone of this black peppery Baltic porter first brewed in 1881, a full 29 years after the Żywiec brewery was founded by the Hapsburg family.

> "Not all chemicals are bad. Without chemicals such as hydrogen and oxygen, for example, there would be no way to make water, a vital ingredient in beer."
> —DAVE BARRY *AMERICAN HUMORIST AND AUTHOR 1947–*

LUXEMBOURG

BOFFERDING
BASCHARAGE, KÄERJENG
WWW.BOFFERDING.LU

Bofferding Christmas Béier 5.5%

Bofferding, the brewery with the largest share of the Luxembourg beer market, was formed in 1975 by the merger of Bofferding and the Brasserie Funck-Bricher of Luxembourg City, in the southwest of Luxembourg. As well as a neat and tidy pilsner, it has branched out with this festive brunette lager that's bready, nutty, and a little earthy.

FANTÔME
SOY, LUXEMBOURG
WWW.FANTOME.BE

Fantôme Chocolat Saison 8%

Left-field Luxembourg brewer Dany Prignon, eclectic, eccentric, and sometimes overly experimental, polarizes opinion among Belgian beer buffs. As if to emphasize this cocktail of conundrums, Prignon places this hazy golden-amber ale in the saison camp, even though it contains cocoa powder and chile pepper, all of which make for a tart, spicy, and caramel-sweet beer that completely deconstructs the idea of chocolate beer (and saison for that matter).

SIMON
WILTZ
WWW.BRASSERIESIMON.LU

Simon Prestige Champagne-Style Beer 5%

Traditional methods dating back to 1824 are still strictly adhered to at this micro nestled in the woody hills of the Ardennes. If a solid but unspectacular lager is the brewery's bread and butter, Prestige is the smart cutlery brought out only on special occasions. Champagne-style beer brewed using spelt, open fermentation, and Crèmant de Luxembourg sparkling wine. A luxury beer.

ESTONIA

A LE COQ
TARTU, TARTU
WWW.ALECOQ.EE

 A Le Coq Porter 6.5%

In the nineteenth century, Belgian Albert Le Coq carved out a profitable niche by exporting strong porter from Britain to the Baltic. In 1913, he bought a brewery in Estonia, where he began brewing porter. But, by the 1970s, demand for the style had waned, and production ceased. In the 1990s however, new owners revived the toffee-tinged, spicy dark lager and, in so doing, have done Albert proud.

PÕHJALA
TALLINN, HARJU
WWW.POHJALABEER.COM

Öö Baltic Porter 10.5%

Pioneering Estonian craft brewery whose expat Brit head brewer is ex-BrewDog. Hops are used with abandon, but Öö is a beautifully dark Baltic porter whose mash-up of roastiness, smoke, dark fruits, chocolate, and a comforting alcoholic warmth is a symphony in the glass.

TANKER
VAIDA, HARJU
WWW.TANKER.EE

Sauna Session Speciality Beer 4.7%

Ryan Suske arrived in Estonia and found it hard to find the beers he'd enjoyed back in San Diego, so he began brewing his own. He soon hooked up with a couple of others, and the brewery grew quickly. This beer is full of of fruitiness, berries, and herbs before a sweet finish.

ÕLLENAUT
SAUE, HARJU
WWW.OLLENAUT.EE

Eesti Rukki Eil Rye Beer 5.3%

Õllenaut's first beers emerged in 2013 and have continued to impress Estonian connoisseurs. This rye beer is a complex little beast with plenty of spice, chocolate, and caramel on the nose, while the palate has a bready character, as well as hints of wood and sweetness.

MALTA

SIMONDS FARSONS CISK
MRIEHEL
WWW.FARSONS.COM

Cisk Lager 4.2%

The sunshine and heat of a Maltese summer's day is well accompanied by this gold-colored sparkling quaffer that wouldn't be out of place in a Munich beer garden. Refreshing, pleasantly bitter, and lemony. Made by a brewery that has been a central part of this Mediterranean island since the 1920s.

LORD CHAMBRAY
GOZO
WWW.LORDCHAMBRAY.COM.MT

Special Bitter 3.8%

The isle of Gozo is home to this ambitious craft brewery that started brewing in 2014. Naturally, like everyone and their mother, they produce an IPA, but this is their Anglophile bitter with English hops in the mix. The result is a dark gold quaffer with a good balance of honeyed, sweet malt, and some bitterness from the hops.

Winter Ale 8%

Malta's winters are not as inclement as those places where sipping a winter warmer is akin to wearing an extra sweater, but this rich and resonant seasonal ale with local carob honey in the mix will still nourish the occasional chilly day by the Med.

HUNGARY

FÓTI KÉZMÜVES SÖRFÖZDE
FÓT
WWW.FOTISORFOZDE.HU

Keserü Méz Premium Lager 6%

This so-called "hop lager" is bright and affable in the glass, grassy and lemony on the nose, and bittersweet and fruity on the palate with a notable bitter finish. The name of the beer translates as *Bitter Moon*, which is a reference to Polanski's movie of the same name, with Hugh Grant in the starring role.

THE AMERICAS

Above: The Deschutes Brewery in Bend, Oregon, is the sixth largest craft brewery in the US with its most celebrated beer a dark one.
Below: Stone Brewing's Liberty Station World Bistro & Gardens is an imaginative reinvention of a US naval training center.

INTRODUCTION
THE AMERICAS

America has reinvented a lot of wheels—movies, music, politics—but for decades beer was less a wheel than an Achilles heel on a foot covered in warts, and all the warts were yellow, fizzy, and bland. Then, between the late 1970s and the tail end of 2015, the country witnessed a brewing revolution that the Founding Fathers, and indeed a pumice stone, would've raised a glass to. In three decades, the boundaries of American beer were targeted, tested, and torn as the tide turned and crashed like a tsunami against the mass-produced lager styles. Frustrated and reactionary students saw homebrewing legalized in 1978 and went from enthusiasts to pioneers for what the world would coin a "craft beer" movement. It was a glorious, rousing response, embracing barrel-aging beers, making cans sexy, and hailing the hop like no one else in history.

Toward the end of its righteous reawakening, though, the American scene went from stunning to a bit silly. After reinventing age-old European styles, celebrating everything from stout to sours and giving us hop-driven delights like American pales or IPAs, the PR noise got in the way. Beard yeast, moon dust, smoked goats' brains, and scrapings of a 35-million-year-old whale fossil had made it into the beer, and if there was yeast on a kitchen sink, some eager upstart with a start-up was throwing it in a fermentation tank.

This wasn't necessarily a disaster, not least because many of the wilder experiments were launched by brewers with a quality range. But as beautifully unmitigated as it was, America's inspirational unshackling saw the wrestling ropes stretch too far and snap. Some of the newbies, with all the best intentions in the world, couldn't maintain consistency, and while America's beer bubble didn't burst, it got a little squashed.

As some fell by the wayside and the conglomerates turned heads and bought their way into craft, the growth slowed, and some onlookers predicted a catastrophic decline. Mercifully that wasn't to be. The enthusiasm the country had engineered sustained a new national

and global affection for better beer, and the survivors steadied the ship and kept moving it forward. Albeit a little slower.

There are now more than 5,000 US breweries, and it remains the most fertile, innovative, and savviest beer nation on the planet. Domestically, "craft" enjoys nearly a 15 percent share of the beer market, which is modest but miraculous in the context of the timescale. Having championed American ingredients, the likes of Sierra Nevada and Samuel Adams have cultivated an international customer base for its beer, while brews from Colorado, Portland, and California are ingrained in the global beer-geek checklist.

Such has been the success of the hop-driven beers that any country with a drinking culture will stock a pale ale or an IPA that is American-inspired. A consequence has been hop price hikes and shortages, but the adaptable American brewers have simply rolled out new spectacular saisons and sours.

The weirdness won't stop of course—cannabis and purple Peruvian corn have made the brewing news and sound lame—but the main players now combine PR stunts with more focused purpose, which should ensure longevity for tasty beer.

USA WEST COAST

21ST AMENDMENT BREWERY
SAN FRANCISCO, CALIFORNIA
WWW.21ST-AMENDMENT.COM

Hell or High Watermelon Wheat Beer 4.9%
A curveball beer produced by a terrific Bay Area brewery, which is located just minutes away from the San Francisco Giants baseball stadium. A wonderfully refreshing wheat beer brewed using 200 pounds of fresh watermelon, which provides a unique fruitiness.

ALAMEDA BREW HOUSE
PORTLAND, OREGON
WWW.ALAMEDABREWHOUSE.COM

Irvington Juniper Porter 5.1%
From the achingly trendy part of Portland known as Beaumont-Wilshire comes this smooth, full-bodied porter finished with a flurry of juniper spice. Imagine a thinking drinker's gin-inspired "depth charge" and prepare to be enlightened and entertained by it.

ALASKAN BREWING COMPANY
JUNEAU, ALASKA
WWW.ALASKANBEER.COM

Alaskan Smoked Porter 6.5%
An enchanting Alaskan interpretation of German rauchbiers, which is also a classic vintage ale that definitely improves with age. Brewed with malt that has been languidly smoked over indigenous alder wood for three days, it conjures up caramel, dried plums, and port flavors, yet thankfully sidesteps the stifling smokiness of its German counterpart. Quite simply incredible.

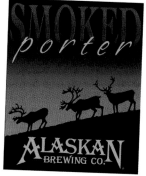

Alaskan Amber 5.3%
An early amber-hued pioneer of American craft beer that has been in the grizzly grip of locals since the 1980s. An accessible alt bier alternative, with an easy-drinking allure.

THE ALE APOTHECARY
BEND, OREGON
WWW.THEALEAPOTHECARY.COM

Sahalie Sour Beer 9.3%
Wood and time are the extra ingredients in use at this unique brewery situated several miles outside the beer-crazy town of Bend. Former Deschutes brewer Paul Arney ferments and matures his beers in oak vessels, allowing all manner of bugs to do their work. Once in bottle, with sugar and yeast for repriming, we have the likes of the tart and tantalizing Sahalie, which is the flagship beer of the Ale Apothecary.

ALESMITH BREWING COMPANY
SAN DIEGO, CALIFORNIA
WWW.ALESMITH.COM

AleSmith Wee Heavy 10%
Brewery founder Peter Zein specializes in hoppy, West Coast warps of Belgian and British ales. Anything but wee, this big, brawny, and balanced Scotch ale will put some bellow in your bagpipes.

Speedway Stout Imperial Stout 2%
Nothing gets a Californian beer buff more animated than this divine dark and velvet-textured imperial stout. After it's brewed in small batches using copious quantities of coffee beans supplied by a local roaster, it is matured in bourbon barrels. Espresso astringency softened by vanilla notes, a touch of wood, and a smug mellow alcohol glow. A signature classic from an excellent artisan aficionado of ale.

ALMANAC
SAN FRANCISCO, CALIFORNIA
WWW.ALMANACBEER.COM

Farmer's Reserve Sour Fruit Beer 7%
The two guys behind Almanac work with local farms to source the fruits that go into their Farmer's Reserve series (strawberries, blackberries and citrus for starters but not all at the same time). They don't have a brewery, and local firms produce a wort to their spec, which is then fermented and blended and aged in wood. Expect varying degrees of tart fruitiness, dryness, and deep complexity.

ALPINE BEER COMPANY

ALPINE, CALIFORNIA
WWW.ALPINEBEERCO.COM

Chez Monieux Fruit Beer 5.8%
A cracking kriek beer chock-a-block with Michigan cherries and decanted into oak barrels that have previously housed red wine. Fifteen months of maturation tames the face-twisting tartness. Sweet, sour, and fruity.

Exponential Hoppiness Imperial IPA 11%
In 2014, Alpine was bought by fellow San Diego brewery Green Flash, a deal that has enabled its beers to reach more people. Beers such as this ever-popular annual release Imperial IPA, where an ever-doubling dose of American hops infuses it with a herbal high, mellowed by the late addition of oak chips and measured maturation. Devilishly drinkable.

ANCHOR BREWING CO.

see Brewery Profile pages 186 to 187
SAN FRANCISCO, CALIFORNIA
WWW.ANCHORBREWING.COM

Liberty Ale IPA 6%
Here come the hops. Anchor's nod to IPA is a measured, marked departure from the loony lupulin efforts of its West Coast neighbors. Brown-sugar-dusted grapefruit flavors spring from a cookie base.

Anchor Small Beer Bitter 3.3%
A rare thing indeed is a Californian session beer. Small in strength but not in flavor, this classic beer is cut from the mash of Anchor's Old Foghorn barley wine.

Anchor Steam Beer 4.9%
First brewed in 1896, Anchor Steam hasn't always been this good. In fact, until Fritz Maytag knocked it into shape in 1971, it was pretty lousy. Not anymore. A San Franciscan classic, brewed using fresh citrusy North American hops and conditioned like an alebut at a slightly lower temperature. This is one of the world's best and most enduring beers.

ANDERSON VALLEY BREWING COMPANY

BOONVILLE, CALIFORNIA
WWW.AVBC.COM

Barney Flats Oatmeal Stout 5.8%
Anderson Valley is a bucolic solar-powered brewery in beautiful Boonville, which is called "Boontling," where locals speak their own dialect. This is a creamy, lightly roasty oatmeal stout with hints of espresso, cherries, and toffee mashing in with a creamy mouthfeel and a dry finish.

BALLAST POINT BREWING

SAN DIEGO, CALIFORNIA
WWW.BALLASTPOINT.COM

Sculpin IPA 7%
This is one of the boldest flavored IPAs on the West Coast, with hopping at five different stages producing a beer shimmering with waves of apricot, peach, mango, and lemon on both the nose and palate. In 2015, the US craft beer world was stunned when Ballast Point was bought by Constellation Brands for $1 billion.

Yellow Tail Pale Ale 4.6%
This is the brewery that Jack White built, and its runaway success owes much to this West Coast take on a German kölsch. Citrus sweetness on the nose and slightly tangy, it's adorned with 5% wheat, Tettnang, and Liberty hops, and yeast collected in Cologne, Germany. All in all, this pale specimen is a real catch you don't want to put back.

BEACHWOOD

LONG BEACH, CALIFORNIA
WWW.BEACHWOODBBQ.COM

Melrose IPA 7.1%
Surfing may have gone the way of the dodo at Long Beach, but Beachwood's divine mix of a BBQ accompanied by its own beer means that the Long Beach style of chilling out continues. Melrose is its dank and sticky West Coast IPA, brimming with tropical fruit and citrus with a dry finish to encourage more sipping. One to savor on long summer days, preferably in a coastal setting and next to palm trees.

ANCHOR BREWING CO.

1705 MARIPOSA STREET, SAN FRANCISCO, CA 94107

WWW.ANCHORBREWING.COM

Even though he sold Anchor Brewery in 2010, Fritz Maytag remains the man who saved this jewel-in-the-crown of US craft breweries from getting lost in the mists of beer-soaked time. In 1965, on a complete whim, he bought a majority stake in the Steam Brewery. It was, if truth be told, a ludicrous idea. For a start, Fritz had no prior knowledge or experience in the brewing of beer, nor even a particular interest in the stuff, so what he has achieved with this now iconic brewery is remarkable.

What's more, his new brewery was in shambles, selling just 100 kegs a year. "It was the last medieval brewery in the world," chuckled Fritz. "There was no refrigeration at all; everything was pumped and gravity-pulled. It was dusty, rundown, ramshackle, very primitive, and the beer tasted pretty bad. I first set eyes on it on a Wednesday, and by the end of the week I had bought the brewery."

To buy any small brewery, let alone a tumbledown one, producing an odd, long-forgotten "steam" beer style, was pure folly. During the 1950s, a wave of consolidation had swept through the American beer scene and culled the number of breweries from 407 in 1950 to just 280 in 1961, with only half of those independently run. The likes of Pabst, Schlitz, and Miller were gobbling up market share like hungry Pac-Men and, quite frankly, it was no time to be a minnow in the 1960s.

But Fritz, heir to the famous Maytag washing-machine empire, had some money in the family coffers and an appetite for a challenge. But the beer's historically lousy reputation initially hamstrung sales. While some restaurant and bar owners even went so far as to inform Fritz that the Anchor Brewery had in fact closed some years before.

"People enthused about Anchor, but that had more to do with the history than the beer," he recalled. "We were a tiny little brewery making quite a traditional beer, but standards had slipped, and it wasn't as traditional as I thought it should be. It was sour, and I wasn't happy with it."

By 1968, Fritz had acquired sole ownership of Anchor and set about restoring some pride in the beer. He sought advice from other brewers—both big and small, and attended brewing conferences where he listened and learned, while, back at the brewery, he buried his head in brewing tomes and transformed it from a "medieval" operation into one of the most modern brewhouses in the world.

"We were very proud of how we modernized things," he told us. "Modern technology is a wonderful thing when used right. We centrifuged. We flash pasteurized—it heated the beer, sending it from ice cold to 160°F and back again without harming the beer at all. Beer can become like stale bread. If you don't keep it fresh, then it's no good."

Fritz went back to traditional basics. Sugar was taken out of the brew kettle, whole hops—and lots of them—were introduced alongside two-row imported barley, while additives and adjuncts were unceremoniously shown the door. The new beer made its bottled debut in 1971, and, consistency being the key, sales shifted ever upward.

Fritz then began making other beers. A porter was unleashed in 1972, Liberty Ale followed in 1975 alongside an Old Foghorn barley wine and a Christmas Ale. In the same year, Anchor began turning a profit, but demand was beginning to outstrip what the original brewery could supply.

Determined to maintain local links, Fritz chose a site in San Francisco—a former coffee roastery in the Potrero Hill district—and built a brand-new brewery in 1979.

Anchor and Maytag's tale has become folklore among North America's craft beer movement, and quite right too. By proving that the small guy can thrive in the shadow of big business, Anchor's success laid the foundations on which a thriving craft brewing movement has been built. Having cut a lonely swathe for so long, it was with open arms that Fritz welcomed the craft brewing cavalry in the eighties. "We'd been doing it for years, and we were saved by the competition," admits Fritz. "Between us all, we've met the tremendous demand for small craft beer."

Today, as the US craft beer revolution continues, Anchor remains as vital as ever. Since its sale in 2010, Anchor has remained in the city and has continued making great beers as well as adding more to its portfolio. This includes Anchor California Lager and an IPA, the first in its history.

Above left: Gleaming copper kettles house hops and wort that are added at regular intervals to the vessel through a hatch in the top.

Above right: Fritz Maytag revived the Anchor Brewery in San Francisco in 1965, and it has been going strong ever since.

Opposite: Steam Beer and Liberty Ale are some of Anchor's bestselling brews.

* KEY BEERS

Anchor Porter 5.6%
Anchor Steam Beer 4.9%
Christmas Ale varies
Liberty Ale 6%
Old Foghorn 8%

BEAR REPUBLIC BREWING COMPANY

CLOVERDALE, CALIFORNIA
WWW.BEARREPUBLIC.COM

⭐ 🍃 **Racer 5 IPA** 7.5%

The joy of Racer 5 is in its immaculately hoarse hoppiness, highly mineral mouthfeel, rasping middle, and a comforting warm finish. An idolized, intelligent IPA from a brilliant brewpub, whose brewer Rich Norgrove also races stock cars in his spare time.

BEND BREWING

BEND, OREGON
WWW.BENDBREWINGCO.COM

🍃 🍺 **Elk Lake IPA** 6.5%

Having being founded in 1995, this is the second oldest brewpub in the beer-savvy town of Bend, but its beers are still pretty much at the peak of their game as this citrusy, piney, grassy IPA with a bittersweet finish demonstrates so well.

BRIDGEPORT BREWING

PORTLAND, OREGON
WWW.BRIDGEPORTBREW.COM

⭐ 🍺 **BridgePort IPA** 5.5%

Set up by the winemaking Ponzi family and head brewer Karl Ockert, BridgePort was a pioneer of Portland's utopian beer scene. Its IPA, first brewed in 1996 and considered by many to be the northwest's finest, accounts for three-quarters of the brewery's production. Double-fermented and brewed using a quintet of hops, it offers glorious balance when compared with other West Coast efforts. Simple and elegant, this is a damn drinkable drop.

THE BRUERY

PLACENTIA, CALIFORNIA
WWW.THEBRUERY.COM

🍃 🍺 **Humulus Lager** 7.2%

Orange County brewing stars The Bruery produces all manner of intriguing beers, especially in the family of sours. However, it's this crisp and fruity lager that gets the taste buds going. It's heavily hopped with the clean lager yeast allowing the bold colors of the hops to show through.

BUOY BREWERY

ASTORIA, OREGON
WWW.BUOYBEER.COM

🍺 🍴 **Czech-Style Pilsner** 6.2%

Buoy makes its beers in a former canning factory on the edge of the Columbia River in the old fishing town of Astoria where sea lions often slumber outside the brewery's restaurant. Try this take on a European classic, with its sweet malt juiciness, brisk carbonation, spicy Saaz, and dry crispy finish.

CALDERA

ASHLAND, OREGON
WWW.CALDERABREWING.COM

🍺 🍴 🍽 **Ashland Amber** 5.6%

Caldera is another veteran of the Oregon brewing scene, having produced its first beers in 1997. Now with two taphouses in Ashland (one of which houses the brewery), it produces a diverse range of beers. The Amber has an appetizing caramel sweetness, which is balanced by a zingy fruitiness before finishing dry and bitter. An ideal, easy-drinking quaffer.

CASCADE

PORTLAND, OREGON
WWW.CASCADEBREWING.COM

🍷 🍺 **Apricot** Sour Ale 7.2%

You could call Cascade Brewing's Barrel House in Portland's Eastside the house of sours, such is the brewery's dedication to making beers with a tartness and a tingle that come from up to 14 months spent in oak wine barrels with different yeasts and bugs. Apricot Ale, as the name suggests, is a fruity, funky, crispy little number and a perfect balance of sweet and sour.

CLOUDBURST BREWING

SEATTLE, WASHINGTON
WWW.CLOUDBURSTBREW.COM

🍃 🍺 🍴 **Happy Little Clouds** Pilsner 5.3%

Founded in 2015 by former Elysian brewer Steve Luke, this lively little brewery produces an intriguing selection of beers. This is called a "Bastardized German Pilsener," which presumably refers to the dry-hopping, which produces a grassy, citrusy lager with a crisp mouthfeel and long dry finish.

THE COMMONS BREWERY
PORTLAND, OREGON
WWW.COMMONSBREWERY.COM

Flemish Kiss Sour Ale 6.3%

Commons' home is an old red-brick warehouse where French, Belgian, and German beer styles (some obviously twisted beyond recognition) rule the roast. Flemish Kiss started off life as a pale ale before Brettanomyces worked its funky magic. The result is an earthy, citrusy, tart beer that deserves more than one glass.

CRAFTSMAN BREWING COMPANY
PASADENA, CALIFORNIA
WWW.CRAFTSMANBREWING.COM

Triple White Sage
Belgian Ale 9%

Never mind the Botox, Los Angelinos should be stuffing their faces with the creative quaff of Craftsman Brewing. Brewer Mark Jilg has been casting pearls before swine for nearly two decades, braving the grim, glitzy gridlock in a 1940s Studebaker delivery truck and brewing some awesome idiosyncratic ales. Sat alongside a pale ale brewed with poppy seeds, a Cabernale brewed with grapes, a pre-Prohibition lager, and a smoked dark lager, Triple White Sage is a bombastic Belgian ale that brings honey, coriander, sage, grassy hops, and a touch of mint to the party. Fantastic.

CRUX FERMENTATION PROJECT
BEND, OREGON
WWW.CRUXFERMENTATION.COM

Doublecross Belgian Strong Ale 11%

Former Deschutes brewmaster Larry Sidor started Crux in 2011 with the aim of using barrels to add character to his ales (hence, no doubt, the affixing of "Project" to the brewery name). Doublecross spends time in oak wine barrels used for Pinot Noir, which helps to produce a rich and luxurious beer featuring vanilla, wood, preserved fruit, candy sugar, and roasted nuts. A classic.

DESCHUTES BREWERY
BEND, OREGON
WWW.DESCHUTESBREWERY.COM

Black Butte Porter 5.2%

Deschutes is the sixth-biggest craft brewery in the United States but the only one whose success has been founded on a dark beer. Beautifully balanced bitterness, chocolate-tinged sweetness, and a slightly smoky finish, like coffee brewed on a bonfire.

The Abyss Barrel-Aged Imperial Stout 11.1%

Once a year Deschutes releases this sumptuous and silky imperial stout, some of which will have spent time slumbering in various wooden barrels. The result is a midnight-black beer with a limitless seduction of molasses, licorice, chocolate, mocha coffee, vanilla, and dried fruits.

DRAKE'S BREWING COMPANY
SAN LEANDRO, CALIFORNIA
WWW.DRINKDRAKES.COM

Drake's IPA 7%

The nautically themed Drake's brews some big, buccaneering beers, many of them barrel-aged, yet lupulin-loving landlubbers will happily walk the plank for this hearty, heavily hopped swashbuckling sip, which was first brewed in 2002, though the brewery opened its doors in 1989.

ELYSIAN BREWING COMPANY
SEATTLE, WASHINGTON
WWW.ELYSIANBREWING.COM

Jasmine IPA 6.3%

Cup of tea? No? How about this instead, where the fruitiness and hoppiness of an IPA meet the aromatics of jasmine to produce an elegant beer that can be enjoyed as a refreshing quaff or served at the dining table. In January 2015, beer geeks and industry observers were slightly stunned, to say the least, when Anheuser-Busch bought the company.

FIRESTONE WALKER BREWING COMPANY

see Brewery Profile pages 192 to 193
PASO ROBLES, CALIFORNIA
WWW.FIRESTONEWALKER.COM

Pale 31 Pale Ale 4.6%

Plowing a lonesome yet seriously lovely furrow amid the vineyards of Californian wine country, Firestone Walker bigs up British beer styles. It has pioneered a barrel-brewing system similar to the Burton Union, which, during primary fermentation, amplifies the hop character and softens the malt with vanilla and wood notes taken from the oak. All the best bits of British and American brewing can be found in this phenomenal pale ale.

FISH BREWING COMPANY

OLYMPIA, WASHINGTON
WWW.FISHBREWING.COM

Organic Wild Salmon Pale Ale 5%

Petite but prolific producer of powerful beers. This is a particularly pleasant pale ale in which Cascade hops leap high amid a stream of caramel sweetness. It's crisp, it's refreshing, and it raises money to protect our aquatic brethren. The beers first appeared in Washington in 1993.

FORT GEORGE

ASTORIA, OREGON
WWW.FORTGEORGEBREWERY.COM

Vortex IPA 7.7%

Fort George is situated in a 1920s building that was once home to a business repairing cars. Now, an eclectic range of beers is produced on site (there's also a restaurant and bar where brewery specials can be found), with Vortex being the brewery's piney, citrusy, grassy, pleasingly bitter IPA.

FULL SAIL BREWING COMPANY

HOOD RIVER, OREGON
WWW.FULLSAILBREWING.COM

Full Sail Amber Amber Ale 6%

Full Sail converted a brewery from a former fruit cannery on the banks of the windsurfing wonderland that is Hood River in 1987, and it is now one of the top 30 largest breweries in the USA. For years, the wind in Full Sail's sails has been this excellent multi-award-winner. Robust yet refreshing.

Session Premium Lager 5.1%

In the heartland of heavy-hopped ales, this retro pre-Prohibition lager does what it says on the label. Ideal for a dedicated sipping session on the brewpub's spectacular sundeck after a long day pretending that you can windsurf like the rest of them.

GREEN FLASH

SAN DIEGO, CALIFORNIA
WWW.GREENFLASHBREW.COM

Le Freak Belgian Strong Ale 9.2%

Ever since they started in 2002, there's been a palpable hop buzz about Green Flash, which, along with the activities of fellow San Diego brewery Stone, has led some to suggest a substyle of San Diego IPA. Le Freak ignores the furor, being a perfect marriage of a Belgian tripel and imperial IPA. The resulting nuptials are fruity, spicy, minerally, and juicy before a dry bitter finish.

HAIR OF THE DOG
PORTLAND, OREGON
WWW.HAIROFTHEDOG.COM

Hair of the Dog Adam Adambier 10%

Only the brave or bonkers would hazard Hair of the Dog's behemoth, boutique bottle-conditioned beauties at breakfast. Drooled over by discerning drinkers, Adam is a complex interpretation of Adambier, an elusive German beer style. A warm, smoky, fruity, constantly evolving ale that flirts with barley wines and harvest ales.

Hair of the Dog Fred Barley Wine 10%

A golden-hued, malt-driven tribute to the late, renowned, and much missed beer writer Fred Eckhart that betters in the bottle. Brewed with rye grain, ten hop varieties, and when it comes to maturation, scant regard for Father Time.

Hair of the Dog Rose Tripel 8%

Honey-cloaked take on a Belgian tripel with a hoodwinking drinkability. Like all Hair of the Dog's beers, Rose gets better if left alone for a while to let time weave its tasty magic, then smugly consumed in celebration of one's restraint.

HALE'S ALES
SEATTLE, WASHINGTON
WWW.HALESBREWERY.COM

Mongoose IPA 6%

Having first poked his mash fork about at the now-defunct Gale's Brewery in Hampshire, England, Mike Hale brews upstanding English ales of impeccable character, of which the rounded, malty Mongoose IPA is one.

HERETIC BREWING
FAIRFIELD, CALIFORNIA
WWW.HERETICBREWING.COM

Evil Twin Red IPA 6.8%

Gloweringly red in the glass with hints of chestnut blending in, this is one of Heretic's most popular beers. It has a rich malt character, though tendencies to oversweetness are kept in check, while the hops add a certain earthiness with a citrusy and bracing bitterness in the finish.

HOPWORKS URBAN BREWERY
PORTLAND, OREGON
WWW.HOPWORKSBEER.COM

Galactic Imperial Red 9.5%

Hopworks is a thriving eco-conscious brewery, which manages to use organic raw materials for all its beers. This is a robust and chewy beer, medium bodied, featuring caramel, citrus and pine resin alongside a very dry finish.

LAGUNITAS
PETALUMA, CALIFORNIA
WWW.LAGUNITAS.COM

Czech Pils Pilsner 6%

Founder Tony Magee describes his Czech pils thus: "While an ale might steal your car or try to date your daughter and keep her out all night for who-knows-what purpose, this well-bred pilsner would offer to clean your house while you're on vacation and leave fresh scones and coffee for you when you return." Well, that's one way of describing a decent pils.

Lagunitas IPA 6.2%

Renowned as much for his extremely amusing tasting notes as his collection of gorgeous giggle juice, Tony Magee has built his esoteric ale empire on this excellent IPA. Pine needles, eucalyptus, and marmalade, with maple sweetness.

Lagunitas Maximus IPA 8%

Imperial IPAs don't come much more imperial than this. It will water your eyes, terrorize your taste buds, and put hairs on your body where there really shouldn't be any.

FIRESTONE WALKER BREWING COMPANY

1400 RAMADA DRIVE, PASO ROBLES, CALIFORNIA CA 93446

WWW.FIRESTONEWALKER.COM

Anyone who has driven through California will know that it is daunting drinking territory for anyone more used to drinks and flavors that emanate from a smaller, perhaps subtler European sensibility. The state's beers, like its burgers, cars, and scenery, are a lot bigger than they are on the other side of the Atlantic. A lot bigger.

For a more timid palate, the West Coast infatuation with intense IPAs is particularly intimidating. Heavily hopped and boldly flavored, Californian IPAs will knock your bowler hat off with Oliver Hardy-esque disdain and give your senses the kind of warm California welcome last witnessed when Reginald Denny drove into town.

But fear not, for respite and refuge from these beefy beers can be found at an Anglophile ale-making enclave, deep in Californian wine country, between Los Angeles and San Francisco.

Surrounded by vineyards, the Firestone Walker brewery goes against the grain—and the grape—by brewing beautiful, balanced beers laced with clichéd British restraint. "We really focus on drinkability and balance, and that can be a little pedestrian for the beer geeks, but we're a traditional regional brewer," says Matt Bryndilson, Firestone Walker's head brewer. "We tend to stick with cleaner hop flavors and not the earthy, grassy, and vegetal aromas that you can find in other Californian beers."

Adam Firestone, the grandson of the eponymous tire-making titan, and his English brother-in-law David Walker set up Firestone Walker in 1996. They had witnessed the Californian wine boom of the 1980s, in particular the harmonious marriage of Old World winemaking traditions and New World techniques, and thought that what worked for a tulip glass would work for a tankard too.

Sadly, Adam and David's first attempt at brewing was far too ambitious. "They wanted to do oak-fermented ales. So the original concept

Opposite left: Firestone Walker, founded by Adam Firestone and David Walker in 1996; Matt Bryndilson, Firestone Walker's head brewer, who oversees a focus on drinkability and balance.

Opposite right: The head brewer at Firestone Walker, Matt Bryndilson.

Right: In the brewery's bottling hall, where classics such as Britain-inspired Union Jack IPA, are readied to emerge into the world.

was to take chardonnay barrels and use beer in them," recalls Matt. "But the beer oxidized, and it was basically all malt vinegar."

The wayward wine barrels were subsequently dispatched from the brewery in favor of a unique adaptation of the iconic nineteenth-century Burton Union system, much favored by nineteenth-century British Burton-on-Trent-based brewers.

The system, which separates beer from surplus yeast using a row of linked oak casks and troughs, was tweaked by Firestone Walker and christened (rather aptly) the "Firestone Union." Using forty 50-gallon, medium-toast American oak barrels, the system amplifies the hop character, and the oak imparts delicate notes of vanilla, chocolate, and wood.

Batches of oak-fermented beer are blended into all Firestone's beers. The Double Barrel Ale, or DBA, is the system's signature beer and Firestone Walker's most successful. Rich, fragrant, bracing, and brisk, it's classic English-style pale ale piqued with hop spice and underscored with soft, warm malt flavors.

As well as Double Barrel, Adam and David have rolled out the bright-eyed, bushy-tailed Pale 31, Pivo Hoppy Pils, and—to placate the hop-hungry masses —Union Jack, an intense, dry-hopped yet drinkable IPA

that shakes you by the hand, not the neck. There is also the nitro series, and in 2016 Luponic Distortion was launched, when every three months Matt gets the chance to produce an IPA with different experimental hops.

Then there are Firestone Walker's vintage ales and bespoke barrel-aged beers that have pricked up the ears of craft ale connoisseurs. In 2006, to commemorate a decade of brewing, a limited edition strong ale was released called "Ten"; a glorious gathering of high-gravity beers aged in different barrel formats and blended using the expertize of local winemakers. Ten years later, 20 years was celebrated with XX, with barrels being hand-selected from Kentucky spirits producers.

"We've learned a lot from winemakers about toast levels, oak, and we're moving beer in and out of barrels," says Matt. "We're not trying to make Belgian beers with fruit or bugs, but I'm interested to see what oak aging does to the beers. So we're taking very clean beers and aging them in all kinds of whiskey and wine barrels, blending them like wine, and experimenting with racking and different toast intensity. The consumer is pushing breweries to go outside of the lines," he adds. "But we don't intend to lose sight of drinkability."

* KEY BEERS

DBA Pale Ale 5%
Pale 31 4.6%
Union Jack IPA 7.5%

LAURELWOOD PUBLIC HOUSE & BREWERY
PORTLAND, OREGON
WWW.LAURELWOODBREWPUB.COM

Red Elephant IPA 7%

If you're flying out from Portland International Airport, don't forget to call in for a livener at Laurelwood's airside bar (there's also one on the other side). Or just drop into one of the brewery's several bars in town and lap up this lasciviously luscious IPA, with its pine, tropical fruit, and citrus notes, all wrapped up with an engaging bitter finish. There's also an organic Green Elephant IPA.

LOGSDON FARMHOUSE ALES
HOOD RIVER, OREGON
WWW.FARMHOUSEBEER.COM

Peche 'n Brett Sour Ale 10%

If you thought the peach was a humble little fruit, the kind of fruit that wouldn't say boo to a goose, then think again. The locally sourced organic peaches that go into the brewery's Seizoen Bretta have a muscular and robust effect, creating a beer with the kind of complexity more usually seen in quantum physics.

LOST ABBEY BREWING
SAN DIEGO, CALIFORNIA
WWW.LOSTABBEY.COM

Angel's Share Ale
Barley Wine 12.5%

For distillers, the angels' share is the spirit that evaporates in the wooden barrels in which their whiskey resides. For Lost Abbey, it's the name of a massively potent barley wine that spends at least six months in wood. The result is a beer positively cacaphonic with wood, vanilla, light toffee, coffee, caramel, dried fruit, and chocolate notes. A real treat to sip with care.

Cuvée de Tomme
Sour Red 11%

In search of enlightening Belgian-style elixirs, Lost Abbey's brewmaster Tomme Arthur pushes more envelopes than a mailman on crack. One of several sought-after seasonal releases, Cuvée is the bourbon-barrel-aged baby of bonkers Brettanomyces yeast and sugars sought from sour cherries, barley, raisins, and candy sugar. It's a sumptuous sip with layer after layer of flavor revealing hints of vanilla and fruit, as well as a mouth-tingling sourness and tartness.

MAD RIVER BREWING
BLUE LAKE, CALIFORNIA
WWW.MADRIVERBREWING.COM

Steelhead Extra Pale Ale 5.6%

Founded in 1989, Mad River is one of the veterans of the Northern California beer scene. However, time has not wearied them, as sips of this ultrapale beer, one of their first, demonstrate: there's a delicate floral nose before it dives into a juicy maltiness, light citrus, and a dry finish.

MAGNOLIA PUB & BREWERY
SAN FRANCISCO, CALIFORNIA
WWW.MAGNOLIAPUB.COM

Magnolia Old Thunderpussy Barleywine 11.2%

Dave McLean, one of San Francisco's main microbrewing missionaries, crafts Californian-accented British beer styles on legendary Haight Street. It's a terrific brewpub, and this rich and fruity extreme IPA is a terrific, tawny tinted beer. Seek it out if you can, and devour it with gusto.

MAUI BREWING
LAHAINA, HAWAII
WWW.MAUIBREWINGCO.COM

Coconut Hiwa Porter 6%

Who would have thought that porter, which developed in eighteenth-century London, would one day be married with naturally toasted coconut to produce such a slinky, silky, chocolate, mocha-like beer that makes the soul feel so good? No one in eighteeenth-century London, for sure, though Captain Cook might have had an idea.

MIDNIGHT SUN BREWERY
ANCHORAGE, ALASKA
WWW.MIDNIGHTSUNBREWING.COM

☑ 🍺 🍴 Kodiak Brown Ale 9%
Alaskan brewer with attitude, artistic labels, and a bevy of Belgian beers and cask seasonals. This chestnut-hued beer, brewed with Northwest Perle and Willamette hops, was one of the brewery's first when it opened in 1995, and it has remained popular, as drinkers plump for its caramel sweetness, gentle roastiness, dried fruit goodness, and long dry finish.

MOONLIGHT BREWING COMPANY
SANTA ROSA, CALIFORNIA
WWW.MOONLIGHTBREWING.COM

🍺 🍴 🍷 Death & Taxes Lager 5%
Breweries don't come much more bucolic than this. Set in a wonderfully rustic corner of the Sonoma Valley, Brian Hunt's small operation brews top-class beers, of which this bracing black lager, adorned with mild molasses and a nutty finish, is very much one.

NINKASI BREWING COMPANY
EUGENE, OREGON
WWW.NINKASIBREWING.COM

🌐 🍷 ☑ Tricerahops Double IPA 8%
Monstrous by name, monstrous by nature. This is a brutally hopped double IPA in which notes of pine, grapefruit, caramel sweetness, and tropical fruit spark off in all directions like so many neurons, while the crisp mouthfeel and dry bitter finish add the trimmings.

NORTH COAST BREWING
FORT BRAGG, CALIFORNIA
WWW.NORTHCOASTBREWING.COM

★ 🍴 🍷 Brother Thelonious
Abbey Ale 9%
North Coast's brawny beers may share their coastal home with a former US military fort dating from the civil war, but they're lovers, not fighters. This robust, dark homage to jazz legend Thelonious Monk is as smooth as his music and spirals up notes of mole-like spicy chocolate, figs, and fall fruit.

🍷 🍺 ★ Old Rasputin Russian Imperial Stout 9%
Ra-Ra-Rasputin stares out from the label of this rich and spirituous imperial stout, which has been part of North Coast's portfolio since 1995. Think roasted coffee beans, butter toffee, nuts, milk chocolate, earthy hops, a long bitter finish—and pour yourself one. Every year the brewery puts some Old Rasputin in bourbon barrels and the ABV climbs to 11.2%.

PELICAN PUB & BREWERY
PACIFIC CITY, OREGON
WWW.PELICANBREWERY.COM

🍺 🍴 🍺 Kiwanda Cream Ale 5.2%
Amid the ale flurry of IPAs and sour beers, the cream beer style is a little lost, its delicacy and subtlety seemingly working against it. However, Pelican has done its bit to keep it going with a light and delicately fruity beer that has a gentle bittersweet finish. It might not be a beer to storm the barricades with, but sometimes, in between the hop monsters, all you need is subtlety.

PIZZA PORT
SAN DIEGO, CALIFORNIA
WWW.PIZZAPORT.COM

🍷 🍺 Oats Oatmeal Stout 6%
This dynamic brewpub has five outlets in Southern California, all of them with their own brewing kit, so there's a lot of Pizza Port to pick from. This is their oatmeal stout from the first brewpub in Solana Beach; gentle and delicate and meticulous in the way its many malts create a creamy, slightly roasty assemblage of chocolate and toffee.

ROGUE ALES
NEWPORT, OREGON
WWW.ROGUE.COM

 **Old Crustacean** Barley Wine 10.6%

Rogue is one of the pioneering West Coast hop-heady breweries whose beers remain packaged in tall screen-printed bottles and are marketed with a mischievous glint in the eye. One of the strongest is this beast of a barley wine. Unfiltered and unfined, it's intense, immense, malty, and dark.

Shakespeare Stout 5.8%

Ebony liquid with a towering ivory head lacing long into the glass. Dark chocolate bitterness, mellow mocha, and a delicate roasted oats and malt accent combine to produce a mild, bitter finish and aftertaste. This is a perfectly balanced beer.

Smoke Ale Rauchbier 7%

Inspired by the fall of the Berlin Wall, brewmaster John Meier built a German rauchbier using delicate smoke aromas, an orange-amber hue, peaty malts, and a spicy hop finish.

RUSSIAN RIVER
SANTA ROSA, CALIFORNIA
WWW.RUSSIANRIVERBREWING.COM

Blind Pig IPA 6.25%

Bringing orange, peaches, grapefruit flavors, and a bag full of balanced bitterness to the party, Blind Pig is believed to be the original double IPA that started a major trend. If you're a hardened hophead, you'll be like a pig in the proverbial.

Pliny the Elder IPA 8%

This is the beer all double IPAs want to be when they grow up. Intoxicating hop oils on the nose, a cacophony of citrus fruit on the palate, and a peppery, tangy finish that stays longer than the mother-in-law. A lupulin-lover's wet dream.

Supplication
Brown Ale 7%

Blissful bottle-conditioned Belgian brown ale. Aged with sour cherries and wild and crazy yeast in French oak Pinot Noir wine barrels for a year. Tart, oaky, and complex.

SIERRA NEVADA BREWING
CHICO, CALIFORNIA
WWW.SIERRANEVADA.COM

Sierra Nevada Celebration Ale
IPA 6.8%

Cockle-warming winter ale with one foot in the IPA family. Comforting, hoppy, and earthy chocolate notes mingle with lots of lemon and leechee hop flavors. Best drunk in the glow of a roaring fire or surrounded by other warming festive clichés.

Sierra Nevada Pale Ale 5.6%

Having sown the seeds of the now-blossoming West Coast beer scene, this quintessential American pale ale enjoys and deserves legendary status among the craft-brewing community. A superb showcase for the spicy, fruity Cascade hop. A classic.

Narwhal Imperial Stout 10.2%

As dark as the depths of the ocean through which the narwhal swims, this magnificent imperial stout is smooth and creamy, full of dark flavors such as coffee and alcohol-soaked raisins, while the long finish is warming, bittersweet, and coffee-dry.

SOCIETE
SAN DIEGO, CALIFORNIA
SOCIETEBREWING.COM

The Gleaner Saison 7.1%

Some would argue that saison is whatever you have at hand to make a tasty, refreshing beer. At Societe, California sagebrush is to hand when the Gleaner is made. There's spicy pepperiness, soft carbonation, a medium-bodied mouthfeel, and hints of ripe apricot and lemon before the long dry finish.

SPEAKEASY
SAN FRANCISCO, CALIFORNIA
WWW.GOODBEER.COM

Prohibition Ale 6.1%

When you drink this beer, you could take yourself back to a time of floozies, bathtub gin, rum runners, and Al Capone grinning on the front page. On the other hand, you could just immerse yourself in its lush aromatics of juicy citrus and caramel sweetness as well as the creamy mouthfeel and dry finish.

STONE BREWING COMPANY
ESCONDIDO, CALIFORNIA
WWW.STONEBREW.COM

Arrogant Bastard Ale IPA 7.2%

This unapologetically hedonistic, herbaceous ale oozes resin aromas and oils. Enormously astringent, it's an in-yer-face IPA that dares you to drink it.

Ruination Double IPA 2.0 8.5%

Pioneering West Coast double IPA, whose second "incarnation" (more dry hopping) was released under the 2.0 moniker in 2015. The result? More tropical fruit, more piney resins, more intensity—here's one beer that's not afraid to express itself.

Smoked Porter 5.9%

Colossal in character and big in both attitude and flavor, Stone's unashamedly aggressive beers blew the doors off a subdued San Diego beer scene in 1996. Malts smoked over peat shape this shimmering ebony-hued twist on German rauchbier. A thinking drinker's Islay whisky depth charge.

SUDWERK
DAVIS CALIFORNIA
WWW.SUDWERKBREW.COM

California Dry Hop Lager 5%

German-style lagers are the beers that get the guys at Sudwerk up in the morning, albeit with their own imprint. Take California Dry Hop Lager, for instance, where the brisk crispness of a helles is carpet-bombed with lots of Amarillo, Simcoe, and Cascade hops to create a juicy, citrusy thirst-quencher.

TELEGRAPH BREWING
SANTA BARBARA, CALIFORNIA
WWW.TELEGRAPHBREWING.COM

California Ale Belgian-Style Ale 6.2%

Even though the brewery says that this beer is a tribute to the ales of the nineteenth century, there's more than a hint of the jazziness, maltiness, and fruity spiciness of a Belgian ale. Whatever you want to call it, it's a damn fine beer that fills your glass with joy.

TERMINAL GRAVITY BREWING
ENTERPRISE, OREGON
WWW.TERMINALGRAVITYBREWING.COM

Terminal Gravity IPA 6.7%

Amid the uplifting oblivion of Eastern Oregon, Terminal Gravity conjures up some seriously superb beers from a modest brewhouse. The brewpub serves a boisterous Black IPA, a big, ballsy barley wine, and this flagship brew: a brawny bottle-conditioned beer with a weighty texture, notes of citrus, ginger, and rosemary, and a finish so beautifully bitter it's bound to tilt your head sidewise.

UPRIGHT BREWING
PORTLAND, OREGON
WWW.UPRIGHTBREWING.COM

Five Saison 5.5%

Yet another reason to move to "Beervana," as Portland is known. Upright specializes in farmhouse-style beers, one of which is this saison. On the nose there's ripe apricot and lemon, while the carbonation is brisk and the finish has a firm bitterness.

USA SOUTH & CENTRAL

(512) BREWING COMPANY
AUSTIN, TEXAS
WWW.512BREWING.COM

Pecan Porter 6.8%
British- and Belgian-style beers are at the heart of what these Texan beer technicians do. Pecan Porter, as the name might suggest, is slightly nutty (local pecans are used in the brew), alongside a caramel-like sweetness, smooth mouthfeel, and dry finish. There's also (invariably) a Double Pecan Porter.

AUGUST SCHELL BREWING COMPANY
NEW ULM, MINNESOTA
WWW.SCHELLSBREWERY.COM

Bock 6.1%
A toffee-tinged, amber-colored, sweet-tempered tipple from America's second oldest brewery, dating back to 1860. Easy to drink and ideal for bock-drinking neophytes and mainstream lager swiggers looking to take the next craft-learning leap.

AVERY BREWING COMPANY
BOULDER, COLORADO
WWW.AVERYBREWING.COM

Avery IPA 6.3%
Amid the laid-back, tofu-munching locals of bohemian Boulder, family-owned Avery crafts some terrific, bombastic beers—especially the high-octane Belgian ales. The IPA is richly resinous, and copious Columbus, Simcoe, Cascade, and Centennial hops deliver a pine-powered punch. A holy mother-pucker.

CAPITAL BREWING
MIDDLETON, WISCONSIN
WWW.CAPITALBREWING.COM

Autumnal Fire Doppelbock 7.8%
Capital is one of the mainstays of Wisconsin independent brewing, having first opened its doors in 1984. Autumnal Fire is its once-a-year treat, available only in September, but this warming and malty-rich doppelbock is well worth looking out for.

CASEY BREWING & BLENDING
GLENWOOD SPRINGS, COLORADO
WWW.CASEYBREWING.COM

East Bank Saison 6.5%
There's a clue in the name: Troy Casey gets his beer brewed elsewhere, and then the wort is brought to him, and fermentation takes place in oak barrels with various yeast strains. Then the fun (or blending) starts. This is a saison with added local honey, making for an eminently complex beer featuring green apple, tropical fruit, peach, wood, and funk, alongside a tart and spritzy mouth feel.

CIGAR CITY BREWING
TAMPA, FLORIDA
WWW.CIGARCITYBREWING.COM

Jai Alai India Pale Ale 7.5%
As well as producing a rollicking range of fine beers, such as this intensely flavored IPA with its mash-up of orange-led aromas and flavors and assertive bitterness, Cigar City is the first brewery to have its own air-side brewing kit and pub at Tampa Airport. Aficionados have been known to make stopovers just to sample the beers.

CIVIL SOCIETY BREWING
JUPITER, FLORIDA
WWW.CIVILSOCIETYBREWING.COM

Blondes Make Me Hoppy Golden Ale 4.9%
Civil Society is three friends banding together to run a brewery and taproom, whose walls are dotted with artifacts from the founders' families. This is a gleaming gold in color, with a sweet fruitiness on the nose, more fruit on the palate, an appetizing bittersweetness, and a long dry finish.

CROOKED STAVE
DENVER, COLORADO
WWW.CROOKEDSTAVE.COM

Surette Provision Saison 6.2%
Crooked Stave is noted for its incredibly complex and nuanced sours, and this is their riff on the classic northern French/Belgian saison. It's dark gold in color with a juicy fruit nose, alongside hints of white wine and hay; it's a dry and crisp beer with a refreshing tartness and the kind of funkiness that would bring James Brown back from the grave in an instant.

LA CUMBRE BREWING
ALBUQUERQUE, NEW MEXICO
WWW.LACUMBREBREWING.COM

Elevated IPA 7.2%

A lot of hops go into this beer (at last count seven varieties, including the poster children of the hop revolution: Simcoe, Citra, and Mosaic). The result could be dreadful, but instead it's a stunning explosion of fruity aromatics and flavors, allied to an assertive bitter finish, making it a serial award-winner.

DESTIHL BREWERY
BLOOMINGTON, ILLINOIS
WWW.DESTIHLBREWERY.COM

Here Gose Nothing
Leipziger-Style Gose 5.2%

Even though the brewery only opened in 2013, such has been its success that within three years it was looking at building a much larger production site. One of the beers responsible for its growth has been this spicy, minerally, refreshing take on the gose style, which is part of its Wild Sour series.

FUNKY BUDDHA
OAKLAND PARK, FLORIDA
WWW.FUNKYBUDDHABREWERY.COM

Floridian Hefeweizen 5.2%

Even though Funky Buddha is best known for Maple Bacon Coffee Porter, it also demonstrates its brewing versatility with less outrageous but just as delicious beers such as this fruity, refreshing, crisp, and unctuous hefeweizen. Ideal to sip as the Floridian sun sets.

GOOSE ISLAND BEER COMPANY
CHICAGO, ILLINOIS
WWW.GOOSEISLAND.COM

Goose Island IPA 5.9%

An intelligent, accessible copper-hued IPA. Sidesteps saccharine malt sweetness in favor of a deliciously dry cookie base, upon which a rich, succulent, herbal hop character is laid.

Sofie Saison 6.5%

Chicago goes rural Belgium with this bright gold booster of a saison that has had wild yeasts added before being aged in wine barrels with orange peel. Dry, tart, effervescent, citrusy, spicy, and peppery and creamy in its mouthfeel, this is an elegant beer.

GREAT DIVIDE BREWING COMPANY
DENVER, COLORADO
WWW.GREATDIVIDE.COM

Oak Aged Yeti Imperial Stout 9.5%

Picture the scene: an enormous yeti walks into the Great Divide brewery tap, an old dairy in north Denver, pads up to the bar, and says: "Can I get some nachos, a glass of milk, some beef jerky, two pale ales, and .... er .... a bottle of your opaque, opulent, and robust Russian imperial stout, the one that's had its intense coffee and chocolate character mellowed by French oak aging?" "Sure thing," replies the barman, "but why the big paws?"

Titan IPA 6.8%

Deep golden, heavyweight hop hitter that'll throw your taste buds on the ropes with jabs of grapefruit, freshly cut grass, and fruity esters thrown from a sweet, shortbread canvas.

HOPS & GRAIN
AUSTIN, TEXAS
WWW.HOPSANDGRAIN.COM

The One They Call Zoe Lager 5%

Sustainability looms larger in the mindset of Hops & Grain, with used grain going to local farmers (and being used to make dog treats for the taproom) as well as employees being encouraged to use bicycles to get to work. Zoe is a lager with a clean body and a light bitter finish.

JESTER KING
AUSTIN, TEXAS
WWW.JESTERKINGBREWERY.COM

Le Petit Prince Farmhouse Table Beer Saison 2.9%

Located in the countryside outside Austin, Jester King is the monarch of Texan spontaneously fermented beer. Ever since it opened in 2010, its modus operandi has been to use wild yeast, barrel aging, and blending to create a portfolio of world-class beers. Le Petit Prince is that rarest of beasts—a Belgian-style table beer with low alcohol but plenty of character.

LEFT HAND BREWING
LONGMONT, COLORADO
WWW.LEFTHANDBREWING.COM

Milk Stout Nitro Milk Stout 6%

In the past nitro beers were a swear word in brew nerd circles, but the new-wave ones are widget-less and give certain beers a smooth experience—such as this luscious milk stout, which has hints of mocha, vanilla, and a gentle roastiness.

Oktoberfest Märzen Lager 6.6%

Loosen the lederhosen or dust down the dirndl and then reach for this cookie-like, slightly spicy, and bracing take on the beer that dominates Munich, Germany, in fall. With this, you can do it at home.

LIVE OAK BREWING CO.
AUSTIN, TEXAS
WWW.LIVEOAKBREWING.COM

Hefeweizen 5.3%

The beer styles of central Europe feature heavily in the thoughts of the guys that run Live Oak, if the preponderance of helles, pils, oktoberfest, Berliner weisse, and grodziskie are any clue. The hefeweizen has the regulation bananas, vanilla, and cloves, alongside a brisk carbonation that is refreshing.

MINNEAPOLIS TOWN HALL BREWING
MINNEAPOLIS, MINNESOTA
WWW.TOWNHALLBREWERY.COM

Masala Mama India Pale Ale 5.9%

Piney, resinous, and piquant proof that the West Coast doesn't have the monopoly on well-balanced IPAs. This has three American hops and caramel malt.

NEW BELGIUM BREWING
see Brewery Profile pages 202 to 203
FORT COLLINS, COLORADO
WWW.NEWBELGIUM.COM

Abbey Dubbel 7%

When it's not hanging about on podiums at major beer competitions, this delightful dubbel keeps itself busy being auburn-hued and smooth. Conjures up banoffee-pie flavors and some herbal notes.

La Folie Sour Red Ale 6%

Wood-aged, sour red Flanders ale that dawdles about in French oak for up to three years. Brewed in homage to New Belgium's "Follow Your Folly" mantra, it's dry, tremendously tart, and an ideal apéritif.

NEW GLARUS BREWING COMPANY
NEW GLARUS, WISCONSIN
WWW.NEWGLARUSBREWING.COM

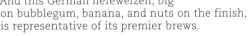

Dancing Man Wheat 7.2%

Quaint and quirky amid the undulating hills of Wisconsin, New Glarus is America's Little Switzerland, complete with chocolate, fondue, chalets, useful pocket knives, cuckoo clocks, and other lazy national stereotypes. And this German hefeweizen, big on bubblegum, banana, and nuts on the finish, is representative of its premier brews.

Wisconsin Cherry Beer 5%

More than a pound of Montmorency cherries make it into each 750ml bottle. Arguably America's finest fruit beer, it also hosts Wisconsin-farmed wheat, Belgian-roasted barley, unruly Belgian yeasts, and year-long-aged Hallertau hops that have mellowed and mingled in oak. A textured tart, sparkling, almond-tinged cherry explosion, best sipped slightly chilled from a champagne flute.

ODELL BREWING COMPANY
FORT COLLINS, COLORADO
WWW.ODELLBREWING.COM

5 Barrel Pale Ale 5.2%

A strapping 36 IBU aromatic pale ale, filtered through a bed of whole flower hops before being inundated with even more of the little green guys. Lovely.

OSKAR BLUES BREWERY
LONGMONT, COLORADO
WWW.OSKARBLUES.COM

Dale's Pale Ale 6.5%

This is a historic beer not because it was drunk by Abraham Lincoln's dad but because, back in 2002, it was the brewery's first beer to go into a "craft" can, a pioneering move at the time. Now, everyone and their mother puts beer in cans. It also tastes good, with a judicious balance of sweet cookie-like malt and citrus-flecked hops before its bitter finish.

Ten FIDY Imperial Stout 10.5%

If the thought of an assertively hopped pale ale in a can was strange enough, the wildness really came on when this hefty hit of chocolate, mocha, caramel, and hops began to hit the can a few years after Dale's. Whether in can or on draft, this is one rich tapestry of a beer.

ST. SOMEWHERE BREWING COMPANY

TARPON SPRINGS, FLORIDA
WWW.SAINTSOMEWHEREBREWING.COM

Saison Atherne 7.5%

One of very few brewers flying the flag in Florida, St. Somewhere brings boutique Belgian-style ales to the sun-kissed hordes. This saison, brewed using chamomile, rosemary, and black pepper, pours a sunny gold and exudes herbs, spice, and all things nice.

SAINT ARNOLD BREWING COMPANY

HOUSTON, TEXAS
WWW.SAINTARNOLD.COM

Saint Arnold Divine Reserve
Weizenbock 8.4%

One can't imagine a problem that has not been solved or at least eased by the Divine Reserve series of beers from Houston. Saint Arnold, founded in 1994 and Texas's oldest brewery, releases a Divine Reserve every year, to huge acclaim. Following in the footsteps of a first-class barley wine and impressive IPA comes this weizenbock, well endowed with flavors of bananas, chocolate, and spice.

SPRECHER BREWING

GLENDALE, WISCONSIN
WWW.SPRECHERBREWERY.COM

Black Bavarian Schwarzbier 5.86%

A jewel of a German-leaning brewery, founded in 1985 by Randy Sprecher and making some of the best micro brews in Milwaukee. A creamy cultured and midnight-black mash-up of coffee, caramel, molasses, and chocolate.

STEEL TOE BREWING

ST. LOUIS PARK, MINNESOTA
WWW.STEELTOEBREWING.COM

Lunker Barley Wine 13.5%

Set up in 2011, this is a family-owned business that produces a good range of quaffable beers. Lunker is part of its barrel-aged series, an English-style barley wine that has spent time in rye whiskey barrels. The result is a beer resonant with caramel, toffee, vanilla, and woodiness—a beer, like a steel toecap, not to be trifled with.

SURLY BREWING COMPANY

BROOKLYN CENTER, MINNESOTA
WWW.SURLYBREWING.COM

Surly Bender Brown Ale 5%

Deftly bridges the gap between a brown ale and a porter. Aromatic American hops conspire with some Belgian malt and, to give it added texture, oatmeal to produce a very drinkable dark beer.

TOMMYKNOCKER BREWERY

IDAHO SPRINGS, COLORADO
WWW.TOMMYKNOCKER.COM

Tommyknocker ButtHead Bock Doppelbock 8.2%

Do not be hoodwinked by the chirpy goat-riding, slightly camp fellows on the label because this big, bucking bock is a German giant of a beer. Auburn-colored and medium-bodied, with nutty chocolate and a sweet malt finish. It rocks.

TYRANENA BREWING COMPANY

LAKE MILLS, WISCONSIN
WWW.TYRANENA.COM

Devil over a Barrel Bourbon Imperial Oatmeal Coffee Porter Oatmeal Porter 8%

In addition to some top-class core and seasonal beers, this whimsical Wisconsin brewery has earned acclaim for its limited-edition "Brewers Gone Wild" collection: a series of "big, bold, and ballsy beers." While this cracking coffee stout, infused with vanilla and peppery spice, is hard to get hold of, the BGW beers are well worth hunting down.

UINTA BREWING

SALT LAKE CITY, UTAH
WWW.UINTABREWING.COM

Bière de Mars
Bière de Garde 7.2%

It's a long way from Salt Lake City to the rural heartlands of northern France, but, with this sprightly floral beer, Uinta has managed to bridge the distance (with not a Mormon in sight). Aged in Chardonnay barrels and released once a year, this is a divine and complex beer.

NEW BELGIUM BREWING

500 LINDEN, FORT COLLINS, CO 80524
WWW.NEWBELGIUM.COM

Do you detest your job? Spend your "working" day staring into the distance, half-heartedly shifting desktop icons from one corner of the computer screen to the other? Wish you could do something, absolutely anything, else? Well, may I suggest you go to work at New Belgium?

Located in the lovely, laid-back town of Fort Collins (a second brewery was opened in Asheville, NC, in 2016), New Belgium is a utopian, environmentally friendly beervana, where everything and everyone appears to have been smeared in a high definition cinematic "happy" visual sheen. Since 2013, the brewery has been 100 percent staff-owned, and if you work there for 12 months you receive a New Belgium cruiser bike to pedal cheerily to your day's "work" in the office. However, the bikes symbolize more than merely a

merry mode of transport. While on a cycling trip through Belgium, back in 1988, that founder Jeff Lebesch first became enchanted by the country's eclectic beer. Enlightened, inspired, and armed with a souvenir strain of brewer's yeast, Jeff returned to Colorado and began homebrewing some Belgian beers of his own. Six years later, he and his wife, Kim Jordan, turned pastime into profession and began brewing commercially from their basement and kitchen.

Abbey, a Belgian ale, was the first beer to be brewed and bottled, followed by Fat Tire, an amber ale inspired by the Belgian beer Palm. Such was Fat Tire's initial success, driven by word of mouth and funky labels, that it was soon being peddled faster than it was being brewed and, before long, the newfangled New Belgium had outgrown its basement and moved into a local rail depot, where it stayed for two years.

But sales kept going upward and onward. In 1995, Jeff, Kim, and a handful of eager employees moved into the current home—a state-of-the-art brewery that employs traditional brewing principles. Since then, New Belgium has metamorphosed from a basement producing a humble eight and a half barrels a week into the fourth-largest craft brewer in America.

Left: Even the brewhouse is constructed from eco-friendly materials, with solar and wind power providing energy.

Opposite top left: New Belgium employees are entitled to a company bicycle after 12 months' service.

Opposite top right and *Opposite:* La Folie and Fat Tire are two of the Belgian-inspired brews at New Belgium.

But what of the beers? Well, first and foremost, there's Fat Tire. The sweet-sided malty, mainstream amber ale has an enormous following across more than 16 states. It's responsible for two-thirds of New Belgium's sales, and while some connoisseurs regard its reputation as somewhat inflated, its phenomenal popularity has afforded head brewer Peter Bouckaert the freedom to experiment elsewhere.

Peter has hailed himself the "Jackson Pollock of brewing."

"I take my can of paint and drip it all over the canvas," he says. "We do everything different here. There's no rule book or parameters. Instead of looking at a beer as lots of separate influences, our beers are greater than the sum of their parts. We use a lot of different yeasts and spices."

Bouckaert, a Belgian-born brewer formerly of Alkan-Maes and Rodenbach breweries, brews more than a dozen beers, mostly with a distinct Belgian accent. "The brewing process can be a little one-dimensional. You need to think about it from a different angle," adds Peter. "Just putting more hops in doesn't make a more interesting beer. It's more involved. You can tweak any one thing in the brewing process—people ignore the mash process, but that's absolutely key."

Unbeknown to the vast majority of Fat Tire followers, Peter brews an excellent ester-emboldened abbey ale, a Flemish dubbel ale named 1554, a top-class tripel, and several IPAs under the Voodoo Ranger name. But it's the liquid embodiment of New Belgium's "Follow Your Folly" mantra that excites the beer buffs the most. A wood-aged Flemish sour ale, La Folie is a spontaneous fermenting ale, very much in the Rodenbach mold, aged in French oak for up to three years with the help of wild yeast strains. Blended and released as a limited-edition vintage every year, La Folie is a forceful yet delicately tart frisson of fruit flavors and well worth getting on your bike for.

* KEY BEERS

1554 Brussels Black Ale 5.5%
Abbey Belgian Dubbel 7%
Fat Tire Amber Ale 5.3%
La Folie Sour Red Ale 7%
Voodoo Range IPA 7%
Voodoo Ranger Imperial IPA 9%

USA NORTH & EASTERN

THE ALCHEMIST
STOWE, VERMONT
WWW.ALCHEMISTBEER.COM

Heady Topper Double IPA %

After Hurricane Irene destroyed its brewpub in Waterbury, Alchemist moved to a new site and focused on one beer. Heady Topper is seen as one of the most boldly flavored double IPAs in the USA and has become a must-have icon for beer geeks. More recently it's been joined by Focal Banger and Crusher.

ALLAGASH BREWING
PORTLAND, MAINE
WWW.ALLAGASH.COM

Allagash Curieux
Tripel 9.5%

Synonymous with beautiful boutique Belgian-style beers, the East Coast-based Allagash made its name on the back of a wonderful wheat beer. But it's this bourbon-barrel-aged tripel in its swanky corked bottle, touched with vanilla and a smidgen of smoke, that charms.

BAR HARBOR
BAR HARBOR, MAINE
WWW.BARHARBORBREWING.COM

Cadillac Mountain Stout 6.7%

Dark, dry stout from a marvelous Maine-based micro. As if it's been brewed to the soothing, soulful sounds of Isaac Hayes. It's smooth, slightly smoky, and satin-black, like the Walrus of Love's bed sheets.

BELL'S BREWERY
KALAMAZOO, MICHIGAN
WWW.BELLSBEER.COM

Hopslam Double IPA 10%

Hopslam is released once a year and is a monstrous assemblage of six different hop varieties, with the brewers' favorite Simcoe added during dry-hopping. The result is a fight club of grapefruit and floral hoppiness on the nose.

Two Hearted Ale IPA 7%

This hoppy and impressive IPA opens with orange, gives a bit of grapefruit, then finishes off with a fine floral flourish. Hearty indeed and very tasty.

BOSTON BEER COMPANY
BOSTON, MASSACHUSETTS
WWW.SAMUELADAMS.COM

Cream Stout 4.9%

Smoother than the patter of a master salesman, this is Boston's homage to the sweet stouts of the UK. A cream mouth feel, luscious roastiness, chocolate, and coffee plus a delicate sweetness.

Samuel Adams Boston Lager 4.8%

When craft brewers stormed the gates of big, bland beer in the mid-1980s, the Boston Beer Company's Jim Koch was in the front chariot, holding the reins in one hand and this Vienna-style lager in the other.

Utopias Barley Wine 25%

It's a beer, Jim, but not as we know it. It's one of the strongest beers ever brewed, possibly the most unusual and perhaps the most expensive. Utopias' beers are not pilsners, bocks, or weiss biers but ports, brandies, and whiskies. Utopias doesn't look like a beer, it doesn't smell like a beer, and it certainly doesn't taste like a beer, but … beer it is. Crimson in color, with the texture and taste of a fine brandy, it is brewed with a trio of noble hops, three varieties of malt, several different types of yeast, and a splash of maple syrup, before being aged and matured in whiskey, Cognac, or port barrels for up to ten months.

BROOKLYN BREWERY
BROOKLYN, NEW YORK
WWW.BROOKLYNBREWERY.COM

Brooklyn Black Chocolate Stout
10.1%

Some of the flavors in this velvet-smooth imperial stout: chocolate, port, dried plums, a bit more chocolate, coffee, chocolate again, figs, chocolate, mocha, chocolate, hints of toast, and, last but not least, chocolate.

Brooklyn Lager 5.2%

In 1996, when the brewery breathed life back into Brooklyn beer, it led with this assertive amber-gold Viennese-style lager. Wonderfully floral, a sturdy bitterness, a kiss of caramel, and a long, smooth finish.

Sorachi Ace Saison 7.6%

Stunning showcase for the Japanese hop variety Sorachi Ace, with lubricious waves of lemon meringue and lemongrass interacting with malty sweetness. A real feast of a beer.

CAMBRIDGE BREWING
CAMBRIDGE, MASSACHUSETTS
WWW.CAMBRIDGEBREWINGCOMPANY.COM

Tall Tale Pale Ale 5.7%
Established in 1989, this is the oldest brewpub in the greater Boston area, and Flower Child IPA is a classic, extensively hopped, and dry hopped with a portfolio of American hops— Simcoe, Centennial, Cascade, Chinook, and Amarillo among them. Honey and pale malts combine in a heady floral mix.

DC BRAU
WASHINGTON, DC
WWW.DCBRAU.COM

The Public Pale Ale 6%
Amber in color, this perky pale ale has a fruit bowl of aromatics, suggestive of ripe orange and mango; the fruitiness continues on the palate, joined by a bracing bitterness and hints of caramel sweetness.

DOGFISH HEAD CRAFT BREWERY
MILTON, DELAWARE
WWW.DOGFISH.COM

90-Minute IPA 9%
In the late 1990s, while other brewers were adding hops once, twice, or thrice during the brewing process, Sam Calagione experimented with continual hopping. A continual stream of hops was added using a converted tabletop football game that languidly shook the little green guys into the boil over the course of 90 minutes. The result? An IPA that's absurdly hoppy without being overly bitter. If you think this is big, try the 120-minute IPA at 21%.

Chateau Jiahu Barley Wine 8%
Properly mental and a little Asian, this barley wine is a living legacy of twelfth-century China and takes the sugars from rice, honey, muscat grapes, hawthorn fruit, and chrysanthemum flowers then feeds them to sake yeast for a month's fermentation.

Raison d'être Strong Belgian Ale 8%
Dark, ruby-red Belgian ale fermented with Belgian yeast, Belgian beet sugar, and raisins. Smoke and no small amount of poke, funky and phenolic, vinous and voluptuous. Lovely.

EVIL TWIN
BROOKLYN, NEW YORK
WWW.EVILTWIN.DK

Imperial Biscotti Break
Imperial Stout 11.5%
Even though he started planning his beers in Denmark, Evil Twin's genius Jeppe Jarnit-Bjergsø (the other twin, as if you didn't know, is Mikkel Borg Bjergsø of Mikkeller) is now firmly ensconced in New York, from where he can get his beers brewed by various US breweries (notably Westbrook). Once in the glass, this ultradark beer unleashes a towering torrent of chocolate, coffee, almonds, vanilla, and licorice, all of which make it a memorable experience.

No Hero Oatmeal Stout 7%
This is brewed at Two Roads in Connecticut and is a super-smooth oatmeal stout with hints of coffee, chocolate, and a light roastiness. A toasty winter warmer.

FAT HEAD'S BREWERY
MIDDLEBURG HEIGHTS, OHIO
WWW.FATHEADSBEER.COM

Head Hunter IPA 7.5%
Founded in 1997, Fat Head's now has several taprooms throughout Ohio (as well as one in Portland, Oregon). Head Hunter is its much-awarded IPA, a truly virtuous expression of hop goodness with oodles of fruitiness, a balance of malt, and a long bitter finish.

FLYING DOG BREWERY
FREDERICK, MARYLAND
WWW.FLYINGDOGALES.COM

Snake Dog IPA 7.1%
You might want to check yourself when it comes to drinking this monster of an IPA. At 7.1%, it's not sessionable, but with such a smooth hop character (grapefruit, grass) and juicy malt with a dry, bitter finish, you will want more than one.

Old Scratch Amber Ale Lager 5.5%
An ace multi-award-winning amber ale whose subdued toffee-apple sweetness makes it superb in the summer.

FOUNDERS BREWING
GRAND RAPIDS, MICHIGAN
WWW.FOUNDERSBREWING.COM

Breakfast Stout 8.3%

Founders is one of the largest breweries in Michigan and a serial award-winner for beers such as this luscious Breakfast Stout, a self-styled double chocolate coffee oatmeal stout that has an abundance of coffee and chocolate on both nose and palate, though its grainy dry finish straightens things out.

GREAT LAKES BREWING
CLEVELAND, OHIO
WWW.GREATLAKESBREWING.COM

Dortmunder Gold Lager 5.8%

Greener than a queasy Kermit, Great Lakes' unrivaled environmental awareness has not been at the expense of brewing excellence. As proved by this distinctively dry Dortmund-style lager, bronze in color, laced and lathered in the head with a minerally middle, and a robust, crisp flourish.

HARPOON BREWERY
BOSTON, MASSACHUSETTS
WWW.HARPOONBREWING.COM

Leviathan IPA Imperial IPA 10%

Harpoon was one of the leading chariots fighting for choice in the early 1990s, having been inspired by the ales of Europe. First brewed in 2008, this imposing imperial IPA is a monster of hop-forward aromas, plenty of citrus, and the kind of dry finish usually seen in the Sahara.

HILL FARMSTEAD
GREENSBORO, VERMONT
WWW.HILLFARMSTEAD.COM

Everett Porter 7.2%

Even though it's hidden away in northern Vermont, the crowds flock to Hill Farmstead to fill their growlers and buy bottles of what is seen as some of the best beer in the US. Founded by Shaun Hill in 2010, the brewery produces highly accomplished beers, many of them named after members of his family. Everett was Hill's great uncle, and he is remembered with a smooth and eloquent porter, which has a delicate roastiness, dark chocolate, licorice, and smoke—a complex and thoughtful beer.

HOPPIN' FROG
ARKON, OHIO
WWW.HOPPINFROG.COM

B.O.R.I.S. The Crusher Oatmeal Imperial Stout 9.4%

This is the kind of beer that small villages can fall into and never be seen again, such is the darkness of its color. It's mighty fine on the flavor front as well, with intense roastiness, a creamy mouthfeel, chocolate, coffee, and a robust hoppiness that balances all the sweetness out.

IRON HILL BREWERY & RESTAURANT
WILMINGTON, DELAWARE
WWW.IRONHILLBREWERY.COM

Pig Eyed Porter 5.4%

Iron Hill was founded in 1994, and since then it has added 11 locations in Pennsylvania, New Jersey, and Delaware. Pig Eyed Porter is its regular porter, a coal-black beer with delicate roast notes and a flurry of chocolate alongside an appetizing bitterness.

JOLLY PUMPKIN'S ARTISAN ALES
DEXTER, MICHIGAN
WWW.JOLLYPUMPKIN.COM

La Roja Flanders Red 7.2%

Ales aged for anything between eight weeks and ten months come together for jolly japes in an amber-colored, tart, toffee-tainted peppery embrace.

Oro de Calabaza Belgian Ale 8%

Barrel-aging, open fermentation, and bottle conditioning are what carves a smile on the face of Jolly Pumpkin, with this Franco-Belgian fusion of esters, bananas, spice, and citrus zest being a prime—and potent—example.

KUHNHENN BREWING
WARREN, MICHIGAN
WWW.KBREWERY.COM

Raspberry Eisbock 10.8%

Best served in a champagne flute, this is an exceptional viscous elixir resplendent in more than just a feast of fruit. Hazelnut, chocolate, and almonds vie for attention alongside licorice, pepper on the nose, and a decadent disappearance of warm alcohol at the end. Outstanding, unique, and, alas, ever-so elusive to boot, but a great match for a dessert.

MAINE BEER COMPANY
FREEPORT, MAINE
WWW.MAINEBEERCOMPANY.COM

 Lunch IPA 7%

Another boldly flavored American IPA with tropical fruit, pine, and malt sweetness linking arms and striding forward into the sun. Incidentally, the beer is named after a whale that has swum off the coast of Maine since 1982. One day it appeared with a big chunk out of its fin and was nicknamed lunch from then on.

MATT BREWING COMPANY
UTICA, NEW YORK
WWW.SARANAC.COM

Saranac Adirondack Lager Amber Lager 5.5%

Founded in 1888 in Utica, New York, at the foothills of the Adirondack Mountains, Matt Brewing launched this reasonably hoppy amber ale in its centennial year. Back then, it was a bold move, but the brewery believed in the beer, and it's worked out amazingly well for it. Today, it makes some pretty aggressive beers, but the Adirondack is still good, and makes just as remarkable a statement.

NEW HOLLAND BREWING CO.
see Brewery Profile pages 208 to 209
HOLLAND, MICHIGAN
WWW.NEWHOLLANDBREW.COM

 Dragon's Milk Stout 9%

Worshippers of barrel-aged beers flock to Holland, a town with more than 150 churches, to kneel at the altar of this creative craft brewer. Dragon's Milk plucks up some Dutch courage with tannins and toffee, raisins, vanilla, and a complex finish. A potent drop.

 Pilgrim's Dole Weizen/Barley Wine 10%

Wonderful "wheat wine" brewed with a 50/50 blend of wheat and barley malt. This rich and fascinating brew includes citrus and caramel flavors, akin to a fruity crème brûlée.

BREWERY OMMEGANG
COOPERSTOWN, NEW YORK
WWW.OMMEGANG.COM

Ommegang Three Philosophers Belgian Ale 9.8%

A Belgian-style farmhouse built on a former hop farm in upstate New York, Ommegang bangs the Belgian-style ale drum with zeal and gusto. Of the five flagship beers, Three Philosophers is the funkiest and fruitiest. A luscious, languidly matured love child of Lindemans cherry lambic and a dark ale, it's all chocolate, dark fruit, and toasted malts matured and delivered in a beautiful bottle. Check it out with cheese or a cigar. Or even both.

OTHER HALF BREWING
BROOKLYN, NEW YORK
WWW.OTHERHALFBREWING.COM

 Mosaic IPA 7%

Brooklyn is home to this small brewery that was founded in 2014 and has developed a strong local following. One favorite is this elegant IPA, which acts as a cheerleader for Mosaic, so expect plenty of tropical fruit and citrus, alongside a rigorous malt backbone and a bitterness on the finish.

SCHMALTZ BREWING COMPANY
CLIFTON PARK, NEW YORK
WWW.SCHMALTZBREWING.COM

He'Brew Genesis Dry Hopped Session Ale
Pale Ale 5.6%

One for the chosen ones, this "interdenominational" pale ale stuffs three American hop varieties under its yarmulke alongside some mellow malt sweetness. Great with a salt beef bagel. Proper kosher.

SIXPOINT BREWERY
BROOKLYN, NEW YORK
WWW.SIXPOINT.COM

Resin Double IPA 9.1%

Resin by name, resinous by nature. This stunner of a double IPA has plenty of resiny pine notes alongside the flurries of tropical fruit and malt sweetness. The finish is bitter too. It's a big beer in many ways and as noisy as a Brooklyn native.

NEW HOLLAND BREWING CO.

66 E. 8TH STREET, HOLLAND, MI 49423

WWW.NEWHOLLANDBREW.COM

The folks at New Holland Brewing believe that craft brewing is an artistic pursuit. They're on a steady course, making good, reliable, balanced beers that are a genuine celebration of the brewer's art.

New Holland is a story of two childhood friends, Brett VanderKamp and Jason Spaulding, who roomed together at Hope College, a small liberal arts school in the west Michigan town of Holland. Jason studied physiotherapy, and Brett studied geology. After graduation, Brett headed to Colorado, where he realized the potential of craft beer and decided to introduce it to his home state.

So, in 1996, Brett came back to Michigan and teamed up with Jason again. The two pursued their dream of brewing beer in the unlikeliest of places. Holland is a staunchly conservative Dutch

Reform community. It's located in Ottawa County, which, until recently, even banned the sale of beer and wine on Sunday. Most people contemplating a brewery would look someplace else.

But young people have the gifts of optimism and determination, not to mention a different perspective. They reasoned that the area was starving for new business; besides, a new bar hadn't opened in Holland for years. Yes, money was an obstacle, but Brett and Jason said to themselves, "This is America. Let's do it."

Lo and behold, they did. It turned out that as straitlaced as Holland was, starting up a brewery there was very easy. By June 1997, they were open for business, brewing beer in an old factory they'd converted to a brewhouse. They opened a small taproom, and, before long, word spread about New Holland Brewing's liquid gold. It gained a following not just in the Holland area but also across the state.

In September 2002, John Haggerty came on board as head brewer. John had attended brewing school in Berlin and, having been part of large-scale brewing, wanted to work at a smaller operation where he could have more influence. He and New Holland were a perfect match. (He left in 2012 to start his own brewery.)

The slow, steady growth that New Holland had enjoyed so far was about to explode. In December 2002, they opened a second facility in downtown Holland, with a small brewery for making experimental batches, 20 taps to serve their fresh beer, and a restaurant. By 2006, they outgrew their original production facility and opened another across town.

Opposite: New Holland, where craft brewing is seen as an artistic pursuit.

Right: New Holland was one of the first breweries in Michigan to barrel-age its beer, and it now has more than 220 barrels where its beers slumber and dream.

The brewery now turns out eight year-round beers, four seasonals, and a rotating series of high-gravity beers. But the brewing fun really begins with the experimental beers it produces, plus the ones that it brews for special occasions only.

New Holland was one of Michigan's first breweries to join both the barrel-aging and high-gravity brewing trends. Sitting in storage are more than 220 bourbon barrels filled with beer in various stages of fermentation. The plan is to develop a library of beers that customers can someday enjoy while comparing the same label across multiple vintages. Not content with beer, they have also added a two-barrel distillery.

In 2008, Brett and other local business owners started a grassroots effort to overturn local restrictions banning the sale of beer on Sundays. The "Say Yes to Sunday" campaigners had to negotiate a convoluted procedure that required them to win two separate elections: the first to put the question of Sunday sales on the ballot; the second to lift the ban. In the end, voters sided with Brett and his friends, and another silly beer law has disappeared from the books.

Now New Holland continues to thrive with its delicious range of beers, as beer connoisseurs go especially crazy over Dragon's Milk, its luscious and palate-pleasing bourbon barrel-aged 11% imperial stout.

* KEY BEERS

Dragon's Milk Bourbon Barrel-Aged Imperial Stout 11%
Mad Hatter IPA 7%
White Hatter White Pale Ale 5.5%

SLY FOX
POTTSTOWN, PENNSYLVANIA
WWW.SLYFOXBEER.COM

Pikeland Pils 4.9%

European beer styles get the juices flowing in this long-established (1995) brewing company, and on a hot day nothing can beat swig after swig of this crisp pilsner, with its crisp mouthfeel and delicate bitter finish.

SMARTMOUTH BREWING
NORFOLK, VIRGINIA
WWW.SMARTMOUTHBREWING.COM

Farmer's Tan Hoppy Saison 5.6%

"Very flat, Norfolk," Noel Coward is meant to have said. He might have said something different if he'd gone to Norfolk in Virginia, especially if he'd partaken of a few glasses of this boisterously hopped saison.

SMUTTYNOSE
HAMPTON, NEW HAMPSHIRE
WWW.SMUTTYNOSE.COM

Bottle Rocket IPA 6.5%

Extremely well-constructed IPA that pours at the Porstmouth Brewpub, the sister company of Smuttynose. Light mahogany in color with a tan head that laces with grassy herbal aromas, orange jelly, and spice from a malt base.

Wheat Wine Ale 11.9%

Wheat wine? Imagine a cross between a barley wine and a wheat beer and you might be getting there. Smuttynose was the first to create one, and its annual release is still eagerly awaited. Expect the richness of a barley wine, the tartness of a wheat beer, all with a funky fusion of hops.

STILLWATER ARTISANAL
BALTIMORE, MARYLAND
WWW.STILLWATER-ARTISANAL.COM

Saison 6.8%

Founded by former DJ Brian Strumke, Stillwater makes its beers in different breweries around the world, so he is a true gypsy brewer. This is his riff on Wallonian saison, though with lots of American and New Zealand hops added, making for a spicy, dry, and fruity beer.

STOUDTS BREWING CO.
ADAMSTOWN, PENNSYLVANIA
WWW.STOUDTSBEER.COM

Gold Munich-style Helles 5%

A fiercely traditional brewery, created more than 20 years ago by Carol and Ed Stoudt and specializing in Germanic and, later, Belgian beers. When it comes to brewing, Carol's the one who wears the lederhosen, and this five-time winner at the Great American Beer Festival is a hell of a helles. It showcases the Perle, Hallertau, and Saaz hops with spice up front, followed by a brusque, bitter conclusion. A perfectly refreshing classic drop.

THREES BREWING
BROOKLYN, NEW YORK
WWW.THREESBREWING.COM

Vliet Pilsner 5.2%

2014 saw the opening of this neighborhood brewery and bar, with the emphasis on producing German- and Belgian-influenced beers alongside modern American classics. Vliet is a crisp, minerally, grassy, and hop German-style pilsner that enlivens the palate with each sip.

THREE FLOYDS BREWING COMPANY
MUNSTER, INDIANA
WWW.THREEFLOYDS.COM

Dreadnaught IPA 9.5%

Mention Three Floyds to well-informed beer buffs, and they will start drooling and shooting eyeballs from their faces. Probably. Since beginning life in an Indiana warehouse back in 1996, where the beers were fermented in open vessels shaped like Samuel Smith's famous Yorkshire Squares, Three Floyds has embraced innovation, none more so than in this massive, muscular mouthful that stuns the senses with cluster bombs of citrus, grapefruit, and freshly cut grass. A cult classic.

Gumballhead Wheat Beer 4.8%

Capable of slaking a thirst from a hundred yards, Gumball bounces about the tongue leaving a trail of coriander, lemon, lime, and dry-hopped bitterness in its wake. Drink it when the sun comes out to play.

TROEGS BREWING CO.

HARRISBURG, PENNSYLVANIA
WWW.TROEGS.COM

 Nugget Nectar Amber Ale 7.5%

Long-running Pennsylvanian purveyor of enigmatic artisan ales with a loyal following, both locally and in the ethereal land of beer bloggers.

TWO ROADS

STRATFORD, CONNECTICUT
WWW.TWOROADSBREWING.COM

Road 2 Ruin Double IPA 8%

Four friends came together in 2012 to found this nifty little brewery that produces a goodly selection of great beers. This double IPA is a hophead's dream, with plenty of tropical fruit and pine resin alongside a lean malt spine.

URBAN CHESTNUT

ST. LOUIS, MISSOURI
WWW.URBANCHESTNUT.COM

Zwickel Lager 5.2%

Zwickel is a Bavarian specialty, served unpasteurized and unfiltered, and usually rarely seen outside the small breweries of Franconia. Urban Chestnut's version is hazy gold in color, with a grainy and grassy hop nose, and bittersweet on the palate. Definitely one to seek out when in Missouri.

VICTORY BREWING

DOWNINGTOWN, PENNSYLVANIA
WWW.VICTORYBEER.COM

Prima Pils 5.3%

A bracing, appetizingly bitter, and mouth-filling German-style pils that begs to be imbibed on a summer's day.

Storm King Imperial Stout 9.1%

Begun by two childhood friends, Bill Covaleski and Ron Barchett, Victory now enlightens educated elbow-benders across the region and beyond with a hugely diverse range of excellent ales. Storm King is its bold and big-flavored imperial stout, whose long dry finish is reminiscent of the Sahara on a good night.

VON TRAPP BREWING

STOWE, VERMONT
WWW.VONTRAPPBREWING.COM

Golden Helles 4.9%

Yes, the hills above Stowe are alive with the sound of brewing as the Von Trapp family added a brewery to the Lodge, which attracts thousands of tourists a year. It remains true to its Central European heritage, with lager very much on the brewing menu. This crisp and bittersweet beer boasts subtle citrus before its dry, quenching finish.

WEYERBACHER BREWING

EASTON, PENNSYLVANIA
WWW.WEYERBACHER.COM

Insanity Barrel-Aged Barley Wine 11.1%

This is Weyerbacher's barley wine after it's spent time in whiskey barrels, creating a rich and spirituous beer full of vanilla, chocolate, fire, and smoke. Treat this beer with respect, and ask it kindly if it would care to be poured into a glass.

YARDS BREWING

PHILADELPHIA, PENNSYLVANIA
WWW.YARDSBREWING.COM

Philadelphia Pale Ale 4.6%

Philadelphia is one of the great beer cities of the USA, and Yards has been slaking locals' thirsts since 1994. This is its signature beer, crisp and citrusy, bitter and well balanced all the way down the glass.

Above: The Big Rock Brewery in Calgary is one of the longest-established craft breweries in Canada.
Below: In its Montreal brewpub, Dieu du Ciel! serves its own award-winning microbrews to a highly appreciative clientele.

INTRODUCTION
CANADA

It's best not to adopt a broad-brush approach when describing Canada's beer scene. You may as well cast all Canadians as maple-syrup munching ice hockey fans who live in igloos.

Much like the nation itself, Canadian brewing can be carved up into several distinct provinces, each with its own bespoke beer scene shaped by cultural history, demographics, and, crucially, varying levels of bureaucratic red tape.

The mass-marketed beers of Labatt and Molson remain ubiquitous across The Great White North, but mainstream beer sales have been in decline for several years, and craft beer's share of the whole market has grown from just 4 percent in 2008 to more than 10 percent in 2017.

The number of breweries has grown steadily in that time, and now there are more than 650 breweries in Canada with the highest concentration found unsurprisingly in Ontario, Quebec, and British Columbia.

The predominantly French-speaking province of Quebec, the largest of the Canadian provinces, may have come to the craft brewing party later than others, but, *mon dieu*, it has certainly made up for lost time.

What catalyzed the Quebecois craft beer scene was both a built-in Gallic appetite for epicurean adventuring and also attractive tax and distribution legislation for small brewers that gave them an advantage over their Canadian counterparts in other regions.

But, more importantly, the beer was good. From day one, Quebec's microbrewing movement, pioneered by Unibroue and McAuslan, has been built on solid Francophone foundations and has long been home to some of the most impressive Belgian-style ales on this side of the Pond.

While Quebec's older brewers have emulated Belgium's anarchic approach to brewing by embracing unusual ingredients, barrel-aging, and funky microorganisms, the North American influence is acutely evident among a new wave of regional brewers who are contributing much to a beer scene that remains Canada's most creative.

In neighboring Ontario, where brewers are locked into tighter legislation, the growth of great beer has been more gradual and the styles more straitjacketed, but brewers, numbering more than 170 now, are loosening their buckles and brewing outside classical European lines, while Toronto, the region's capital, boasts a brilliantly vibrant beer bar scene.

British Columbia is considered the cradle of Canada's craft beer movement, having pioneered microbrewing back in the 1980s. But it wasn't until 2013, when new legislation allowed breweries to sell their beer through their own tasting rooms, that the British Columbia beer scene really hit its straps—and the vast majority of the province's 135 breweries have opened since that time.

The BC beer scene is strong on collaboration, camaraderie, and celebration of localism—using indigenous ingredients such as pumpkins and boysenberries. Having initially been influenced by English styles, it is unsurprisingly taking cues from what's going on below it, across the border, in the Pacific Northwest and California—where the hop is hailed with plenty of zest and experimentation is rife.

CANADA

À LA FÛT
SAINT-TITE, QUEBEC
WWW.ALAFUT.QC.CA

Ruine-Papilles IPA 6.3%
Microbrewery and bar in the small town of Saint-Tite. A whole range of beers is produced, including regulars, seasonals, and Belgian-inspired beauties. This is a regular, a grandstanding IPA that wraps up light orange, grapefruit, and caramelized malt to produce one big embrace of taste.

ALLEY KAT BREWING CO.
EDMONTON, ALBERTA
WWW.ALLEYKATBEER.COM

Fireside Mild 3.5%
Who says winter seasonals need to be big beers? This annual offering has an appealingly sweet, malty nose that carries a hint of chicory coffee, plus a balanced and malty body that's neither too sweet nor disappointingly thin, with notes of molasses, carob, and coffee.

Olde Deuteronomy Barley Wine 10%
Given the paucity of barley wines in Canada, it's inexplicable that this splendid example is only sporadically brewed. Toffee-ish malt blends with spicy hop in the foreground, while sweet and complex fruitiness in the body segues to moderate bitterness and a lengthy, warming finish. Ideal for cold northern Alberta winters.

AUVAL
VAL D'ESPOIR, QUEBEC
WWW.AUVAL.CA

Nordet IPA 6%
Classic American IPA from another thriving microbrewery in Quebec. This is amber in color and gives off ripe peach, a tingle of citrus, and the hint of a pine forest after a shower of rain. It's bitter, juicy, dry, and fruity. A thoroughly enjoyable IPA.

BEAU'S ALL NATURAL BREWING
VANKLEEK HILL, ONTARIO
WWW.BEAUS.CA

Lug-Tread Golden Ale 5.2%
Father and son Tim and Steve Beauchesne founded Beau's in 2006 and have always taken an eco-friendly stance, using only organic ingredients, locally sourced where possible. Lug-Tread is its most popular product, a golden ale that is lagered kölsch-like, with the result being a thirst-quenching drop with subtle fruit and a crisp finish.

BELLWOODS
TORONTO, ONTARIO
WWW.BELLWOODSBREWERY.COM

Farmageddon Saison 6.7%
Even though it was founded only in 2012, such has been the popularity of this brewpub with Toronto's craft beer cognoscenti that it got permission to expand to a second production facility in 2016. One of the beers that gets Torontonians raving is this Brett-infused barrel-aged saison, which is fruity, earthy, and vinous, though each yearly batch can have a different character.

BIG ROCK BREWERY
CALGARY, ALBERTA
WWW.BIGROCKBEER.COM

Mosaic Lager IPA 5.5%
One of the pioneers of Canadian craft beer, which started in 1985, after founder Ed McNally despaired of ever finding a decent beer to drink in Calgary. McNally retired in 2012, but the brewery continues to thrive. The use of Mosaic hops gives this golden beer a citrusy character, which dovetails well with the distinctly dry finish.

LE BILBOQUET
SAINT-HYACINTHE, QUEBEC
WWW.LEBILBOQUET.QC.CA

MacKroken Flower Scotch Ale 10.8%
Proof that the Quebecois brewing scene is not just about massively hopped IPAs comes with this big-hearted, kilt-wearing beer that trills with deep malt notes, caramel, chocolate, honey, and a creamy mouthfeel.

BLACK OAK
ETOBICOKE, TORONTO
WWW.BLACKOAKBEER.COM

Red Eye Coffee IPA 7.5%
No chance of snoozing off when you drink deeply of this amber-hued coffee-infused IPA, with the citrusy notes from the hops playing around with caramel-like coffee (real beans are added) before it finishes bittersweet. Intriguing seasonal from a brewery that was founded in 1999.

LE CASTOR
RIGAUD, QUEBEC
WWW.MICROLECASTOR.CA

Yakima IPA 6.5%
You don't need a crystal ball and a small booth on a pier to guess what this beer is about, given its name. Yes, it's a powerfully hopped IPA, a beer with the entire West Coast's Yakima hop production seemingly emerging from the nose, before it becomes perfectly integrated with its crisp malty background and a bittersweet finish.

CENTRAL CITY BREWERS & DISTILLERS
SURREY, BRITISH COLUMBIA
WWW.CENTRALCITYBREWING.COM

Red Racer IPA 6.5%
This is the kind of beer that friends order in a bar, clink glasses of, sniff, and rhapsodize about the citrus and pine notes on the nose, the citrus on the palate, and the dry bittersweet finish—vital parts of this beer that have made it one of Central City's beery bestsellers.

CHARLEVOIX
BAIE ST. PAUL, QUEBEC
WWW.MICROBRASSERIE.COM

Dominus Vobiscum Tripel 9%
The name of this fine tripel translates from Latin to "The Lord be with you," and after a couple of half-liter bottles, perhaps He or She will be! A spicy-fruity aroma foretells of the tropical fruitiness and peppery spice flavors to come, all wrapped up in a drying, warming finish.

LE CHEVAL BLANC
MONTREAL, QUEBEC
WWW.LECHEVALBLANC.CA

Chiquita Session Hopfenweiss 4%
No sooner does hopfenweiss become a regular beer style than Le Cheval Blanc takes it and makes it into a session beer, and a mighty fine one at that, with tropical fruit, Weissbier yeast, and a spicy finish.

COUNTY DURHAM BREWING CO.
PICKERING, ONTARIO
WWW.ONTARIOCRAFTBREWERS.COM

Red Dragon Amber Ale 4.7%
Yes, it's amber in color, and, like most ales of its stylistic ilk, it's full-bodied, has a malt sweetness, some fruit, hints of roast, and a dry finish, all of which combine to make it a very satisfying quaff.

DIEU DU CIEL!
MONTREAL, QUEBEC
WWW.DIEUDUCIEL.COM

Herbe à Détourne Tripel 10.2%
After opening as a brewpub in 1998, Dieu du Ciel! swiftly gained a name for its vibrant range of beers. This is its tremendous take on a Belgian tripel, released annually between January and April and pulsating with citrus.

Péché Mortel Imperial Stout 9.5%
This "mortal sin" is an intense experience, with real coffee providing the espresso accents to a full, rich, and formidable imperial stout already rife with notes of chocolate, roasted malt, and dark fruits.

Rosée d'Hibiscus Wheat Beer 5%
As the name might indicate, hibiscus flowers provide the flavoring for this rose-colored wheat beer, imbuing it with a subtle floral character, light notes of citrus and gooseberries, and a dry finish.

DRIFTWOOD BREWERY
VICTORIA, BRITISH COLUMBIA
WWW.DRIFTWOODBEER.COM

Fat Tug IPA 7%
Lively hop-centric brewery that opened in 2008 and has kept growing since. Fat Tug features five fulsome American hops, all of which radiate intense citrus and tropical fruit notes, while a hefty malt backbone keeps the fruitiness from tugging this beer into fruit juice territory.

DUNHAM
DUNHAM, QUEBEC
WWW.BRASSERIEDUNHAM.COM

Assemblage No. 1 Sour Beer 5.5%
Not one beer but two go into making this spicy, lightly vinous, and funky sour —it's a blend of Dunham's saison/witbier hybrid Propolis and an American-style pale ale, which is then aged in wine barrels to the accompaniment of Brettanomyces. It's slightly tart, quenching in the mouth but pleasingly dry in the finish.

FOUR WINDS
DELTA, BRITISH COLUMBIA
WWW.FOURWINDSBREWING.CA

Nectarous Sour Beer 5.5%
Family-owned outfit that opened only in 2013 but whose beers have already been scooping up the awards—beers such as this luscious dry-hopped sour, which is part of the brewery's Zephyrus range. Peach, mango, and passion fruit fly out of the glass, while the palate is light-struck with citrus, tartness, and a gentle bitterness, all of which create a refreshing dance on the tongue.

GARRISON BREWING CO.
HALIFAX, NOVA SCOTIA
WWW.GARRISONBREWING.COM

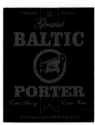

Grand Baltic Porter 9%
Deep regal purple in color, this soulful seasonal beer has a nose that speaks to the molasses added to the boil, plus sweet black coffee, dark chocolate, and a whiff of burned toast. In the body, it's rich and coffee-ish, with notes of blackstrap molasses, burned toffee, and black licorice.

Imperial I.P.A. 7%
Piney, spicy, and citrusy hoppiness are present and correct in this West Coast-style imperial, which is accompanied with aplomb by the malt front and the almost chewy finish that will keep you coming back.

GREAT LAKES
TORONTO, ONTARIO
WWW.GREATLAKESBEER.COM

Karma Citra IPA 6.6%
A fresh hoppiness frolics in the glass with the glee of a happy child whenever this incisive IPA is poured. Tropical fruit, citrus happiness, homely grassiness, and a bracing bitterness in the finish makes for one of the most popular beers from this vintage Toronto brewery, which was founded in 1987.

HALF PINTS BREWING CO.
WINNIPEG, MANITOBA
WWW.HALFPINTSBREWING.COM

Burly Wine Barley Wine 10.5%
Like many of Half Pints' beers, this seasonal sipper has a duality to it, with a more malty, British-style front and a singularly American, peppery, citrusy middle. A formidably warming and bitter finish leaves the distinct impression of a bracing barley wine, regardless of inspiration.

Humulus Ludicrous Double IPA 8%
This big beer announces itself with a full and perfumy nose carrying notes of burned orange peel and a malty, caramelly front. Hops arrive in force soon after, but always in balance and never quite dominating, all the way to a gently bitter, slightly toffee-ish finish. Such subtlety in a so-called "double" IPA is rare indeed.

HIGH ROAD
TORONTO, ONTARIO
WWW.FACEBOOK.COM/HIGHROADBREWING

Bronan IPA 7.1%
Curtis Bentley and Rob Doyle are veterans of the Toronto brewing scene and opened High Road in 2015. This is their Vermont-style IPA, which means that it is lush and luscious, fulsome and fruity, and blessed with a long bitter finish that makes you want more.

HOPFENSTARK
L'ASSOMPTION, QUEBEC
WWW.HOPFENSTARK.COM

Post-Colonial IPA 6.5%
Amber-colored American-style IPA with a complex perfumey aroma, pungent flowery citrus notes preceded by caramelly malt held in check by fresh lemon and grapefruit notes. Fruity, brisk, and fantastically funky.

Saison du Repos Saison 6%
Founded in 2006, Hopfenstark's beers are influenced by styles from all over the world, such as this take on the Wallonian farmhouse classic. It's a big, bold saison, with plenty of fruit and spice on the nose, while a funky fruitiness leads to succulent tartness on the palate.

MABRASSERIE
MONTREAL, QUEBEC
WWW.MABRASSERIE.COM

Tribal Pale Ale 5.5%
Co-op-owned brewery and tap that brews its own beers as well as ones from members of the co-op. Tribal is a fresh and fulsome American-style pale ale with a succulent sweep of citrus and the kind of dry finish that lingers longer on the palate.

MCAUSLAN BREWING CO.
MONTREAL, QUEBEC
WWW.MCAUSLAN.COM

St-Ambroise Oatmeal Stout 5%
As good as oatmeal stout gets, this ebony offering has a rich aroma of coffee, raisin, and plum, followed by a silken, mocha-ish body, with plenty of gentle roast and a hint of smoke. Simply outstanding.

St-Ambroise Stout Impériale Russe 9.2%
This is the brewery's tribute to the strong and midnight-black beers that were consumed with gusto at the imperial Russian court in the eighteenth and nineteenth centuries. Brewed once a year (so buy two, one to age) and bourbon-wood-aged, the beer has smoke, espresso, chocolate, and vanilla too.

MILL STREET BREWERY
TORONTO, ONTARIO
WWW.MILLSTREETBREWERY.COM

Tankhouse Ale 5.4%
Although identified as neither bitter nor pale ale, this is certainly more the former, with a lightly roasty, faintly cocoa-ish nose, and fruity (raisins, red apple), earthy, hoppy body that ends with a satisfying bitterness.

LES BRASSEURS DU NORD
BLAINVILLE, QUEBEC
WWW.BOREALE.COM

Boréale Blanche Wheat Beer 4.2%
The brewery is coy about the extra spice they add to this Belgian-style wheat beer, but one sip is enough to let you know it's ginger, and a fairly generous portion at that. Mixed with the orange peel and coriander, it makes for a truly thirst-quenching summer tipple.

PIT-CARIBOU
L'ANSE-À-BEAUFILS, QUEBEC
WWW.PITCARIBOU.COM

Horreum Alpha Saison 4.5%
The wild world of farmhouse ales gets an injection of Brettanomyces for this easy-drinking and refreshing saison. Golden in the glass, it's herbal, spicy, lightly bitter, and dry in the finish. Another winner from a brewery that was founded in 2007.

UNIBROUE

Without question, the most widely recognized
Canadian craft brewer in the world today is Unibroue.

Born in the suburbs of Montreal, the beers of the
Quebec brewer, with such irreverent and, to some,
impenetrable names as Maudite ("Damned"), and
La Fin du Monde ("The End of the World"), are
sold far and wide, from Los Angeles to Paris, says
Canadian beer writer Stephen Beaumont.

Although known today for brewing strong
Belgian-inspired ales, Unibroue has origins going
back to one of Quebec's earliest craft breweries,
the Massawippi Brewing Company. Known for
a pale ale of dubious reliability, Massawippi
was on the precipice of failure in 1991, when it
was rescued from near bankruptcy by a retired
hardware magnate named André Dion.

Looking forward to semiretirement when
he sold off his holdings in 1990, he remained
restless and was soon listening to offers from
other businesses, including a coalition of Québec
microbrewers with an interest in organizing a
distribution network for their brands. Would Dion,
they enquired, consider getting behind the idea?
He would, he did, and Unibroue was born.

Although the distribution idea ultimately went

nowhere, the brewing bug had bitten Dion, and
it was not long before he found himself traveling
to Belgium in search of beers he could import to
Quebec. It was during one of these trips that he
discovered the Riva Brewery in West Flanders.

Recognizing the potential in Riva's wheat beer,
Dion decided that his interests would be better
served by buying the recipe for the beer and
brewing it on the other side of the Atlantic, rather
than merely acting as the importer. However,
when he returned home, recipe in hand, he
found that the provincial government had placed
a moratorium on the issuing of new brewery
licenses. Luckily, Massawippi was ripe for picking.

Not long after, Massawippi pale ale fell by the
wayside in favor of brands such as Blanche de
Chambly—the wheat beer modeled after Riva's
original—Maudite and La Fin du Monde, and
the brewery itself was relocated to the Montreal
South Shore community of Chambly. Dion's
apparent strategy was simple: "hire young people
with no brewing industry experience, so they
have no bad habits," he once said—brew beers of

ALE
ON LEES
9% alc./vol.

1PT. 9.4 FL.OZ.
750ML

BOTTLE. REFERMENTATION

Left & opposite: Painterly labels and witty beer names are all part of the Unibroue story.

Below: La Fin du Monde is Unibroue's fine tripel, full of Belgian-style spice and hops.

unusual character and market them heavily using beautiful imagery and Quebecois symbolism.

It didn't take long for Dion's new brewery to make its presence felt internationally, selling in America, France, and, audaciously, Belgium, as well as in other European nations. But it was in the rough-and-tumble world of Quebec beer sales that Unibroue made the most noise, going toe to toe with the country's third-largest brewing company, the Ontario-based Sleeman Breweries.

Best known for a golden cream ale packaged in a clear glass bottle, Sleeman was desperate to make a name for itself in the Quebecois market, and Dion appeared equally determined to stop them, launching a competing and rather out-of-character golden lager, called simply U, and bottling it in clear glass.

Ultimately, John Sleeman, founder and CEO of Sleeman Breweries, made Dion an offer he couldn't refuse, and Unibroue joined the Ontario company's stable of regional cross-Canada breweries in 2004. Two years later, the hunter became the hunted, and Sleeman, along with its

Unibroue subsidiary, fell to the control of Japan's Sapporo Breweries.

Most Unibroue aficionados will assert that little has happened to change the character of the brewery's beers since the Sapporo purchase, especially when it comes to head brewer Jerry Vietz, rated as one of the most accomplished brewers in the country. The heavy metal band Megadeth obviously concurred: in 2016, they collaborated with him to produce À Tout Le Monde, a dry-hopped Belgian-style saison, which, like the band's music, was a massive hit.

* KEY BEERS

Don de Dieu Belgian Strong Pale Ale 9%
La Fin du Monde Tripel 9%
Maudite Amber Ale 8%
Noire de Chambly Dark Ale 6.2%
Terrible Dark Ale 10%
Trois Pistoles Dark Ale 9%

PHILLIPS BREWING CO.
VICTORIA, BRITISH COLUMBIA
WWW.PHILLIPSBEER.COM

Chucklehead India Red Ale 6.5%
Matt Phillips founded his brewery in 2001, using credit cards to finance his dream. It's certainly worked, as the brewery now also has a soda company, distillery, and maltings. Chucklehead (or Coulrophobia, as it was known) is an amber-hued delight of citrus, hops, hearty maltiness, and a long bitter finish.

PRINCE EDWARD ISLAND
CHARLOTTETOWN, PRINCE EDWARD
WWW.PEIBREWINGCOMPANY.COM

Sydney Street Stout 5.3%
There are four breweries on Prince Edward Island, but PEI is the veteran, having been founded in 1997, when it was originally called Murphy's. Sydney Street is a perky and bittersweet stout with a mix of chocolate, toffee, and roast notes alongside a smooth and full-bodied mouthfeel.

PROPELLER BREWING
HALIFAX, NOVA SCOTIA
WWW.DRINKPROPELLER.CA

ESB 5%
When London brewery Fuller's brewed the first ESB in the early 1970s, little did they know how this beer style would spread around the world. Here in Nova Scotia, Propeller's ESB is a regular among its well-made beers, featuring caramel, chocolate, bitterness, and a soothing mouthfeel that makes it a beer to keep revisiting.

BRASSEURS RJ
MONTREAL, QUEBEC
WWW.BRASSEURSRJ.COM

Belle Gueule Weizenbock 7.2%
This is part of the Belle Gueule brand, which also features a dunkelweizen and a hefeweizen, so we know we're in capable hands when it comes to producing Bavarian specialties. Malt leads the way, alongside the classic banana-and-cloves weizen signature, with the added luxury of chocolate notes on the nose and palate.

REBELLION
REGINA, SASKATCHEWAN
WWW.REBELLIONBREWING.CA

IPA 6.7%
Some say that this is the best IPA in the province of Saskatchewan, with its intense barrage of pine and juicy citrus and tropical fruit notes alongside a pleasing bitterness in the finish. A quality quaff for happy hopheads.

STONE CITY ALES
KINGSTON, ONTARIO
WWW.STONECITYALES.COM

Uncharted IPA 7%
The historic city of Kingston is home to this small brewery and taproom that was founded in 2014. Despite the relative newness of the brewery, awards have been showered on this rousing IPA, which blooms with tropical fruit, citrus juiciness, and plenty of delectable hop character.

STORM BREWING CO.
VANCOUVER, BRITISH COLUMBIA
WWW.STORMBREWING.ORG

Imperial Flanders Red Sour Ale 11%
This is a brute of a Flemish red ale, a crimson tide of lambic-style lavishness that has spent at least a year in old oak barrels. It's tart and mouth-puckering, funky, and chunky on the palate, but there's also a cherry-like sweetness and vinous fruitiness that add to the complexity.

LE TROU DE DIABLE
SHAWINIGAN, QUEBEC
WWW.TROUDUDIABLE.COM

Dulcis Succubus Sour Beer 7%
Brewpub whose name comes from the Devil's Hole, which is a big hole in the ground close to Shawinigan and leads to hell. There are no such dark thoughts, however, in the approach of Le Trou de Diable to brewing, as they produce a goodly amount of beers. This is a saison that has spent time in wine barrels in the company of Brettanomyces and is tart and fruity, vinous and woody, and much more complex than a hole in the ground.

Saison du Tracteur 6%
Juicy, and lubricious, and brimming with passion fruit, orange, and spice and blessed with a crisp carbonation, this is a soulful saison that would be ideal after a day in a tractor plowing the land.

LES TROIS MOUSQUETAIRES
BROSSARD, QUEBEC
WWW.LESTROISMOUSQUETAIRES.CA

Doppelbock 8.6%

Quebec-based micro that looks to Belgian brewing traditions for inspiration but is also influenced by German beer styles, as is evident by this beast of a big-hearted doppelbock. Chocolate, coffee, molasses, and orange all make their appearance before its cookie-dry finish. A wallop of a beer to be studied carefully.

UNIBROUE
see Brewery Profile pages 218 to 219
CHAMBLY, QUEBEC
WWW.UNIBROUE.COM

★ **La Fin du Monde** Tripel 9%

Filled with fruitiness, bracingly strong, and afforded great depth by a solid spiciness and drying, rather than bittering, hop, this is less a Belgian-style tripel than it is a Belgian-inspired, very Quebecois interpretation. Delicious.

★ **Maudite** Amber Ale 8%

Generously spiced with coriander and possibly something else unidentifiable, this strong Belgian-inspired ale possesses sufficient fruity malt to qualify as a great dinner accompaniment, yet enough spicy, warming strength to work also as a fitting nightcap.

★ **Terrible** Quadrupel 10%

Ignore the Quebecois tongue-in-cheek, this wonderfully potent ale is anything but terrible. Expect notes of black licorice, Asian spice, molasses, and alcohol in the aroma and a complex body offering spice, dark chocolate, espresso beans, and blackstrap molasses.

WELLINGTON BREWERY
GUELPH, ONTARIO
WWW.WELLINGTONBREWERY.CA

Iron Duke Strong Ale 6.5%

This is a malty delight of an ale, with an almost syrupy toffee nose and a winey body that offers stewed fruit, hints of cocoa, and a touch of coffee on the warming, satisfying finish.

WILD ROSE BREWERY
CALGARY, ALBERTA
WWW.WILDROSEBREWERY.COM

Electric Avenue Lager 5%

Even though this brewery is based deep in the Canadian north, where winters are brought in by a battalion of brass monkeys, when the sun shines, the monkeys vanish, and it's time for this refreshing, highly quaffable lager.

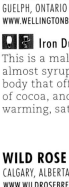

"Give my people plenty of beer, good beer, and cheap beer, and you will have no revolution among them."

—QUEEN VICTORIA BRITISH MONARCH, 1819–1901

ARGENTINA

ANTARES BREWING
MAR DEL PLATA, BUENOS AIRES
WWW.CERVEZAANTARES.COM

Imperial Stout 8.5%
US- and English-influenced chain of brewpubs producing this immense, full-bodied, sweet and spicy stout brewed with pilsner, chocolate and caramel malts, and Cascade and Fuggles hops.

ARAUCANA CERVEZA ARTESANAL
EL BOLSÓN, RÍO NEGRO
WWW.CERVECEROSCASEROS.COM.AR

Negra Bock 7.2%
Small brewery that was founded in 2005 and which brews beers with a definite German influence. Here is one: dark amber in color, subtly fruity, grainy and cookie-like, with a dry finish.

BEAGLE
USHUAIA, TIERRA DEL FUEGO
NO WEB ADDRESS

Beagle Fuegian Negra Stout 7.8%
The southern-most brewery in the world produces excellent bottle-conditioned Beagle ales, named after Darwin's ship of the 1830s. These include a bitter/pale ale, IPA, and this tawny-colored and fruity stout.

PERU

BARRANCO BEER COMPANY
LIMA
WWW.BARRANCOBEER.COM

Heiss Weiss Hefeweizen 4.8%
Craft beer is a relatively new concept in Peru but it is growing, especially in Lima, where the majority of breweries reside. This busy brewpub has been going since 2013 and Heiss Weiss is its creamy Bavarian-style wheat beer, packed with traditional banana and clove notes and a refreshing mouthfeel.

BRAZIL

BADEN BADEN
CAMPOS DO JORDÃO, SÃO PAULO
WWW.BADENBADEN.COM.BR

Red Ale Especial Barley Wine 9.2%
1999 was the year Baden Baden was founded in the Alpine lookalike town of Campos do Jordão. In 2007 the brewery was bought up by Kirin, but little seems to have changed, and the beer range remains impressive. Red Ale Especial is a robust and fruity barley wine that demands respect.

BODEBROWN
CURITIBA, PARANÁ
WWW.BODEBROWN.COM.BR

Perigosa Imperial IPA 9.2%
The name of this beer translates as 'dangerous," which is a very apt description of the pitfalls that lie ahead if one drinks too much of what is a pleasing, well-made imperial. Citrus and tropical fruit notes billow out of the glass like papal smoke and also make their presence felt on the palate alongside a high bitterness.

CERVEJARIA COLORADO
RIBEIRÃO PRETO, SÃO PAULO
WWW.CERVEJARIACOLORADO.COM.BR

Vixnu Imperial IPA 9.5%
This veteran of the Brazilian craft brewing scene was founded in 1995 (and has since been acquired by AB InBev) and made its name with a mixture of US-style beers and ones that used local ingredients, such as local honey and cassava. This is its resinous and rapturous imperial IPA, which has a notably bracing bitterness in its finish.

DUM CERVEJARIA
CURITIBA, PARANÁ
WWW.DUMCERVEJARIA.COM.BR

Petroleum Imperial Stout 12%
Intensity of flavor is the name of the game for this black-as-midnight imperial stout that has oatmeal and cocoa in the mix. It's rich and spirituous, full-bodied and smooth, roasty and chocolaty, with a big bitterness in the finish.

EISENBAHN
BLUMENAU, SANTA CATARINA
WWW.EISENBAHN.COM.BR

Eisenbahn Vigorosa Weizenbock 8%
Named after a Blumenau brewery that opened and closed in the early 1900s, Eisenbahn has become the largest craft brewery in Brazil, which led to it being bought by Cervejaria Sudbrack (Brasil Kirin) in 2011. It was built in 2002 by Juliano Mendes, a disillusioned beer drinker with a love for ambitious European beers, such as this effervescent, unfiltered wheat double bock with toasted whole-grain bread, bananas and chocolate.

TUPINIQUIM
PORTO ALEGRE, RIO GRANDE DO SUL
WWW.CERVEJATUPINIQUIM.COM.BR

Monjolo Imperial Porter 10.5%
Many beers (including collaborations with Stillwater and Evil Twin) emerge from the creative minds behind this up-and-coming micro that was founded in 2014. This is its beefy yet smooth-talking imperial porter, with coffee, licorice, and chocolate on the nose and palate, plus a full-bodied texture.

THE CARIBBEAN

DESNOES & GEDDES JAMAICA
KINGSTON, JAMAICA
WWW.REDSTRIPE.COM

Dragon Stout Foreign Stout 7.5%
A rumbunctious sweet and syrupy stout with a color akin to navy rum. Mostly drunk chilled in Jamaica, it gains complexity when taken slightly warmer. Toast and roasted malt, chocolate, and a dry bitter finish.

Guinness Foreign Extra Stout 6.5%
Never mind all that twee fiddle-fiddling Oirish, "do-you-know-the-way-to-Tipperary" nitro-keg nonsense. If drinkers want a proper Guinness, then this black-cherry-flavored, jet-black sweet, and slightly sour stout is genuine, uncut liquid craic.

Red Stripe Lager 4.7%
Here's a joke for you: "My wife went to the West Indies to drink a crisp, clean lager first brewed in 1927 and named after the red stripe that runs down the uniform trousers of the police force." "Jamaica?" "No, she went of her own accord." She likes slightly malty lagers, especially when it's hot.

MEXICO

CUCAPÁ
MEXICALI, BAJA CALIFORNIA
WWW.CUCAPA.COM

La Migra Imperial Stout 8.5%
Founded in 2002, this is a pioneer of a growing band of Mexican craft brewers, and its beers are well regarded both in its home country and over the border to the north. This is a luscious imperial stout.

INSURGENTE
TIJUANA, BAJA CALIFORNIA
WWW.CERVEZAINSURGENTE.COM

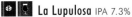

La Lupulosa IPA 7.3%
There's a blast of hops on the nose of this citrus bomb of an IPA, a swoop of malt sweetness, fruit, and a bitter finish.

MINERVA
ZAPOPAN, JALISCO
WWW.CERVEZAMINERVA.MX

Imperial Tequila Ale Strong Ale 7%
The historic city of Zapopan is home to this independent brewery. This self-styled Imperial Tequila Ale (it spends time in former tequila barrels) is orange amber in color with hints of fruit and tequila.

PRIMUS
MIGUEL HIDALGO, MECIO
WWW.PRIMUS.COM.MX

Tempus Doble Malta Altbier 7%
Primus make a tempting range of beers, many of which are influenced by German brewing culture. (For instance, they made the first ever alt in Mexico.) This is an 'imperial alt', toasty, roasty and bittersweet.

WENDLANDT
ENSENADA, BAJA CALIFORNIA
WWW.WENDLANDT.COM.MX

Perro Del Mar IPA 7%
Even though it was founded in 2014, Wendlandt was quickly voted Mexico's best new brewery at the prestigious Copa Cerveza Mexico. This presumptuous and muscular IPA also took home a gong.

AUSTRALIA

&

NEW ZEALAND

Above: The guys from Altitude Brewing in Queenstown, New Zealand, take the ethos of their brewery name very seriously.
Below: Piratical pale ales and imperious IPAs are the order of the day at Australia's Pirate Life in Adelaide.

INTRODUCTION
AUSTRALIA & NEW ZEALAND

It should come as no surprise that, in a country covered with a lot of desert, most Australians still "crack open a tinny" of something light, fizzy, and cold.

Beer choices have historically proved scarce here, the first Europeans discovering a distinct lack of brewing ingredients when they landed, and it wasn't until hops arrived on convict ships in the late 1700s that brewing could start properly.

That said, in lieu of barley and hops, those first brewing efforts utilized an eclectic mix—of gooseberries, tree bark, corn, and possibly the odd flamin' galah with it—and it seems this invention is alive and well today. Granted, nearly 90 percent of the beer sold here won't deviate from the lager styles that quench the sun-drenched, but a recent craft revolution has inspired plenty of brewing creativity.

Coopers deserves a special mention, and having always challenged the flavor monotony and monopoly of mainstream lagers, the brewery continues to fire out beer with flavor and inspire homebrewing. Equally inspiring in the earlier days were the likes of Little Creatures and Redoak, who have been instrumental in rejuvenating the reputation of flavorsome Australian beer. But there's much more besides. Today the country is bubbling over with new breweries.

Along with the pioneering beer fans making the stuff, one of the heroes of the scene is the Galaxy hop, growing a long, long way from the European and American hop heartlands, but very close to the hearts of Australian brewers.

The versatile hop features in many of the beers you'll discover in this chapter and produces beer full of passion fruit, peach, and clean citrus.

Meanwhile, the Aussies are becoming adept at session beers. "See Fosters," you might say, but along with a manageable ABV and beers that are very welcome cold, the new batch of brewers are not presenting this without the flavor you actually desire. It's an area of brewing to keep an eye on over the coming years as drinkers react to the trend in brewing to amp up the alcohol content—Nomad's IPA and Hoppy Pale are fine examples.

Next door, the New Zealanders are focusing that zeal on their brewing. Benefiting from an untouched botanical beauty, the Kiwis' burgeoning small-scale scene means there are nearly as many beers as sheep here—but not quite. For a country that had two breweries up until the late 1990s, it is a remarkable turnaround.

The global affection for hop–driven beers has played into Kiwis' hands. This naturally robust island has dodged some of the hop blights other brewing nations have suffered, and some of the native botanicals have earned rave reviews, particularly the Nelson Sauvin—a dynamic dual-purpose variety whose fruity "new-world wine" character works equally well in punchy India pale ales and Pacific pales as it does in delivering the delicate aromas associated with lighter lagers.

But hop-driven beers are only part of the story. The likes of Tuatara, 8 Wired, Liberty, Moa, Garage Project, and Yeastie Boys are becoming familiar names to global beer lovers for beers right across the flavor spectrum.

They're inspiring new boys, the likes of Altitude, for example, to scale the dizzy heights, with new startups and contract brewers emerging all the time.

AUSTRALIA

3 RAVENS
THORNBURY, VICTORIA
WWW.3RAVENS.COM.AU

Little Raven Double IPA 8%

The Melbourne suburbs is home to 3 Ravens, which was founded in 2003 but was taken over by new owners in 2013. This double IPA is part of the Little Raven limited release program, boldly hopped with Mosaic, Citra, Simcoe, and Amarillo, all of which suggest it might double as breakfast fruit juice until you experience the soft yet firm bitterness present in the finish.

4 PINES
MANLY, NEW SOUTH WALES
WWW.4PINESBEER.COM.AU

Pale Ale 5.1%

Speedos swapped for cargo shorts and you'll be ready to leave the sandy paradise of Manly Beach for the nearby brewpub of 4 Pines, which is where it all started for them. Experimental beers will be on offer here, as well as this robust Pale Ale, which has waves of grapefruit, pine, and a rounded maltiness to create a perfect balance.

BENTSPOKE BREWERY
CANBERRA, AUSTRALIA CAPITAL TERRITORY
WWW.BENTSPOKEBREWING.COM.AU

Crankshaft IPA 5.8%

Until he opened Bentspoke's brewpub in 2014, Richard Watkins was the highly renowned brewer at Wig & Pen. His experience obviously served him well, as Bentspoke's beers are highly prized in Canberra's quaffing community. Crankshaft is a well-hopped IPA, a riot of citrus and pine, before a cookie malt spine keeps things in order.

BIG SHED BREWING
ADELAIDE, SOUTH AUSTRALIA
WWW.BIGSHED.BEER

Golden Stout Time Sweet Stout 5.4%

Sweet-tooth sufferers step right up. This luscious stout has added toffee and honeycomb in the mix, making it taste much like the famous Australian ice cream Golden Gaytime while still keeping the sternness of a stout.

BILLABONG BREWERY
PERTH, WESTERN AUSTRALIA
WWW.BILLABONGBREWING.COM.AU

4 Hop Ale Best Bitter 3.8%

Born out of a brew-your-own bar begun in 1993, Billabong has been winning awards and weaning Western Australians off bland bubbly booze for a few years now. As well as brewing some gorgeous beers such as this remarkably balanced and tasty best bitter, which is hopped at four different stages of the boil, Billabong has gone against the grain, quite literally, with some award-winning gluten-free beers that you don't have to suffer wheat allergies to enjoy.

J. BOAG & SON
LAUNCESTON, TASMANIA
WWW.JAMESBOAG.COM.AU

James Boag's Premium Lager 5%

Now part of Lion Nathan, Boag livened up its lager line a few years ago with some delectable Tasmanian beers. This devilish beauty is fermented at a lower temperature, lagered longer and has a big dose of late hopping.

BOATROCKER
MELBOURNE, VICTORIA
WWW.BOATROCKER.COM.AU

Ramjet Imperial Stout 10.2%

Initially released as a special in 2013, this potent and powerful dark destroyer of a beer spends time in whisky barrels, a diversion that adds to its appeal. It's creamy and toasty and chocolaty. In 2016, a coffee-infused Ramjet was unleashed on the world.

BOOTLEG BREWERY
MARGARET RIVER, WESTERN AUSTRALIA
WWW.BOOTLEGBREWINGCO.COM

 Raging Bull Porter 7.1%

Surrounded by vineyards in the staunch wine region of Margaret River, Bootleg has been converting cork-sniffing, plonk-spitting tourists since 1994. This dark porter will prick up the ears of Malbec and Musar drinkers, with notes of sweet caramel, coffee, chocolate, and dried plums.

BREWCULT
MELBOURNE, VICTORIA
WWW.BREWCULT.COM

Milk and Two Sugars
Sweet Stout 7.2%

Gypsy brewer Steve Henderson makes some fascinating beers. With some, he indulges in his love of hops; others, like this creamy, soothing coffee-infused sweet stout, are a bit more left-field. (He's also made a porter that was aged in balsamic barrels.)

BRIDGE ROAD BREWERS
BEECHWORTH, VICTORIA
WWW.BRIDGEROADBREWERS.COM.AU

Beechworth Pale Ale 4.8%

Bridge Road is an innovative small-batch brewery in the historic town of Beechworth, founded by former winemaker Ben Kraus after an inspirational beer-drinking sojourn in Europe. However, he can do American-style pale ales too, as this crisp and aromatic hop refresher proves.

BRUNY ISLAND BEER
BRUNY ISLAND, TASMANIA
WWW.BRUNYISLANDCHEESE.COM.AU/BEER

Farm Ale Golden Ale 4.5%

Young brewery that shares space with Bruny Island Cheese Company and very much focuses on using Tasmanian ingredients for its beers. This gold-colored ale has tropical fruit and citrus notes, which combine elegantly with a nutty, smooth, and malty character.

BURLEIGH
BUREIGH HEADS, QUEENSLAND
WWW.BURLEIGHBREWING.COM.AU

Twisted Palm Pale Ale 4.2%

Given that Burleigh is the only brewery situated in the beautiful surrounds of the Gold Coast, it seems only natural that this beer, which bursts with tropical fruit and citrus notes, comes to hand when it's time for a drink.

COLONIAL BREWING COMPANY
MARGARET RIVER, WESTERN AUSTRALIA
WWW.COLONIALBREWINGCO.COM.AU

I.P.A. Australia 6.5%

Another small-batch brewing infiltrator working its magic in wine country, Colonial began beermaking in 2004 and excels in the crafting of artisan ales. This is an awesome, piney, grassy, American-style IPA steeped in a cacophony of citrusy hops.

COOPERS BREWERY
ADELAIDE, SOUTH AUSTRALIA
WWW.COOPERSBREWERY.COM.AU

Coopers Sparkling Ale 5.8%

While other big Australian breweries jumped on the bland bottom-fermenting bandwagon, Coopers of Adelaide steadfastly kept hailing the bottle-conditioned ale in style, and in doing so provided inspiration for the legion of new-wave breweries in Australia. This is the beer that Coopers is built on. A deep auburn-colored cloudy beer with lots of sediment, it is brewed using a top fermentation that Thomas Cooper implemented in 1862. A honeyed hop aroma followed by a full-bodied fruity, raspberry-ish note, with a mild hop bite.

Coopers Vintage Ale 7.5%

Christmas pudding, port, and dark toffee are just some of the tasting notes applied to vintage batches of what is arguably Australia's finest beer. Packed with cooked plum and toffeelike flavors and balanced by hints of sour cherry and chicory, it is reckoned by Coopers that two years of rest will bring out the best in it.

FERAL BREWING COMPANY
PERTH, WESTERN AUSTRALIA
WWW.FERALBREWING.COM.AU

Feral White Witbier 4.7%

Don't be put off by the wild hog on the label, as the beers from this Western Australian micro are anything but, ahem, boorish. What you get is a hazy, lightly hopped, and spicy Belgian wit.

Feral Hophog Pale Ale 5.8%

True to the brewery's Undomesticated Yet Sophisticated slogan, this American-style pale ale will drive hopheads wild with its spike of pine needle, searing citrus aroma, and bready malt background.

FORTITUDE BREWING
EAGLE HEIGHTS, QUEENSLAND
WWW.FORTITUDEBREWING.COM.AU

Pacer 2.8 Pale Ale 2.8%

In a beer world seemingly bossed over by supercharged IPAs and mind-bendingly strong imperial stouts, it's often good to come across a beer that's low in alcohol but high in flavor, which is what this citrusy pale ale from Queensland is.

GAGE ROADS BREWERY
FREMANTLE, WESTERN AUSTRALIA
WWW.GAGEROADS.COM.AU

Sleeping Giant IPA 5.4%

Go-getting micro with beers brewed by fussy bastards who first caught the brewing bug working in a brewpub. They set up their own brewery after becoming frustrated by the fact that the number of people who could experience their esoteric ales was severely limited. This dry-hopped IPA, firmed up superbly with five Australian malts, is just one of its fine brews.

HAHN
SYDNEY, NEW SOUTH WALES
WWW.LIONNATHAN.COM.AU

Hahn Premium Lager 5%

A nice, easy-drinking beer made with Munich hops from a brewery with Germanic roots. Purists may scoff at this beer, but when things are hotter than a flaming galah, its crisp, back-of-the-throat bitter bite is a simply superb thirst-quencher.

HARGREAVES HILL
LILYDALE, VICTORIA
WWW.HARGREAVESHILL.COM.AU

Pale Ale 4.9%

Founded in 2004 by a former pianist and his opera-singing wife who swapped warbling and ivory-tinkling for making melodious malty lagers and ales. The original brewery was destroyed in 2009, but a new brewhouse was found in Lilydale, and the brewery has gone from strength to strength. This Pale Ale hits top grapefruit and citrus notes with a cookie-backing vocal.

HAWKERS
RESERVOIR, VICTORIA
WWW.HAWKERS.BEER

Hawkers IPA 6.5%

Until founding Hawkers in 2015, Joseph Abboud was best known as the chef at Melbourne's popular Middle Eastern restaurant Rumi. However, a trip to Lebanon led to an encounter with the beers of 961 Brewery, which inspired him to start up Hawkers. With this rumbunctious ale, expect grapefruit, passion fruit, and pine working together with a cookie-like maltiness.

HOLGATE BREWHOUSE
WOODEND, VICTORIA
WWW.HOLGATEBREWHOUSE.COM

 Wild Red Ale Flemish Red 6%

After traveling around the USA and Europe and sampling plenty of beers, Paul and Natasha Holgate returned home, and, in 1999, a brewery was born. A variety of beers is available, some of them cask-conditioned; this is Holgate's tribute to Rodenbach, a complex wood-aged beer with a quenching tartness.

HOP NATION
MELBOURNE, VICTORIA
WWW.HOPNATION.COM.AU

The Chop IPA 7%

It's not an unfamiliar story in Aussie beer. A couple of winemakers change liquids and go into brewing, which is what happened with Hop Nation. Brewing their luscious liquids at Hawkers first, they found a brewery in 2016 and added wood-aging to their skills. The Chop, however, eschews wood and is a bright and boldly flavored IPA influenced by all the various styles the founders had tasted on their travels.

JAMIESON BREWERY
JAMIESON, VICTORIA
WWW.JAMIESONBREWERY.COM.AU

Beast IPA 7%

It's only little, but the Jamieson family-run hotel brewery has made a big impression in Melbourne and beyond with a range of impressive, adventurous bottled ales. The biggest and most boisterous is this IPA, inspired by the ales of the Pacific Northwest and heaving with five hop varieties. Bitter yet balanced.

KAIJU BEER
DANDENONG SOUTH, VICTORIA
WWW.KAIJUBEER.COM.AU

Aftermath Double IPA 9.1%

Microbrewery that was originally called Monster Mash, but after a legal battle with an energy drink company they named themselves after the monsters in *Pacific Rim*. Not ones to do things by half, they announced themselves in 2013 with this monstrously drinkable double IPA, which features tropical fruit and citrus worked in tandem with a malty, toffeelike backbone.

KNAPPSTEIN ENTERPRISE WINERY & BREWING
CLARE VALLEY, SOUTH AUSTRALIA
WWW.KNAPPSTEIN.COM.AU

Knappstein Reserve Lager 5.6%

When the Knappstein winery moved into the former home of Enterprise Brewery in 1970, it was surely only a matter of time before the winemakers succumbed to curious temptation and breathed life back into the building's brewing past. In 2006, nearly a hundred years after the brewery first fired up its kettles, this luscious grapefruit-tinged lager with notes of lychee and pear was unleashed in a sharply designed bottle and label combo. Maybe those pesky winemakers aren't so bad after all.

LITTLE CREATURES
FREEMANTLE, WESTERN AUSTRALIA
WWW.LIITLECREATURES.COM.AU

Little Creatures Pale Ale 5.2%

Inspired by the American craft-brewing revolution, especially the Sierra Nevada business model, Little Creatures began fashioning an array of intriguing ales on the Fremantle shore back in 2000. (They also now have a brewery in Geelong.) This, the biggest Little Creature, has made its way to the United States and Europe on the back of a hazy hue, succulent malt and lychee, and citrus-flavored finish.

LORD NELSON BREWERY HOTEL
SYDNEY, NEW SOUTH WALES
WWW.LORDNELSONBREWERY.COM

Nelson's Blood Porter 4.9%
Pours black with a portlike red shimmer, a rolling roasty mouthfeel, and a rich espresso finish.

Three Sheets Pale Ale 4.9%
This big, grandiose brewpub is something of a Sydney beer-drinking institution, having been around since the 1980s, longer than any other on-premise institution. In a building that dates back to the 1830s, it brews half a dozen year-round ales. Three Sheets, a golden aromatic pale ale, is the most popular of the Lord Nelson offerings.

MALT SHOVEL BREWERY
SYDNEY, NEW SOUTH WALES
WWW.JAMESSQUIRE.COM.AU

James Squire Stowaway IPA 5.6%
Having helped develop Coors Light while brewing in his native USA, brewmaster Chuck Hahn arrived at Malt Shovel in 1998, and he's been digging himself out of a hole with some excellent craft ales ever since, which are all branded with the James Squire name (he is thought to have been the first Aussie brewer.) An intense yet not overly outrageous IPA, earthy, dry-hopped with English Fuggles and robust malt, and a floral finish.

MASH BREWING
HENLEY BROOK, WESTERN AUSTRALIA
WWW.MASHBREWING.COM.AU

Copy Cat IPA 6.8%
Mash is located in the Swan Valley just outside Perth, an area where food and drink are taken seriously. Mash has been around since 2006, but it's only in the last several years that its beers have been winning awards and making friends. Copy Cat is its well-amplified American-style IPA bursting with tropical fruit and pine.

MATILDA BAY BREWING COMPANY
PORT MELBOURNE, VICTORIA
WWW.MATILDABAY.COM.AU

Longshot Brown Ale 6%
Dispatch all thoughts of brown ale's flat-cap-and-whippets image. Matilda Bay pounces on this classic style with the agility of a panther, producing a sleek and burnished bittersweet beer, which is enlivened by the addition of coffee.

Redback Hefeweizen 4.7%
When this trailblazer first stuck its head above the parapet in the dark beer-drinking days of the 1980s, it caused a stir with this hazy hefe full of yeasty fruit and spice. Even though it's now owned by Carlton & United Breweries, its penchant for pioneering hasn't waned, so keep an eye out for Matilda's more maverick efforts.

MILDURA THEATRE BREWERY
MILDURA, VICTORIA
WWW.MILDURABREWERY.COM.AU

Storm Pale Ale 4.5%
A brewpub based in an impressive 1930s theater whose beers tread the boards of taste with confidence. US-influenced blood-orange pale ale that is heavily flavored with Amarillo and Cascade hops. It is assertive and a little astringent but with enough malt to balance it out.

MODUS OPERANDI
SYDNEY, NEW SOUTH WALES
WWW.MOBREWING.COM.AU

Former Tenant Red IPA 7.8%
Grant and Jas Wearin took a mobile home around the US in search of craft beer and returned home thinking of nothing but starting a brewery. That dream came true in 2014, and the accolades and awards followed—not surprising when you consider this boombox of a red IPA with its aromatic tropical fruit notes alongside a deep spicy caramel character.

MOO BREW
BERRIEDALE, TASMANIA
WWW.MOOBREW.COM.AU

Moo Brew Dark Ale 8%

Based in a winery in gorgeous countryside outside Hobart, Tasmania, Moo Brew has a sleek selection of beers, which are packaged in stylishly shaped bottles. This seasonal special is silky and velvety, tantalizing with chocolate and coffee before its dry, bitter finish.

MORNINGTON PENINSULA
MORNINGTON, VICTORIA
WWW.MPBREW.COM.AU

Russian Imperial Stout 9.5%

Located in a factory that used to produce golf balls and founded in 2010, this is a thriving brewpub popular with traveling beer geeks. As well as its regulars, the brewery produces a series of imperial beers, one of which is this smooth and creamy brew with plenty of chocolate, roast grain, dark fruit, and coffee on parade, followed by a dry finish.

MOUNTAIN GOAT BREWERY
MELBOURNE, VICTORIA
WWW.GOATBEER.COM.AU

Organic Steam Ale 4.5%

In 2015, Mountain Goat was bought by Asahi, but founders Cam Hines and Dave Boningham have stayed on. This is one of their most popular beers, a crisp and refreshing drop serves as an excellent starter beer for those new to the craft beer scene.

Summer Ale 4.7%

Cam and Dave began this Melbourne micro in the late 1990s after originally brewing in Dave's backyard. It accrued its moniker because it's a big, hairy animal that's never going to fall over and it's forever on the front hoof in terms of marketing and flavorsome brewing. Summer Ale is their light and breezy session beer with hints of passion fruit leading to a dry finish.

MURRAY'S CRAFT BREWING COMPANY
BOBS FARM, NEW SOUTH WALES
WWW.MURRAYSBREWINGCO.COM.AU

Wild Thing Imperial Stout 10%

Since founding the brewery in 2006, craft beer enthusiast and owner Murray Howe has not been scared to drag Australian drinkers out of their schooner-swilling comfort zone, as this intensely dark imperial stout demonstrates. Coffee, malt sweetness, and hop bitterness all come together and make sweet music on the tongue.

NAIL BREWING
BASSENDEAN, WESTERN AUSTRALIA
NAILBREWING.COM.AU

Clout Stout
Imperial Stout 10.5% (ABV varies)

Clout Stout tastes as it sounds: big and bold, a lubricious Imperial stout that is almost decadent in the way notes of vanilla, chocolate, coffee, and caramel simmer away on both the nose and the palate. It's an annual special from Nail, whose brewer John Smallwood has been a leading light in the Western Australian craft beer scene for two decades.

PADDY'S BREWERY
SYDNEY, NEW SOUTH WALES
WWW.MARKETSHOTEL.COM.AU/PADDYS-BREWERY

Paddy's Original Pilsner 4.5%

Located in a bustling mainstream pub next to the Olympic site in Sydney's Homebush Bay, Paddy's installed a brewery in 2001, and within three years it was named Champion Small Brewery of the Year. Spicy, floral, pale-straw-colored Czech pilsner swathed in distinctive spicy Saaz hop and reputedly using a yeast from a brewery in Pilsen. A cultured, educated alternative to VB and Foster's.

PIRATE LIFE
ADELAIDE, SOUTH AUSTRALIA
WWW.PIRATELIFE.COM.AU

IIPA Imperial IPA 8.8%

Mosaic, Centennial, Simcoe and Columbus all work in riotous harmony for this big, bold, and brash beer, with a sturdy malt backbone providing the balancing sweetness before the long bitter, and dry finish.

Pale Ale 5.4%

There's a zip and a lust for life in the way Pirate Life approaches the beer world, which might have something to do with the fact that brewers Jack Cameron and Jared Red Proudfoot once did apprenticeships at BrewDog, while Jack's dad, Michael, (now CEO) also worked with BrewDog. Its pale ale is a riot of tropical fruit and resiny pine notes alongside an orangy fruitiness and a long dry finish.

PRANCING PONY
ADELAIDE, SOUTH AUSTRALIA
WWW.PRANCINGPONYBREWERY.COM.AU

India Red Ale 7.9%

Founded in 2013 by long-term homebrewer Frank Samson, this is a go-ahead brewpub whose beers keep winning awards. India Red Ale is one of those, being awarded Supreme Champion in the International Beer Challenge in 2016. It's brown-red in color, pulsating with plenty of tropical fruit and citrus on the nose, which then joins in with a juicy malty body and plenty of bitterness to create an immensely satisfying beer.

REDOAK BOUTIQUE BREWERY
SYDNEY, NEW SOUTH WALES
WWW.REDOAK.COM.AU

Baltic Porter 8.7%

Initially inspired by founder David Hollyoak's encounter with a Baltic porter in a small Polish café in the 1990s, this is a rich and luscious, bittersweet, and booming take on a style of beer that is rare in its home countries.

Framboise Froment 5.2%

Founded in 2004, Redoak continues to stoke the coals of craft ale convention by bravely brewing a hugely ambitious and award-winning range of unusual beer styles. This is Redoak's flagship beer, brewed with hand-picked raspberries from Victoria's Yarra Valley. Tart, sweet, and sour with a flint-dry fruit finish, it is definitely one you must try.

Global IPA 6.5%

Yes, there are hops from the USA here but also varieties from the UK, Australia, New Zealand, and Germany, all of which contribute to layers of flavor and a bracing bitterness in the finish.

RIVERSIDE
PARRAMATTA, NEW SOUTH WALES
WWW.RIVERSIDEBREWING.COM.AU

88 Robust Porter 6%

We might not be in early nineteenth-century London but as you taste this smooth sipper with its chocolate and coffee notes, chances are that images of massive vats and porters popping into the pub for a quick one will swirl around like smoke. All this from a brewery in the western suburbs of the capital city, Sydney.

"Buy a man a beer and he wastes an hour.
Teach a man to brew and he wastes a lifetime."
—ANONYMOUS

ROCKS BREWING

ALEXANDRIA, NEW SOUTH WALES
WWW.ROCKSBREWING.COM

The Hangman Pale Ale 4.9%

Founded in 2008, but with their own brewery in the Sydney suburb of Alexandria only since 2014, the names of Rocks' beers have an earthiness to them (The Governor, The Convict etc). The Hangman is an American-style pale ale with rumbles of American hops, citrus and pine notes emerging from the glass, while there's a long stretch of bitterness in the final flourish.

SAILORS GRAVE

ORBOST, VICTORIA
WWW.SAILORSGRAVEBREWING.COM

Down She Gose 4.5%

2016 saw the first beers emerge from Sailors Grave, who are based in a former butter factory. As if to show their intentions for the future, their main beer is this tart and quenching gose, which also uses local seaweed. Other beers brewed include an alt, an IPA (naturally), and a grapefruit and marigold saison.

LA SIRÈNE

MELBOURNE, VICTORIA
WWW.LASIRENE.COM.AU

Super Saison 8%

Artisanal brewery based in inner city Melbourne, whose founder Costa Nikias comes from a winemaking and scientific background. His passion is for rustic and distinctive ales, especially classic Belgian and French farmhouse styles, such as Super Saison, a stronger than usual version of the classic style with the heft of alcohol, spice, brisk carbonation and a hint of orange.

SOUTHERN BAY BREWING COMPANY

MOOLAPI, VICTORIA
WWW.SOUTHERNBAY.COM.AU/

Hop Bazooka IPA 5.8%

This is a palate-rousing treat of tropical fruit and pinelike resins from a brewery that dates back to 1987 and whose beers weren't spectacular, but a change of direction in 2012 brought forth hop-head delights like this.

STONE & WOOD

BYRON BAY, NEW SOUTH WALES
WWW.STONEANDWOOD.COM.AU

Stone Beer Stein Lager 7.2%

Once a year Stone & Wood gets together to produce this intriguing limited-release interpretation of a stein lager where hot rocks are added to the brew, with the result being a rich and smooth beer with hints of caramelization.

TWO BIRDS

MELBOURNE, VICTORY
WWW.TWOBIRDSBREWING.COM.AU

Taco Speciality Beer 5.2%

Old friends Jayne Lewis and Danielle Allen began their brewing career in 2011 as gypsy brewers, making friends with their boldly flavored beers, but it wasn't until 2014 that they got their own brewery and bar. Taco contains corn, lime peel, and cilantro leaf, which when working with the Citra and Amarillo hops create a bright, zesty beer.

"Give me a woman who loves beer and I will conquer the world."

—KAISER WILHELM GERMAN EMPEROR 1859–1941

ALTITUDE BREWING

QUEENSTOWN, OTAGO

WWW.ALTITUDEBREWING.CO.NZ

New Zealand has history when it comes to ale-inspired adventuring. When British explorer Captain James Cook first left Britain, he packed his ship *Endeavour* with four tons of beer for the journey.

Turns out, that wasn't enough. He ran out of beer on the voyage, and, no sooner had he dropped anchor in Dusky Sound, than he began brewing his own using molasses and manuka and rimu, sprucelike native plants that successfully saved his sailors from scurvy.

Similarly, explorer and reformed teetotaller Ernest Shackleton left New Zealand on his heroic yet ultimately unsuccessful expedition to the South Pole in 1907 with, among his ton of liquor, two barrels of New Zealand beer from the J. Speight brewery in Dunedin.

Just a couple of hundred miles northwest of Dunedin in Queenstown, modern day outdoor-loving Kiwis reach for the Mischievous Kea.

Positioned in the shadow of the snowcapped Remarkables mountains on the shore of Lake Wakatipu, Queenstown is the country's extreme sports capital, a place of extraordinary rugged beauty attracting global adrenaline junkies.

Thrill-seekers may know it as the birthplace

of the bungee jump and wine connoisseurs as prime Pinot Noir country, but adventurous beer drinkers know it as home to Altitude Brewing, an exploratory ale-making operation that began brewing back in 2013.

It was the brainchild of Queenstown local, adventurer, skier, and long-time homebrewer Eliott Menzies, who, having broadened his beer horizons while living in the UK ten years earlier, returned to New Zealand just as its fledgling craft beer movement was getting into its stride. Using Kiwi hops and other local ingredients, Eliott began to experiment, creating new styles and twists on European classics.

By 2009, with hundreds of recipe ideas fermenting in his brain and four years of amateur experimentation under his belt, he locked himself away for six months in a tiny spot near Kaikoura to perfect an IPA recipe—and the result was the now-iconic The Mischievous Kea IPA. "I lived the life of a slightly weird backcountry boffin," recalls

Eliott. "I didn't just want to tip a whole load of hops into an IPA and hope for the best. I wanted to remodel an English IPA with all the character the best Kiwi hops could deliver. It needed to suit the Queenstown environment and be the go-to beer for everyone that's having a rad time in the outdoors—refreshing, rewarding, satisfying."

Brewed using Pacific Jade, Pacifica, Motueka, and Nelson Sauvin hops, and jam-packed with a range of Canterbury malts, it was first released at the home of craft beer in Queenstown: Atlas Beer Café. It was here an Englishman named Eddie Gapper, recovering adman and then teacher at a local adventure tourism college, sank his first pint of the Kea. As Victor Kiam used to say, he liked it so much he bought into the company.

"Like a lot of Queenstowners, I ended up here sort of by accident, fell in love with the place, and then met another good dude that had a similar dream. It's a bit of a change from my previous life, but I certainly don't miss the desk job."

Armed with Eliott's brewing nous and Eddie's experience in advertising, the unlikely duo embarked on a mission to improve the liquid lives of local adventurers with an award-winning stable of eight core styles, including a hazy German hefeweizen and a velvety stout, alongside an experimental range featuring delights such as a barrel-aged saison and an elderflower IPA. The good people of Queenstown showed their appreciation, and now Altitude has become a cornerstone of the community—supporting the local mountain bike club at events, brewing the Tenacious Timber XPA to raise funds to remove wayward pine trees, and supporting local charities with their "1% for the Wakatipu" program.

"Whatever we brew, we make sure it's super drinkable," said Eliott. "Queenstown can be a transient place, but whether they're here for a weekend or live here, people still want a local beer, so catching a Kea in Queenstown is now an essential way to wind down after an awesome day sky-diving, skiing, snowboarding, or throwing yourself off a bridge with nothing but a bit of elastic attached to your leg. Queenstown's an amazing place, and a glass of characterless mainstream beer simply doesn't do it justice."

Opposite left and right: Eddie Gapper and Eliott Menzies are aiming high with their super-drinkable beers.

Above & below: Eddie Gapper loved his first-ever drop of The Mischevious Kea so much that he invested in the brewery.

* KEY BEERS

Goldpanners Profit Golden Ale 4.4%
Persistent High Hefeweizen 4.9%
Posturing Professional Pale Ale 5%
The Mischievous Kea IPA 5.5%
The Moonlight Track Peated Stout 6.5%

NEW ZEALAND

ALTITUDE BREWING
see Brewery Profile pages 236 to 237
QUEENSTOWN, OTAGO
WWW.ALTITUDEBREWING.CO.NZ

The Mischievous Kea IPA 5.5%
A complex hybrid of New World hop-forward and old-English toasty, bitter IPA styles. A judiciously selected quartet of Kiwi hops keeps it native, and its full, robust body comes courtesy of six different malts, and a closely monitored mash. A stupendous ale.

EMERSON'S BREWING COMPANY
DUNEDIN, OTAGO
WWW.EMERSONS.CO.NZ

Emerson Pilsner 5%
Energized by what he drank as an 18-year-old on a jaunt to Europe with his father, founder and brewer Richard Emerson has been at the forefront of New Zealand craft brewing since 1993, and his beers are permanently on the podium at national and international brewing competitions. A crisp and citrusy Kiwi classic using Saaz hops that are grown in New Zealand.

London Porter 5%
A voluminous velvet mouth-filler that's a lot chunkier and richer in character than the ABV would suggest. Brewed using malt plumped with sweetness, rather than parched, it makes for a delightful milk-chocolate-laden dessert of a beer.

EPIC BREWING COMPANY
OTAHUHU, AUCKLAND
WWW.EPICBEER.COM

Epic Pale Ale 5.4%
Brewing beers that are bigger, badder, and better, Epic is a brash Auckland brewer that's clearly inspired by the high-octane USA craft-brewing community. The claim to fame of its flagship pale ale is that each bottle is imbued with the equivalent of 15 hop flowers, and, judging by the explosion of grapefruit on both the nose and palate, it may well be true.

FORK & BREWER
WELLINGTON
WWW.FORKANDBREWER.CO.NZ

Godzone Beat IPA 5.9%
Former Thornbridge man Kelly Ryan is the person in charge of the brewing at this lively brewpub, which features beers from fellow Kiwi brewers as well as ones brewed on the premises. Godzone Beat is an award-winning IPA, medium-bodied, pulsating with tropical fruit, and ending with a subtle bitterness.

GARAGE PROJECT
WELLINGTON
WWW.GARAGEPROJECT.CO.NZ

Death from Above IPA 7.5%
In 2011, three friends started what they called a nano-brewery in the Aro Valley. The plant has grown to become a micro, and Garage Project is well-known for its bold beers such as this Indochine pale ale, which marries citrusy hops with mango, Vietnamese mint, and chile—it really shouldn't work, but it does.

HALLERTAU
RIVERHEAD, AUCKLAND
WWW.HALLERTAU.CO.NZ

Porter Noir Wood-Aged Porter 6.6%
Named after the German noble hop, which also gave its name to the New Zealand hop now known as Wakatu, this is a busy and popular brewery and pub that was at the forefront of Kiwi craft brewing. Porter Noir is aged in Pinot Noir barrels with the result being a beer that brings chocolate and vinous notes together.

INVERCARGILL BREWERY
INVERCARGILL, SOUTH ISLAND
WWW.INVERCARGILLBREWERY.CO.NZ

BiMan Pilsner 5.2%
New Zealand's southernmost brewery was created by father-and-son team Gerry and Steve Nally back in 1999. Initially installed in a cowshed, the brewery outgrew its original home and moved into bigger premises in Invercargill; in 2012 they moved again. The core beers, supplemented by a flurry of seasonals, include a pale ale, a superb stout, a honey pilsner, and this sprightly hopped floral pilsner with fruity traces of litchis, melon, and lime.

LIBERTY

RIVERHEAD, AUCKLAND
WWW.LIBERTYBREWING.CO.NZ

C!tra Imperial IPA 9%

Look at the name of this beer, and you think it's yet another pale ale dosed liberally with Citra. Look again, and the exclamation mark instead of an i suggests something else is going on—and it is. This heavily hopped imperial IPA is flush with grapefruit and tropical fruit, with a honeyed maltiness balancing all the fruit. Strong bitterness in the finish.

MOA BREWERY

BLENHEIM, MARLBOROUGH
WWW.MOABEER.COM

Moa Imperial Stout 10.2%

Josh Scott founded Moa in 2003, turning his back on the family's winemaking business, preferring the grape to the grain. He has never looked back. Moa has become known for a series of elegantly branded and perfectly made beers. This tremendous Imperial stout is aged in French oak barrels and comes out of it with mocha, chocolate, roast, and woody notes, with a delectable sweetness in the background.

NORTH END BREWERY

WAIKANAE, WELLINGTON
NO WEB ADDRESS

Oud Bruin

Flanders Brown Ale 7%

Started life in 2013 using other breweries to make award-winning beers, but 2016 saw it set up in its own brewery in a small town on the Kapiti Coast. This is its tasty take on an East Flanders brown ale with dried cherries and dried plums. The result is a rich, tart, and fruity beer with a refreshing sourness lurking in the background.

RENAISSANCE BREWING

BLENHEIM, MARLBOROUGH
WWW.RENAISSANCEBREWING.CO.NZ

Elemental Porter 6%

Prize-winning porter, with chocolate and cappuccino notes, courtesy of a thriving brewery based in Marlborough. Set up in 2005 by Brian Thiel and Andy Deuchars, brothers-in-law from San Diego, Renaissance brews a range of styles from pale ale to barley wine.

THREE BOYS BREWERY

CHRISTCHURCH, CANTERBURY
WWW.THREEBOYSBREWERY.CO.NZ

Three Boys Wheat 5%

Another micro, this time headed up by former scientist Dr. Ralph Bungard, who caught the brewing bug after a vacation romance with Yorkshire real ales. Packaged in seriously dapper bottles, Three Boys beers taste as good as they look, especially this hazy, straw-colored slightly sour wit brewed with coriander and citrus zest.

TWISTED HOP BREWERY

CHRISTCHURCH, CANTERBURY
WWW.THETWISTEDHOP.CO.NZ

Twisted Ankle Dark Ale 5.9%

Originally a boutique brewery and bar in central Christchurch run by a pair of young expat English mash-fork-waving beer missionaries, Martin Bennett and Stephen Hardman, who served several of their beers cask-conditioned. The devastating Christchurch earthquake of 2011 saw them without a home, with an industrial unit being leased first before moving into their current home in 2012, the year which also saw the reopening of a new pub. Twisted Ankle is a savory carbonated plum-colored brew.

YEASTIE BOYS

WELLINGTON
WWW.YEASTIEBOYS.CO.NZ

Gunnamatta IPA 6.5%

Stu McKinlay and Sam Possenniskie set up the Yeastie Boys in 2008, basing themselves in Wellington, though the beers are contract brewed for them by Invercargill Brewery (they have also had some made at BrewDog for the UK market in the past.) This is one of their signature beers, a potent IPA with Earl Grey tea, all of which makes for a floral, citrus beer with a long, dry finish.

ASIA & REST

OF

WORLD

JAPAN

BAEREN
KITAYAMA MORIOKA CITY, IWATE
WWW.BAERENBIER.COM

Ursus Weizenbock 7%

German-style beers call the shots at this micro that was set up in 2001. Hazy gold in color, this has banana and breadiness on the nose, while each sip reveals a light sweetness, more banana, a medium body, and a moderately bitter finish.

BAIRD BREWING CO.
see Brewery Profile pages 244 to 245
NUMAZU, SHIZUOKA
WWW.BAIRDBEER.COM

Baird Kurofune Porter 6%

A robust yet refined and super-smooth porter decked in dry chocolate and spicy bitter coffee.

 Baird Rising Sun Pale Ale 5.1%

West Coast American pale ale with all the heavily sugared grapefruit character one would expect. For such a delicately balanced pale ale, it travels wonderfully well across the Pacific Ocean.

BRIMMER
KUJI, KANAGAWA
WWW.BRIMMERBREWING.COM

Porter 5.5%

Scott Brimmer opened this go-ahead micro in 2011, with the aim of making beers he would like to drink himself. This eponymous porter is creamy, smooth and silky, subtly roasty, and happy to dance on the tongue for as long as you like.

ECHIGO BEER BREW PUB
NIIGATA, NIIGATA
WWW.ECHIGO-BEER.JP

Echigo Stout 7%

When Japanese brewing laws were relaxed in 1994, an established sake brewer was one of the first to take advantage. Within a year, Echigo became Japan's inaugural brewpub, and four years later brewing began on a bigger scale at a larger brewery site. The brewpub is a little out of the way, but Echigo's beers are widely available in cans, and the sleek stout, all muscular malt and creamy coffee notes, is the pick of a pretty good bunch.

FUJIKANKOKAIHATSU CO./SYLVANS RESTAURANT
KAWAGUCHIKO, YAMANASHI
WWW.FUJIZAKURA-BEER.JP

Fujizakura Rauchbock Smoked Beer 7%

A medium-bodied beer with a full waft of beech wood smoke plus earthy malt and peppery hops.

Fujizakura Weizen Hefeweizen 5.5%

Set in the shadow of Mount Fuji, the Sylvans Restaurant is a massive brewpub, restaurant, and garden complex inspired by German brewing traditions. Its excellent beers can be found in Tokyo.

HARVESTMOON
MAIHAMA, CHIBA
WWW.IKSPIARI.CO.JP/HARVESTMOON/HARVESTMOON.HTML

Schwartz 4.5%

The phrase "nailing it" comes to mind with each sip of this interpretation of the classic beer style from Eastern Germany; it's roasty, bittersweet, chocolaty, and has a finish as long as the arm of the law.

HIDA TAKAYAMA BREWING AGRICULTURAL CO.
TAKAYAMA-SHI, GIFU
WWW.HIDATAKAYAMA.CO.JP

Hida Takayama Weizen 5%

Brilliant brewery in the little town of Takayama, perched high up in the idyllic mountains of the Gifu prefecture, which makes beers with attitude at altitude. Soft, spritzy Bavarian-style, banana-laden beer. Like all its beers, it is stored in a stubby bottle.

HITACHINO NEST
NAKA CITY, IBARIKI
WWW.HITACHINO.CC

Hitachino Espresso Stout 7.5%

An unbelievably delicious and mellow coffee stout brewed with caramel and roasted black and chocolate malt. Deep dark fruit flavors on the finish. Superb.

Hitachino Saison du Japon 5%

The Kiuchi Shuzou company was established in 1823 in the tiny hamlet of Kounosu (Nest) as a producer of Japanese sake. But, in 1996, the company branched out into brewing beer. Having won numerous international awards, its range of bottle-fermented beers and bottles adorned with a funky-looking owl have developed a strong following in the United States. This is an intriguing beer made with saison yeast and with added koji rice and yuzu.

HYOUKO YASHIKI NO MORI BREWERY (SWAN LAKE)
AGANO-SHI, NIIGATA-KEN
WWW.SWANLAKE.CO.JP

 Swan Lake Amber Ale 5%
Located in the Niigata-Ken prefecture of Japan, Swan Lake's stock is continually on the rise, with its beers continuing to scoop medals at competitions both at home and abroad. Misty reddish copper, tight off-white head, and gentle aroma of cookie-like malt, fresh peach, and dried plums. Perfumed hop bitterness and caramel tang.

ISE KADOYA BREWERY
ISE, MIE
WWW.BIYAGURA.JP

Peach Lambic 5.5%
While Ise Kadoya made its latest brewing bow in 1997, it claims that its beer-making heritage dates back to the late nineteenth century. One wonders what they would have made of this tart, funky, white peach sour beer, but we certainly liked it, especially when served as a light apéritif.

IWATEKURA
ICHINOSEKI, IWATE
WWW.SEKINOICHI.CO.JP

Iwate Kura Oyster Stout 7%
The Iwate prefecture, situated at the northern tip of Japan, is renowned for its oysters, and the brewery is said to cast the local mollusks into the brewing of its smooth, satin stout. The oysters help to clarify the beer and add to the slightly salty, metallic mouthfeel.

MINOH BEER
MINOH, OSAKA
WWW.MINOH-BEER.JP

Bosuzaru Black IPA 6%
Founded in 1997 and now run by the two daughters of the original founder, this is a thriving business whose beers attract awards like iron filings to a magnet. With this dark brown black IPA (and let's forget all the controversy about the name for a minute), Minoh has created a deeply refreshing beer packed with hop and dark grain flavors and aromas.

Weizen Hefeweizen 5.5%
Grab a schnitzel and wail for a wurst and then take a deep draft from a glass of this Bavarian-style beauty, with its bustle of bubblegum, cloves, bananas, and breadiness on the nose and palate. Lederhosen optional.

MOKU MOKU
NISHLYUBUNE, IGA-SHI
WWW.MOKU-MOKU.COM

Smoked Ale Rauchbier 5%
Owned by a farm cooperative and located to the east of Osaka, Moku Moku is well known for making beers with a smoky signature, hence the brewery name: a reference to the smoke screen used by Ninja warriors. This awesome ale is the smokiest of them all but not outrageously so. Smooth, a little syrupy, and brewed with Scottish peated malt.

OTARU BEER
OTARU, HOKKAIDO
WWW.OTARUBEER.COM

Otaru Dunkel 5.2%
Look closely under Otaru's kimono and you'll find a pair of German lederhosen. Founded in 1995 by Akio Shoji, Otaru headhunted German brewmaster Johannes Braun, who brews according to the Reinheitsgebot laws using Otaru's extremely soft, Pilsen-esque water. Slow decoction brewing gives this dunkel caramel and toffee-apple tones.

BAIRD BREWING

SHIZUOKA

WWW.BAIRDBEER.COM

The Japanese craft-brewing industry is only three decades old, and Baird Brewing, established in 2001, has been instrumental in driving the country's thriving beer scene. Bryan Harrell tells us more.

In 1994, regulations on the issue of brewery licenses were eased from a required 2 million liters (around 530,000 gallons/17043 beer barrels) to just 60,000 liters (15,850 gallons/511 beer barrels), making it possible for small breweries to start up. While 60,000 liters yearly is a bit much for a brewpub, small regional breweries began to open in Japan, albeit at a slow pace. By the turn of the century, more than 300 had opened, most being operated by joint ventures between local governments and private interests or additional new businesses that had been set up by sake brewers.

However, things weren't easy. Craft beer in Japan was unnecessarily expensive, and, despite most breweries having access to trained European or American brewers, regular employees could not maintain the methods necessary to make beer of a quality similar to that of mass-produced products. While the public was interested in trying the new "local" beers, most fell short, and, by the end of the decade, the stage was set for a talented American brewer to steal the show.

Bryan Baird, a native of Ohio, opened Baird Brewing in 2001, together with his business partner and wife, Sayuri Baird, a native of southern Japan. They chose to settle in the town of Numazu in Shizuoka Prefecture, on the Pacific coast, two hours south of Tokyo.

Here the pace of life is slower than in the capital, and the winters are warm and clear. They found a small storefront just opposite the town's thriving fish market, and built a brewpub on the second floor, and added a small brewery at the back of the building.

Baird initially brewed on a tiny setup, in 30-liter (7-gallon) batches. A visit to the Baird Fishmarket Taproom was akin to going over to the house of a great homebrewer whose wife happened to be a great cook. Sayuri ran the kitchen, turning out interesting dishes that combined the best parts of Japanese and American home cooking. Dishes made with fresh local fish and vegetables combined with American-style seasonings were perfect matches with Bryan's well-balanced characterful ales.

Bryan still insists on using top-quality floor-malted Maris Otter malts and whole flower hops, along with a variety of brewing techniques inspired by the US homebrewing revolution of the 1970s. He had apprenticed at Redhook, near Seattle, and brought with him to Japan a high level of passion to brew the best beer possible. Baird Brewing is well-known in Japan and is recognized by Japanese craft beer enthusiasts as one of the country's best producers.

"I never thought of launching this craft-brewing business in the USA. I've been a long-time student of Japan and have lived here a while. My primary motivation, before beer even, was to create a business endeavor in Japan," explains Bryan. "So, pursuing craft brewing in Japan is how I can marry two of my great life passions—characterful beer and Japanese culture."

Bryan notes that Japan is a well-educated and affluent society with a huge population in a small area. The social environment is also favorable because there is a great reverence for craftsmanship and no pseudo-moral demonization of alcohol in Japanese society. As such, Japan has a fairly relaxed and uncomplicated legal structure regarding alcoholic beverage production. Specifically, there are no restrictions on shipping, distribution, and sales between prefectures and no limitations on the ability to both manufacture and retail beer or on internet sales of beer.

When asked what approach Baird Brewing has taken to achieve its remarkable success, Bryan explains it in very simple terms. "Craft beer, to me, means beer of character. My own equation for this when I create a new beer is that character is the sum of balance and complexity. This is a simple equation, but, as with most simple things, it is easier said than done. I work toward this goal by solid commitment to three things: the best ingredients, natural carbonation, and appropriate temperature. I also store and serve the beer at the appropriate temperature."

In 2014, work was completed on a brand new brewery in the Shuzenji area of Izu city, the brewery's third expansion since opening in 2016.

Meanwhile there are now six taprooms where Baird's beers can be sampled and enjoyed.

Above: Bryan Baird and his wife, Sayuri, started Baird Brewing in 2001.
Opposite: Baird Brewing's Rising Sun Pale Ale is a US-inspired brew.

* KEY BEERS

Baird Kirofune Porter 6%
Baird Rising Sun Pale Ale 5.1%

OUTSIDER BREWING
KOFU, YAMANASHI
WWW.OUTSIDERBREWING.JP

Drunk Monk Tripel 8%
Nifty little brewpub based at Hops and Herbs, where a scintillating selection of beers is brought into the world. Belgium is on the mind of the brewers with this fruity tripel, which has dried fruits, orange, brown-sugar sweetness, light spice, and a full body.

SAPPORO
TOKYO
WWW.SAPPOROBEER.JP

Sapporo Yebisu Joël Robuchon Yoin no Jikan Pilsner 5.5%
Sapporo was founded in the northern city of the same name back in 1876 and claims to be Japan's oldest brewery. Its flagship lager, often drunk from a funky-looking can, wrestles with Asahi and Kirin in terms of sales, but thinking drinkers enjoy this crisp and refreshing all-malt pilsner.

SHIGA KOGEN BREWERY
NAGANO, NAGANO
WWW.TAMAMURA-HONTEN.CO.JP

Kogen House Kangunu Imperial IPA 8%
Named after Japan's largest ski resort. Shiga Kogen is a sake producer that branched out into beer in 2004. This enormous tikka-tinged Imperial IPA has huge eucalyptus and mint aromas, with earthy undertones.

SHIMANE BEER CO.
MATSUE, SHIMANE
WWW.SHIMANE-BEER.CO.JP

Enmusu Stout 5%
Appetizing stout with a dryness, roastiness, coffee acidity, chocolate, caramel, and a hint of condensed milk all making an appearance. Another example of the excellent way Japanese craft brewers take on European beer styles and get it right.

YO-HO BREWING COMPANY
SAKU CITY, NAGANO
WWW.YOHOBREWING.COM

Yo-Ho SORRY Umami IPA 6.5%
Seasonal beer from one of the pioneers of the Japanese craft brewing boom and indicative of its interest in producing beers a little out of the ordinary. This is brewed with dried bonito flakes, whose savory, soy-sauce-like meatiness complements the citrus and grass IPA character. Serve with sushi, naturally.

Yo-Ho Yona-Yona Tokyo Black Porter 5%
Very dark brown, almost black, porter-style beer. It has a lightly tanned, long-lasting head. The aroma is a pleasant mix of chocolate, espresso coffee, and roasted malt, with a hint of woodiness, giving a slightly oaky smell and a slightly sweet floral element from the hops. Texture is smooth, medium-to-full-bodied, and crisp, with a dry feeling on the palate. Carbonation is medium, giving a slight bubbly sensation on the tongue.

YOROCCO BEER
ZUSHI, KANAGAWA
WWW.YOROCCO-BEER.COM

Cultivator Belgian Ale 6%
This gold-colored beer came about after the brewmaster made a trip to Canada and returned inspired by some of the beers he'd tasted. Belgian yeast is used, as are American hops, and the result is a complex beer with spice, lemons, and grapefruit, and all things nice.

ZAKKOKU KOBO
OGAWA, SAITAMA
WWW.CRAFT-BEER.NET/ZKM.HTML

Kobo Cats Eyes Sour Beer 5.5%
No cats' eyes were involved in the making of this tart and Flemish-inclined beer, which has citrus and cherry and is gently sour. It's light in its sweetness, has a hint of wood and earth, and fills the mouth with the luminosity of a lantern in a cave.

Opposite above: Careful monitoring goes on at the Yo-Ho Brewing Company in Saku City.

Opposite below: Yo-Ho welcomes visitors too.

CAMBODIA

CAMBREW BREWERY
SIHANNOUKVILLE
NO WEB ADDRESS

Black Panther Stout 8%

First commissioned by the Cambodian Government in the 1960s about 170 miles west of Phnom Penh, the Angkor Brewery was knocked off its stride in the 1970s then bought by Carlsberg in 1991. Surrounded by bland lagers, this punchy, rich, toffee-tainted stout is one of Southeast Asia's more complex contributions to world beer.

SRI LANKA

LION BREWERY
BIYAGAMA
WWW.LIONBEER.COM

Lion Stout 8.8%

In a country where humidity and heat are high, it's a wonder why Sri Lankans love their stouts so much, but they do—a lot. Perhaps it's because this is one of the world's most impressive stouts, brewed high up in the mountainous tea-plantation region. Plenty of rich and chocolate cookie notes, with licorice, spice, dried plums, and cappuccino.

ISRAEL

DANCING CAMEL ISRAEL
TEL AVIV
WWW.DANCINGCAMEL.COM

Olde Papa Babylonian Old Ale 7.5%

English-style old ale is the influence for this dark brown beer, though date honey is also used in the mix alongside English hops. It's honeyed and nutty, caramel-like, and full-bodied and finishes off with a moderate bitterness.

KENYA

EAST AFRICAN BREWERIES
NAIROBI
WWW.EABL.COM

Tusker Lager 4.2%

This consistent Kenyan thirst-quencher is the largest beer brand in East Africa. Pale gold and instantly refreshing, with a delicate citrus nose, it's an ideal "sunset" beer and named in memory of the brewery's founder George Hurst, who was killed by a rogue elephant a year after the brewery was founded. Brewed with barley grown in Kenya.

MOROCCO

BRASSERIES DU MAROC
CASABLANCA
WWW.1STMAROC.COM

Casablanca Beer Lager 5%

This clean and simple lager is not to be drunk with one's thinking fez on, as it is a simple-thirst quencher, but is none the worse for that.

NAMIBIA

NAMIBIA BREWERIES
WINDHOEK
WWW.NAMBREW.COM

Hansa Urbock Bock 7%

A robust and earthy bock with a chewy, no-nonsense malt profile. Not what you'd expect from a country where the mercury soars, but the legacy of the two German founders, who started brewing in the 1920s, lives on. Brewed only once a year, in May.

SOUTH AFRICA

CAPE BREWING
PAARL, WESTERN CAPE
WWW.CAPEBREWING.CO.ZA

Cape of Good Hops Imperial IPA 7.5%

Full-bodied and smashing it out of the veldt, this is an ardent imperial IPA that makes use of a brace of American hops to create fruity character, which balances beautifully with subtle malt sweetness.

COPPERLAKE
SUNRELLA, GAUTENG
WWW.COPPERLAKE.CO.ZA

India Pale Ale 6%

Brewpub that was founded in 2012 and whose IPA is a dish of tropical and citrus fruit; copper in color, there is also a pine-like resinous quality and a malt sweetness to balance things out.

DEVILS PEAK
CAPE TOWN, WESTERN CAPE
WWW.DEVILSPEAKBREWING.CO.ZA

King's Blockhouse IPA 6%

USA-style IPAs get everywhere as this Cape Town classic demonstrates: floral, piney aromatics on the nose and a judicious balance between the juicy citrus, malt sweetness, and the dry, bitter finish.

MITCHELL'S BREWERY
KNYSNA, WESTERN CAPE
WWW.MITCHELLSBREWING.COM

Ninety Shilling Scotch Ale 5%

In 1983 Lex Mitchell kick-started Africa's first microbrewery in the Western Cape town of Knysna, and Mitchell's is now the country's second largest. This spicy homage to the Mitchell family's Perthshire roots is one of several predominantly British-style unpasteurized beers.

Raven Stout 5%

Creamy and soft lactose-imbued ebony ale firmed up with plenty of hops; it's fulsome and full-bodied and as well-balanced as an acrobat on the highwire.

SAB MILLER
SANDTONA
WWW.SAB.CO.ZA

Castle Milk Stout 6%

Until a merger in 2002 with SAB Miller, this sturdy, sweet stout was part of South African Breweries—set up back in 1895 to slake the thirst of the mining community in the Johannesburg region. Despite the decline in mining and a climate that lends itself to light lagers, it remains huge in South Africa and is still a top-five selling beer.

"A fine beer may be judged with only one sip, but it's better to be thoroughly sure."
—CZECH PROVERB

BEER & FOOD

THE ORIGINS OF BEER & FOOD

Matching beer with a meal is far from a modern phenomenon. Indeed, beer was once safer than water, so back in the day if you wanted something to wet a whetted appetite, ale was a go-to alternative.

The Spanish covered their beer with their first tapas dishes to keep the flies out; the Pilgrims celebrated their first Thanksgiving banquets with weird brews; the first European monks paired Trappist tipples with abbey cheese; and King Henry the VIII demanded it at his wedding feast—and that man liked a wedding.

Somewhere along the way, vine beat barley in the drink and dining battle. The Romans gave the grape an early air of sophistication, but the crafty French, whose admirable stab at marrying fine dining with wine, encouraged the rest of us to ditch our original alcohol ally at the dinner table.

Over the last decade beer has clawed its way back up the tablecloth. As the passion for varied and complex beer styles has advanced, the idea of matching it with meals has been embraced by foodies. We're no longer required to spit out our breadsticks when the waiter in a Michelin-starred restaurant suggests an IPA with the main. While it's not quite universal, any chef worth his salt now accepts that you can't ignore beer.

Beer is unlikely to knock wine off its perch in the haughty haute-cuisine hangouts. After all, wine's mark-up on a bottle is too tasty for a restaurateur to ignore. But the street-food movement has at least provided a new urban playing field. Vertical eating around a taco truck has made a can of quality beer a very useful side arm, and the generation of diners shunning "high dining" has embraced this affordable cult of casual dining. This is the stronghold for beer, and as foodies ask more questions about ethically sourced and straight-from-farm apparently-happy-to-die chickens, they demand more truths about artisanal beer. Without generalizing, street-food styles play to beer's strength: quality pizzas, pulled pork, burgers, chicken, Asian food, Mexican food, American food, chargrills, spicy sauces and salsas, rich meat, and complex toppings. These are culinary attributes that can be quenched by beer with its complex offering of sweet, sour, bitter, and carbonated profiles.

We've learned to not be one-dimensional in our pairings, but in our bid to champion the sophistication of the practice, some of us inadvertently attributed slightly complicated rhetoric and rules to the process. Most people can discover something they like in the list just given, and beer emphatically works with these dishes, so if you're a skeptic, start there.

Beyond that, if we're honest, the only rule when matching beers with food is to avoid overpowering one with the other; try to combine the intensity or subtlety of a dish with an appropriate beer. This should ensure you enjoy both in equal measure. So, a light beer like a pilsner or lager will work nicely with a lightly seasoned fish or salad dish; and yes, a tried-and-tested spicy IPA is always better than wine with a curry.

While we try to simplify the pairing approach, though, we should also emphasize the new complexity in beer choice. When we first started shouting about beer and food, we didn't have access to the range we have today, with huge double IPAs using six hop varieties that can take on a big cheese; or British-brewed witbiers using Belgian ale and American hops that work beautifully with a dessert. Thanks to some beer enlightenment, most of us now understand style alone doesn't confine a beer's flavor, ensuring the intricacy of that witbier can make it equally useful next to a salad or a fish dish.

Taste is subjective. We all discover things we enjoy about the beer and food we consume independently, so the best approach is to get a batch of interesting beers, cook up something you love eating, and pair the two. The benefit of drinking with food is you can taste-test beers with some safe sustenance along the way, rather than dangerously drinking four strong beers on an empty stomach. Like all the best things in life (television, wearing slippers, being in bed), you can make the recipes that follow at home, enjoying your own fascinating culinary adventure without breaking the bank.

BEER & CHEESE

Wine and cheese are a lazy convenience that ends most of our epicurean evenings, but the marriage is past its best, so it's high time you started playing away with beer. Not convinced? Ask a farm laborer if he'd go for a pint of bitter over a glass of Bordeaux with his lunch. Go on. Ask. No, wine falls well short of the compatibility required, and even the sincerest sommelier would might beer is best when you're chopping up the cheese. Beer has a breadth of qualities to take it to another level—bitter, sweet, fruity, floral, rich, light, even the low or high carbonation, all the assets to compete with and pay homage to the fromage.

PAIRINGS

Duke of Wellington cheese: Far from old boots, this blue cheese is packed with subtle brilliance. It is produced by the Yorkshire family cheesemongers Cryer & Stott and proves so tasty it has even been served to the queen. Using French Roquefort Penicillin and with 15 weeks' maturation, there's a slightly buttery taste, making it a great introduction to the spiky flavors of blue cheese.

WITH

Roosters Yankee: Blue cheese is sharp and salty, and one option is to go at it with a carbonated and bitter IPA to scrub the palate after each mouthful. Or you could tone it down a little and go for a Roosters Yankee. Brewed in Yorkshire, this pale ale blends Cascade hop with a soft Golden Promise malt for a lighter touch.

Original Barwhey: The producer of this Scottish cheese, Tricia Bey, says, "I'm often asked to do wine and cheese tastings, and my heart always slightly sinks because I know beer—a bitter with caramelly/nutty tones—goes much better." We agree Tricia, especially with this cheese, which starts hard and tart but crumbles into creamy caramel and nuts.

WITH

Dark Island Reserve: Porters are a go-to beer with cheese and The Orkney Brewery's Dark Island Reserve is big on chocolate malt, having been finished in Scottish whisky barrels to give it incredible complexity. The toffee tones of the beer match the caramel of the cheese, and the oak tanins cut through the cream.

SOME GENERAL GUIDELINES
Soft-rind cheese: Summer ale, helles, kölsch, pilsner, tart fruit beer
Mild cheese/goat cheese: Wheat beers, honey beers, amber lagers, Champagne beers
Blue cheese: Barley wine, porter, imperial pilsners, American IPA
Hard cheese: Stronger British bitters, Belgian golden ales, American pale ale, oude bruin
Sheep's cheese: Saison, bière de garde, amber lager, Vienna lager, märzen
Wash-rinded (pongy) cheese: Trappist/abbey ale, doppelbock, tripel, gueuze.
Mountain cheese: Dunkelweizen, fruit lambic, doppelbock, dubbel, sour red ale
Smoked Gouda-style cheese: Rauchbier, smoked porter, barrel-aged beer

Old Weydeland: Treur Cheese is based in the rural area of Holland's Woerden, right in the historic heart of the area where Dutch Gouda is made. Old Weydeland is the famous black Gouda—soft and rich and aged for 16 months to give it a lingering spicy and slightly smoky quality.

WITH

De Molen Heen & Weer: The cheesemakers are close to the Belgians, so contrast the salt here with a sweet Belgian tripel. This one has bags of sugared fruit but with a nice hit of alcohol. "Heen & Weer" means back and forth, which is exactly what it inspires you to do with cheese and beer.

Époisse: Tricky to talk cheese and ignore the French. they know their cheese like they know their onions. Époisse is a soft brine-washed cheese, hugely pungent and creamy but with fruity tang. It demands a beer such as Orval, which can compete with the nose and the palate.

WITH

Orval: A Trappist classic that reminds us that the monks are masters of beer and cheese matching, with form in making both at the monastery. The beer is fruity and full on, almost port-like and almond tinged.

BEER & CHOCOLATE

Chocolate is a good deal more than small beans to William Curley, a champion in the world of quality confectionery as a luxury pâtissier and chocolatier.

When asked about pairing beer with his creations, the response was unequivocal. "I've always felt chocolate pairs better with beer than something like wine," says William. "They share a terroir, both come from grain, and beer has the characteristics that complement the chocolate. When I make chocolate it's an obvious process of trying to find flavors that pair well, you don't want them to conflict."

William has plenty of experience on the sweeter side of life, working in Michelin-starred restaurants around the world before setting up his celebrated chocolate stores, including a presence in Harrods in London. His chocolates contain thought-provoking ingredients and when he first approached the process of beer matching it was a natural step for him.

As with his chocolate, he prefers to take the beer pairings beyond conventions and has worked with a diverse set of brewers, including the outstanding Siren Craft Brew in Berkshire and celebrated London brewery The Kernel.

His chocolate is both high quality and ethically sound, and the fact that he's prepared to pair it with beer is evidence this can be a top-notch way to indulge in the two experiences. Quality Street this is not. But beer is versatile enough to pair with all styles of chocolate if your tastes are not quite so indulgent.

"The key is to not be too serious," adds William.

MUSCOVADO CARAMEL
WITH
THE KERNEL IPA

"Muscovado is an easy combination with beer, it has a depth and malty character."

Kernel's IPA has that depth in its malt backbone but the additional burst of bitterness from the Citra hops cuts through the rich chocolate.

RASPBERRY TRUFFLE
WITH
GEUZE MARIAGE PARFAIT

Lambic beers have a long association with chocolate pairings, and this is an awesome exponent of the match up. Again, William's chocolate has a rich quality that ensures the sour notes are perfectly balanced. The beer is a classic of the style, unfiltered, and unpasteurized, it possesses a pretty punchy sour and dry quality.

The four-time winner of the Academy of Chocolate's "Best British Chocolatier," he brings a creativity to his chocolate boxes that mirrors new wave craft brewing.

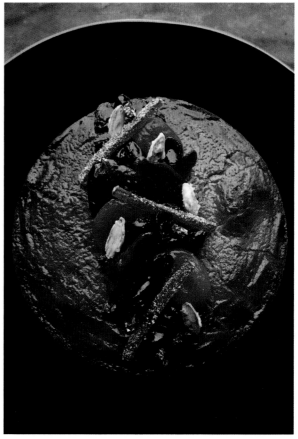

LEMON CURED CARAMEL

WITH

SIREN AMIGOS BRITÁNICOS

"The brewers have a similar approach to beer as I do to chocolate. There's a massive burst of flavor with the beer. It blew me away, a totally different experience."

The beer is brewed with lime, honey, and chile, which is as thought-provoking as the flavors running through the chocolate.

BLACK BUN

WITH

SIREN ODYSSEY 001

A belter of a chocolate, which includes a very subtle hint of whiskey and a slight crunch to it. When paired with the Siren beer from the Odyssey range, which is rested in bourbon barrels and brewed with soft brown sugar, this is one of the best food and beer matches we've found.

BEER & BURGERS

MEATliquor owners Scott Collins and Yianni Papoutsis have made a righteous business of burgers and know how to match them with beer—indeed, they have championed some of the best new brews in their bars.

If you make the meat pilgrimage to one of their many restaurants, you'll find a drool-inspiring selection of burgers that can annihilate any empty stomach and remind you: life is short, and burgers are necessary. The Dead Hippie, for example, rates as one of our favorite meat sandwiches of all time, and while the Triple Chili Challenge tests the boundaries of sanity—nailing a chili burger, dog ,and fries in less than ten minutes —all the food is properly tasty. Meanwhile the beer is carefully curated to pair with the massive flavors in the food.

When it comes to making your own at home, the team has plenty of advice, but burger genius and co-owner Yianni Papoutsis recommends his take on the BBQ effort. If there's a more essential food—and beer—moment than the BBQ and a beer, we have yet to find it.

For Yianni, a burger from the alfresco grill demands quality meat and a simple approach, as the Backyard Burger proves. He suggests you ask the butcher for a dry-aged chuck steak.

BACKYARD BURGER

5½ ounces freshly ground dry-aged chuck steak
Generous pinch of salt and pepper
1 ½-inch slice large white onion
1 burger bun
2 slices American-style cheese
1 squirt Heinz tomato ketchup
1 squirt French's mustard
2 or 3 slices dill pickle

1) Light and bring the coals to the correct heat so there is a white ash over them.

2) Form the chuck steak into a ball then squash it on wax paper to create the burger patty. It should be bigger than your bun to allow for shrinkage during cooking.

3) Place the patty on the oiled preheated BBQ grill and cover the top side with a healthy dose of salt and pepper. Place the thick slice of onion on the BBQ too.

4) Cut the bun in half and toast the cut sides over the BBQ. This will take only a few seconds. When the bottom of the burger has formed a good brown crust, it will lift easily off the BBQ without sticking. Flip it and cook the other side. It won't take nearly as long.

5) Flip the onion when it starts to brown.

6) Lay a couple of slices of cheese over the burger while it's on the BBQ.

7) Squirt some Heinz tomato ketchup and French's mustard on the bottom of the bun.

8) Add a couple of slices of dill pickle too.

9) Add the burger on your bun base and stack the onion on top. Put the top half of your burger bun on top and serve immediately.

BEER

Everybody loves sunshine, and if it's out while you BBQ, then a crisp lager will do. But it's a burger, so feel free to go big. The thick juicy meat requires carbonation, so bittering hops are going to help when it comes to a contrast with the sweetness of meat and ketchup.

HOBO CRAFT CZECH LAGER

For those not ready to inflict big bitterness on their palate, here is the perfect lager. A pilsner style made with soft malt and noble hops to provide a little more meat in the mouth and some complex character to stand up to a burger.

MOOR CONFIDENCE AMBER ALE

Moving up the flavor gears a bit, this has a pleasant malt to match with the meat and brings in some spicy American hops to amp up the bitterness, with citrus and pine coming right to the fore.

MAGIC ROCK CANNONBALL IPA

As the name suggests, this beer explodes on the tongue and contrasts with each bite of the burger. With six hops, it's big on the bitterness so perhaps one for the brave. At 7.4% ABV, you'll possibly need to move onto something lighter after the burger course.

BEER & MEATBALLS

Italian American concept Capish! was launched in 2012 by chef Rachel Taylor on the Roman Road Market in East London. Conjuring up quality classics on the streets, her meatball subs with their ethically sourced ingredients quickly built a reputation, encouraging her to find a permanent home with Ed Mason at their bar Mason & Co. Ed happens to be partnered with Hackney-based brewery Five Points, and the union ensures Rachel has great beer on tap to pair with the food.

INGREDIENTS

PICKLED JALAPEÑO SALSA

7 ounces fresh jalapeños, sliced
1 white onion, coarsely chopped
1 cup white wine vinegar
1 cup water
3 tablespoons sugar
1½ tablespoons sea salt

MEATBALLS

7 ounces free-range ground pork
7 ounces aged ground beef
  (you want at least 20% fat, not lean ground beef)
4 eggs
3½ ounces Parmesan cheese
2 cups breadcrumbs
4 garlic cloves
1 tablespoon dried oregano
1 bunch flat leaf parsley, finely chopped.
1 glug good extra virgin olive oil
salt and pepper

MARINARA SAUCE

4 cups canned plum tomatoes
  (San Marzano if possible)
1 bunch fresh basil
1 glug good extra virgin olive oil
salt and pepper

PROVOLONE CHEESE SAUCE

3½ tablespoons butter
6 tablespoons flour
1¼ cups whole milk
7 ounces provolone cheese
  (you can also use a strong cheddar/Gruyère
  instead of provolone)
1 squeeze lemon juice
fresh nutmeg, grated

METHOD

PICKLED JALAPEÑOS

(CAN BE STORED FOR UP TO A MONTH IN THE REFRIGERATOR)

Make a basic brine—equal parts vinegar and water, 2 parts sugar to salt. Boil the brine in a pan and then mix with your chopped jalapeño peppers and onion. You can use other chiles if desired, but test their heat first! Let cool and lightly blend with a stick blender to make your salsa.

MEATBALLS

Mix all the ingredients together and knead gently until everything incorporates. Be firm but light-handed, you don't want to overwork the mix. Roll the meatballs between your palms until they have a smooth surface with no cracks. Heat a skillet with some olive oil and fry your meatballs. You don't want to cook them through, just add some color, so you need a good hot pan.

MARINARA SAUCE

Use a stick blender to blend the tomatoes with olive oil in a pan. Add the fresh basil, stalks and all, salt, and pepper and simmer on low heat until you're ready to add your meatballs.

Use tongs to drop your browned meatballs into the hot sauce and let simmer for 1½ to 2 hours on low heat, stirring occasionally. When meatballs are almost cooked, prepare the cheese sauce.

PROVOLONE CHEESE SAUCE

Make a roux with equal parts butter and flour, then add the milk slowly until you have a smooth béchamel sauce. Stir in the cheese until fully incorporated. Finish the dish off with a squeeze of lemon juice and some grated fresh nutmeg.

"I love beer," says Rachel. "It's why Ed and I set the bar up. Our food is all about big flavors and works best with a drink that complements. Beer is perfect. The wide-ranging flavor profiles of beer mean you can pretty much find a different one to pair with any of our dishes."

SANDWICH ASSEMBLY

Slice a quality sub roll down the middle and lightly toast. Toasting brings out the sweetness of the bread and adds some extra resistance to the sauciness. Grab two of your meatballs and cut them in half. Layer some fresh arugula, the four meatballs, flat side down, and then add an extra spoonful of marinara. Finish with your cheese sauce and the best grated Parmesan you can find. Add your jalapeño salsa to spice things up and cut through the richness of all that sauce.

BEER

When juggling beer choices with your meatballs, try to keep it crisp and light to contrast the rich meat and sauces of the dish.

BIRRIFICIO ITALIANO TIPOPILS

A pilsner style but with lively bitter accents and gestures thanks to the four hops. The combination means it cuts through the rich sauces and slakes the thirst but you're interested enough to want another if the meatballs stick around long enough.

FIVE POINTS PALE ALE

A lower ABV at 4.4%, this dials up the bitterness with Amarillo and Citra hops delivering a slightly lighter zest. It retains the carbonation to contrast the spice and rich meat of the dish and starts matching flavors in the glass with those on the plate.

ALPINE BEER COMPANY DUET IPA

Stepping up again in bitterness, this small-town brewery found in the foothills of the Californian Alpine mountains has been brewing brilliant beer since 1999. It is available at Mason & Co. and provides a pleasant sweetness to counter the bitterness of its Simcoe and Amarillo hops.

BEER & SCANDINAVIAN FOOD

Since learning how to bake and brew, humans have always recognized the value of a decent sandwich paired with a pint. The chaps at Øl & Brød (beer & bread) have proved particularly enthusiastic proponents of this combination, setting up a restaurant in Copenhagen entirely devoted to the open sandwich.

Indeed, owners Patrick Andersen and Skovsgaard Bjerg might argue there hasn't and never will be anything better than sliced bread. Brewers Mikkeller seem to agree because when the chefs approached the beer gurus, Mikkeller quickly provided financial backing and launched the restaurant concept next to their own beer bar.

Since inception, the restaurant has earned plenty of plaudits for perfecting traditional smørrebrød (open sandwich), and as the name would suggest, whatever they serve on a plate they like to pair with a smashing selection of beers. The sandwiches here are as comforting as the brews—smoked salmon and scrambled eggs, shrimp and dill, potato with pickled onions and bacon, chicken, venison. Anything goes—especially the cod roe. But we've opted for the pickled herring because you don't get more Nordic than this dish.

PICKLED HERRING OPEN SANDWICH

FOR THE HERRING
4 big filets of matured herring
7 tablespoons water
¾ cup white wine vinegar
½ cup superfine sugar
6 cloves
4 bay leaves
20 black peppercorns
2 star anise

FOR THE MAYONNAISE
6 eggs
2 teaspoons Dijon mustard
juice of 1 lemon
salt
1 cup sunflower oil

4 slices rye bread
butter
3 tablespoons capers
watercress for garnish

FOR THE HERRING
Add the vinegar and sugar to the water and bring to a boil. When boiling point is reached, add the cloves, bay leaves, black peppercorns, and star anise. Let the water cool, then pour the mixture over the herring and place it in the refrigerator for at least a week.

When you're ready to prepare the dish, hard boil 4 eggs by cooking in boiling water for 8 minutes. Let them cool, then cut into slices.

FOR THE MAYONNAISE
Whisk 2 egg yolks with mustard, lemon juice, and a bit of salt. Add sunflower oil while mixing until you get the right consistency.

TO SERVE
Spread butter on the rye bread. Place the herring on one half of the rye bread. On the other half of the bread, spread the egg slices and add a little salt and pepper, leaving a small space in the middle for the watercress garnish. Place some dots of mayonnaise over the egg and spread some capers over them.

Finish the smørrebrød with the freshly cut watercress.

BEER

This is a fish dish, so you can keep it light and clean with a pilsner or a kölsch. Lifting the cloves and bay leaves with a spicy saison can work, and Mikkel Borg Bjergsø, the man behind Mikkeller, suggests a Belgian pale, dry but with softer ,slightly sweet citrus notes to accompany the fish.

MIKKELLER HVA SÅÅ?!
A Belgian pale ale that has a subtle spice and a dry quality to it that really offsets the oil in the fish. With a little carbonation and a bitter finish, the beer leaves the palate ready for another mouthful.

TO ØL GOSE TO HOLLYWOOD
Keeping things great and Danish, this salty but sour gose is light and fresh and brewed with California oranges to add a citrus twist to other botanical flavors in the dish.

THORNBRIDGE TZARA
Fermented like an ale but matured like a lager, the beer is crisp but full with a fruity palate that matches the spice and breaded malty notes to complement the bread. This is a beer that would work with most sandwiches in fact. Even Marmite.

BEER & MEXICAN FOOD

Once a movement that saw diners flirt with digestion disaster, street food has recently coaxed serious foodies from stuffy silver service to trucks in the sunshine. Whether it's an alfresco adventure or returning to a bit of casual dining indoors, Mexican cuisine has flourished in this culture.

One of London's finest exponents is Bad Sports, a taqueria that turns out tasty tacos paired with cracking drinks. The success of Bad Sports helps reaffirm our own view that Mexican food and beer is one of the finest matches around, and coowner Liam Davy often turns to a beer when he has a taco on the go.

"Tacos and beer are a natural combination," says Liam. "Spicy, sharp, intense, and normally inexpensive, a cold beer is almost always the ideal accompaniment. Most of our tacos at Bad Sports are nicely balanced and not too greasy and meaty. However ,whenever I eat this one, you can only drink a beer with it."

On the dish, Liam adds, "Cheeseburger tacos are allegedly a Mexico City thing rather than an American bastardization. This recipe is an adaptation of Alex Stupak's from Empellón Taqueria in New York. The Kewpie mayonnaise gives it a savory kick, while the sour guacachile balances the richness of the meat and cheese."

CHEESEBURGER TACOS

Makes 3 tacos

3 corn tortillas (preferably homemade)
⅓ ounce diced white onion, plus more for garnish
vegetable oil.
5 ounces rare breed ground steak,
   with a decent fat content
1 tablespoon Kewpie mayonnaise
1¼ ounces queso de Oaxaca (any
   melting cheese will do, including cheddar)
1¼ ounces guacachile (green salsa, see opposite)

TO GARNISH
Pickled red onions, jalapeños
diced white onion, salt and lime wedges

1) Warm the tortillas in a hot dry pan. Keep warm by wrapping them in a dish towel.

2) Fry the diced onion in a little vegetable oil until softened and slightly browned. Add the ground meat and cook until brown and slightly crispy.

3) Add the grated cheese and continue to mix with the meat until it has melted. Take the pan off the heat, and keep warm while you make the tacos.

4) Put one-third of the Kewpie mayonnaise on each tortilla, then layer with the burger mixture and then a drizzle of guacachile.

5) Garnish with pickled onions, jalapeños, raw onion, and a pinch of salt. Serve with lime wedges on the side.

GUACACHILE (GREEN SALSA)

In a blender add:

7 avocados, peeled and pitted
1 cup lime juice
7 tablespoons water
8 jalapeños (or other green chiles)
1 onion, chopped
1 garlic clove
pinch sea salt
pinch sugar

Blend and refrigerate until ready to use.

BEER

The obvious choice here is a light lager style. But when selecting a crisp beer to clean the palate and work against the full flavors, find something with a bit of spice to match the heat of the dish.

SIGNATURE BREW ANTICIPATION

This Japanese rice beer has a useful touch of complexity. Light but with a sweetness about it that complements the meat in the dish and enough of a crisp finish to counter the spice.

BEAVERTON NECK OIL IPA

Another popular pairing at Bad Sports, this is a sturdy but session-able IPA. Lots of citrus on the nose but a balanced and refreshing hit on the palate with enough to cut through the oily food without overpowering the flavors.

PABST BLUE RIBBON

At Bad Sports they have a "dressed" Tecate Mexican lager, which includes a squeeze of lime and a decent slug of Valentina hot sauce. Apply the same treatment to a Pabst Blue Ribbon, a light-bodied, carbonated beer best served ice cold.

BEER & VEGAN FOOD

Beer and beans—a flatulent combo no doubt, but incredibly tasty and by suggesting the pairing the folks at Oproer provide further evidence there are no boundaries with beer and food pairings. Based in Utrecht, Netherlands, Oproer has combined its brewing business with vegan values to award-winning effect, with the chefs committed to sourcing plant-based and organic produce and pushing a philosophy of considerate cooking and consumption. They use seasonal and fresh ingredients from local farmers, and the bread is made from the spent grains from the brewery (bostelbrood). It's commendable stuff, and the process of pairing the food with beer is high on the kitchen's agenda.

Mark Strooker is one of the owners, and as well as food, he knows his beer, having previously set up contract brewer Rooie Dop before joining forces with the creators of Ruig Bier to open Oproer.

"As our beers are constantly evolving, so is our food," says Mark. "Every month we create a new menu. The Oproer restaurant started as an encounter between the brewers and our chefs, with the common goal of creating an exciting taste experience by combining craft beers with quality food."

BORLOTTI & CANNELLINI BEAN STEW

1 cup dry borlotti beans
1 cup dry cannellini beans
1¼ cups water
¼ cup olive oil
1 white onion, minced
2 garlic cloves, minced
½ teaspoon smoked paprika
Salt e
1½ tablespoons margarine
1 teaspoon cornstarch, dissolved
    in 2 tablespoons water
3½ tablespoons red wine
2 tablespoons tomato paste dissolved in
1 cup boiling bean water
¼ teaspoon ground cloves
2 bay leaves
½ teaspoon ground black pepper

Soak the beans overnight. Rinse beans in cool water, pour them into a large pot, and cover with 2 inches water. Bring to a boil, then reduce heat and cover. Simmer for 2 hours or until beans are tender. When beans are cooked, drain but do not discard the water. (You can substitute the beans with 5½ cups each canned borlotti beans and canned cannellini beans. The bean cooking water can be replaced with 1¼ cups vegetable broth.)

Pour the olive oil in to a large skillet. On low heat, add the white onion and garlic and cook softly until the onion is soft and golden, approximately 5 minutes. Add the smoked paprika and cook on low heat for 20 seconds. Boil the bean water and add to the beans. Add salt to taste. Bring back to a boil and add the margarine. Dissolve the cornstarch in 2 tablespoons cold water. Add the red wine and simmer for 10 minutes.

In a separate pan, boil 1 cup water and dissolve 2 tablespoons of tomato paste in it, along with ¼ teaspoon ground cloves. Add it to the stew with the bay leaves and black pepper. Simmer on low heat for 1 hour. Stir occasionally to make sure the stew does not stick to the bottom of the pan. Adjust taste with salt and pepper and check thickness, adding more water if necessary.

MILLET

1½ cups millet grains
2½ cups vegetable broth
2 tablespoons olive oil
 or margarine
salt

Toast the millet in a dry cooking pan on medium heat for 2 minutes stirring continuously. Add hot broth and bring to a boil. Cover with a lid and simmer until all the water is absorbed by the millet, 10 to 15 minutes. Remove from heat and let stand for 10 minutes with the lid on. Add salt and olive oil and fluff the millet with a fork.

OVEN ROASTED SHALLOTS

10 shallots
olive oil
salt

Peel the shallots. Toss them with olive oil and salt. Roast the shallots in the oven on a parchment paper-lined baking tray, at 350°F for 20 to 25 minutes until the shallots are brown and tender.

BEER

Delicate beers are often advisable with vegetable dishes, but despite its vegan nature, this is a hearty and spicy meal, so aim for a vegan-friendly beer with character as well.

OPROER 24/7 INDIA SESSION ALE
(NETHERLANDS)

The chefs and brewers at Oproer recommend the IPA with their dish, and the 24/7 cleverly combines the bitterness of an IPA with low alcohol; light, clean, refreshing, and as the name would suggest, a session-able quality.

MAISEL'S WEISSE
(GERMANY)

A refreshing German hefeweizen that delivers a decent dose of carbonation and a dry, citrus finish but with it a softer, spicy side adding clove and banana to the mix.

MEANTIME YAKIMA RED

An amber ale again combining the light, refreshing touch required for the vegan dish with a touch of weight. The light toast from the malt is offset by a crisp fruit and a subtle citrus and floral bitterness provided by the five Yakima hops.

BEER & SPANISH FOOD

This dish has been created by Nacho and Esther Manzano, owners of the two-Michelin-starred Casa Marcial and one-starred La Salgar in Spain. Fair to say they make the right kind of meal out of Spanish cuisine. There are some obvious accents to pair with beer when it comes to Spanish dishes, not least the cured meats and fattier or carb-driven tapas, and these all make for marvelous matches.

In this dish, Nacho and Esther take a more nuanced approach with a complexly seasoned and sauced vegetable. Nacho specifically paired with Alhambra Reserva 1925, which makes for an interesting dynamic because, in his own words: "We matched with the bitter flavors of the dish. The eggplants are slightly roasted, and that is the reason we choose Alhambra Reserva 1925; it gives the best complement to the dish. The recipe is made with walnuts and black garlic which also pair perfectly with the flavor of the beer."

ROASTED EGGPLANT WITH GREEN WALNUTS, SOUR CREAM, AND BITTER NOTES

FOR THE EGGPLANT
2 eggplants
pinch of salt
1 teaspoon mild olive oil

Split the eggplants along their length and open them. Add table salt and very little oil and roast them at 325°F for 22 to 25 minutes. Take the eggplants out of the oven and peel them. Set aside the skins. Dry the eggplants under a salamander broiler for 2 minutes on each side, with the elements raised so the eggplants do not receive direct heat. Do the same with the eggplant skins to dry out completely. Set aside.

FOR THE EGGPLANT POWDER EGGPLANT SKIN
dried eggplant skins from 2 eggplants
½ teaspoon ground coffee beans
4 ounces rosemary
4 ounces thyme
4 ounces sage
2 dried pine cones

Put the eggplant skins on a stainless-steel tray. Put rosemary, thyme, and sage together with the pine cones inside a deeper gastronorm tray and place the tray with the skins over them. Light the pine cones and cover with another gastronorm tray to steam the skins. Once smoked, grind the eggplant skins to a powder in a food processor. Mix ½ teaspoon eggplant powder with the ground coffee.

FOR THE SOUR CREAM
2 teaspoons yogurt
3½ tablespoons cream
1 tablespoon lime juice

Mix the cream with the lime juice.
Add the yogurt.

FOR THE BITTER NOTES
Rind of 1 lemon
¾ cup water
¾ cup sugar

Blanch the lemon rind three times. Cut into
julienne strips. Make a simple sugar syrup with
the water and sugar. Immerse the rind in the
syrup for 3 minutes. Transfer to a dehydrator
and dry out for 12 minutes.

FOR THE COFFEE SAUCE
1 cup espresso coffee
½ teaspoon instant coffee
¾ ounce simple syrup
½ teaspoon modified corn starch

Mix the espresso with the instant coffee. Add
the syrup, then reduce and thicken with the
corn starch.

TO SERVE
green walnuts
black garlic
chicory or endive
arugula shoots

Dress the chicory with a little oil and cider
vinegar and a drop of coffee sauce. Make spots of
sour cream on the plate. Cut the black garlic into
julienne strips and place a piece over each sour
cream spot, together with a little lemon rind
and a piece of green walnut. Finish with arugula
shoots to enhance the bitter flavors.

BEER
This is an obvious dish for the vegetarian, but
it comes from a warmer clime, so crisp, bitter
lagers are useful. It helps to have something
a little meaty in the glass. British bitters are
excellent pairings here because,
although the flavors of the eggplant
can be subtle, the wider ingredients
really play into its hands.

ALHAMBRA RESERVA 1925
Since Nacho and Esther chose this
beer, you'd be missing a trick if you
didn't try it. Behaving like lager with
a delicate crisp bitter quality, it also
has a rich, sweet body, so it slices

through elements of the
dish but complements as
it goes, cleaning the palate
for the next mouthful.

LONDON PRIDE
A classic British bitter, this has
the perfect level of fruit and hop-
bitterness and with the sweet weight
and subtle nuttiness from
the malt this proved a
fantastic ally to the dish.

HILL FARMSTEAD ARTHUR
This saison goes in a different
direction, but has something of a
fermented-vegetable note about it,
in a good way, and it really works
with the sour of the cream and the
general bitter qualities of the dish.

BEER & DESSERT

Ollie Dabbous enjoyed a staggering introduction to the competitive world of London restaurants when, a mere year after opening, he'd earned a Michelin star. The success lies in his passion for flavor. The food is far from frilly.Instead, Ollie relies on a commitment to seasonal fare and a passion for what tastes good. Taste permeates every element of the menu, so quality beer, as with everything, is important at Dabbous.

Beer works beautifully with desserts it can match the sweetness and cut through the sugar. Ollie's dessert not only plays to this strength but also incorporates beer into the recipe.

"Whether, food, wine, or beer, we only want to serve the customers what we think is a fantastic product," says Ollie. "This is a fun dish but also a dish full of contrasts: hot and cold, crunchy and smooth, sweet and sour. Nuts are typically served alongside beer in many bars, so it felt like an obvious choice. It's nice to have something cool and floral, such as a pale ale, to cut the salt and savoriness of the nuts. The lime and ginger also add to the fresh taste. There are so many different styles of beer that they can match with a vast array of flavors: anything from citrus and floral to earthy and musky. I like the diversity when it comes to pairing. It is usually wine, but something different provides a nice change and may well be a better match."

HOT CASHEW NUT BUTTER
WITH CHILLED GINGER BEER

CASHEW NUT BUTTER
2½ cups cashews, toasted
½ cup (packed) raw brown sugar
7 tablespoons salted butter, diced
7 tablespoons milk
7 tablespoons whipping cream
½ ounce vanilla beans

Coarsely chop half the nuts and set aside. Heat together the milk
and cream with the vanilla. Caramelize the sugar in a hot pan, then
add the butter followed by the hot milk and cream, then mix to
obtain a smooth butterscotch. Let cool slightly then blend half the
butterscotch with half the cashews to form a coarse textured puree.
Mix in the remaining sauce and nuts.

GINGER BEER FOAM
½ cup sugar
7 tablespoons lime juice
1 ounce ginger, peeled and grated

Bring the lime juice and sugar to a boil, then add the ginger. Remove
from the heat, and cover with plastic wrap.

2 cups Einstök white ale
3 leaves gelatin
⅓ cup superfine sugar
¼ teaspoon xanthan gum
5 ounces pasteurized egg white

Soak the gelatin then dissolve it in a little of the beer. Mix together
with the remaining beer, sugar, xanthan gum, and 1 cup of the
ginger and lime syrup; blend with a heavy duty blender to combine.
Strain, then blend in the egg whites just to combine; do not work in
too much air. Place in a culinary gas gun/blowtorch and charge with
two gas cylinders; keep chilled until required.

ASSEMBLE
Heat the cashew mix in a pan. Place 3 to 4 tablespoons in the
bottom of a half–pint beer tankard.

Squirt on top the ginger beer foam on top and serve immediately to
maximize the temperature contrast.

BEER
The ambidextrous nature of
beer makes it a perfect partner
for your dessert, both sweet and
bitter squeezing into one sip.
Since these qualities apply to
most beer styles, feel free
to experiment.

EINSTÖK ICELANDIC
TOASTED PORTER
Having used Einstök
in the recipe, it makes
sense to stay with the
brewery; the rich and
smooth mouthfeel
of the porter turns to
bitter-mocha chocolate
and makes it a useful
beer with this and a
host of other desserts.

MAGIC ROCK CLOWN JUICE
A witbier blending the best
Belgian yeast with
assertive American
hops. The result is
a beer that takes on
sweet with bitter
and matches ginger
with coriander and
orange spice.

FIRESTONE WALKER DOUBLE JACK IPA
Weighing in at 9.5% ABV, this is
a beer that'll send you off to bed.
A strong malt backbone plays to
the sweet elements of the dish,
but the hops bombard the sugar
with big spicy bitterness.

GLOSSARY

Abbey ale
Belgian strong ale brewed by or under license from monasteries, although not all have monastic links.

ABV (alcohol by volume)
A measurement of the alcoholic strength of beer, it is expressed as a percentage, e.g. 5% ABV.

Adjuncts
Any ingredient other than barley, hops, yeast, or water that is added to beer. It usually refers to cereals and sugars that may be introduced for special flavors.

Alpha acid
The naturally occurring acid present in the cone of the hop plant. It gives bitterness to beer.

Alt, Altbier
Old-style beer from the Düsseldorf area of Germany, similar in style to British bitter or pale ale.

Aroma
The "nose" of a beer is what gives an indication of the malt, hops, and possible fruit content. Combined with finish and mouthfeel, it is used to assess the taste and flavor of a beer.

Barley
The most commonly used grain for brewing and one of the main ingredients in beer.

Barley Wine
Extra-strong ale that originated in Britain but is now produced by brewers worldwide, particularly in Belgium and the United States.

Berliner Weiss
Weaker at around 3 to 4% ABV and often spiked with fruit syrup to ease the acidity. Berliner Weiss remains relatively rare in its hometown, but as a tart, top-fermented beer laced with lactobacillus and brettanomyces, it's riding the funky and sour retro-wave in both America and Europe—with many new German craft brewers resurrecting this remarkably refreshing beer.

Bière de Garde
French "keeping beer" was a style originally associated with the farmer brewer of French Flanders, who brewed in spring and stored the beer for use during the summer to refresh farm laborers. It is now brewed year-round.

Bitter
British-style beer that is usually well hopped. Best Bitter is a stronger version.

Blonde/Blond Ale
European name for a light-colored golden ale, often French or Belgian in origin.

Bock
German term for a strong beer that was once brewed only seasonally. Stronger versions include Doppelbock and Eisbock.

Bottle conditioning
A process in which beer is bottled with live yeast in order to improve in condition, to mature, and to develop additional strength.

Brettanomyces
A semiwild form of yeast used in the brewing of Belgian Lambic beers and some porters and stouts.

Brew kettle
Vessel used to boil wort with hops during the brewing process.

Brew pub
A pub that brews and sells its own beer on the premises.

Brown ale
A traditional British beer, low in alcohol, which was often mixed with Mild. Newer versions of the style made by US brewers tend to have a higher hop content.

Burtonize/Burtonization
A process of adding salts such as gypsum and magnesium to ape the hard brewing water found in Burton-on-Trent, England.

Carbon dioxide (CO₂)
A gas that is naturally produced during fermentation of beers that are conditioned in either the cask or bottle. When beers are filtered in a brewery, carbon dioxide may be added.

Cask ale
Ale that is brought to maturity in the cask, either at a brewery or in a pub cellar. Maturation times can vary from a week to more than a year.

Condition
A beer's condition is denoted by the level of carbon dioxide present, which gives the brew its sparkle.

Copper
Vessel used in the brewing process to boil the sugary wort with hops. Traditionally made of copper, it is now often made of stainless steel. Also known as a brew kettle.

Decoction
Part of the brewing process in which some of the wort is removed from the vessel then heated to a higher temperature and returned to the vessel in order to produce more complex flavors by improving enzyme activity and increasing sugar levels.

Doppelbock/Double bock
An extra-strong German-style bock, often of an ABV around 7.5% or more.

Dortmunder
A style of bottom-fermented golden ale originating in Dortmund, Germany.

Draft Beer
Beer that is served direct from a cask or bulk container and drawn to the bar. Also known as draught in the United Kingdom.

Dry hopping
A process of adding hops to the finished brew to improve the beer's bitterness, aroma, and flavor.

Dubbel/Double
A Belgian-style abbey ale that describes a strong dark ale.

Dunkel

Means "dark" in German and describes dark lagers and dark wheat beers.

Eisbock

The strongest available version of bock.

Enkel

Means "single" in Dutch and describes a beer of modest strength.

Esters

Natural flavoring compounds that impart fruit and spice flavors by turning sugars into alcohol and carbon dioxide.

Extra Special Bitter (ESB)

A bigger and bolder version of bitter, often with additional hop character, this beer style is enjoying a renewed popularity in the USA and UK, with new brews appearing quite regularly.

Extreme beers

A phrase originating in the United Kingdom to describe beers that push the limits by means of taste and flavor due to unusual ingredients, wild yeast fermentation, oak-barrel aging, or a very high hop or alcohol content.

Fermentation

The process that converts malt sugars to alcohol and carbon dioxide by the action of yeast. Ale is made by warm fermentation, lager by cold fermentation, often called top and bottom fermentation, respectively.

Finish

The aftertaste of a beer; the impression left at the back of the tongue and the throat.

Foeder

An oak barrel used to mature beer, used in particular by Rodenbach in Belgium.

Golden ales

Pale ales with a moderate hop content, rarely exceeding 5 percent. These accessible ales straddle the line between lager and bitter, introducing many novice beer drinkers to the delight of craft brews. Referred to as blonde ales in the United States.

Gose

Laced with lactic acid, coriander, and salt, Gose is an eighteenth century regional specialty that nearly died in the 1960s. Sharp, sour, sometimes served with syrup, and synonymous with the East German city of Leipzig, Gose has made a refreshing return.

Grand Cru

A term often used by Belgian brewers to describe their finest brew and one that is typical of their house style.

Grist

The name applied to ground malt (or other grains) that, when combined with warm water, forms the wort used in the brewing process.

Gueuze/Geuze

A type of beer formed by blending young and old Belgian Lambic beers to produce a refreshing beer.

Hefeweizen

Hefe means "yeast" in German, and this is a naturally conditioned German-style wheat beer with yeast sediment.

Helles

A German-style beer, meaning "light," applied to a pale beer, either a lager or a wheat beer.

Hops

Climbing plant with cones containing acids, resins, and tannins that produces aroma and bitterness in beer, to complement the natural sweetness of malt. There are many different varieties, each known for its different flavoring properties.

IBU/International Bittering Units

A scale for measuring the bitterness of beer, which is a complex calculation that is based on the ratio and weight of hops, alpha acids, wort, and alcohol in a brew.

IPA/India Pale Ale

A heavily hopped beer which was first brewed in Burton-on-Trent, England, in the nineteenth century to survive the long journey to India, bound for soldiers and civil servants based there. Now produced by several brewing nations, including the heavily hopped versions found in the United States.

American IPA

The Americanization of India Pale Ale is the most significant event to have shaped beer in the last thirty years, and it's been the backbone of the global craft brewing revolution. The Americans not only reinvented IPA by cranking up the aroma and bitterness, but they also doubled it, tripled it, made it imperial, and even took it into the black. More than two hundred years after English brewers were exporting heavily hopped ales and porters to India, American-style IPAs are being brewed all over the world—even in their original British birthplace.

Kellerbier

German for "cellar beer," this is a hoppy, lightly carbonated lager, often unfiltered.

Kölsch

A type of top-fermented light golden ale first brewed in and around the city of Cologne in Germany.

Kräusen

The addition of partially fermented wort to beer in the lager cellar to stimulate a strong secondary fermentation.

Kriek

A Belgian Lambic beer in which cherries are fermented, imparting a tart, fruity flavor.

Lager

A range of beer styles created by bottom-fermenting (or cold-fermenting) in tanks where the temperature is just above freezing. As yeast settles at the bottom of the tank, a slow secondary fermentation occurs, carbonation increases, and a thirst-quenching beer emerges. Lager means "to store" in German.

Lambic

A style of Belgian beer originating from tiny, rural breweries in the Payottenland region. It is fermented using airborne wild yeasts that cause spontaneous fermentation. When cherries or raspberries are added, the beers are known as kriek and framboise, or frambozen.

Lauter
A vessel used to run off and filter the wort from the grain once the mashing has taken place.

Liquor
The term used by brewers for the water that is used durng the mashing and boiling process.

Maibock
A German beer style usually denoting a strong, often pale lager that is brewed to mark the beginning of spring.

Malt
Grains, usually barley, that have undergone partial germination, and are then dried and cured, or toasted in a kiln, when the seed contains high levels of starches. The starches are converted into fermentable sugars during the brewing process.

Märzen
Traditional Bavarian seasonal lager brewed in March and stored until fall when it is drunk at the Munich Oktoberfest. These days it is also brewed year-round.

Mash
The mixture created when the grist is steeped in hot water during the beer brewing process.

Mash tun
Vessel in which malted grain is mixed with "liquor" to start the brewing process.

Méthode Champenoise
A form of bottle conditioning that follows the method for making Champagne by going through a secondary fermentation using added yeast and fermentable sugars. Beers made in this way are usually produced in Champagne-style bottles and can mature for several years.

Microbrewery
A small brewery brewing small batches of beer for local distribution and consumption. The craft beer revival in the United Kingdom and the United States began in such breweries 20 to 30 years ago.

Mild
A British beer style, low in alcohol, developed to quench the thirst of farmer types. Since the 1960s, it has become less available in British pubs, although CAMRA (Campaign for Real Ale) has been instrumental in ensuring its survival as a beer style.

Mouthfeel
This is the texture or weight of the liquid on the tongue as the beer flows over it. Distinct from flavor or taste.

Noble hops
Name given to a group of German and Czech hops hailed for their aroma rather than bitterness: Hallertau, Zatec (Saaz), Spalt, and Tettnang.

Nonik Glass
A beer glass in both half pint and pint sizes that has a characteristic bulge two-thirds of the way up to aid grip.

Oktoberfest
An enormous annual two-week beer festival held in the Bavarian city of Munich, with some beers even brewed specially for the occasion.

Oud Bruin
A Belgian beer style from Flanders meaning "old brown." These beers have an aging period of up to one year.

Pasteurization
A heat treatment process that kills bacteria and stabilizes beer. It can sometimes dull the final flavor.

Pilsner/Pils
A golden, hop-filled lager first brewed in the Bohemian city of Pilsen, now part of Czechia.

Porter
A dark beer that is characterized by dark chocolate malty flavors and a strong hop flavoring.

Quadrupel
A particularly potent, dark Trappist-style beer first created at the Koningshoeven monastery in the Netherlands back in 1991. Now a term used to describe dark, high-strength beers too strong to be dubbed a dubbel or tripel. Also known sometimes as Abt.

Rauchbier
German-style lager originating from the Franconia area, made from malt and smoked over beech wood fires.

Reinheitsgebot
The German beer purity law of 1516 stated that beer must not contain anything other than water, yeast, malt, and hops. It is still adhered to by many German beer makers.

Sahti
Finnish sahti is one of the world's oldest and most bizarre beer styles. The mash, made up of a variety of grains including rye and barley, is filtered through a bed of juniper twigs, seasoned with juniper berries instead of (and/or in addition to) hops and fermented with baker's yeast from where it gets its banana undertones. Tasting like a slightly loony lovechild of a German Hefeweizen and a Belgian lambic, Sahti is heady and hazy with a resinous aroma of pine needles, mint, and cloves and a tart tingle on the palate. Having first been the exclusive domain of the ambitious homebrewer, Sahti brewing has, of late, been undertaken by ambitious brewers eager to explore esoteric, quasi-extinct ale styles.

Saison
A Belgian-style beer that was traditionally brewed in winter for drinking in the summer months. Nowadays it is often produced all year round.

Schwarzbier
Meaning "black beer" in German, this is a dark, opaque style of lager.

Scotch ale
Strong, malty beer style that originated in Scotland as a "pint of heavy" but is now more likely to be brewed in France, the United States, and Belgium, where some of the strongest versions are produced.

Seasonal beers

Beers brewed for a limited period each year, traditionally produced to suit climatic seasons examples include German Märzens and French Saisons, or to celebrate a holiday (Christmas seasonals) or an event, such as Oktoberfest.

Sour ales

Beers from Flanders that undergo an aging process of between 18 months and two years in oak tuns, resulting in a sharp, acetic flavor.

Sparge

"Esperger" in French means to "sprinkle." This is a process by which the grain is rinsed after mashing, to flush out any remaining malt sugars.

Spice/Herb Beers

Before hops, brewers balanced out their grain base with herbs and spices. Today, in their unwavering pursuit of flavor, modern brewers are embracing unusual, esoteric ingredients with wild-eyed gusto, using bacon and beet; Egyptian bread and Turkish figs; South American leaves laced with caffeine and sea buckthorn; wormwood; asparagus; chile and bog myrtle. Some of these beers taste great. Others less so.

Steam beer

Amber-colored, all-malt beer known as California Common and introduced to the West Coast in the latter part of the nineteenth century. Synonymous with San Francisco, where Fritz Maytag revived the style at his Anchor Brewery.

Stein

A traditional glass or ceramic German drinking tankard seen in bierkellers all over the country. "Stein" means stone.

Stout

A strong dark beer style, usually top-fermented, that is made using highly roasted grain.

Trappist beers

Beers made in seven breweries controlled by Trappist monks in Belgium (Achel, Chimay, Orval, Rochefort, Westmalle, Westvleteren) and one, La Trappe (Koningshoeven), in the Netherlands.

Tripel

The strongest beer of the Belgian abbey ale style, although a few quadrupels have been developed in the United States, especially to fit the extreme beer mold. Generally used as a description for a very strong ale.

Tun

A vessel in which the mash is steeped (mixed with "liquor") during the brewing process.

Urbock

The strongest of bock beers and among the strongest beer in the world.

Urtype

Meaning "original type" in German, this is a term used for a beer that is an authentic interpretation of an established style.

Vienna red/lager

Reddish lager with a sweet, malty aroma that was the first lager beer brewed in Austria during the nineteenth century.

Vintage ales

Connoisseur beers that benefit from being cellared, laid down, and left to improve over time, becoming more complex in flavor over the years. The fine port and Cognacs of the beer world.

Weiss, weisse

"White" in German, meaning a wheat beer.

Wit, witbier

"White beer," meaning wheat beer, used to describe some Belgian and Dutch beers.

Wheat beer

Beer made from a blend of wheat and barley malt. Also known as Weizen (wheat) or Weiss (white) in German, blanche in French, or wit in Dutch and Flemish. Often pale and cloudy in appearance, creamy in texture, and sweet on the finish.

Wood-aged beers

Beers stored and aged in wooden rather than metal kegs to add flavor. Whiskey, sherry, port, and bourbon barrels have all been used to create beers that are enjoying increased popularity, particularly in the United Kingdom, United States, and Belgium.

Wort

An extract created by the mashing process in brewing and containing fermentable sugars. It is boiled with hops, then cooled prior to fermentation.

Yeast

A natural fungus that is an active agent in the brewing process, attacking sweet liquids such as wort to convert malt sugars into alcohol and carbon dioxide.

Yorkshire squares

Square fermenting vessels associated with traditional brewing in Yorkshire, England. Still used at Samuel Smith's brewery and at Black Sheep in Masham. They are said to produce fine well-balanced beer.

Zoigl beer

An old-fashioned farmhouse lager beer style brewed only by communal breweries in five towns in the Oberpfälz wald region of Germany, close to the Czech border. The towns are: Eslarn, Falkenberg, Mitterteich, Neuhaus, and Windischeschenbach.

BEER DIRECTORY

BEER FESTIVALS

1. Annafest
For many, this phenomenal 10-day Franconian beer festival dating back to the mid-nineteenth century can't be bettered. On a wooded hill on the outskirts of Forchheim, more than 20 bierkellers and breweries pour their fabulously fresh bottom-fermented beer into stone mugs amid music and lots and lots of sausages. And, rather inappropriately, a fairground.
Where? Forcheim, Bavaria, Germany
When? July
www.anna-fest.de

2. Villaggio della Birra
A beautifully bucolic beer festival held amid the undulating hills of Tuscany and an ideal way to explore Italy's esoteric and increasingly excellent beers.
Where? Tuscany, Italy
When? September
www.villaggiodellabirra.com/eng

3. Boreft Beer Festival
Every fall, the cream of Europe's artisan beermakers descend on Bodegraven, the home of De Molen, for two days of quality, cutting-edge beer courtesy of the likes of Del Ducato, Alvinne, Buxton, etc. …
Where? Bodegraven, Netherlands
When? September
www.brouwerijdemolen.nl

4. Indy Man Con
Held in the hugely impressive Grade II-listed Victorian baths in Manchester, IMC is an intimate and atmospheric showcase of the best of Britain's thriving beer scene alongside some cracking brewers from the continent too.
Where? Manchester, England, UK
When? September
www.indymanbeercon.co.uk

5. Craft Beer Rising
Held in the old Truman Brewery in London's Brick Lane, this festival is a bit cooler and craftier than the classic CAMRA cask ale festival, delivering street food, music, whisky, and the best of UK independent and regional brewing.
Where? East London, England, UK
When? February
www.craftbeerrising.co.uk

6. Firestone Walker Invitational Beer Fest
Each year, just 50 of the world's best brewers are asked to bring their beers to Paso Robles for this elite and intimate event. Tickets are expensive, rare, and like catnip to Californian craft beer lovers, so keep an eye on the website for release dates.
Where? Paso Robles, California, USA
When? June
www.firestonebeer.com/brewery/invitational-beer-fest.php

7. International Festival of Small Breweries
Rightly revered among Belgian's informed ale imbibers, this Walloon festival is a wonderful way to familiarize yourself with the independent, New-World Belgian scene as well as similar outfits from elsewhere in Europe.
Where? Marbehan, Wallonia, Belgium
When? October
www.brassigaume.be

8. Copenhagen Beer Celebration
Cult cuckoo brewer Mikkeller has made a lot of friends as he's trotted the globe over the last ten years, and he brings some of them together in Copenhagen every May—and gets them to bring their most left-field liquids.
Where? Copenhagen, Denmark
When? May
www.mikkeller.dk/category/copenhagen-beer-celebration

9. Shelton Brothers: "The Festival"
This beer geek's nirvana, organized by one of America's most knowledgeable importers, visits a different American state every year, bringing together some of Europe and America's cult craft heroes including Cantillon, Drie Fonteinen, and Hill Farmstead.
Where? Varies
When? October
www.sheltonbrothers.com/festival

10. Slunce ve Skle
Love lager? Then head to "Sun in the Glass," where the top bottom-fermenting beers from Czechia and beyond, as well as ales too, pour generously among a lively, good-times crowd.
Where? Pilsen, Czechia
When? September
www.sluncveskle.cz

11. Zythos Beer Festival
An awesome introduction to Belgium's beer scene, Zythos showcases more than a hundred breweries, 600 beers, and no small amount of rowdy "conviviality."
Where? Brabanthal, Leuven, Belgium
When? April
www.zbf.be

12 .Toer de Geuze
Every two years, Lambic lovers make a cheek-puckering pilgrimage to Payottenland and Brussels for a two-day tour of the region's growing number of blenders and brewers.
Where? Brussels & Payottenland, Belgium
When? May (every other year)
www.horal.be/en/toer-de-geuze

13. Oktoberfest
The biggest beer festival on the planet and a must-visit—even if you don't like beer that much—it lasts for more than three weeks.
Where? Munich, Bavaria,Germany
When? September (ends on the first weekend of October)
www.oktoberfest.de

14. Great American Beer Festival
Like obsessive Elvis impersonators going to Graceland, the world's beer cognoscenti (and a whole load of jocks wearing caps) breathlessly converge on the Denver Convention Center to meet the best beers in America.
Where? Denver, Colorado, USA
When? September
www.greatamericanbeerfestival.com

15. Beervana
For more than 15 years, and over two days as part of a wider Wellington food festival, Beervana has enthusiastically captured the growing Kiwi craft brewing scene—and even invited some Australian brewers over too.
Where? Wellington, New Zealand
When? August
www.beervana.co.nz

16. Festival of Barrel Aged Beer
The Windy City, boasting more than 300 beers, hosts a lip-puckering, funk-filled festival dedicated to the wonders of wood and the marvels of microorganisms.
Where? Chicago, Illinois, USA
When? November
www.illinoisbeer.com

BEER KNOWLEDGE

Here's a list of resources for finding out more about beer, wherever you live.

UK

MAGAZINES
Original Gravity:
originalgravitymag.com

BLOGS
Beer Geek Blog: beergeekblog.co.uk
Beer Therapy: realbeer.com/blog
Boak and Bailey's Beer Blog:
boakandbailey.com
Brew Geekery: brewgeekery.com
Called to the Bar:
maltworms.blogspot.co.uk
CAMRGB: www.camrgb.org
Craft Beer London:
craftbeerlondon.com
HonestBrew:
honestbrew.co.uk/beer-banter
Inside Beer: insidebeer.com
Martyn Cornell's Zythophile:
zythophile.co.uk
Pete Brown's Beer Blog:
petebrown.blogspot.com
Protz on Beer: protzonbeer.co.uk
The Northern Beer Blog:
seanliquorish.co.uk/blog
Shut Up About Barclay Perkins:
barclayperkins.blogspot.co.uk
Total Ales: totalales.co.uk/blog

EUROPE

BLOGS

BELGIUM
Belgian Beer Geek:
belgianbeergeek.be
Belgian Smaak: belgiansmaak.com
CZECHIA
Evan Rail's Beer Culture:
www.beerculture.org
FRANCE
Top of The Hops:
www.topofthehops.fr
ITALY
Fermento Birra fermentobirra.com
NORWAY
Knut Albert:
knutalbert.wordpress.com
NETHERLANDS
The Dutch Beer Pages:
dutchbeerpages.com

USA

American Homebrewers Association:
homebrewersassociation.org
New York Craft Beer Guide
nycraftbeerguide.com
Ratebeer: ratebeer.com

MAGAZINES
All About Beer: allaboutbeer.com
Beer Advocate: beeradvocate.com
Beer Street Journal:
beerstreetjournal.com
Craft Beer & Brewing Magazine:
beerandbrewing.com
DRAFT: draftmag.com

BLOGS
Appellation Beer:
appellationbeer.com/blog
Beer Guy PDX:
beerguypdx.blogspot.co.uk
Beer Me: beermebc.com
Beer Pulse: beerpulse.com
Beervana: beervana.blogspot.com
Brew Studs: wearebrewstuds.com
Brewbound: brewbound.com
Brewpublic: brewpublic.com
Brookston Beer Bulletin:
brookstonbeerbulletin.com
Brulosophy: brulosophy.com
Craft Beer Austin:
craftbeeraustin.com/beer-blog
Craft Beer: craftbeer.com
Drink Up Columbus:
drinkupcolumbus.com
Full Pint: thefullpint.com
Good Beer Hunting:
goodbeerhunting.com
Guys Drinking Beer:
guysdrinkingbeer.com
Mike's Craft Beer:
mikescraftbeer.com
MyBeerBuzz:
mybeerbuzz.blogspot.com
New Jersey Craft Beer:
newjerseycraftbeer.com
Oh Beautiful Beer:
ohbeautifulbeer.com
San Diego Beer News:
westcoastersd.com
The Beeroness: thebeeroness.com

CANADA

MAGAZINES
TAPS: The Beer Magazine:
tapsmagazine.com
Canadian Beer News:
canadianbeernews.com
The Growler: thegrowler.ca

BLOGS
Beer et Seq:
www.beeretseq.com/
Stephen Beaumont
Beaumontdrinks.com

AUSTRALIA

Australian Brews News:
brewsnews.com.au
Beer & Brewer: beerandbrewer.com
Beer Cartel: beercartel.com.au/blog

BREWERY INDEX

BEERS INDEX

GENERAL INDEX

PUBLISHER'S ACKNOWLEDGMENTS

PICTURE CREDITS
The publisher thanks the many breweries from around the world that kindly provided images of their beers, labels, logos, and facilities reproduced here.

Many thanks also to Katie Lawrence and Nikki Mehta for their painstaking picture research.

Special photography:
Simon Murrell/Jacqui Small
Endpapers, Pages 1, 4, 7-8, 21, 23, 24 (Tulip/Thistle, Snifter), 25 (Goblet/Chalice, Weizen), 38-39 (Map background), 40-41.

John Carey/Jacqui Small
Pages 2, 6, 12, 14, 18

Maps
Pages 39-39, 47, 79, 99, 119, 131, 139, 155, 167, 173, 183, 213, 227 Shutterstock/Boreala; 183 Shutterstock/Raevsky Lab

The publisher also thanks the following:
Page 24 Riedel Glassware; Page 24, Dartington Glassware (Flute); Page 25, Dartington Glassware (Pilsner); Page 24 ThinkStock by Getty: Zerbor (Noninck pint glass, dimpled mug); Page 25 ThinkStock by Getty: Zerbor (Stein); Page 36 Shutterstock/Kazoka; Pages 38-9 Shutterstock: Boreala; Page 43 Moorhouse's; Page 46 top Harvey's; Page 46 bottom Brewdog; Page 50-51 Beavertown; Pages 56-7 Fuller's; Page 62 Anspach & Hobday; Pages 68-9 Thornbridge Brewery; Page 76 Estrella Damm; Page 78 top Arterra Picture Library/ALAMY; Page 78 bottom Cantillon; Page 98 top Erdinger; Page 98 bottom Althstadhof;

Pages 84-5 Cantillon Brewery; Pages 102-3 Bayerischer Bahnhof Brewery; Page 118 top Pilsner Urquell, bottom Kocour Brewery; Page 126-7 Matuška Brewery; Page 130 top Grado Plato, bottom Lambrate; Pages 134-5 Birrificio Baladin; Page 138 Nogne Ø Brewery; Page 145 Mikkeller; Page 154 top Les Brasseurs du Grand Paris, bottom Deck & Donohue; Page 165 Brauerei Locher; Page 166 top De Molen, bottom Oproer; Page 172 top Barcelona Tourist Board, bottom ThinkStock by Getty: Toni Flap Page 180 The Ale Apothecary; Page 82 top Deschutes, bottom Stone Brewing Liberty Station; Page 182 top Deschutes Brewery; Page 182 bottom Stone Brewing Company; Page 183 Shutterstock/Raevsky Lab Pages 186-7 Anchor Steam Brewery; Pages 192-3 Firestone Walker; Pages 202-3 New Belgium Brewery; Pages 208-9 New Holland Brewing Co; Page 212 top Big Rock Brewery, bottom Brewery; Dieu du Ciel! Brewery; Page 224 Brewcult logo; Page 226 top Altitude Brewing, bottom Pirate Life; Pages 236-7 Altitude Brewing; Page 240 Yo-Ho Brewing Company logo; Pages 244-5 Baird Brewing; Page 247 Yo-ho Brewing Co; Page 250 Peter Cassidy/Jacqui Small; Page 253 Peter Cassidy/Jacqui Small; Pages 254 left Cryer & Stott, right Barhwey Cheese; Page 255 left Old Weyderland cheese, right Jacqui Small/Lisa Linder; Page 256 chocolate images Jose Lasheras/Jacqui Small; Page 257 Jose Lasheras/Jacqui Small; Pages 258-9 Meat Liquor; Page 261 Mason and Co; Page 262 Mikkeller; Pages 264-5 Bad Sports; Pages 266-7 Oproer; Pages 268-9 Casa Marcial; Page 270 Dabbous; Page 288 Steve Ullathorne

A NOTE ABOUT THE AUTHORS

Ben McFarland and Tom Sandham are award-winning spirits experts, writers and performers—and the authors of *The Thinking Drinker's Guide to Alcohol* (Sterling Epicure). McFarland has been named Britain's Beer Writer of the Year three times (2004, 2006, 2011) and Sandham is the author of *World's Best Cocktails* (Jacqui Small). Both write regularly on the beer world for a wide range of publications, including the *Daily Telegraph*, the *Spectator,* the *Guardian* and *Time Out*. They have performed sold-out shows at the Edinburgh Festival for seven consecutive years. Visit them at **thinkingdrinkers.com** and follow them on Twitter @ **thinking drinks**.